www.wadsworth.com

wadsworth.com is the World Wide Web site for Wadsworth Publishing Company and is your direct source to dozens of online resources.

At *wadsworth.com* you can find out about supplements, demonstration software, and student resources. You can also send e-mail to many of our authors and preview new publications and exciting new technologies.

wadsworth.com
Changing the way the world learns®

Music Listening Today

By Charles R. Hoffer

University of Florida

Wadsworth Publishing Company

I(T)P® An International Thomson Publishing Company

Belmont, CA ■ Albany, NY ■ Boston ■ Cincinnati ■ Johannesburg ■ London ■ Madrid ■ Melbourne
Mexico City ■ New York ■ Pacific Grove, CA ■ Scottsdale, AZ ■ Singapore ■ Tokyo ■ Toronto

Music Editor: Clark Baxter
Senior Development Editor: Sharon Adams Poore
Editorial Assistant: Melissa Gleason
Marketing Manager: Jay Hu
Print Buyer: Stacey Weinberger
Permissions Editor: Robert Kauser
Production: Gary Palmatier, Ideas to Images
Designer: Gary Palmatier, Ideas to Images
Photo Researcher: Laurel Anderson, Photosynthesis
Copy Editor: Elizabeth von Radics
Illustrator: Ideas to Images
Cover Designer: Gary Palmatier
Cover Photographer: Jeffrey Aaronson/Network Aspen
Compositor: Ideas to Images
Color Separator: Summerfield Graphics
Printer: Courier/Kendallville

About the cover: An adventurous audience enjoys a performance at the Moab Music Festival. This natural amphitheater, known as "the Grotto," is in Canyonlands National Park. The piano made a special trip up the Colorado River for the event.

The art and photo credits on page 362 are an extension of this copyright page.

Printed in the United States of America

1   2   3   4   5   6   7   8   9   10

For more information, contact Wadsworth Publishing Company, 10 Davis Drive, Belmont, CA 94002, or electronically at
http://www.wadsworth.com

International Thomson Publishing Europe
Berkshire House
168-173 High Holborn
London, WC1V 7AA, United Kingdom

International Thomson Editores
Seneca, 53
Colonia Polanco
11560 México D.F. México

Nelson ITP, Australia
102 Dodds Street
South Melbourne
Victoria 3205 Australia

International Thomson Publishing Asia
60 Albert Street
#15-01 Albert Complex
Singapore 189969

Nelson Canada
1120 Birchmount Road
Scarborough, Ontario
Canada M1K 5G4

International Thomson Publishing Japan
Hirakawa-cho Kyowa Building, 3F
2-2-1 Hirakawa-cho, Chiyoda-ku
Tokyo 102 Japan

International Thomson Publishing Southern Africa
Building 18, Constantia Square
138 Sixteenth Road, P.O. Box 2459
Halfway House, 1685 South Africa

Library of Congress Cataloging-in-Publication Data
Hoffer, Charles R.
    Music listening today / by Charles R. Hoffer.
        p.   cm.
    Includes index.
    ISBN 0-534-51360-3
    1. Music appreciation.   I. Title.
MT6.H565M87   1998
781.1'7— dc21   98-42563
                                                          MN

To Mimi

vi

Brief Contents

Contents

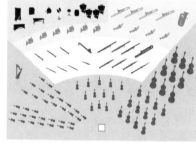

Orchestra seating diagram 38

Part II MUSIC AROUND THE WORLD 47

Africa and the world 61

Middle East 65

Part III WESTERN MUSIC BEFORE 1750   75

Ludwig van Beethoven
174

Preface

Over the past several years, I have had the opportunity to talk with many students and instructors about their music appreciation textbooks. Their comments varied widely, of course, but five attributes arose again and again. I concluded that most people involved with the course believe, as I do as an instructor, that an ideal appreciation text today should do the following:

1. **Provide a solid grounding in Western art music**. *Music Listening Today* covers Bach, Beethoven, Brahms, Bartók, and a wide selection of other composers through a judicious selection of exemplary works. Its repertoire ranges from Gregorian chant to electronic music, and includes works by men and women writing in a variety of styles.

2. **Include a substantial sample of music from different cultures around the world and in the United States**. As the American student body becomes more diverse and increasingly more connected with the rest of the world, contemporary music appreciation courses can no longer be confined to Western art music. *Music Listening Today* devotes two chapters to popular music, one chapter to music for stage and film, and four chapters to folk and ethnic music. The folk music chapters appear well within the book rather than at the end where, as an apparent afterthought, they are easier to ignore.

3. **Help students listen to music perceptively**. Students today are surrounded by music, but rarely do they know how to really listen to it. *Music Listening Today* contains more than seventy Listening Guides to aid students in focusing their attention as they listen. In addition, much of the first chapter is devoted to improving listening skills. Many additional Listening Practice Exercises and suggestions also appear in the ancillary *Study Guide*.

4. **Present information in a clear, concise, and interesting way**. "Classical" music is not a significant part of the lives of most college students; if it were, courses in music appreciation would be unnecessary. Because of this fact, the first chapter of *Music Listening Today*, "Music Listening and You," seeks to relate music to everyday life. For example, the first work readers encounter in the book is from the *Star Wars* film series. Throughout the book the music selected consists of attractive examples of each genre or style.

   In addition, useful and interesting information about topics appears in margin notes, biographical sketches of composers are set apart, and "enrichment boxes" expand on important topics. Music terminology is limited to what is useful to general students, and key points are set off by bullets, numbers, or headings. In short, *Music Listening Today* is user-friendly.

5. **Include these four attributes in a cost-effective package**. Time is limited in a one-semester course. An expensive package that includes a lengthy textbook and a large CD collection does not meet the needs of either instructors or students, who can cover only a portion of the material. *Music Listening Today* is less than 400 pages in length and includes two compact discs bound into the book's covers, with three additional CDs available separately. This package gives the students a book they can read and understand on their own. At the same time, it assures instructors that their students always have easy access to the recorded music included in the course. And it does this at a budget-sensitive price.

THE PACKAGES

Music Listening Today is packaged to suit the needs of traditional classrooms as well as online and other nontraditional instruction. The basic package consists of the book and two CDs that contain a representative sample of its repertoire.

Other packages are available consisting of the *Study Guide*, the multimedia CD-ROM, and the three additional music CDs.

ANCILLARY MATERIALS

Several ancillary items are available for students and instructors.

Study Guide

The *Study Guide*, co-authored with Dr. Mary Ray Johnson, an instructor at Santa Fe Community College, includes the following material to help students learn independently:

◆ Brief overviews of the seven main parts of the book

◆ Brief reviews of the major points of each chapter

◆ Many practice exercises in listening, with answers available

◆ Suggestions for listening to the works presented in the book, as well as three simplified scores for listeners to follow

◆ Flash cards of musical terms

◆ Sample test questions

The *Study Guide* also contains three special sections: One provides an overview of the multimedia CD-ROM, the second is for students in distributed/nontraditional learning courses, and the third offers suggestions for attending concerts.

Multimedia Software

This ancillary, prepared by Dr. Darrell Bailey, professor of music at Indiana University Purdue University Indianapolis, provides on CD-ROM a Windows-compatible program that accesses the book's music CDs to provide helpful visual images and text on the computer's screen. As one listens to a given piece of music, the software displays a graphic of the work that allows the listener to see the structure of the music. An arrow moves from left to right, pointing out characteristics of the music as they occur, allowing the viewer to become more aware of the features of the music as they unfold. Brief text commentary and the notation of the theme appear at key points synchronized with the music. This commentary closely parallels the text and *Study Guide*. Captions are also linked to a glossary of musical terms. In addition, the software contains icons that can be linked directly to complementary sites on the Internet. When combined with the *Study Guide*, this package is not only effective in distributed/distance-learning and nontraditional situations, it also helps all students to develop their listening skills and understand music better.

Online Learning

For fully utilizing Internet resources, as well as assisting students who cannot regularly attend class, *Music Listening Today* introduces a dynamic Web site to use interactively in conjunction with the text, CDs, *Study Guide*, and CD-ROM. The site allows author commentary, course guides, supplemental material, and ideas to be shared in discussion forums. The site is updated regularly to facilitate discussion about music and deliver useful information to classrooms worldwide. For further information visit the Wadsworth music Web site at: **http://music.wadsworth.com**.

Additional Music CDs

Three compact discs are available in a separate album that covers the balance of the musical selections not included on the two core CDs bound with the book. Together the five CDs, prepared by Sony Music Special Products, cover all the works discussed in the many Listening Guides of *Music Listening Today*.

Videotape on Orchestral Instruments

The videotape *The Orchestra and Its Instruments*, which includes Benjamin Britten's *Young Person's Guide to the Orchestra*, is available to instructors for class and library use. It allows students to see the various instruments as they are being played—not just hear them.

Instructor's Manual

The *Instructor's Manual* provides many suggestions for teaching the material covered in the textbook, plus a large sample of objective questions. Also included are many Listening Guides for works that space limitations prevented including in the book. A special feature of the *Instructor's Manual* is a guide to teaching the course in nontraditional settings.

Computerized Testing

Test banks for Windows, Macintosh, and DOS are available. These test banks allow instructors to create, edit, store, and print examinations.

ACKNOWLEDGMENTS

I would like to thank the following professors for their reviews of the manuscript: Ann Anderson, University of Minnesota, Duluth; Mark Anderson, Foothill College, California; Mary Kay Bauer, Western Carolina University; Lynn Hizer, Shepard College, West Virginia; Kenneth Keeling, Carnegie Mellon University; Leslie Lambert, Santa Fe Community College; Connie Mayfield, Kansas City Community College; Ken Peterson, Aims Community College, Colorado; Edward Thompson, Judson College, Illinois; Linda Trucks, Jefferson State Community College, Missouri; and Rick Waldron, Everett Community College, Washington.

I wish to thank Susan Lehrman, who provided valuable help and assistance when it was needed. I want also to recognize the following persons for their part in making *Music Listening Today* a reality: Clark Baxter, music editor at ITP, for his superb overall vision for the book and constant encouragement; Gary Palmatier, Ideas to Images, for his outstanding imagination and talent in designing the book; Elizabeth von Radics for her thorough and highly competent editing of the manuscript; and Darrell Bailey for his innovative ideas, generous sharing of expertise, and dedication in creating the multimedia disc.

I especially want to thank my wife, Mimi, for her loving patience during the many hours I spent in front of the computer. In addition to co-authoring the *Study Guide*, as an experienced instructor of music appreciation courses she was able to offer many valuable suggestions and was very helpful in reading the manuscript and giving encouragement.

Charles R. Hoffer

Music Listening and You

Imagine the world without music—no singing or whistling,
no tapes or compact discs, no music in movies, no marching bands,
no dancing, no hymns, and no organ at baseball games.
The world would certainly be a bleaker place.

Why? The answer to that question will help you understand two
truly fundamental facts about music and human life:

1. **Music is important to the quality of human life.**
2. **People have created different types of music for different purposes.**

These facts have much to say about why and how we listen to
music and what we choose to listen to.

EXISTING ≠ LIVING

Why do people sit at home or in a concert hall and listen carefully to works of music? When you think about it, listening to music only for the sake of hearing it is not a practical thing to do. It doesn't help you earn money, make running easier or faster, or keep you healthy. Listening to music doesn't make much sense until a deeper question is raised:

Are practical, utilitarian activities all there is to life? Don't people want more out of life than eating, sleeping, and working? Don't all of us want times in our lives that seem to rise above everyday existence? Don't we want lives lived in color rather than black-and-white?

Here is an everyday example of this fact: You could leave the walls of your room or apartment bare. But you don't. Your room is more than just a shelter from cold and rain and heat, so you hang posters to break the monotony of the plain walls. You make the room more liveable, more attractive, and less like a monk's cell. Turning a room into a home is an example of an important truth about human beings: Living is more than existing.

Where does music come into the picture of making life more than existence? That's an easy question. And the fundamental fact is: *Music contributes to the quality of life.* It is not the only thing that makes our lives more than physical existence, of course, but it has a significant place and role in enriching human expression and feeling.

Do people need music? Not in the sense that they need to eat and sleep. But they do need it in terms of a rich human life. Humans need music, beauty, gentleness, sensitivity to others, and all the civilizing elements that create a life of substance.

People enjoy music for the same reasons they enjoy growing flowers, wearing attractive clothes, or admiring a sunset.

The psychologist Abraham Maslow (1908–1970) identified music as a source of what he termed "peak experience" in life.

THE USES OF MUSIC

People use music in many different ways. They use it to express their feelings when they sing and whistle and dance. They use it to heighten the drama of a motion picture. Often, people use music as a "sonic background" while studying, working, or driving a car. And people find intellectual and psychological satisfaction in listening carefully to music—a use that pertains directly to this course.

Are some uses of music better or more valid than others? Not really. Some music is better for unifying the crowd at a football game, but other music is better for expressing love. Some music is more rewarding to listen to in a contemplative way, and other music is very danceable. People find or create music that is effective for a particular activity, and the music differs according to its purpose.

Film music is discussed in chapter 45.

The hammer and the screwdriver are both useful tools, but they are different from each other. It's like that with types of music.

ART MUSIC: MUSIC FOR LISTENING

Music created for the intellectual and psychological satisfactions it provides is termed *art music*. It is usually the kind composed for performance in concert halls and opera houses. Often it is called "classical music," although that is not an accurate term as musicians use the word *classical*.

The word *art* describes objects that are created with uncommon skill and devotion. Often the word *fine* is coupled with *art* to distinguish between objects that can be made by most people and those that demand extraordinary skill, effort, and talent. A symphony by Beethoven or a painting by Rembrandt are examples of *fine art* because they show exceptional artistic talent and devotion.

Crafts such as needlepoint and basket weaving are often referred to as "folk arts."

"I KNOW WHAT I LIKE"

Everyone likes at least one kind of music. Usually, it is the type of music with which they are most familiar—and it is often the only kind they listen to. The saying *I know what I like* is true. But so is the phrase *I like what I know*. It is not surprising that people feel more comfortable and competent with the music they know. The problem with stopping at this comfort level, however, is that it usually confines you to only a tiny bit of the rich world of music.

Consider this analogy: Suppose you had the chance to advise a person from a foreign country about what to see on a tour of the United States. You might suggest seeing the part of the country where you live, and that would be fine. But is that all a visitor should experience of the United States? What about its other great cities and natural wonders? The analogy with music seems clear. There is a vast and varied world of music out there. Why confine yourself to just one small portion and miss out on other kinds of music that could enrich your life? The more people know about music, especially art music, the more quality they add to their lives.

LEARNING TO LISTEN

How can you improve your ability to hear music, especially art music, more fully? Here are some suggestions.

Hearing and Listening Are Not the Same

Most people use the word *listen* in a very casual way. Being conscious of how music sounds is far from really listening to it. When musicians talk about listening, they mean an activity requiring concentration. There is an important fundamental point here: *Listening to music is much more than just hearing its sounds.* Unless you really

Remind yourself often of this crucial fact as you progress through the course.

grasp the basic difference between listening and hearing, chances are you will hear music only superficially and, as a result, will find limited meaning and satisfaction from listening to it.

Listening for Musical Features

Acquire the habit of describing the features of the particular work you listen to. Don't just let the sounds wash over you; don't stop with being aware of only that some music is playing. Don't daydream or think about other things or visualize scenes while listening to the music.

Instead, as you listen, decide something about:

◆ The nature of the melodies and themes

◆ The texture of the music

◆ The nature of the rhythm and its patterns

◆ The changes in dynamic levels

◆ The dominant timbres

◆ The use of form and other musical practices

Over time you will get better at noticing and describing these aspects of music. But try to determine these six points even if you are not sure your answers are correct.

Different Ways of Listening

At least three different modes are possible, and each has its place when listening to music. One mode involves listening for the sensuous qualities in a musical work, for the physical effect it produces. The chills that run down a listener's spine when an orchestra or choral group reaches a climactic point in a musical work is evidence of music's sensual power.

A second mode of listening centers on the expressive power of music. A musical work may give an impression of sadness, but it does not describe what has caused the sadness. The emotional responses produced by music are general, not specific.

The fact that music does not express definite meanings is one of its assets. Words are often too conventional and inflexible to allow for full expression. But a musical work may be heard by a thousand people, and each will hear it in a slightly different way, because each of us lives a different life.

A third mode of listening might be called "sheerly musical." It consists of listening for what happens in the music: what notes are being played or sung, at what speed, in what combinations with other notes, on what instrument, with what degree of loudness, and so on. This mode provides another avenue of interest and satisfaction for listeners. It is also the mode in which you become aware of the skill and imagination that musicians bring to creating interesting combinations of sounds. This mode usually requires some training to achieve, something this course and book seek to provide.

This point can be illustrated by the three Chinese characters shown below. At first glance these symbols look about the same to someone who doesn't read Chinese. But a person competent in that language notices the differences and knows that the character on the left means "painting," the one in the center, "daytime," and the character on the right, "book."

Sidenotes:

Fantasizing may be enjoyable, but it takes your attention away from the music.

All of these musical terms are explained in the following three chapters.

Adopting the habit of listening for specific features applies to all kinds of music from all parts of the world.

Sensuous means "of or appealing to the senses."

The "sheerly musical" mode involves the intellect as well as feelings.

To a degree, listening to art music perceptively is an acquired skill. It usually doesn't just happen.

As in learning to read Chinese, we need to develop our ability to hear what is taking place in a musical work.

The three modes of listening are not mutually exclusive, of course. People switch back and forth among them as they listen. They can feel the rich warmth of a particular chord, and then respond to the romantic power of a flowing melody, and also understand that the music uses a certain form.

Listening perceptively is an active experience. It requires that listeners mentally participate in the process.

Listener Expectations

Everyday life has taught us not to listen carefully. People learn to ignore the sounds of traffic, clocks ticking, and air-conditioners turning on and off. People learn to "tune" music too. They must, because music is heard nearly everywhere—in airports, supermarkets, dentists' offices, and while driving the car. From cleaning house to jogging, music accompanies almost every activity. People would become mentally exhausted if they listened intently to all the music they heard each day.

What's more, most people don't listen carefully to popular music. Instead, they get most of what it has to offer by "absorbing" it, much as they absorb the impression of a wallpaper pattern. It is not a question of which kind of music is better. Popular music and art music simply have different uses, and therefore they have different listening requirements.

And what are those differences?

♦ Most art music is not played as loudly as popular music. To a novice listener, art music must seem pretty pale when heard at its more restrained level of sound.

♦ Most popular music consists of short pieces that last only a few minutes. The time span of many works of art music is *much* longer. To someone not used to it, listening to art music may seem like watching a videotape of a basketball game in slow motion.

You should develop a casual style of listening for most of the music you hear in everyday life. You should also learn to listen in a contemplative, thoughtful way to art music.

♦ Popular music does not usually contain the development of themes or the other sophisticated musical practices of art music. It is simpler and doesn't require as much effort to understand what it offers.

♦ With the exception of stage productions, art music is presented without theatrics, flashing lights, or gyrating performers.

Most popular music is heard in situations that focus on activities other than music. The opposite is true for art music.

The Importance of Memory

Memory is absolutely essential for understanding music. At any particular moment, only one sound can be heard. What was sounded before that moment exists only in your memory. What will be heard in future moments can only be a guess based on what was heard previously. When listening to a work for the second or third time, your guess about what will be sounded later relies partly on a memory of previous hearings.

The careful analysis of an artwork requires more time, of course.

It's not like this with what you see. An entire painting or piece of sculpture can be seen in a second or two. If memory were to be made an essential part of looking at a painting, it might be done something this: An unfamiliar picture is covered except for one thin, vertical band. You can see the picture only as the open band moves across the painting from one side to the other. Your comprehension of the picture would result from (1) your memory of what you've seen, (2) the portion you could see at the moment, and (3) your guess about what would be revealed by the open band in succeeding moments.

Not only is hearing the same work several times a good way to remember it better, it also helps in acquiring positive feelings for the work.

Would this be a difficult way to see a picture? Definitely! But that is the way music is perceived, and that is why memory is so important in listening to music. In the foregoing analogy, the more often you see the band drawn across the picture, the better your recall of the fragments and the more accurate your comprehension of the whole. That is why hearing a musical work several times, especially a complex one, is necessary for understanding it.

The Importance of Responding

People respond to almost everything they experience in life. They notice and have feelings about animals, possessions, and pieces of music. Each note in a musical work evokes at least some response *if it is noticed*. A changed rhythm, a note in a chord, or the instrument playing a melody affects a listener's feelings. A willingness to respond to what is heard in music is nearly as important as remembering it.

You can't respond to something you don't hear.

Listening to music with no feeling must be something like watching a basketball game in which the baskets have been removed. Likewise, listening to music with no feeling has little point. The psychological satisfaction is missing, and only a sterile, intellectual experience remains.

How can you become more responsive to musical sounds? It seems simple, but just *trying* to be more sensitive to what you hear is a good first step. Open yourself up to the qualities of music.

You can also play a short section of a work, say, five seconds, and then ask yourself, *What kind of response did I have to that portion of the music?*

Using the Listening Guides

The Listening Guides as well as the other aids in this text will help improve your skill in listening to music. Listening Practice Exercises also appear in the *Study Guide*. These exercises ask you to listen and then make a judgment about an aspect of the music. In some cases, you are asked to compare the features of two different works.

A MUSICAL GUIDED TOUR

Listening Guides help keep your attention on the music, especially when listening to long works.

A Listening Guide is something like a map that one buys for a walking tour of the points of interest in a city or a national park. The map tells you what street or trail to walk along and informs you about what you see. A Listening Guide takes you on a musical tour.

The Listening Guides in this book have several features. The elapsed times from the beginning of the work are listed at the left margin. These times apply to the recording on the compact discs (CDs) that accompany this book. It is not necessary to follow the times while listening; but because they offer an idea of how much time will pass between features of the work, the timings can prove helpful.

To the right of each time is a brief description of a feature of the music. These descriptions may refer to the form of the music, the instruments playing, the quality of the rhythm, or other noticeable elements in the music. The notation for the main themes is sometimes provided as a visual representation of what is heard. It is not expected that you can read music, but the suggestions offered in the enrichment boxes in chapters 2 and 3 will help you understand notation.

A different recording of the same work will not have exactly the same timings, but they will be approximately the same.

Getting Started: The Theme from *Star Wars*

Talking and reading about music is useful up to a point, but then the time comes for listening to examples. The CDs included with this book include the main theme from the *Star Wars* films. Because it is familiar to you, it is a good work with which to begin listening carefully to music.

Although the composer, John Williams, originally created this work to enhance the film, he also succeeded in writing music that people find interesting to listen to apart from the film. In fact, there is much more to this music than can be perceived in just one hearing.

The music is associated with the characters and situations in the *Star Wars* films, so its various sections have different personalities. For example, the music for the beautiful Princess Leia sounds very different from the music for the space ship.

"Star Wars: Main Title" is presented in a simple Listening Guide—simple because it points out only the main sections of the music. Also, it uses as few musical terms as possible because they have not yet been introduced.

By early 1997 *Star Wars* had grossed more money than any film in the history of motion pictures up to that time.

No notation is presented in this Listening Guide, however. Notation appears in the Listening Guides from chapter 2 on.

L I S T E N I N G G U I D E

John Williams: "Star Wars: Main Title"
CD 1 Track 1

0:00	**1**	The music begins with a short fanfare.
0:08		The main theme begins. It is strong and marchlike in character, and trumpets and other brass instruments are prominent.
0:26		The main theme continues, played by the violins and other string instruments.
0:49		The main theme returns, played by the full orchestra over more-elaborate accompanying music.
1:17		The music becomes quiet, but after a while it begins to build.
1:43		Many repeated notes are played loudly in a strong rhythm pattern.
2:01	**2**	The character of the music changes as it is associated with the battle portion of *Star Wars*.
2:21		The main theme returns in a more militant style. It follows a similar pattern to the one earlier featuring the horns, then the strings, followed by the full orchestra. The music then grows softer as it leads to the next section.
3:13	**3**	Princess Leia's theme is played by the lower strings. It has a warm and passionate quality.
4:05		The main theme returns, played by the full orchestra and continued by the strings.
4:38		The brass instruments are featured as they loudly play again a portion of the battle music. The music then grows slower and more quiet.
5:16		A closing section *(coda)* begins, featuring the brasses. The music is slow and powerful.
5:46		After a drumroll is clearly heard, "Stars Wars: Main Title" concludes in a decisive manner.

John Williams

John Williams was born in 1932 in New York City, but at the age of sixteen moved with his family to Los Angeles. His father was a musician, so music was a logical career choice for John. He studied at UCLA, intending to become a concert pianist. After three years in the U.S. Air Force, he spent a year at the Juilliard School of Music in New York, still concentrating on piano, and then returned to Los Angeles, where he studied composition with the noted Mario Castelnuovo-Tedesco.

Soon Williams was in demand as a pianist-arranger, starting in television in 1958. He composed music for nearly every kind of TV program, ranging from *Wagon Train* to *Gilligan's Island* to *Mod Squad*. By the 1970s he had become a major composer in American films. His first highly regarded score was for *The Reivers*, a film based on William Faulkner's final novel, set in Mississippi in 1905. This was soon followed by *Jane Eyre*, which is set in the Yorkshire countryside of England. His efforts continued in the 1980s and 1990s, reaching a total of more than seventy-two film scores by the beginning of the decade, and his composition of film scores has continued unabated.

Williams's attention has not been confined to music for television and films, however. From 1980 to 1993, he was conductor of the Boston Pops Orchestra. In addition, he has composed a number of concert works, as well as adapted some of his film music for orchestra.

Best-Known Works
Film scores:
- *Star Wars* and its sequels
- *Superman*
- *Close Encounters of the Third Kind*
- *Jaws*
- *The Towering Inferno*
- *Indiana Jones and the Temple of Doom*
- *Dracula*

THE GOALS OF MUSIC APPRECIATION

We return to the main theme from *Star Wars* in the final chapter of the book. By then you will have acquired additional information and listening skills that will help accomplish the main goals of a music appreciation course and textbook:

♦ To increase your ability to listen to music perceptively. Hearing the notes and rhythms—the elements of musical works—is what listening to music is all about.

♦ To acquire basic, useful information about music: its styles, forms, terminology, and historical contexts.

The result of achieving these two goals will expand and enhance the quality of your life. The more you know and can hear, the greater the chances that your feelings about art music will become more positive. It is hoped that with increasing knowledge about art music will come an ever increasing enjoyment that will lead to still greater competence and interest in a continuously growing cycle. In music, positive attitudes, listening skill, and knowledge reinforce one another.

A *coda* is a closing section of a musical work.

C o d a

What does music have to do with adding quality to our lives? Perhaps the American patriot and second president of the United States, John Adams, summarized best the value of the arts in a letter he wrote to his wife, Abigail, in 1780 during the hard times of the Revolutionary War:

I must study politics and war, that my sons may have liberty to study mathematics and philosophy, geography, natural history and naval architecture, navigation, commerce, and agriculture, in order to give their children a right to study painting, poetry, music, architecture, statuary, tapestry, and porcelain.

Rhythm

2

Music is a time art. Paintings and pieces of sculpture occupy space, but the "canvas" of music is time. Because all music occupies time, all of it has rhythm, even when it's not a toe-tapping rhythm that makes it easy to mark the time. The term for the orderly flow of music through time is *rhythm*. It is a comprehensive word that includes beat, meter, and tempo.

The word *rhythm* comes from a Greek word meaning "flow."

BEAT: THE MUSIC'S PULSE

The *beat* is the regular pulse found in most music. It is what people tap as they listen, and it is most easily heard in marches and dance music when it is marked by the drum sound. Although the beat can be felt most of the time in a musical work, it is not always sounded overtly.

Furthermore, not all music has a beat, although most of the music we hear in the United States today does. It is central to most of the music of the Western world. In fact, our sense of meter depends on the presence of beats.

Usually, beats are heard and felt in a steady, even succession. If they are erratic, the effect is something like listening to a person who says a few words very rapidly, and then some more words very slowly, and then some words moderately fast, and so on. It is tiring and irritating to listen to someone talk with such changes of speed. The speed with which beats occur in music can change within a piece of music, but usually the changes are gradual and occur by design of the composer and performer.

Throughout a piece of music, a drum doesn't need to tap the beat, although it often does in dance music and marches.

METER: THE PATTERNS OF BEATS

The human mind has the tendency to seek out patterns in what is heard and seen. It is easier to remember a telephone number like 555-1212 instead of one like 555-2719, because 1212 has a pattern.

When people hear groups of beats, even though the beats may be exactly as strong as one another, their minds tend to group them into twos, threes, or fours; only occasionally are groups larger than four. Instead of beat-beat-beat-beat-beat-beat and so on, the mind tends to perceive **beat**-beat-beat **beat**-beat-beat or **beat**-beat **beat**-beat **beat**-beat. The grouping of the beats (*not* the notes) into patterns is called *meter*.

Meter is very evident in group cheers and rap music. Here is an example of a cheer (the *1* represents the more strongly stressed beat or the *downbeat*):

A well-known number by the Glen Miller band in the late 1930s was "Pennsylvania 6-5000," the telephone number of a New York hotel.

Whether the meter is perceived in twos or threes depends on the nature of the music.

    1   2   **1** 2 **1** 2   **1** 2
Two bits, **four** bits, **six** bits, a **dol**lar,

    1 2 **1** 2 **1** 2   **1** 2
All for **Den**ver **stand** up and **hol**ler!

Here is an example of meter in a poem, "The Raven" by Edgar Allan Poe:

    | ᴗ | ᴗ | ᴗ | ᴗ
Once u**pon** a **mid**night **drear**y,

    | ᴗ | ᴗ | ᴗ | ᴗ
As I **pon**dered **weak** and **wear**y,

The Notation of Rhythm

Music existed long before a system for writing it down was devised. In fact, even today most folk music and jazz are rarely written down. In other words, the sounds used in music and the notation of those sounds are two quite different matters. Hearing the rhythm and other elements of music is clearly the more important and valuable of the two. Knowing about the notation of rhythm, however, usually helps in learning and understanding music better.

Although the applications of the system of notating rhythm can be quite complex, the basic system is rather simple: It consists of various combinations of note heads, stems, and flags.

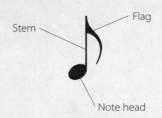

As the combinations progress from an empty oval to a solid head with a stem and flag(s), each note is sounded one-half the length of time that the previous note sounds.

A whole note ○ usually receives four beats.

A half note ♩ usually receives two beats.

A quarter note ♩ usually receives one beat.

An eighth note ♪ usually receives half a beat.

A sixteenth note ♬ usually receives a quarter beat.

And the opposite is also true: As the notes change from solid heads, stems, and flags toward empty ovals, the length of the note played doubles. Therefore, all other things being equal, a passage of music that contains notes with many filled-in heads and flags is probably going to move quickly.

As can be seen from looking at the different note lengths, the system for notating rhythm is built on a 2:1 ratio, with note lengths being either one-half or double the length of the other. The 2:1 ratio is even carried over into the use of the dots that are

sometimes placed to the right of a note. The dot to the right of a note tells a performer to increase the length of the note by one-half. So a note that is two beats long becomes three beats when a dot is added. Dotted notes are used extensively when the beat is divided into threes instead of twos.

The note with a solid head and a stem ♩ (a quarter note) is most frequently used to represent the beat, although any note can be used for that purpose. For example, the following three lines of notes sound exactly alike when performed, even though they look different from one another. The reason they sound the same is the different numbers at the beginning of each line. This vertical combination is the meter signature or time signature.

The top number of a meter signature usually indicates the number of beats in the measure, and the bottom number usually indicates the type of note that should receive one beat. In the first example above, the eighth note (♪) receives the beat; in the middle example, it is the quarter note (♩); and in the last example, it is the half note (♩). The notation of rhythm, including silences, called rests, is described more fully in the appendix.

The familiar song "Jingle Bells" has an easily felt two-beat meter. The beats are marked with short vertical lines.

Jin - gle bells,   jin - gle bells,   jin - gle all the way.

> Horizontal beams are often used in place of flags when two or more notes occur in the same beat. Beams help the eye to group notes when reading music notation.

Beats normally follow a metrical pattern. The meter of a piece of music is indicated in music notation in two ways. One is by a *meter signature* or *time signature*. Usually, they are placed at the beginning of a work or section. In some twentieth-century works, however, the meter changes every few measures, and so meter signatures are sometimes found within the work.

The other way in which music notation indicates the pattern of beats is by vertical lines that enclose the beats in the pattern. These units of rhythm are called *measures*.

> Beats normally adhere to a regular pattern. If they don't, the music has not been arranged correctly. For example, the punctuation of a sentence like *Every piece of. Music can be enjoyed, for its sounds. And rhythm.* tends to obscure its meaning.

Two-beat meter		
Beat Beat	**Beat** Beat
Measure	Measure

> Measures are also called *bars*, possibly because their vertical lines look something like bars on a window.

Music students learn that the first beat of a measure is normally performed more strongly than the other beats in the measure. That is why it is the first beat.

Syncopation

Sometimes the emphasis, called *accent*, is deliberately placed off the beat. *Syncopation* happens either by adding the emphasis where it is not expected, or by removing the emphasis from where it is expected. Here is an example of syncopation from a spiritual:

Lit - tle Da - vid   play on   your   harp.   Hal - le - lu,   Hal - le - lu!

Syncopation   Syncopation

In the example, the words *on* and *Hal-* occur halfway through beats instead of on the beat. The syncopation could be removed from the melody and the accent would fall normally, but the song would lose much of its character.

TEMPO: THE SPEED OF BEATS

Another important aspect of rhythm is *tempo*, which is the speed of the beats. The tempo of a piece of music can be indicated in two ways. One is by a metronome marking such as ♩ = 84. A metronome is a clocklike device (either windup or electronic) that indicates the beat with audible ticks and/or a flashing light. Metronomes can be set to provide exactly the desired number of beats per minute. With a few exceptions, most tempos in music range between one and three beats per second.

The other way of indicating tempo is through the use of words, which are usually in Italian. These verbal descriptors are general, such as *very fast*, *moderate*, and *slow*. Because the terms are general, the tempo of a work marked *Allegro* will

> *Tempo* means "time" in Italian.

differ somewhat from one performer or conductor to the next. The words indicating tempo not only provide guidance for performers, they also appear in concert programs and liner notes to identify the large, independent sections, or *movements,* of instrumental works.

The following are the more common terms for tempo.

Italian Term	Meaning
Largo	Very slow, broad
Grave	Very slow, heavy
Adagio	Slow, leisurely
Andante	"Walking," moderate tempo
Moderato	Moderate
Allegretto	Little allegro, moving easily
Allegro	Moderately fast, moving briskly
Allegro molto	Much allegro, very brisk
Vivace	Lively
Presto	Very fast
Prestissimo	As fast as possible

Other words are often attached to the indication of tempo. These usually describe the style of the music, not the tempo. Examples of additional words include *con fuoco* (with fire or force), *sostenuto* (sustained), and *con brio* (brusque). Sometimes modifiers such as *meno* (less) and *piu* (more) are added. Two Italian terms affecting tempo that have close parallels in English are *ritardando* (*ritard* or slow down) and *accelerando* (accelerate or speed up).

Georges Bizet

Georges Bizet (1838–1875) first learned music from his parents and was admitted to the Paris Conservatory at about the age of ten. By age seventeen he composed Symphony in C, which was not performed until 1935. He was awarded the Prix de Rome and began composing music mostly for the theater and opera. For a variety of reasons, much of his music was not well received, and he earned his living arranging music and giving piano lessons.

After serving in the national guard in the Franco-Prussian War in 1870, Bizet was commissioned to write incidental music for Daudet's play *L'Arlésienne (The Woman of Arles)*. The play was not successful, but fortunately Bizet's music survived.

Most of Bizet's fame is the result of his opera *Carmen*. Its plot is built around the gradual decline of Don José, a simple honest

> Today *Carmen* is perhaps the best-known and best-loved opera in the world.

soldier, caused by his infatuation with Carmen, a Spanish gypsy girl who worked in a cigarette factory. The music is filled with one colorful and beautiful work after another. At first it was not well received and was condemned for its "obscene" text. Apparently, the patrons of the Opera Comique, which was somewhat of a family theater, did not enjoy watching Don José's life being ruined by the amoral Carmen.

Bizet had poured enormous effort into *Carmen* and was worn out by months of rehearsal and tension. His sensitive nature was simply unable to tolerate its initial cool reception. He died three months after it its premiere.

Best-Known Works
Orchestra:
- Symphony in C
- *L'Arlésienne*, Suites 1 and 2
Opera:
- *Carmen*

Notes and beats are not the same thing. Although a tempo may be slow, many notes can be played during the beat, giving the impression of much motion. On the other hand, the tempo may be fast but if the duration of the notes is long, it reduces the sense of movement. Of course, all things being equal, more notes are heard when the tempo is fast than when it is slow.

Rhythm in Bizet's Farandole

Georges Bizet ("Bee-*zay*") composed twenty-seven pieces of music to go with the play *L'Arlésienne (The Woman from Arles)* by Alphonse Daudet. Later his friend Ernest Guiraud arranged the music into two suites. *Farandole* is from Suite No. 2.

For the main melody, Bizet chose an old song called "Marche de Turenne" from the Provençe region of France. The tune is still sung at Christmastime in English under the title "The March of the Kings."

Bizet's *Farandole* has both a marchlike and a dancelike theme. Notice that the march and the dance have different meters, as you can see from key signatures of the music notation in the musical examples. As you listen, try counting the march **1**-2-3 **1**-2-3 instead of **1**-2 **1**-2. You will quickly sense that the music is in two-beat meter, because the three-beat pattern just doesn't seem to fit.

Some marches have been written for processions or coronations and they are slower. Marches at football games are usually played at a much faster tempo than military marches.

L I S T E N I N G   G U I D E

Georges Bizet: *Farandole* from *L'Arlésienne*, Suite No. 2

CD ① Track ④

0:00   ④ The full orchestra plays the opening theme at a lively march tempo in a strong four-beat meter. The first three notes of the theme seem to emphasize the solid rhythm of the music.

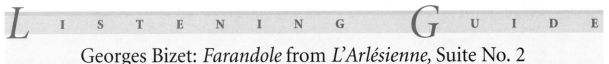

0:33   ⑤ The tempo of the music becomes more rapid as the second theme enters. The rhythm is not quite as strongly felt in the second theme, because the sounds are not as forceful as in the first. The music grows in intensity as it moves along.

1:16   The strings play the second theme. The tempo remains fast.

1:27   The strings play the first theme again, but this time at the faster tempo used for the second theme.

1:38   The woodwinds play the second theme again.

1:44   The tempo is still quite fast, but the four-beat meter returns as the strings continue with the opening theme.

1:55   The woodwinds take up the second theme again.

2:17   ⑥ The full orchestra combines both the first and second themes as the marchlike rhythm of the music continues.

3:07   *Farandole* concludes in a flurry of sound.

POLYRHYTHM

African music has a well-deserved reputation for its exciting rhythms. "Mitamba Yalagala Kumchuzi" is a good example of this fact. It comes from the Zaramo tribe of the coastal region near Dar es Salaam in Tanzania in East Africa.

What makes the rhythm of this music exciting is the appearance of several rhythms at the same time, what is referred to as *polyrhythm*. When hearing "Mitamba Yalagala Kumchuzi" for the first time, it may seem like one of the drummers is lost and coming in at the wrong time. Not so. Instead, he is playing a different pattern. As the music progresses, other performers join in with their own particular patterns. Although you might expect rhythmic confusion because of the different patterns occurring at the same time, instead the effect is exhilarating.

L I S T E N I N G   G U I D E

Africa: "Mitamba Yalagala Kumchuzi"
CD 1 Track 7

0:00   7 The music starts with one drummer playing two sounds, high and low. Other drummers soon enter, and several different rhythmic patterns are heard at the same time. Rattles enter.

0:44   A singer begins and is soon answered by other singers. The rhythmic patterns continue in the drums and rattles.

1:00   The lead singer exchanges portions of the music with the other singers in an overlapping call-and-response arrangement.

1:33   Although the music continues, often for an hour or more, the recording fades.

African music is described in chapter 9.

Rhythm is not the only interesting feature of "Mitamba Yalagala Kumchuzi." The recording was made with five goblet drums, four cylindrical drums, and tines rattles. Each of the two types of drums has its own distinctive quality of sound, and these different qualities add to the music. The call-and-response pattern between the vocal soloist and the group also contributes to the African quality of the music.

C o d a

Rhythm is the heartbeat of music. Like the human heartbeat,
it is not an intellectual phenomenon. It does not lend itself well to
cerebral discussions. Instead, it is learned and understood
through listening to and making music.

Melody and Harmony

3

It is obvious that most music contains sounds that are higher or lower than others. These differences in high and low sound are the second important element of music.

PITCH: THE HIGH AND LOW OF SOUNDS

As used in music, the word *pitch* refers to the highness or lowness of a sound. It is the result of the number of vibrations made by the sound-making instrument—the human vocal cords, the reed of the clarinet, the string of the violin, and so on. The greater the number of vibrations, the higher the sound. For example, a sound-producing medium vibrating 440 times per second produces the standard pitch for the note A above middle C.

Pitches by themselves are not music. To be useful in music, pitches must meet one of three conditions:

◆ Be a part of a series of pitches that forms a logical unit of music—melody.

◆ Be a part of two or more logical series of pitches sounded in contrast with each other—counterpoint.

◆ Be a part of several pitches sounded at the same time—harmony.

In many cultures pitch is described in terms of large/ small or masculine/feminine.

This pitch is easily sung by females and children and can be played on many different instruments.

MELODY: PITCHES IN A COHESIVE SERIES

The first of these conditions—a series of pitches that forms a cohesive entity—is referred to as *melody*. The important words here are *cohesive* and *entity*. The pitches must seem to belong together and be a unit—an entity. Not just any sequence of pitches will do.

What causes some melodies to be memorable and emotionally moving and others to seem forgettable and senseless? No one really knows, although from time to time scholars attempt to provide general melodic guidelines. For example, a series made up of the same pitch sounded again and again in a drone has little chance of being a melody that anyone will want to sing or listen to; it lacks musical interest and variety. On the other hand, a melody in which the pitches seem to have little relationship to each other won't work either; it lacks a sense of unity. A good melody seems to achieve the perfect balance between unity and variety.

Melodies are what people generally remember in music. It's what they whistle, sing, and focus their attention on when listening to music. No doubt you can easily recall the opening melody from *Star Wars*. Some melodies over the centuries have acquired names of their own. In many Protestant churches, the Doxology is sung to a melody named "Old Hundredth." The names of the melodies of hymns are often given in the hymnals just under the title.

Two other terms are sometimes used as synonyms for *melody*. The word *tune* is a less formal term, the implication being that a tune is less serious and complex than a melody or theme. A *theme* identifies an instrumental melody that plays an important role in a musical work. We heard a theme in the opening melody of *Star Wars*.

Many melodies are known by their words, such as "Take Me Out to the Ball Game" and "Anchors Away!" Some melodies have two or more different sets of words. What we know in the United States as "My country 'tis of thee . . ." ("America") is the national anthem of Great Britain, where its words are "God Save Our Glorious Queen."

The topic of how composers work with themes in music is covered in part IV.

A theme is of interest both for its musical qualities and what the composer does with it during the course of the piece. In some cases, quite average themes have become the basis for great musical works. A prime example of this is the famous four-note theme in Beethoven's Symphony No. 5, which is presented in part IV.

Features of Melodies

We can better understand melodies by considering their various dimensions and features.

Length   Some melodies are short and concise; others stretch out over many measures. The themes in *Star Wars* are clear and to the point, but in contrast the melody for Joachin Rodrigo's *Concierto de Aranjuez,* discussed in chapter 4, seems more flowing.

Range   Some melodies stay within a narrow range of pitches. Others spread out over a wide pitch distance.

Steps and leaps   Some melodies, like the beginning of "Row, Row, Row Your Boat," move by small steps from one note to the next. Other melodies leap to a note a distance

Pitches in Music Notation

The representation of pitch in music notation is partly graphic. The horizontal lines and the spaces between them provide a visual image of the distance from one pitch to another. Both lines and spaces are used to represent pitches.

Middle C

The five lines and their spaces make up the staff. The higher a note is placed on the staff, the higher it sounds. The clef (French for "key" and meaning the key to the musical piece) sets the general level of pitch for the five lines. For example, in the treble clef, which is indicated by the symbol 𝄞, the inside curl goes around the line for G above middle C. In the bass clef indicated by 𝄢, the two dots straddle the line for F below middle C. The relationship between the two clefs can be seen when they are combined, as shown here.

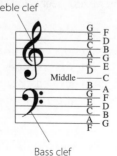

Treble clef

Middle

Bass clef

Only the first seven letters of the alphabet are used in music. The notes can be modified by a sharp (♯), raising the pitch one half-step, or a flat (♭), lowering the pitch one half-step. Knowing the names of notes is not essential to appreciating music.

Much as words are read on the page, notes placed one after another in a row are to be performed sequentially. Notes that are aligned vertically on the page are sounded at the same time as a cluster or group, called a chord. Chords, too, are read from left to right across the page.

Therefore notation gives you a visual representation of what the music sounds like. It can help you sense and remember what you hear.

away. As we all know from the occasional strain of singing "The Star-Spangled Banner," it opens with several leaps that carry it over a considerable range:

The word *leap* may seem like an exaggeration for any note that is not adjacent, but it is the appropriate term.

O ___ say can you see, By ___

Contour Each melody has its own outline, or contour, just as each city has it own skyline. In fact, melody is often referred to as the "line" or "melodic line." Here is the contour for the first several measures of "The Star-Spangled Banner":

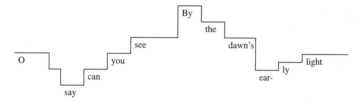

And here is the contour of "America":

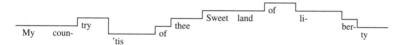

Decorative notes In some melodies each note seems solid and unadorned. The Shaker hymn melody is a prime example of a straightforward, undecorated melody. "Simple Gifts" is an American Shaker song from around 1840. Notice that the melody moves in a steplike progression complemented by infrequent leaps.

We will hear the opposite in decoration in the melody for Rodrigo's *Concierto,* which has many ornamented notes.

Aaron Copland

Aaron Copland (1900–1990) was born in Brooklyn, New York, the son of Russian Jewish immigrants. His family had little money, and he took his first music lessons from an older sister. He studied books and scores at the New York Public Library. After graduating from high school, he studied piano and harmony in New York.

In 1921 Copland went to the American School of Music at Fontainebleau in France. The teacher there was a remarkable woman named Nadia Boulanger. (She and her sister Lydia Boulanger are discussed in chapter 35). He became the first of a long list of young American composers to study with her.

Copland became interested in jazz in the late 1920s, and several of his compositions contain elements of jazz. In the early 1930s, his music tended to be more abstract. He began to be concerned, however, about the

Copland was an unassuming man who cared much for people.

gap between the music-loving audiences and contemporary composers. Copland wrote, "It made no sense to ignore them and to continue writing as if they did not exist. I felt that it was worth the effort to see if I couldn't say what I had to say in the simplest possible terms."

His efforts at greater simplicity were successful, and he was able to retain the interest and respect of trained musicians while at the same time pleasing the general concert-going public. In addition to his music, he lectured at many universities and wrote several very readable books about music for persons who are not musicians.

Best-Known Works
Orchestra:
  A Lincoln Portrait
  El salón México
Ballet:
  Billy the Kid
  Rodeo
  Appalachian Spring
Film scores:
  Of Mice and Men
  The Red Pony
  Our Town
Songs:
  Old American Songs (2 sets)

L I S T E N I N G   G U I D E

Shaker Melody, arranged by Aaron Copland: "Simple Gifts"
CD 1 Track 8

0:00 **8** The strings play a short introduction, and the singer begins:

'Tis the gift to be sim-ple, 'tis the gift to be free, 'Tis the

gift to come down where you ought to be

'Tis the gift to be simple, 'tis the gift to be free,
'Tis the gift to come down where you ought to be.

The melody for the next two lines is very similar to that of the first two lines:

And when we find ourselves in the place just right,
'Twill be in the valley of love and delight.

0:32 **9** The singer sings a contrasting section of the song:

When true sim-pli-ci-ty is gained, to bow and to bend we shan't be a-shamed.

When true simplicity is gained.

The concluding line is sung with almost the same melody that concluded the first half of the song:

To bow and to bend we shan't be ashamed

0:41 The melody of the second two lines returns, but with new words and a few small changes:

To turn, turn will be our delight,
'Till by turning, turning come round right.

0:58 The opening four lines are repeated exactly.

1:27 A short concluding section is played by the strings.

1:40 "Simple Gifts" ends with an "Amen" cadence.

The Shakers were a religious sect that earned their name from the fact that they shook when they felt the spirit of God. They lived a simple, celibate life and developed a number of communities in New England and Kentucky. They are known today for the simple, elegant furniture they designed.

What Affects the Impression of a Melody?

Just about everything affects the impression a listener gains of a melody.

Accompanying music The accompanying music is like the setting for a play or film. Its purpose is to contribute to the overall effect of the play. Effective accompanying music helps make a melody more pleasing and interesting, to sound its best. The opposite is true of accompaniments that overwhelm the melody or do little to make it sound better.

Aaron Copland's arrangement of the American Shaker song "Simple Gifts" demonstrates the skillful use of chords in contributing to the effect of the melody.

He makes the setting clear and simple in keeping with the mood of the music and its text. The simplicity of the music also makes the chord changes easier to hear.

Tone quality and instrument characteristics A melody played on a flute gives listeners one impression, but the same melody played on the guitar gives another. A melody may be more suited to one instrument than another. For example, what sounds good when played on a violin may not when played on a trombone, and vice versa. In some cases, the versions played by different instruments are just different, and neither is more appropriate than another. For example, both the song "Simple Gifts" and the variations on that melody by Copland in his ballet music for *Appalachian Spring* merit careful listening.

Appalachian Spring is discussed in chapter 42.

Rhythm The rhythmic properties of a melody have a major effect on its quality. The wrong tempo can destroy the effectiveness of a memorable melody. Imagine singing "Jingle Bells" very slowly. A merry holiday song now sounds like a funeral dirge. On the other hand, a vital rhythm pattern can make an average melody something people want to listen to.

Style of performance If you sing a melody like "America" in short, detached notes instead of a flowing singing style, it will seem like a different song. The manner in which the melody is played or sung can make a big difference.

Quality of performance The same piece played by two performers, one who is exceptionally able and another who is mediocre, can leave listeners with very different impressions of the music. Outstanding concert performers sometimes take pieces made familiar by less competent players and render them in ways that sound refreshing and beautiful. Listeners react as though hearing the music for the first time and are amazed at how much they enjoyed a piece that had always seemed trite.

COUNTERPOINT: MELODIES SOUNDED TOGETHER

The word *counterpoint* comes from the time when notes were called "points." The adjectival form of the word is *contrapuntal*.

Melodies can be combined in one of two ways. One is as a *round*. You have known about rounds since you were in elementary school. In a round exactly the same music is sung, but each line starts at a specified time interval. For example, one group of singers sings, "Are you sleeping? Are you sleeping?" and then the second group follows, singing the same melody and words while the first group continues on with "Brother John, Brother John." The process continues with additional groups joining in until the round is sung a given number of times and the last group concludes singing alone.

When one group or instrumental part periodically follows another exactly, it is called *imitation*. When the imitation continues for an entire song or section of music, it is called *strict imitation* as in a round. The term *round* implies a short song. A *canon* is a somewhat longer and more complex piece than a round in strict imitation.

Canon means "by the rule." When spelled with one *n*, the word has nothing to do with the artillery weapon.

The second way to combine melodies is to design two different and distinctive lines of music to be performed at the same time. The term for this is *counterpoint*. A composer may add a line of counterpoint to an existing melody, or he or she may compose two fresh lines. Usually, the two lines have somewhat different characters; that is part of the reason why counterpoint is interesting to listen to. One line of melody is likely to be more solid and have longer note values than the other.

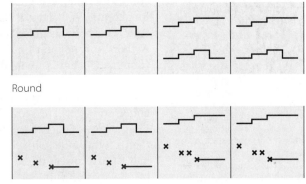

Round

Counterpoint

HARMONY: PITCHES SOUNDED TOGETHER

If melody is the horizontal line in music with its sounds occurring one after another, *harmony* is the vertical line with sounds occurring at the same time. To illustrate this concept, let's return to "The Star-Spangled Banner." Here are the first seven notes in its melody:

Aligned vertically, these same notes form the B-flat major chord, which is the tonic chord in the key of B-flat.

The preceding sentence contains a number of points about harmony that need to be explained.

Key or tonal center Both melodies and harmonies usually have a *tonal center* and are in a *key*. The music tends to move away from and then back to this center. The musical example of "The Star-Spangled Banner" is in B-flat. Like most music we know, our national anthem ends and centers around its tonal center. If "The Star-Spangled Banner" were to end on any note other than B-flat, it would sound incomplete—as if someone had a made a mistake.

> Some melodies end on the third or fifth note of the scale, but "The Star-Spangled Banner" is not one of them.

Modulation Can the tonal center or key change during a musical work? To use the musical term for changing key, can the music *modulate?* Definitely! Not only *can* it change key, but in works longer than a song, it usually *does.* Modulations help make the music sound fresher. If the music goes on too long in the same key, it can become tiring. Most of the music you hear modulates every so often, but usually people aren't aware that the key has changed.

Scales A *scale* is a series of pitches that goes upward or downward according to a prescribed pattern. Most scales contain seven different pitches, but a five-note scale is often found in Asian music and some folk music. Few melodies contain a complete scale one note after another, but generally scales are the underlying "skeleton" of melodies and harmonies. The scale for "The Star-Spangled Banner" is B-flat C D E-flat F G A B-flat. Although an alteration or two can occur in a song (and there is one in "The Star-Spangled Banner"), most of the notes come from that scale.

> "Joy to the World" is one exception to this statement. Its first eight notes are a descending scale.

Chords A *chord* is three or more pitches sounded together. Usually, the notes of chords follow an every-other, checkerboard pattern. For example, the chord for the tonal center in B-flat is B-flat D F, which are the first, third, and fifth notes in that scale. This chord is called the *tonic chord* and is indicated with the Roman numeral I. A chord can be built on each step of a scale, but the I, IV (subdominant), and V (dominant) chords are used more often than the other chords.

> The earlier reference to notes forming the tonic chord on B-flat should be more clear now.

Octaves You may have noticed that the B-flat scale mentioned earlier began and ended on B-flat. The second B-flat is an *interval* (the distance between two pitches) of an octave higher than the lower B-flat. An *octave* is eight notes higher or lower than another note with the same name. Each octave has double (if it is higher) or half (if it is lower) the number of vibrations of the other. When sounded, octaves blend very well with one another.

> The note A above middle C vibrates 440 times per second. With each octave higher, the A on the piano vibrates at 880, 1,760, and 3,250. With each descent, the A vibrates at 220, 110, 55, and 27½— the lowest note on the piano.

Major/minor Two patterns of scales, *major* and *minor,* are traditional in the music of Western civilization. The main difference between the scales is in the third step, which is one half-step lower in the minor scale. The chords based on these scales are also affected by this difference. To listeners, major and minor sound different from one another, but one is by no means better or more pleasing than the other. *Farandole* by Bizet, discussed in the Listening Guide in chapter 2, has a marchlike theme in minor and a dancelike theme in major. It offers you a chance to listen to their particular qualities.

Consonance/dissonance *Consonance* implies agreement and equilibrium. *Dissonance* implies the opposite—tension and disequilibrium. If you push your hand down on a keyboard depressing all the keys under your hand, you will get a very dissonant sound. If you press down every other white key, a rather consonant chord will be sounded. There are no clear standards, however, as to what is consonant or dissonant. These two terms are subjective and relative. Therefore, it is more accurate to think in terms of degrees of consonance or dissonance.

Harmonic progressions and cadences Because music moves through time, so do chords. They have a logic and a sequence, just as notes do in a melody. If you start on C on a keyboard, play the white keys up to B, and then stop without playing the C an octave above where you started, you will be left with an incomplete feeling—somewhat like someone saying to you, "I have a great idea! Why don't we . . . [silence]."

A progression of chords can give listeners the feeling of conclusion or incompleteness. Certain patterns of two chords have become traditional for "punctuating" music. These patterns are called *cadences.* Usually, they appear at the ends of phrases and they give a sense that the music is going to come to a musical comma or period. One familiar cadence is the "Amen" associated with the conclusion of hymns and heard in "Simple Gifts."

Texture and the Ways Pitches Are Used

In music, the word *texture* refers to the basic approaches in the use of pitches. It does not refer to the smoothness or roughness of a melody. The three terms describing texture are discussed below.

The word for a melody alone, with no other accompanying sounds, is *monophonic.*

The term for a melody with accompaniment is *homophonic.*

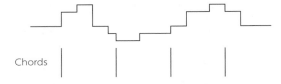

Chords

The presence of two or more lines with melodic character creates a *polyphonic* texture.

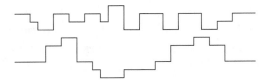

The limits of human hearing range from about 20 to 20,000 vibrations per second.

The word *cadence* is also used to describe the pattern played by the drum in a marching band, but this usage is, of course, quite different from the chord patterns discussed here.

Homophonic and polyphonic textures are relative, and they are sometimes used at different places in the same work. Often composers include musically interesting patterns in an accompanying part, but these parts lack enough melodic character to be considered another line of music. Occasionally, works that are basically polyphonic include portions containing mostly chords, and vice versa.

Bizet's *Farandole*, explored in the context of rhythm in chapter 2, also contains many of the musical elements discussed in this chapter: texture, counterpoint, and major and minor scales.

L I S T E N I N G   G U I D E

Georges Bizet: *Farandole* from *L'Arlésienne*, Suite No. 2
CD 1 Track 4

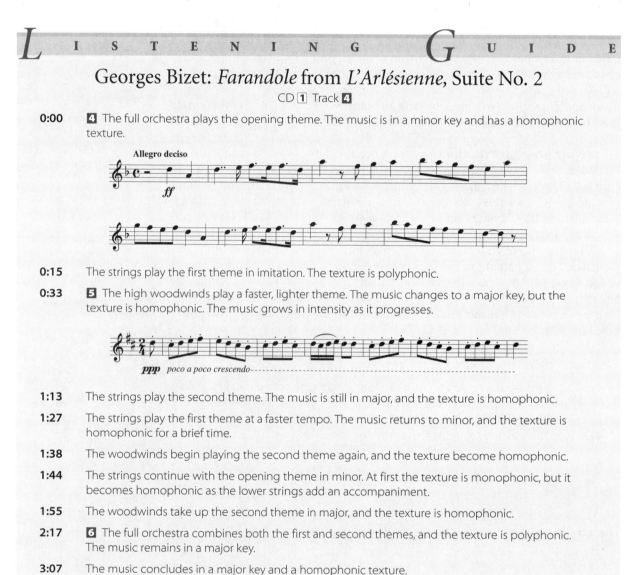

0:00   4 The full orchestra plays the opening theme. The music is in a minor key and has a homophonic texture.

0:15   The strings play the first theme in imitation. The texture is polyphonic.

0:33   5 The high woodwinds play a faster, lighter theme. The music changes to a major key, but the texture is homophonic. The music grows in intensity as it progresses.

1:13   The strings play the second theme. The music is still in major, and the texture is homophonic.

1:27   The strings play the first theme at a faster tempo. The music returns to minor, and the texture is homophonic for a brief time.

1:38   The woodwinds begin playing the second theme again, and the texture become homophonic.

1:44   The strings continue with the opening theme in minor. At first the texture is monophonic, but it becomes homophonic as the lower strings add an accompaniment.

1:55   The woodwinds take up the second theme in major, and the texture is homophonic.

2:17   6 The full orchestra combines both the first and second themes, and the texture is polyphonic. The music remains in a major key.

3:07   The music concludes in a major key and a homophonic texture.

C o d a

Melody and harmony give music its shape, its identity.
If rhythm is like the heartbeat of music, melody and harmony are the face
and body of music. They form what listeners and performers usually
notice and remember most about a musical work.

Dynamics, Timbre, and Organization

4

Loudness and tone quality have a major impact on how music sounds. Whatever the relative importance of the four basic elements of music (pitch, rhythm, dynamics, and timbre), they amount to little unless they are brought together in an organized way.

DYNAMICS: THE LOUD AND SOFT OF MUSIC

Every sound has some degree of loudness, or else it could not be heard. The amount of loudness can range from barely audible to ear splitting, although concert music rarely reaches that level of loudness. The term for the levels of loudness in music is *dynamics*. Sometimes the word *volume* is used for dynamics, but technically speaking it is not the correct term.

Loudness can be measured precisely in terms of *decibels*. A food processor reaches a level of 85 decibels, and a New York subway train produces about 100 decibels, which requires shouting over its noise to carry on a conversation. At 120 decibels, rock concerts reach levels louder than a jackhammer or a chainsaw.

The difference between 100 and 120 decibels may not seem all that much until you consider that the decibel scale is logarithmic; that is, 110 decibels is ten times louder than 100, and 120 decibels is 100 times louder than a subway train.

Dynamic levels in music are indicated only in a general way through the use of terms or symbols representing those terms. The following table lists the commonly used terms and symbols for dynamics.

As with *tempo*, the terms for dynamic levels are in Italian.

Term	Symbol	Meaning	Pronunciation
fortissimo	*ff*	very loud	"for-*tis*-si-moh"
forte	*f*	loud	"*for*-tay"
mezzo forte	*mf*	moderately loud	"*met*-zo *for*-tay"
mezzo piano	*mp*	moderately soft	"*met*-zo *pee*-ah-noh"
piano	*p*	soft	"*pee*-ah-noh"
pianissimo	*pp*	very soft	"pee-ah-*nis*-si-moh"

An increase in dynamic level is indicated by the word *crescendo* ("cre-*shen*-doe"), abbreviated *cresc.*, and shown by the sign ⬌. The opposite of crescendo is *decrescendo* ("*day*-cre-shen-doe"), which is abbreviated *decresc.* and indicated by the sign ⬌.

Not all changes in dynamics are gradual. Some notes are marked to be accented (>) or suddenly emphasized *(sfz)*. Some changes in dynamic level are to be made suddenly and are indicated by the Italian word *subito*.

sfz is an abbreviation for *sforzando*.

Most musical works contain changes in dynamic levels. Such changes are easily heard in virtually every work presented in this book.

TIMBRE: COLOR IN MUSIC

The fourth basic element of sound to be presented in this book is its tone quality, its color, which is known as *timbre* ("*tam*-ber"). Timbre in music is as important as color in a picture.

Every musical instrument and every voice has its own particular tone or timbre. If a trombone, clarinet, violin, guitar, flute, and the human voice sound middle C, which all of them can, each will produce it with a different quality. Furthermore, if two or more of them produce the same pitch at the same time, yet another timbre will result.

Why do people and instruments have their own characteristic tone quality? The reason is a bit complicated, but is worth examining. Almost all musical sounds have pitch (A, D-sharp, G, and so on). But in addition to their fundamental pitch, they also produce small bits and pieces of other pitches, called *partials*, that make up the overtone series for that particular pitch. It's somewhat like getting the accessories (shirt, vest, shoes, cufflinks) that go with a rented tuxedo. The number and the strength of these various partials are what create the timbre of a sound; they make a clarinet sound like a clarinet and a guitar sound like a guitar.

> The overtone series is also called the *harmonic series*.

A pitch can be divided in half either by touching the string at half its length or by dividing the air column in half on a wind instrument by opening a key or changing lip tension. Such a division produces a pitch one octave higher than the fundamental. Divide the string or air column into thirds, and a pitch one octave and five notes higher is heard. Divide it into four parts, and a pitch two octaves higher is sounded. The pattern of pitches produced by dividing a string or other sound-producing mechanism into equal parts is called the *overtone series*.

> The importance of the overtone series is described more fully in chapter 5.

The pattern of the overtone series is exactly the same for every pitch. Here are the first seven overtones for the note C:

Because the timbre of a sound is determined by the number and strength of the partials, the tone quality of instruments can be reproduced on a tone synthesizer. High-quality synthesizers can come surprisingly close to imitating the authentic timbre of an instrument. They cannot produce foolproof imitations, however, because the sounds they produce are too consistent, too perfect.

> Because of the subtleties of sound produced by some instruments, technicians make actual recordings (called *samples*) of an instrument's sounds and enter them into a computer for use in electronically produced music.

The timbre of a pitch played or sung by a human being is not the same from beginning to end. The beginning of a sound may have a distinct hard quality that quickly blends into its basic timbre, which often changes slightly as it is being sustained. In fact, many singers, especially in popular music, make wide changes in timbre as they sing a pitch. These changes usually make the music more interesting and expressive.

> Courses in orchestration and arranging are required in university degree programs for composers.

Composers and arrangers are very conscious of the different timbres of instruments and voices. They know, for example, that the low notes of the flute are mellow, whereas its high notes are more shrill. They also know that adding French horns to a melody played by cellos will give strength and richness to the sound. The possibilities for combinations of timbres are limitless.

ORGANIZATION: ORGANIZED SOUNDS = MUSIC

> Seeing one dot alone has little meaning. But three dots arranged like this
>
> describe a triangle and have more meaning than just three dots.

Everyone who has taken a psychology course knows this basic principle of Gestalt-cognitive psychology: The whole is greater than the sum of its parts. This principle certainly applies to music. Composers work with a virtually infinite universe of possible combinations of rhythm, pitch, dynamic level, and timbre. But music, which is often defined as *organized sounds occurring in a specified span of time*, is more than just its accumulated total of notes and rhythms and timbres. Something more—and better—is created when they are combined and organized by a skillful composer or improviser. The whole truly becomes greater than the sum of its parts.

Consider again the song "Simple Gifts." It reveals a strong sense of organization. It has a three-part symmetrical pattern, and its phrases have a logical forward motion followed by points of repose. Its chords fit the notes of the melody, and their simple character adds to the thought the song is expressing. The rhythms used in "Simple Gifts" fit the words and are organized into patterns. And, best of all, the musical elements combine into a musically satisfying entity. The various combinations of elements really work.

The definition of music as organized sound has two implications. One is that any organized group of sounds occurring in a span of time meets the criteria for music. You may or may not enjoy hearing a particular group of sounds, but so long as they are organized, they fulfill the definition of music.

The other implication is that listeners will understand music better if they can consider how sounds are organized. Why? Because the organization of sounds is the very stuff of music. Listening to music carefully and thoughtfully requires listening for what happens in the music, which in turn means listening for how the elements are manipulated by the composer and performer.

> Ignoring what is taking place in a musical work is a little like watching a football game with no understanding of the action while you sit around waiting for the final score.

Form: Planning in Music

Over the centuries a number of general plans for organizing music have evolved. These general plans are called *forms*.

> Forms were named after they were developed and used often.

Forms developed out of the trials and errors of hundreds of composers over hundreds of years. Musicians discovered, for example, that a three-part pattern with the first and third parts almost the same provide a satisfying logic in a musical work. Someone tried it, and other composers and listeners liked it.

Composing a form is not, however, like filling out a job application in which certain specific information must be supplied. They are not molds waiting for composers to fill with notes. Instead, forms in music are usually constructed around one or more of three broad, general considerations: repetition, variation, and contrast.

Repetition   Because music exists in time, the repeating of ideas in music is probably much more important than in the other fine arts. "Simple Gifts," for example, has a three-part form, with the middle part concluding with music similar to the last two lines of the first part. The first melody, the *a* section of the song, begins, "'Tis a gift to be simple . . ."—the contrasting melody, the *b* section, follows, "When, true simplicity is gained . . ."—and the *a* section is repeated by the singer, "'Tis a gift to be simple . . ."

Alphabet letters are used to designate the parts of a work. When the parts are short, the letters are in lowercase. Therefore, the form of "Simple Gifts" is *a b a'*, or what is termed *ternary form*. The prime (') sign is used to indicate that the material is slightly different from its identifying letter. When longer sections of music are repeated, uppercase letters are used. The second movement of Joaquin Rodrigo's *Concierto de Aranjuez* brings back the opening melody before it concludes, which gives the work a large three-part form. Because its sections are long, they are represented in uppercase letters, *A B A*.

Architecture has been called "frozen music." The three-part patterns represented in the façade and towers of this cathedral at Chartres, France, are similar to the *a b a* form used in music.

Variation   A second broad approach to form is through varying the musical material—to repeat the same basic material but with changes.

Basically, one of three things happens in music: The music you hear can (1) be the same, (2) be somewhat different, or (3) be completely different from what has been sounded.

Contrast   A third broad approach is by contrast. In "Simple Gifts" the *b* portion of the song has a different melody and words. In longer works not only might the contrasting sections have a different melody, but also different tempos, keys, dynamic levels, and instruments as well. Even when a work does not repeat material, it usually contains contrasting sections unless it is quite short.

Because there are many different musical forms, they cannot successfully be discussed in just one chapter. Forms will be presented and discussed at the appropriate places throughout the book.

RODRIGO'S *CONCIERTO DE ARANJUEZ*

Concerto is pronounced "con-*chair*-toe."

Joachin Rodrigo's *Concierto de Aranjuez* is a concerto for guitar and orchestra. It has three movements, and the second movement is featured here. *Concierto de Aranjuez* is a typical concerto in that it features musical exchanges between the soloist and the orchestra and shows off the playing ability of the soloist.

The second movements of concertos usually feature melody.

Most musical works can be examined in terms of how their melodies, rhythms, and timbres are organized. The second movement of *Concierto de Aranjuez* seems especially well suited for such analysis.

Melody   The basic outline of the melody—its "musical skeleton"—consists of a long note and then the melody moves up two notes before returning to the original long note. Next the melody ascends for four notes and then works it way down note-by-note to four notes below where it began. Up to this point, all the melodic movement has been to adjacent notes.

But there is much more than its melodic skeleton. Rodrigo also adds many quick-moving, decorative notes. These notes are especially noticeable when the guitar takes its turn playing the melody. Then three quick, accented notes begin the melody (♪♫), something often found in Spanish music. This short melodic figure is heard frequently throughout the music and contributes to the unity of the

Joaquin Rodrigo

Joaquin Rodrigo (b. 1901) was born in Sagunto, Spain. By the age of three, he was blind. His music studies began at an early age, and they later took him to France, where he studied with the composer Paul Dukas. After his marriage in 1933, Rodrigo returned to Spain, but civil war broke out there in 1936 and lasted three years. During this time he lived in Paris and Germany. He then returned to Spain, and in 1940 his *Concierto de Aranjuez* received a highly successful premiere. He was hailed as Spain's greatest postwar composer. Although he has received many honors and has continued to compose, none of his works has achieved the recognition comparable to that accorded his *Concierto de Aranjuez*.

Rodrigo's style has not changed over his long life. It is Spanish in character, although he seldom includes folk melodies in his music.

Rodrigo composed his *Concierto de Aranjuez* just after the death of his newborn child. He feared that his wife, Vickie, would not live.

It also reveals the French influence of his teacher Paul Dukas. In form, harmony, melody, and rhythms, his music is quite formal and conservative. The dissonances and driving rhythms of other twentieth-century composers seem not to have affected him. At various times, his music is passionate, colorful, and filled with charm.

Best-Known Works
Guitar and orchestra:
Concierto de Aranjuez
Fantasia para un gentilhombre

movement. Such brief figures are called *motives* when they act as a unifying element in a musical work.

The word *motive* has nothing to do with the reasons why the composer wrote the music.

Timbre   Much of the second movement of the *Concierto* has a tender, melancholy quality, due in large part to the tone qualities of the English horn and the guitar.

Harmony   The quiet, uncomplicated accompaniment adds to the tenderness of the music while allowing the melody to be clearly heard.

Rhythm   The rhythm is slow and steady with four beats to the measure. Because this movement features the melody, its rhythm is not as noticeable as it is in many works, including the other movements of the *Concierto de Aranjuez*.

Aranjuez is pronounced "A-*rahn*-hou-ayz." It is the name of the former summer palace of Spanish kings.

Form and organization   The movement has a large three-part or *ABA* form, with the main melody followed by contrasting material and then a return of the main melody. But that's not all. Rodrigo has the music build ever so gradually to a rather lengthy section for the guitar alone. This section also begins quietly but then slowly increases to a truly passionate level of intensity as the orchestra again takes up the theme with its three-note motive. The music just seems to float away as the movement ends.

The section for guitar alone is called the cadenza. *Cadenzas* allow the soloist to play paraphrases of the themes in a free-sounding and often technically stunning style. Cadenzas are almost always featured in one or more movements of solo concertos.

Everything about the second movement of *Concierto de Aranjuez* works. All the elements are organized into a musically satisfying entity. The whole really is greater than the sum of its parts.

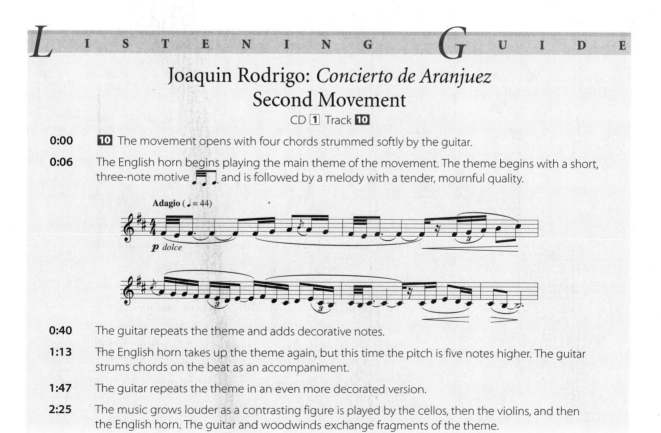

L I S T E N I N G   G U I D E

Joaquin Rodrigo: *Concierto de Aranjuez*
Second Movement
CD 1 Track 10

0:00	**10** The movement opens with four chords strummed softly by the guitar.
0:06	The English horn begins playing the main theme of the movement. The theme begins with a short, three-note motive and is followed by a melody with a tender, mournful quality.

Adagio (♩ = 44)

p dolce

0:40	The guitar repeats the theme and adds decorative notes.
1:13	The English horn takes up the theme again, but this time the pitch is five notes higher. The guitar strums chords on the beat as an accompaniment.
1:47	The guitar repeats the theme in an even more decorated version.
2:25	The music grows louder as a contrasting figure is played by the cellos, then the violins, and then the English horn. The guitar and woodwinds exchange fragments of the theme.

3:57   **11** The guitar plays without accompaniment a version of the theme on its low strings. Chords are interspersed between the phrases of the theme, and the music grows more stern.

4:57   The oboe plays a fragment of the theme and is answered each time by the guitar.

5:33   The flutes and other woodwinds play rapidly repeated notes. The music is louder for a moment, but then becomes very quiet.

5:55   **12** The guitar alone begins a cadenza. It begins softly with persistently repeated notes that have the theme embedded in them.

6:32   The three-note motive is played four times in succession, each time an octave lower.

7:08   The basic pattern of four notes ascending followed by four notes descending begins. The music slowly becomes more intense and passionate.

7:49   **13** The cadenza climaxes as the orchestra enters with a loud, short chord, followed by the guitar's rapidly repeated chords. The orchestra twice exchanges notes with the guitar, and then plays the main theme in an intense, passionate style ending with flute, oboe, and guitar.

9:00   The guitar returns, quietly playing a portion of the theme, with two lines that seem to answer each other.

9:57   The movement seems to fade into space as it closes with the guitar and violins playing high, ethereal notes.

C o d a

How can you tell if you are really hearing what a musical work has to offer?
One way to determine this is by answering these practical questions:

❖ *Does the music seem sensible?*
❖ *Does it move along without seeming to be stagnant?*
❖ *Do you hear details of form, rhythm, and melody?*
❖ *Do you keep your attention on the music most of the time?*
❖ *Do you have reactions to the music as you listen to it?*
❖ *Are you able to follow the Listening Guide*
while listening, without getting lost?

If the answer to most of these questions is yes,
you are hearing much of what the work has to offer.

Orchestral Instruments

5

Sounds are produced when something causes the molecules in the air to rapidly collide and bounce off one another something like balls on a billiard table. What a musical instrument does is control and shape the vibrations in a particular way. In doing this, instruments provide the element of tone color in music.

Most musical instruments can be examined for their capabilities in doing four things: (1) producing their characteristic sound, (2) modifying their basic timbre, (3) playing different pitches, and (4) starting and stopping their sounds. The instruments used in the symphony orchestra can be grouped into families according to the way they produce sound.

STRING INSTRUMENTS

The difference among the four main string instruments in the orchestra is mostly one of size. The *violin* is the smallest and has the highest pitch. It is held under the chin when played. There is no difference between the instruments used for the first and second violin sections. Only the parts written for them differ.

The *viola* ("vee-*oh*-lah") is somewhat larger than the violin but is still played under the chin. Its general range is five notes lower than that of the violin.

The cello ("*chel*-low," officially known as the *violoncello*) rests on the floor when played and is supported between the player's knees. It is one octave lower than the viola.

The *double bass* has several other names: *bass viol, contrabass,* and *string bass.* Players of the instrument stand or can sit on a high stool when playing. With its sloping shoulders, the shape of its body is slightly different from the other string instruments, and its strings are tuned four notes apart.

The *harp* is quite different from the other string instruments. It's a large instrument that sits on the floor with many strings that are strummed or plucked. Its strings are modified to play different pitches through the use of a pedal mechanism.

The strings are the backbone of the symphonic orchestra, with their number equaling that of all the rest of the instruments put together. By far the largest number are violins (about 24 to 30), with at least 12 violas, 12 cellos, and 8 basses.

Sound Production

String instruments produce sounds by vibrating strings. This is done in two ways. One is to draw a bow across the string; the other is to pluck the string with the finger.

The bow was originally slightly arched like the bow used in archery. But over the years, its curve was reduced, and then curved slightly inward toward the hair, which allowed for more flexibility in the types of bowing. The hair on a bow is from the tail of a horse. If you look at it through a microscope, you will see hundreds of tiny depressions in it. The uneven surfaces of the hair catch on the string, causing it to vibrate. Usually, players of string instruments apply rosin to the hair to help it catch the string better.

The guitar is a string instrument, but it is rarely used in symphony orchestras. It is described in the next chapter.

Sometimes professional string players can be seen tapping the bow against the instrument as a form of applause. Often they are faking it when they do, because they don't want to hit a $4,000 bow against a $45,000 instrument— a typical price for a fine string instrument.

Pitchers in baseball often apply rosin to their fingers for better control of the ball.

The violin The horsehair bow drawn across the strings sets them vibrating. The vibrations are conducted through the bridge and amplified by the intrument's hollow body. The position of the player's fingers pressing down on the strings on the fingerboard determines the pitches that are played.

A string vibrating by itself doesn't produce much of a sound. The vibrations need to be amplified, which is the purpose of the body of the instrument. The strings are held off the body by a wooden bridge. The vibrations of the strings are conducted through the bridge to the largely hollow body of the instrument.

Modifying Basic Timbre

The timbre of string instruments can be affected in several ways. One is to rock the left hand back and forth in small, rapid motions. This creates a *vibrato* ("vih-*brah*-toe"), which adds warmth to the tone quality by causing small alterations of pitch. All advanced string players use vibrato when playing.

Another way of affecting the timbre of a string instrument is to place a *mute* over the bridge. This small wood or plastic device softens the sound and makes it more mellow.

The timbre of string instruments is also affected by the way the bow is drawn across the string. More pressure on the bow makes the tone more harsh. Several different styles of bowing are used, each of which affects the tone and expressive qualities of the sounds.

Regulating Pitches

Different pitches are achieved on a string instrument by (1) the particular string being played, (2) the length of string allowed to vibrate, which is regulated by the

The cello Notice the rapid rocking of the left hand to create the small variations in pitch known as *vibrato*.

The double bass The fingerboard is glued to the neck of the instrument but does not touch the hollow body.

player, and (3) occasionally by the way the string is fingered. All orchestral string instruments (except the harp) have four strings. The strings each have a different thickness, are made of different materials, and are tuned five notes apart (except for double basses) by tightening or loosening the pegs at the end of the instrument.

As can be seen in the photos above, the neck extends from the instrument, and a fingerboard is glued on top of it. The player depresses a string firmly against the fingerboard to shorten the string, and thereby makes the pitch higher.

String instruments can also play *harmonics*, which are the notes in the overtone series above the basic pitch. The player can touch the string lightly at various points to create a *natural harmonic*, or use a combination of depressed first finger and lightly touching with the little finger to produce an *artificial harmonic*. Both types of harmonics have a high, ethereal sound.

It is possible to sound two or three notes at the same time on string instruments. These combinations of notes are called *double stops* or *triple stops*.

Some professional-quality double basses have five strings.

The player's fingers must be placed at exactly the right spot, or else the sounds are out of tune.

Starting and Stopping Sounds

The motion of the bow across the string usually determines how long a sound is produced. String players learn several different styles of bowing. Some styles have abrupt, clear-cut beginnings and endings of the sounds, but others are very smooth with less distinct beginnings and endings. Sounds that are made by plucking with the first finger of the left hand, called *pizzicato*, are short and cannot be sustained. Occasionally, the left hand will pluck an open string in flashy solo works.

Woodwind instruments

Some special flutes are plated with gold or platinum.

The *flute* used to have a wooden body, but since about 1900 silver-nickel bodies are now universally favored because of their more brilliant sound. The flute generally plays notes higher than the reed instruments. It has a smaller cousin, the *piccolo*, which sounds one octave higher.

Grenadella is a very heavy wood that comes from the island of Madagascar.

The *oboe* is made of a grenadella wood that has been carefully treated to prevent cracking. The oboe has a distinctive plaintive quality. The English horn is neither English nor a horn. It is basically a large oboe with a bulb-shaped bell. It sounds five notes lower than the oboe.

The *clarinet* has a wide range, but its timbre differs quite a bit from its low notes (very mellow) to its high notes (quite shrill). Clarinets are made from the same wood as oboes. They come in several sizes, including the bass clarinet, which looks like wooden saxophone.

The *bassoon* has a distinctive appearance, which with its reddish brown or black finish looks somewhat like a long bedpost. Like the clarinet, it has a wide range, but it is more than an octave lower in pitch. The *contrabassoon* sounds another octave lower than the bassoon, going almost to the lowest note on the piano.

The saxophone was invented by the Belgian Adolphe Sax in the nineteenth century.

Saxophones have a metal body and a distinctive J shape, except for the soprano saxophone, which has a straight body like a clarinet. Saxophones use a single reed clamped on a mouthpiece and come in a variety of sizes.

A symphony orchestra has two flutes and a piccolo, two oboes and an English horn, two clarinets and a bass clarinet, and two bassoons and a contrabassoon. Saxophones are not regular members of the symphony orchestra.

Sound Production

With the exception of the flute, the woodwinds produce sound through vibrating reeds. The reeds are cut from cane that looks like bamboo. In the case of the clarinet, a single reed is clamped on a mouthpiece. The oboe and bassoon play double reeds, with two reeds being wired together facing each other.

Double reeds

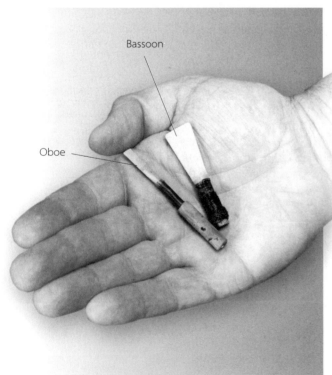

Bassoon

Oboe

The flute produces sound by the "stopped pipe" principle. It is possible to blow across the top of a bottle or jug and produce a sound. The sound is created by the collision of the air going down into the bottle meeting the air coming back out.

Modifying Basic Timbre

All the woodwinds except the clarinet can be played with a vibrato, especially the flute. Only in jazz is a vibrato used on the clarinet.

Advanced oboists and bassoonists make their own reeds, which is somewhat of an art. The cutting and shaping of the double reed has a noticeable effect on the timbre of the instrument.

Regulating Pitches

All woodwind instruments regulate pitch by shortening or lengthening the column of air inside the instrument. This is done by *key* mechanisms that open or close holes. Some of the fingerings are quite complicated, however. The closer an open hole is toward the end of the instrument in the player's mouth, the higher the pitch will be—usually.

The flute To generate various pitches, woodwind instruments use complex keying mechanisms to open and close holes that regulate the length of a column of vibrating air.

Bassoons and clarinets In this photo you can see the thin metal tube, called a *bocal*, that holds the double reed used to produce sound.

The qualification is included in the preceding sentence because all the woodwinds can move into a new and higher level of pitch by either overblowing at the octave (as on the flute) or opening a key that causes the instrument to overblow (as on the oboe, clarinet, and bassoon).

No mutes are used on woodwind instruments.

Starting and Stopping Sounds

Sounds are usually started when air is allowed to go through the instrument as the player's tongue is pulled off the reed, or away from the upper teeth in the case of the flute. Flute players can also use an action called *double tonguing* to articulate notes very quickly. Flutists can also achieve an effect called *flutter tonguing*.

French horns Most high-quality French horns are actually double horns, which makes it easier to play the right notes. A valve regulated by the thumb controls which part of the horn is used.

BRASS INSTRUMENTS

The *trumpet* is the highest-pitched brass instrument. It has three piston valves that change the length of tubing. The *cornet* is similar to a trumpet except that its tubing is more like a cone; the trumpet's tubing is more cylindrical. The configuration of the tubing affects the timbre of the instruments, with the trumpet having a more brilliant quality and the cornet a more mellow timbre.

The *French horn* contains more than 16 feet of tubing that is coiled so that it can be handled more conveniently. It has three or four rotary valves, which are operated by the player's left hand. Rotary valves turn to open up different lengths of tubing instead of moving up and down as piston valves do. Most of the time, players insert their right hand into the bell of the instrument to modify the timbre.

The most unusual feature of the French horn isn't visible. All the other brass instruments utilize the overtone series starting one octave above the fundamental pitch. The French horn uses the overtone series staring two octaves above the fundamental pitch. This means that the notes with the same fingering are closer together and that much precision is needed to produce the desired pitches. The French horn has a rather wide range, however.

The *trombone* is the only orchestral instruments today that uses a slide to regulate the length of its tubing. It sounds one octave lower than the trumpet. The *bass trombone* is somewhat larger than the more common tenor trombone and it can play several notes lower.

The *tuba* is the largest and lowest in pitch of the brass instruments. Its role is similar to that of the double bass in the string section in playing the important bass line. The tuba seldom gets to play solos. Like the double bass, however, when played well it has a pleasing quality.

A symphony orchestra usually has three trumpets, four French horns, two trombones and a bass trombone, and one tuba.

Sound Production

A brass player's lip membranes can vibrate a thousand or more times each second.

All brass instruments produce sound by the membranes of the player's lips vibrating into a cup-shaped mouthpiece. The buzzing sound is then amplified through a metal tube with a flared bell at the end. For ease of handling, the metal tubing on brass instruments is curled once or twice.

Modifying Sound

All brass instruments occasionally use mutes that are placed in the bell of the instrument to alter the timbres. They come in a variety of shapes and materials, including one resembling a rubber sink plunger and another called a "wah-wah mute." A vibrato can be used when playing brass instruments, especially in solo passages.

Trumpets and trombones Brass instruments vary pitch by subtle changes in the player's lips and by mechanically adjusting the length of the tubing through which vibrating air passes. The trumpet has three piston valves; the trombone uses a slide.

Regulating Pitch

The pitches on brass instruments are controlled in two ways. One is by subtle changes in the lips, which produce the different pitches of the overtone series. This phenomenon is best explained by considering the bugle. A bugle has no mechanism for changing pitch. All its different pitches are the result of changes in the tension of the bugler's lips. Only the sounds of the overtone series can be produced, however, the ones heard in bugle calls. All brass instruments can play the "bugle" pitches.

In addition all brass instruments in an orchestra have either a valve or a slide mechanism that allows the player to change the length of tubing. That means that a new overtone series is made available when the length of the tubing is changed. The various combinations of valves and slide positions therefore make it possible for the player of a brass instrument to sound any pitch within the range of the instrument.

It is rather difficult to play the fundamental pitch on a brass instrument, and its quality is not all that satisfying to listen to.

Brass mouthpieces

Tuba

Trombone

French horn

Trumpet

Starting and Stopping Sounds

Brass-instrument players start and stop sounds with their tongue, with the sound beginning as the tongue is pulled back from behind their upper teeth, opening the air stream. They can tongue very rapidly by *double* or *triple tonguing*.

To triple tongue, the player makes the tongue say the syllables "tah-tah-kah" very rapidly.

PERCUSSION INSTRUMENTS

The xylophone is sometimes referred to as "old bones" because it portrays a rattling skeleton in *Danse Macabre* by Saint-Saëns.

Percussion instruments can be divided into those that play pitches and those that don't. The *glockenspiel, xylophone, marimba,* and *vibraphone* are all percussion instruments that have metal or wooden bars arranged like the piano keyboard. They are played with sticks. The glockenspiel has metal bars that produce high tinkling sounds. The xylophone has wooden bars and produces dry, brittle sounds. The marimba is like a xylophone except for hollow tubes hanging below each bar that allow the sound to resonate after the bar has been struck. The vibraphone also has tubes, but in addition has an electrically driven device that adds vibrato to the sounds.

The singular of timpani is *timpanum.*

Timpani are two or more kettledrums of different sizes tuned to different pitches. Five are used in symphony orchestras today, and three are a minimum for works composed after 1800. The player positions the timpani around him or her in a semicircular arrangement. The sticks used in playing the timpani have round, padded heads. Professional players have several pairs of sticks of differing firmness to fit the needs of the music.

The *celesta* looks like a small piano, but it is more like a glockenspiel that is operated from a keyboard. (The piano is described in chapter 6.) *Chimes* sound different pitches. The player strikes the top of the metal tube with a wooden hammer.

The *snare drum* is the most prominent percussion instrument that does not sound a definite pitch. It is constructed around two hollow rings that are five or more inches apart. The rings have calfskin or plastic stretched over them. The bottom surface has several strands of wire, called *snares,* that rattle against it. The snares give the drum its characteristic crisp sound. The snare drum is played with a pair of wooden sticks.

Timpani These large kettledrums are tuned to specific pitches. The player can vary the pitch of each drum with a pedal mechanism.

The *bass drum* is the largest percussion instrument, sometimes having a diameter of four feet or more. It is placed on its side and hit with a single beater with a round, padded head.

The *cymbals* are large metal discs that are struck against each other with glancing blows. A single cymbal can also be suspended and struck with a stick or a wire brush.

The *triangle* is made of metal and is shaped like a triangle. It is struck with a metal beater while suspended. The *tambourine* has a single calfskin head stretched over a wooden or metal hoop. The rim hoop contains small metal discs that rattle when moved. The player shakes the tambourine or hits it against the heel of the other hand to produce sounds.

Percussion players get to play a number of unusual instruments. For instance, they play something called a *whip,* which is actually two flat pieces of wood that are slapped together. They even get to blow whistles and car horns.

Fortunately for the orchestra's budget, percussionists play more than one instrument, but not at the same time. Orchestras have four regular percussion players and hire extras when needed.

Glockenspiel and snare drum

Sound Production

Percussion instruments make sounds when struck or rattled. None of them can sustain sound, something that all string (except the harp), woodwind, and brass instruments can do. Some percussion instruments are hit together, others are struck with a stick or a beater, and a few are operated from a keyboard.

Modifying Sound

Sticks and beaters are made from different materials and in different sizes, and each has an effect on the sound produced. Sometimes wire brushes are used, and sometimes beaters with round, padded heads are required. Drumsticks come in a variety of sizes. The manner in which percussion instruments are struck or rattled varies, and that can alter the sound produced.

Regulating Pitch

Many percussion instruments do not sound definite pitches. But there are a number of percussion instruments that do. One group has wooden or metal bars arranged in the manner of a piano keyboard. The large kettledrums (timpani) regulate pitch with a foot mechanism or handles at the edge of the drumhead that change the tension in the drumhead.

Starting and Stopping Sounds

Sounds on percussion instruments start when the instrument is struck or rattled. Because percussion instruments do not sustain sounds, there is little problem with stopping sounds. An exception involves the ring of the cymbals and the timpani. Sometimes percussion players must dampen the sound of these instruments immediately after being played to keep them from ringing too long and intruding on the music that follows.

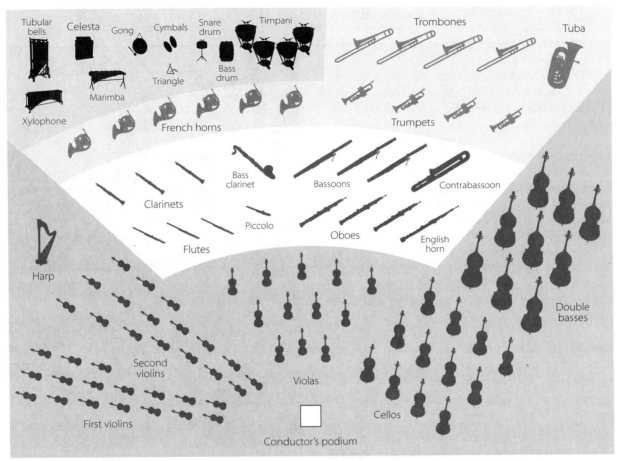

The instruments of the symphony orchestra are grouped into four families according to the way they produce sound: strings, woodwinds, brasses, and percussion. This illustration shows a typical seating plan, although exact number and placement of the instruments can vary.

LISTENING FOR INSTRUMENTS

Being able to identify the timbres of various instruments as you listen helps you understand and enjoy music more. You can learn to do this better by noticing the sounds of instruments as they are pointed out in the Listening Guides and the practice exercises in the *Study Guide*.

The most sophisticated work created to demonstrate instruments is *The Young Person's Guide to Orchestra* by Benjamin Britten, who is discussed more fully in chapter 35. It presents the instruments by families, then a variation of the theme is played by each instrument, which is followed by a short theme played in imitation by each instrument. The work closes with the opening and the short theme sounded together.

View the videocassette "The Orchestra and Its Instruments," which should be available in the media center on campus if you didn't see it in class. In addition, a Listening Guide with approximate timings for this work is included in the *Study Guide*.

Coda

For nearly 200 years, the symphony orchestra has been the most important ensemble in instrumental art music. The particular instruments it comprises therefore have a special place in hearing symphonic music more fully. They provide the palette of musical sounds for composers and listeners alike.

Other Musical Instruments

6

The instruments of the symphony orchestra are often discussed together because they make up a rather standardized musical organization. But these instruments represent only one segment of the instruments used to make music throughout the world. This chapter examines the other important types of instruments.

THE VOICE

It may seem odd to talk about the *voice* as an instrument, although singers often refer to a person's voice as his or her "instrument." But it can be examined using the same categories that were used for orchestral instruments. The reason why we don't usually think of the voice as an instrument is the fact that we are born with it. We learn to use it for talking and to some extent for informal singing without any special instruction, something that is usually needed to play most instruments competently.

Sound Production

The voice produces sound through the vibration of the vocal cords in the larynx, or what is commonly called the voice box. Air and enough tension in the cords are required before these cords can produce sound.

Having enough air for breathing and enough for singing for an audience without the aid of amplification are two quite different matters. Because singing involves sustaining vowel sounds, good singing requires much control over the air. The muscular floor below the lungs, called the diaphragm, must provide a sufficient amount of breath support. The vocal cords must also be tightened, or else no sound can be sustained.

The correct use of breath helps in both speaking and singing, as well as in preserving the voice.

The lungs are not muscles, hence the importance of the diaphragm.

Modifying Basic Timbre

The timbre of vocal sounds is determined by the shape of the oral and nasal cavities inside the head, as well as the cheeks and tongue formation. Each vowel has its particular formation, which is altered by the placement of the throat and tongue and the shape of the mouth and lips. An infinite number of shadings of timbre are possible.

Regulating Pitch

The pitch of a vocal sound is determined by the amount of tension in the vocal cords in relation to their length and thickness. The shorter the cords and the tighter they are stretched, the higher the pitch.

The difference between men's and women's voices is caused largely by the length of the cords. A man's vocal cords are normally about twice the length of a woman's, and they are also thicker. A larger larynx is required for the male's cords, which explains the more prominent Adam's apple.

Starting and Stopping Sounds

Vocal sounds are controlled by the action of the diaphragm in pushing air through the larynx. Sounds can also be choked off in the throat, but that doesn't sound very attractive, so it is usually avoided in singing.

Types of Voices

The four main types of voices can be heard in Handel's "Hallelujah Chorus," which is explored in part III and is included on the CD.

Voices in choral singing are traditionally divided into four classifications. The higher, lighter women's voice is called *soprano*. The darker, lower women's voice is called *alto*. In the case of men, the higher voice is called *tenor* and the lower, deeper voice is called *bass* (pronounced "base"). Solo voices are classified using these four basic terms, plus additional modifiers such as *mezzo, dramatic,* and *lyric*. Most of the terms for classifying solo voices are not as well standardized as the four main classifications.

The voice is an instrument in one other way. Training is normally required to achieve the maximum power, beauty, range, and expression. It is, of course, possible to sing simple songs without any formal training. For almost all persons, however, lessons are needed to sing more-difficult pieces or to have much power without the aid of a microphone.

WIND BAND INSTRUMENTS

Wind bands vary in size from thirty to more than a hundred players. The wide range in the size of a wind, or *concert,* band indicates that its instrumentation is not as well standardized as that of the symphony orchestra. The larger groups usually produce a more massive sound, and the smaller groups achieve greater clarity. The larger bands also use more players on many of the parts.

As the name indicates, wind bands are composed almost entirely of brasses and woodwinds plus percussion. Some bands include one double bass, but no other string instruments.

The sound of a wind band can be heard on the CD in Sousa's "The Stars and Stripes Forever," which is discussed in chapter 41.

Wind bands include a number of instruments not usually found in a symphony orchestra. Additional brass instruments include cornets and euphoniums or baritone horns, which sound one octave lower than a trumpet. Because tubas are difficult to carry while marching, an instrument with the same range and similar timbre was developed in the band of John Philip Sousa. The appropriately named sousaphone is coiled over the player's shoulder and has a large flared bell that faces straight forward.

School bands are common in some provinces of Canada and, more recently, in some schools in Japan and Australia.

Wind bands also include saxophones of different sizes: alto, tenor, and baritone. Many times alto clarinets are used in wind bands, and sometimes the low-pitched contrabass clarinet as well.

The wind band is largely an American institution. Bands are seldom found in schools and colleges in the rest of the world. Most bands in other countries are associated with the military. Even in the United States, the most musically recognized professional bands are the armed services bands in Washington, D.C.

TRADITIONAL KEYBOARD INSTRUMENTS

Harpsichord

The *harpsichord* looks something like a grand piano, but it operates quite differently. Often it has two keyboards, called *manuals,* plus knobs that affect the couplings of strings to the keys. Sometimes the pattern of black and white keys is exactly the opposite of what it is on the piano.

The sound of the harpsichord is more delicate and light than that of the piano. Probably for this reason, it fell out of favor with composers after about 1750, who preferred the more powerful sounds of the piano. It has, however, enjoyed a revival of interest in the twentieth century.

The harpsichord can be heard on the CD containing the Gigue from French Suite No. 5 by J. S. Bach.

Piano

The *piano* is a historically younger instrument than the harpsichord, being first constructed in Italy about 1709. Behind or underneath the strings, depending on the type of piano, is the *soundboard,* which amplifies the vibrations of the strings. Throughout its history, the piano has had a differing number of keys. Today that number is standardized at eighty-eight, although keyboards on electronic pianos often have fewer keys.

There are two types of piano, the upright and the grand. The *grand* piano is long and flat, ranging from 5½ to 9 feet in length. With its longer strings and larger soundboard, the sound of the grand piano is superior to that of the upright piano.

The piano is included on the CD with works by Chopin, Liszt, and Rachmaninoff.

Concert music is therefore always performed publicly on a grand piano. The *upright* piano is the type usually seen in homes, because of its lower cost and smaller size.

Grand pianos usually have three pedals. One pedal holds the dampers off the strings so that they can ring freely. Another pedal holds the dampers off only certain strings, usually those in the lower half of the keyboard. The third pedal moves the entire mechanism so that the hammers do not strike all the strings for each pitch. On an upright piano, this pedal moves the hammers closer to the strings, which makes it easier to play the sounds more softly.

Pipe Organ

Today air is pushed through the organ by an electric blower. Until the nineteenth century or so, the air had to be pumped through by an assistant.

Although it uses a keyboard—usually two or more—the *pipe organ* is a quite different instrument from the harpsichord and piano. Instead of strings the pipe organ has pipes—hundreds and hundreds of them—into which air is pumped. A piano has a set of strings that produces a uniform timbre. The pipe organ has many sets, or *ranks*, of pipes, each with a large complement of pitches and each with a different timbre. In fact, a large pipe organ can have as many as seventy ranks of pipes; medium-sized organs have forty or so. A rank of pipes is activated when a knob is pulled, and combinations of knobs can be set up in advance to be activated with the hand or foot. The number of combinations of timbres in a high-quality organ are enormous.

A pipe organ has several keyboards or manuals; generally, these keyboards have sixty-one keys. The different manuals make it easier for the organist to change back and forth between ranks of pipes.

The pipe organ has been called "the king of instruments." It can be heard on the CD in J. S. Bach's "Little" Fugue in G Minor.

A special feature of a pipe organ is the *pedalboard*, which is played with the feet. The pedalboard looks like a series of blond and black wooden slats that have been arranged in the pattern of the keyboard. It sounds many of the low pitches on the organ. Good organists can execute remarkably difficult passages with their feet on the pedalboard. The feet also control pedals for changing dynamic level that look like accelerators on an automobile.

Organists often have certain shoes for playing the organ, which they don't wear at other times.

The high costs of professional-quality grand pianos and pipe organs has encouraged the adoption of electronic versions of both instruments. Although electronic organs can sound quite good, they are also expensive, so less expensive, and therefore less authentic, instruments are often heard.

Sound Production

Keyboard instruments produce sounds in one of three ways: (1) In the case of the piano, a hammer of firmly packed felt strikes a string. (2) In the case of the harpsichord, a plectrum or quill plucks a string. (3) In the case of a pipe organ, air is released into a pipe.

Modifying Basic Timbre

It is not possible to make obvious changes in the timbre of the piano or harpsichord. Subtle differences are possible, especially on the piano, by the use of the pedal and the manner in which the keys are depressed.

Regulating Pitch

The particular pitches sounded on a piano or harpsichord depend on the keys that are depressed. Unless coupled by some mechanical means, which is possible on larger harpsichords, only the pitch of the depressed key is sounded. The pitch of the strings on the harpsichord and piano depends on how tightly they are stretched. The tension, and therefore the pitch, of a string is regulated by the person tuning the instrument. The tuner twists the tuning pins with a wrench until the correct pitch is achieved.

Keyboard instruments also differ from those found in bands and orchestras in that they can easily sound more than one pitch at a time. This fact means that a keyboard instrument can play both a melody and its accompanying part simultaneously. For this reason, keyboard instruments are basically solo instruments; only occasionally are they played in ensembles consisting of only keyboard instruments.

Many piano duets have been composed, but most of them are for amateurs.

Starting and Stopping Sounds

Sounds on keyboard instruments start when a key is depressed. On the piano and harpsichord, the sounds soon fade or decay; they cannot be sustained. Normally, they end as soon as the damper returns to the string. This action can be delayed by holding down the key, or, more common, holding down a pedal that keeps all the dampers from returning to the strings. Through the skillful use of the pedal, pianists can affect the impression of the music.

Changing Dynamic Level

The harpsichord does not allow the player to alter the dynamic level by the amount of finger pressure; in other words, hitting a key harder does not make it sound louder. The only way to change the dynamic level on a harpsichord is to couple the two keyboards so that the sound is doubled an octave higher on the second keyboard. It's different for the pianist. The piano can be played very softly or very loudly, depending on how firmly the keys are pressed.

The piano's name comes from its capability for making dynamic changes. It was orginally called *pianoforte*.

FOLK INSTRUMENTS

A vast number of musical instruments have been created around the world. Although each has its own unique characteristics, folk instruments have been classified into four broad groups according to the way they produce sounds.

Aerophones

One type of flute found among the natives of Oceana and Hawaii is blown through the nose.

This category comprises instruments that are played by blowing. The most common of these are flutes. Some are played sideways, as we are accustomed to seeing today, but many are played straight in front of the player's mouth.

Actually, the music is wasted on the snakes, which have no hearing. The snakes respond to the swaying body of the charmer.

Some reed aerophones are also found. Some of these use a double reed like an oboe; others have a single reed and mouthpiece like a clarinet. The *pungi* played by snake charmers in India is an example of a reed instrument.

A simple instrument that approaches the buzzing of the lip membranes on brass instruments is animal horns. They are hollowed out and blown from the small end. The Jewish *shofar* is one such instrument.

Aerophone

Ideophones

These are the percussion instruments other than drums. Bells, chimes, xylophones, and rattles are all examples of ideophones.

Membranophones

Membranophones are all the types of drums encountered throughout the world. Drums are constructed from wood, metal, coconut shells, and clay. Some are struck with sticks, others are hit with the hand or fingers, and friction drums are rubbed with a piece of animal hide. Some have straight sides, others taper in, and a few have the shape of an hourglass.

The term *membranophones* is easy to remember because it contains the word *membrane*.

Ideophones and membranophones

Chordophone

Chordophones

This fourth group includes all string instruments. Most of these are plucked—harps, lyres, and zithers. The strings on some chordophones are struck with mallets, and a few are bowed like the violin.

Unlike orchestral instruments, which are quite standardized, folk instruments lack uniformity. They may be similar to one another, but no two are alike. And they are traditionally taught individually, usually by rote. Because there are few instruction books for learning to play them, the way they are played varies widely.

POPULAR INSTRUMENTS

Guitar

Versions of the *guitar* have existed for hundreds of years in different parts of the world, but it probably originated in the Near East. Actually, the acoustic (nonelectric) guitar of today is not all that different from its ancestors. Some of the older versions had four strings instead of the six used today, and guitars have been constructed in many different sizes.

All guitars produce sounds from the strumming or plucking of the strings by the player. The vibrations of the strings are then resonated by the hollow body of the instrument. The neck of the instrument, where the players place their fingers, has metal strips running across it. These strips, called *frets,* help players find the right place on the fingerboard.

The guitar has two relatives. One is the *banjo,* which has a plastic or parchment head stretched over a hoop and no back. The head gives the banjo a brilliant sound. The other is the *ukulele,* a small four-string guitar.

Accordion

The *accordion* is basically a small organ that the player holds between his or her arms. Air is pushed through the instrument by the in-and-out motion of the player pumping air through the bellows. The sounds are produced by small metal reeds, one for each pitch. The short keyboard is used for playing the notes of the melody, while the chords are sounded by pushing the buttons. One button sounds an entire chord. Expensive accordions can produce several somewhat different timbres.

ELECTRONIC INSTRUMENTS

Electronic instruments divide into two groups. One group consists of instruments that electronically alter and amplify the sounds of the player. The *electric guitar* is the most prominent of this type of electronic instrument. Unlike the traditional acoustic guitar, the body of the electric guitar is not hollow, even though it is shaped somewhat like a guitar. Instead, it holds the strings and various control knobs, as well as a lever for adding vibrato to the tones. Players still place their

It is easy to strum a few chords in G major on the guitar. It is not at all easy to play complicated music on it, however. Rodrigo's *Concierto de Aranjuez,* for example, is a very difficult piece to play correctly.

Blues artist B. B. King plays an electric guitar he calls Lucille.

An early digital synthesizer
Today's systems are more compact and can produce more-realistic sounds.

Computers can process about 64,000 bits of audio data *per second;* information data processing can be as much as one thousand times faster than that.

The use of recorded samples is, appropriately, called *sampling*.

fingers on the fingerboard as with the conventional guitar, but there the similarity ends.

The sounds of drums are often altered in popular music by electronic means. As with the electric guitar, electronic drums can produce wider differences in dynamic levels and alter the timbre to some degree.

The other group of electronic equipment is used in creating music. This group includes synthesizers, computers, and tape and disc players. The sky's the limit with such equipment today. Any type of sound and rhythm can be produced. And performances of the music are always flawless! There are no performers in the traditional sense who can affect the musical results—a fact which has both good and bad points.

In the 1950s electronic music was largely confined to the manipulation of magnetic tape. Composers could alter the speed of the tape, splice in other sounds, record different music on two tracks for performance together, and so on.

A generation later technology had moved from analog to digital processing and production. In *analog* music, sounds are recorded in a continuous, uninterrupted form. Dynamic levels, for example, are changed by increasing or decreasing the power.

It is different with *digital* recording, which consists of discrete, noncontinuous bits of information, usually in the form of numbers, that are produced, sorted, or analyzed. How is this possible? Computers can process these bits of data at an incredible rate of speed. It is the same principle used in motion picture film. The reel of film contains thousands of individual pictures. When they are projected at the rate of 24 per second (*much* slower than a computer!), the eye perceives the individual pictures to be a continuous flow.

The complaint about electronically produced music is that it has a certain manufactured quality about it. To overcome this problem, synthesizers can now store recorded samples of the actual complex sounds of instruments, and then have them available anytime the composer wants them. For example, the sound of a snare drum is complex, with its abrupt beginning and ring in the drum after a tap. Technology can come close to imitating it, but not really capture all the nuances of the tap on a drum or the sounds of other instruments. The inclusion of traditional instrumental sounds in the computer memory helps make the electronic music sound more musical.

Coda

The past few years have seen an explosion of interest in the use of images with music through CD-ROM and DVD disks. Multimedia programs can control both sounds and pictures. They offer a real opportunity in the near future for both listeners and composers.

Part II

Music Around the World

Folk and Ethnic Music

What's different about a song of the Huron tribe in America, the music of the Bantu in Africa, the chantey of English sailors, and the Hindu religious music of India? It's a good question, and a topic that merits attention.

WHAT IS FOLK AND ETHNIC MUSIC?

Folk music is different from art music because it is the music of the common people of a particular nation or ethnic group. And because it is the music of a sizable group of people, it has qualities that cause the people of a particular culture to like and remember it. It is music that has been tested by a large segment of people or a nation. If it had not met with their approval, it would have been forgotten and passed into oblivion.

Music also exists that can be identified with a particular group of people but is not the product of those people. Such music is often referred to as *ethnic*. It is also representative of its particular culture, but not of the music of the common people of that culture.

> Western art music is a type of ethnic music because it is a product of a particular civilization. As used in this book, however, *ethnic* refers to non-Western music.

All folk music is ethnic music, because it is the product of a particular culture. But the opposite is not true: Not all ethnic music is folk music, because usually ethnic represents the efforts of a small, elite group of musicians.

KNOWING FOLK AND ETHNIC MUSIC

Why learn about folk and ethnic music? Such music does not appear on programs in the concert halls of Europe and America, nor is it played on radio stations other than educational ones, and even there only rarely. Recordings of most such music are limited, and they are sold only in a few specialized record stores.

In spite of this situation, there are at least three good reasons for learning about folk and ethnic music: (1) Elements of such music often find their way into art music. (2) Folk and ethnic music reflect the attitudes and values of a culture. (3) Today we encounter other cultures and their music more and more.

INFLUENCE OF FOLK AND ETHNIC MUSIC

In both art and popular music, composers and musicians have often been influenced by folk and ethnic music, sometimes more than they like to admit. Occasionally over the past two hundred years, actual folk tunes have been used in symphonies and other concert music. In other cases, even if no actual folk melodies are used, composers have written folklike tunes.

> Melodies from concert music have also appeared occasionally in popular music.

> "Simple Gifts" is discussed in chapters 3 and 4 and it appears again in chapter 42 in *Appalachian Spring*.

But more than melodies are involved here. Composers sometimes appropriate and adapt ideas they hear in folk and ethnic music. They take a rhythmic or melodic pattern and alter it for use in a composition. For example, Aaron Copland drew heavily on elements of square dance music in his music for the ballet *Appalachian Spring;* he also used the American folk song "Simple Gifts."

Reflecting Culture

Music and the other arts are windows to the culture in which they exist. They represent the attitudes and values of a people. The sensitivity and subtlety of Japanese *koto* music, for example, says more about Japanese character and beliefs than can a thousand words.

Knowing the politics, history, and economy of a nation is certainly worthwhile. It is also valuable to have a sense of its character, its cultural "soul." The former provides basic factual information; the latter provides insight into a society's character.

A cultural heritage is kept alive by these ceremonial dancers of the Tsimshian nation, Metlakatla, Alaska.

The Global Village

A hundred years ago, people were born, lived, and died in the same small geographic area. The customs and way of life of that area were all they ever experienced or knew about. How different it is today! The journey across the Atlantic from England to America used to require months on a sailing ship, but now it is covered in just three hours on a supersonic jet. Mail and news, once transported by ship, are now instantaneous via satellite and other technology. A famine or war in some far-off place like Somalia used to be scarcely noticed, if it was known at all. Today such tragedies are seen live on television in vivid color.

It is a fact: People have contact with and are affected by other peoples around the world to a degree that no one could have imagined a hundred years ago. Each year throughout the twentieth century, the people of the world have been drawn closer and closer together. Today we live in a "global village." Provincialism is now as out-of-date as the hoopskirt and the high Prince Albert shirt collar!

It is important therefore to know about and understand the other residents of our global village, including their cultures and their arts. Learning about the music of other peoples is no longer an academic exercise. It has become an essential aspect of being an educated person.

Not only have travel and communication been made vastly quicker and easier, peoples from many diverse cultures are becoming U.S. citizens in ever-increasing numbers. Even small towns in the heartland of America have recent immigrants from Southeast Asia and Latin America; no longer are immigrants confined to large cities such as Los Angeles, Miami, or New York. Ethnic radio stations and newspapers in languages other than English are commonplace. The yellow pages of telephone books list a wide array of restaurants featuring ethnic foods, and mosques and temples now stand beside Christian churches and Jewish synagogues.

Estimates vary, but around the middle of the twenty-first century the traditional majority of Americans of European descent will become a minority.

HOW ARE FOLK AND ETHNIC MUSIC DIFFERENT?

What is different about most folk and ethnic music? What features do most such musics have in common?

Lack of Uniformity

A symphony by Mozart is published in notation. Therefore, when it is performed by competent musicians, it sounds similar from one performance to another. As for musical instruments, a modern B-flat clarinet is very much like thousands of other B-flat clarinets.

The different performances of the symphony would not be identical, of course.

It's different with most folk music. A song may be performed in a particular way by an individual, and another person in the same culture living only a few miles away may perform it quite differently. A homemade musical instrument is truly one-of-a-kind, although it may be similar to other instruments.

The lack of uniformity makes it difficult to determine which version of a song is the authentic one.

Creation

Folk and ethnic music are usually created by an individual, which is also true of art music. But there the similarity ends. In art music the composer is closely identified with his or her composition—Beethoven's Fifth Symphony, Prokofiev's Third Piano Concerto, and so on. On the other hand, the originator of a folk melody is rarely known. In fact, he or she might not even admit to such an accomplishment, because in some cultures songs are supposed to be gifts from the gods. Besides, in folk music no one seems to care who created a song.

Individual Changes

There is another reason why the creator of a song is seldom recognized. Once the song is created, it begins a process of modification. Performers feel perfectly free to make changes, usually small ones. Over the years a song can evolve to become quite different from how it started out. A folk song is a living organism; it is ever changing. That is one of the virtues of folk music.

Importance of the Performers

Because folk music is seldom set in notation, and because modifications are accepted and even encouraged, performers of folk and ethnic music have a much more important role than they do in Western art music. No longer are they confined to the role of being a re-creator of a work from notation. They become at least co-creators of the music.

Improvisation

One of the reasons why performers have such an important role is that often they are expected to *improvise*—to make up music on the spot. However, they do not usually improvise out of thin air—that is, without any guidelines at all. Each type of music (African, Hindu religious, jazz, and so on) has performance traditions and practices that musicians are expected to follow. It's a bit like a basketball team: The players have some plays or plans for scoring and defense, but usually they have to adjust them on the spot, depending on what the other team does. They operate within a system yet have the freedom to try their own ideas when it seems desirable.

Audience

Today we are used to having music performed for an audience, either in person or by listening to a recording. In the case of folk and ethnic music, the audience, if there is one at all, is much less important. In many parts of the world, music is performed at events in which everyone participates; there are few listeners as such. Some of the time, the music is performed as part of a ceremony to appease or thank gods, which makes a human audience irrelevant.

When an audience becomes unimportant, performers no longer need to worry about people *liking* their music. It also removes any commercial considerations, because no tickets or royalties are possible. Therefore, folk and most ethnic music is created for reasons other than to make money.

Subtleties, Shadings, and Sophistication

Each type of music contains a number of small things that add much to its character and are an integral part of the music. For example, in some styles of music the performers "bend" or "shade" certain tones in a melody to make the music more expressive. Such sophisticated subtleties are easily overlooked by someone not familiar with the particular musical style, because the music sounds so different to them.

In general, when a musical style is strong in one element, it is relatively undeveloped in some others. African music, for example, is noted for its rhythms, but its other aspects are less notable. Balinese music contains a kaleidoscope of timbres, but it does not have the harmonic or melodic interest of many other types.

Most folk and ethnic music consists of short works, often songs. True, some African rituals last for hours, but the same music tends to be repeated over and over with only slight variations. Without a system of notation, works of music are usually rather short-winded. This short length allows for little development of themes, something that is important in Western art music.

Shading is an integral part of traditional Japanese music. In Japanese culture it is believed that a melody sung without such inflections lacks expression.

The point about hearing subtle differences is emphasized in chapter 1.

The development of themes is discussed in chapter 19.

Oral Tradition

Much of the world's music is never rendered in notation. Yet some of the music that has existed for thousands of years has not been forgotten or changed in a noticeable way. How is this possible? By passing it from one person or generation to another by word of mouth, what is known as *oral tradition*. It is difficult for those of us who are used to preserving thoughts in writing or through recordings to understand the ability that people can acquire to remember what they hear. When they want or need to, people can recall quite accurately, especially if the song or story is not too long.

Preservation

Until about a hundred years ago, almost no one seemed to care about preserving folk or ethnic music. Western intellectuals did not seem to consider it worth saving, and the musicians who created and performed it seemed happy with what oral tradition had given them. As the twentieth century progressed, interest in preserving and studying folk and ethnic music increased. Today a number of ethnomusicologists with tape recorders and notepads are working and living in many parts of the globe in an attempt to preserve this vast musical treasure.

MUSIC AND CULTURE

All music is a product of a particular culture. As has been pointed out, music and the other arts provide much insight into the character and customs of a people. The cultural difference between a piano concerto by Prokofiev, for example, and a song of the Aleut tribe in Alaska lies in the relative importance of the cultural elements. In the case of the Aleut music (and almost all other folk and ethnic music), a knowledge of language, customs, thought forms, and other aspects of culture is necessary for a full understanding of the music. The Prokofiev piano concerto is much more able to stand alone; it is not as embedded in everyday culture.

It is of course possible to analyze a folk or ethnic work apart from its cultural setting, but the music loses much of its meaning when this is done. In fact, some Indian scholars object to putting Hindu ragas in notation and to discussing only the features of the music. They are correct in their concern for the cultural relevance of the music, but the amount of time one can devote to learning about any given type of music is limited. Therefore, we have no choice but to consider mainly the musical aspects in college-level music courses.

An ethnomusicologist studying Mexican music wanted to hear a certain song that was sung for a particular festival. He located the performer, who didn't want to sing it. "We're not having the festival now," he explained. Finally, the man was coaxed into singing it, but broke into laughter before finishing, because singing the song apart from the festival seemed ridiculous to him.

In folk and ethnic music, sociocultural considerations outweigh musical factors, whereas in art/concert music, the opposite is true.

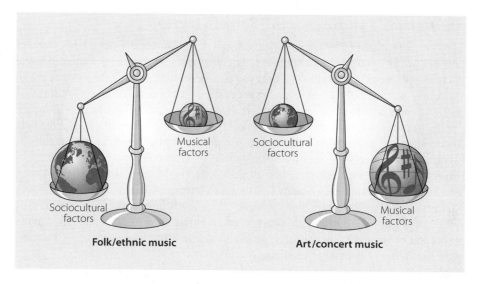

Folk/ethnic music **Art/concert music**

LISTENING TO FOLK AND ETHNIC MUSIC

Listening to folk or most ethnic music requires a somewhat different approach from what is needed for listening to art music. Listening to what happens in a melody and the rhythm of a work is still necessary, but the listener must also consider the cultural factors.

Listen to "Mitamba Yalagala Kumchuzi" again. As you listen this time, keep in mind the sociocultural setting of the music.

One way to think about and listen to folk and ethnic music is to imagine two columns. One column is under the heading *Musical* and the other is under the heading *Sociocultural*. Here is an example that could easily be true of much of the music from East Africa.

Musical	Sociocultural
Drums in several sizes	From East Africa
Polyrhythms	Highly trained drummers
Very steady tempo	Everyone participates
Call-and-response	Male drummers and soloist
Some improvisation	Aspects of a tonal language
Simple melody	Simple dances to music
Phrases often repeated	Performed "by ear"—no notation
African singing style	Instruments of skins and gourds

As with most types of music, several hearings of the same piece are recommended so that you become somewhat accustomed to the style. Keep in mind too that the music was not created as concert music, but it is very effective in relating its message and in representing East African culture.

C o d a

*The banquet of music around the world is incredibly rich and varied.
At first some of it may sound new and strange to you, but give it a chance to
work its magic. Your understanding and appreciation of your fellow residents
of the global village and their music will be greatly increased.*

Folk Music of Europe and the Americas

8

Europe stretches from the Ural Mountains in
Russia several thousand miles west to England and Ireland.
With the settling of North and South America by the various
nations of Europe, the culture of western European civilization was
transported across the Atlantic Ocean and later halfway around the
world to Australia and New Zealand. The immigrants from Europe
came upon lands already occupied by Native Americans in the
north and Incas, Aztecs, and other peoples to the south. Later
slaves were brought to the Western Hemisphere from Africa.

The resulting combination of music from
multiple countries and sources is a wealth of music styles,
with each influencing and enriching the others.

EUROPEAN FOLK MUSIC

European folk music is built around the features presented in part I. These include melody, harmony, timbre, accompaniment, form, subject matter, and rhythm.

Melody

Melodies are built on the seven-note major and minor scales. In addition, many folk melodies use seven-note scales other than major or minor, or what are termed *modes*. A few pentatonic scales are encountered, particularly in eastern Europe. A *pentatonic* scale has five notes in the pattern of the black keys on a piano. Generally, the range of the melodies is about one octave and they do not contain many repeated notes.

Harmony

Accompanying chords are built in thirds, with the three primary chords predominating. The presence of harmony is an important difference between Western music and much of the music of other parts of the world.

Thirds follow an alternating pattern (*ACE, BDF,* and so on). The primary chords are I (tonic), IV (subdominant), and V (dominant.)

Timbre

The style of singing found in Western folk music is natural and relaxed, at least to Western ears. Many folks singers use little vibrato, and no attempt is made to impress listeners with the singer's vocal prowess. The instruments used in folk music are equally unpretentious. The guitar, accordion, harmonica (mouth organ), dulcimer, and other easily transported instruments are generally used.

Although most Western folk music consists of songs, there is a body of instrumental music associated with dances. The fiddle tunes found in western Europe and America are part of this tradition.

The dulcimer looks like a long, flat violin with three strings. It is placed on the player's lap and plucked with a quill. Two of its strings produce a drone.

Accompaniment

Originally, folk music was often performed without any accompaniment. Most of it is now accompanied by an instrument, however, which is often played by the singer.

Traditionally, ballads are sung by one singer.

Form

A characteristic of Western folk music is the singing of different sets of words to the same melody. The musical term the repeating of a song with different verses, or *stanzas,* is *strophic.* Although some European folk songs have twenty or more stanzas, four or five is typical.

Subject Matter

European folk songs include a larger percentage of epic tales and love sentiments than is found in other cultures. One important type of song is the *ballad.* Its words tell a story, often a sad one, in five or more stanzas. In English ballads the singer usually relates a tale about someone else, which gives the song a sense of detachment. In American ballads the singer often sings about himself or herself, but an attitude of detachment is nevertheless retained.

Rhythm

The rhythm of Western folk music is regular and metrical. Traditionally, ballads have a common iambic meter and stanzas of four lines in which a four-foot line alternates with a three-foot line.

"Barbara Allen" is a good example of a ballad as well as of many characteristics of Western folk music. It is the most popular ballad of the Western world and is found of hundreds of versions.

In addition to its metrical rhythm, "Barbara Allen" has a simple melody that is largely built out of the notes of its main chord. It is based on the five-note, or pentatonic, scale. The singer on the recording uses a plain, unemotional style as he accompanies his singing on a guitar.

Samuel Pepys wrote of singing "Barbara Allen" on January 2, 1666, in London. Both the English and the Scotch claim the song, and some ninety-eight versions of it were found in Virginia alone!

LISTENING GUIDE

English Ballad: "Barbara Allen"
CD **3** Track **1**

1. **1** In Scarlet town where I was born,
there was a fair maid dwellin',
made many a youth cry well a-day,
and her name was Barb'ry Allen.

2. Twas in the merry month of May,
when green buds they were swellin',
Sweet William came from the west country,
and he courted Barb'ry Allen.

3. He sent his servant unto her,
to the place where she was dwellin',
"My master's sick, bids me call for you,
if your name be Barb'ry Allen".

4. Well, slowly, slowly she got up,
and slowly went she nigh him,
but all she said as she passed his bed,
"Young man, I think you're dying."

5. He turned his pale face to the wall,
and busted out at cryin',
"Adieu, adieu, my dear friends all,
Be kind to Barb'ry Allen."

6. Well, lightly tripped she down the stairs.
she heard those church bells tollin',
and each bell seemd to say as it tolled,
"Hard-hearted Barb'ry Allen."

7. And she looked east, and she looked west.
She seen his pale corpse a-comin',
"Lay down, lay down that corpse of clay,
that I may look upon him."

8. "Oh, mother, mother go make by bed,
go make it long and narrow.
Sweet William died for me today.
I'll die for him tomorrow."

9. They buried Sweet William in the old churchyard.
They buried Barbara beside him.
Out of his grave grew a red, red rose,
and out of hers a brier.

10. They grew and grew up the old church wall,
'till they could grow no higher.
And at the top, twined in a lovers' knot,
the red rose and the brier.

AMERICAN FOLK MUSIC

Just as English is the predominant language in the United States, the British Isles are the main source of its folk music. Many songs were imported from England, and many others are patterned after British types. The style of performance is also closely related to its English heritage.

One adaptation of the English ballad is the *broadside*. The name comes from the old English practice of printing ballads on large sheets of paper called broadsides, which were sold on the streets. Broadsides were often about current events or famous personalities. About two hundred such songs were circulated in the United States. The poetry of broadsides is not always of superior quality, but it reflects the interests of the people of the time.

The ballad style is found in many American folk songs associated with occupations—sailors, cowboys, lumberjacks, miners, farmers, and so on.

Non-British music came to America with various immigrant groups. In a few cases, such music was incorporated into the culture. For example, "Du, du liegst mir im Herzen" is a German song that has been adopted into the culture; "Alouette" is a French-Canadian example; "Chiapanecas" ("Mexican Clapping Song") is a Latin American contribution that is clapped and stomped at many major-league ballparks.

Some non-British songs have had new words set to their melodies. The Pennsylvania Dutch song "Marjets wann ich uffschteh" became "Go Tell Aunt Rhody." Unfortunately, much non-British music was lost in America. Still, there are various types of American folk music.

Folk music scholars in the early twentieth century found Elizabethan English folk songs better preserved in remote Appalachian hamlets than in England itself.

The word *Dutch* as used in *Pennsylvania Dutch* is a perversion of *Deutsch*, which is the German word for "German."

Work Songs

Songs that accompany labor are not characteristic of American folk music, except for sea chanteys and African American music. "Blow the Man Down" is an example of a sea chantey. Its words hardly convey a deep message:

Chantey is pronounced "shanty."

> *Come all ye young fellows that follow the sea,*
> *to the way haye, blow the man down,*
> *And pray, pay attention and listen to me,*
> *give me some time to blow the man down.*

Occupational Songs

Although few songs accompanied work, many of them were about work. Cowboy ballads, which were modeled after the English ballad, often had a melancholy tone. In "The Cowboy's Lament," the dying young man says:

> *Get sixteen gamblers to carry my coffin*
> *Six purty maidens to sing me a song,*
> *Take me to the valley and lay the sod o'er me,*
> *For I'm a young cowboy an' know I done wrong.*

The development of the railroads provided another source for occupational songs. Some of them are about men who built the railroads ("Drill, Ye Tarriers, Drill"), some describe famous personalities ("John Henry" and "Casey Jones"), and others tell about particular trains ("The Wabash Cannonball," discussed in chapter 44).

"The Ox-Driving Song" tells about the troubles of the teamsters who drove their wagons over muddy roads and washouts:

Joan Baez exemplifies the tradition of the self-accompanied folk singer.

> *When I got there, the hills were steep,*
> *'twould make any tenderhearted person weep*
> *to hear me cuss and pop my whip*
> *and see my oxen pull and slip.*

Dance Music

The most important type of folk dancing was square dancing. If no instruments were available, the dancers sang the music as they danced. Usually, the words had little significance; sometimes words were added simply to complete a line of music. A good example of dance music is "Skip to My Lou":

Flies in the buttermilk, two by two,
flies in the buttermilk, two by two,
flies in the buttermilk, two by two,
skip to my Lou, my darling!

CHORUS:
She's gone again, skip to my Lou,
she's gone again, skip to my Lou,
she's gone again, skip to my Lou,
skip to my Lou, my darling.

My girl wears a number nine shoe,
my girl wears a number nine shoe,
my girl wears a number nine shoe,
skip to my Lou, my darling.

CHORUS

A fiddler

Dance music was often played on fiddles. Most of the tunes, called *hoedowns* or *breakdowns*, were in a fast tempo with two beats to the measure. Their heritage is the reels and hornpipes from the British Isles. Jigs were also popular fiddle music for dancing. Fiddle tunes had some imaginative titles: "Devil's Dream," "Lost Indian," "Orange Blossom Special," "Leather Britches," and others.

The fiddle and the violin are the same—sort of. The difference comes in the way they are played. Fiddlers handle the bow somewhat differently and hold the instrument lower in front of the chest. No vibrato is used. They sometimes tune strings to nonstandard pitches. The instrument itself may be an inexpensive mail-order model or a handmade version.

One old catalog lists a "Special Stradivarius Model" for $9.95, including bow, case, extra strings, instruction book, and fingering chart!

Self-expression

Many songs, in both folk and art music, serve to express deep feelings. The white spiritual "The Wayfaring Stranger" is one example:

I'm just a poor, wayfaring stranger,
A-trav'ling through this world of woe,
Yet there's no sickness, no toil, no danger,
In that fair land to which I go.

I'm goin' there to see my mother,
I'm goin' there no more to roam,
I'm just a-goin' over Jordan,
I'm just a-goin' over home.

"A-goin' over Jordan" refers to dying.

Arrangements

Sometimes composers find songs that they consider worth arranging for concert or recital hall performance. They leave the original melody largely intact and devise an accompaniment for piano or orchestra. Aaron Copland did this with the Shaker song "Simple Gifts." The song comes from the period between 1837 and 1847.

The accompaniment for "Simple Gifts" is in keeping with the text and melody by being open and uncluttered. There are only very brief introductory measures based on the melody for each section of the song. Sometimes the chords are sounded off the beat in a subtle way, but generally everything is plain and understated.

The harmony of "Simple Gifts" is discussed in chapter 3, which also includes a Listening Guide for Copland's arrangement of the song.

NATIVE AMERICAN MUSIC

The Native Americans came to the Americas during the Ice Age more than fifty thousand years ago, when an ice bridge existed across the Bering Strait between Siberia and Alaska. Their music differs very much from that of the English tradition.

The functional nature of Native American music is apparent in the names given to the rituals. A sun dance or a rabbit dance were created for a specific purpose. Sometimes that purpose was to appease or influence spirits, and at other times it was to sing about events in life.

Native American instruments traditionally consisted of a variety of drums, usually played with sticks. Many types of rattles were also developed. Several kinds of flutes were played, especially by the men, who performed love music on them to impress their chosen young women.

The Native American population was never large, and it was spread over a vast land area. Its music differs according to the particular tribe and geographic location.

The Native American population was no more than 1 to 2 million in all of the United States and Canada.

- ♦ The Eskimos and the tribes of the Pacific Northwest developed music characterized by nonstrophic forms, complex rhythms, and small melodic intervals.

- ♦ The tribes of California and the extreme Southwest sing with a harsh vocal sound. Their songs consist of two or more separate sections that are repeated, alternated, and interwoven.

- ♦ A third broad area includes Utah, Nevada, and the interior of northern California. In this region the singing is more relaxed in style, and the songs are made up of paired phrases, with each phrase repeated.

- ♦ A fourth type of Native American culture is distinguished more by language than geography. It consists of the Navajo, Apache, and some western Canadian tribes. Their melodies have a wide range, and male singers freely perform in high, falsetto voices.

Native American dancers and drummers of the Tesuque people perform an ancient hunting ceremony called the Buffalo Dance. Only men sang and danced in most Native American ceremonies.

- ♦ The Pueblo and Plains tribes display more tension in singing and favor a two-part song form.

- ♦ Native Americans in the eastern and southern parts of the United States feature singing responsively, with shouts tossed back and forth between leader and group.

Native American music has not had much effect on the other types of American music for two reasons. First, most Native Americans did not live close to non–Native Americans. They have often lived apart on reservations, and their music has tended to be confined to the tribe.

Second, Native American music is quite different from Western music. In some respects it is more Asian than Western. When one culture incorporates music from another, the two styles are likely to be similar. Some change—but not too much—is accepted in a musical style. In the few instances in which Native American music has been incorporated into compositions, it has been changed quite a bit.

No Native American music was found in concerts before about 1890, and even today there are very few works that show the influence of this music.

AFRICAN AMERICAN MUSIC

In a complex and pluralistic society such as the United States, the sources of the cultural mixture are hard to determine, and so it is difficult to know which aspects of African American music were transplanted from Africa and which were developed in America. In any case, some of the African's rhythmic ideas, call-and-response patterns, love of instruments, and improvisation are now part of American music. Africans brought something perhaps more important than any technical features: a strong interest in music and a desire to involve listeners in the music.

Calls and Hollers

One early and important feature of African American folk music was the spontaneous individual *calls and hollers* heard in the fields and other workplaces. Their purpose was to relieve loneliness and stress, as well as to express feelings. Musically, they were short melodic fragments that were highly decorated. They were mostly improvised. Few calls and hollers were recorded before they largely disappeared, but they played a role in the development of the blues, which led directly to jazz.

<blockquote>Jazz is discussed in chapter 43.</blockquote>

Spirituals

An important form of African American religious folk music was the *spiritual.* Until after the Civil War, these songs existed by oral tradition among blacks. The first book of spirituals containing both words and music was not published until 1867.

During Reconstruction several colleges for the recently freed slaves were established in the South by various church groups. To help raise money by giving concerts, singing groups were formed at these colleges, most notably the Fisk Jubilee Singers at Fisk University in Nashville. Initially, the group sang a variety of songs, but no spirituals. They soon found, however, that spirituals were enthusiastically received by audiences. The Fisk Jubilee Singers was both a musical and a financial success as it toured New York City, Washington, D.C., and Europe.

The Fisk Jubilee Singers
In seven years they raised $150,000, a large amount of money at that time.

Spirituals drew heavily on biblical texts. Some of these texts use Bible stories as thinly veiled parallels to the plight of the African Americans as slaves. The spiritual "Go Down, Moses" is a good example:

> *When Israel was in Egypt's land,*
> *Let my people go.*
> *Oppressed so hard they could not stand,*
> *Let my people go.*

Spirituals were sung with much inflection and subtlety. What is seen in the notation of a spiritual is only the skeletal outline for what was actually sung. In fact, quite a bit of improvising took place during the singing. Spirituals were originally sung by a group, not a solo singer.

Folk Blues

Blues songs were the most important type of secular folk music among African Americans. In contrast to spirituals, blues songs were for individual singers to cry out against life's problems. The topics of the blues ranged from problems with work (too much or not enough), crime, infidelity, loneliness, and rejection. These sentiments were generally sung in a three-line form *(aab)*.

> *My mama told me before I left home,*
> *My mama told me before I left home,*
> *You better let them Jacksonville women alone.*

Furthermore, lines of the blues are harmonized in a rudimentary way. The musical interest was in the way the melody was sung. Blues singers tend to slide between pitches to put more emotion in the music. Many embellishments are also added. Usually, singing blues is accompanied by the guitar. Sometimes it is played in "bottleneck" style by running a knife blade on the strings, which creates a timbre something like a Hawaiian guitar.

Work Songs

Songs created to accompany work are definitely a contribution of African Americans. The song text is not always related to the job at hand; often the words are only to supply a pleasant accompaniment to labor.

Instruments

Particular instruments are prominent in African American folk music, just as they are in Africa. Some instruments are conventional; others are intended to provide sound effects. Included in the latter category are washboards, pans, cowbells, bottles, various clappers, and the gutbucket.

The *gutbucket* is an inverted washtub with a rope pulled through it, which is connected to a stick. The pitch is varied according to the tension the player exerts on the stick and thereby the rope.

*L*ATIN AMERICAN MUSIC

Latin American music includes a wide variety of types, partly because the music of Spain, the parent culture of Central and South America, is so varied. Spanish music includes the music of the gypsies and the Basque people of northern Spain, Arabian influences resulting from six hundred years of occupation by the Moors, and French influence from Provençal. With the Spanish conquests in the New World, elements of its music were transported to the Americas.

In addition to the Spanish and Portuguese colonialism, the music of Central and South America was heavily influenced by African music brought by black slaves. This influence is especially strong in Haiti and the other Caribbean nations of Cuba, Jamaica, and Trinidad, the Guianas on the north coast of South America, and northern Brazil. Central and South America also have large Indian populations, which in some areas have retained their native languages. Recent immigrations from Asia have also played a role in the music of Latin America.

What has resulted from the contacts among these four groups is a varied and wonderfully mixed heritage. Many countries have terms for these mixed cultures, such as *mestizo* (Native American and Spanish), *mulato* (African and Spanish), and *zambo* (African and Native American).

Since the Spanish came to the New World, the various types of music have been adapted so much that it is often impossible to tell the origins of a particular style of music. For example, the *bolero* was originally Spanish, but in Cuba its rhythm became more complex. Among other features that carried over from Spanish music are the frequent use of rhythms having three notes to the beat (called a *triplet*), the presence of a line of harmony moving parallel to the melody but three notes below, and melodies with a narrow range.

The *bolero* is a dance in four beats to the measure containing complex rhythmic patterns.

Mexican music is largely Spanish in character, more so than most Latin American music. Although some Mexican Indians have retained their musical heritage, Indian influence is not significant in Mexican music. The Mexicans have

A mariachi band The name *mariachi* comes from the French *mariage,* because these musicians used to play mainly for weddings during the time of Maximillian and the French rule of Mexico.

a narrative type of song called a *corrido.* Like the English ballad, it relates a happening or tells a story.

Instruments play an important role in Mexican music and are sometimes featured in interludes of songs. The often-heard mariachi band consists of from three to twelve performers playing violins, guitars, trumpets, and other instruments.

Another type of Latin American music is the *son,* which appeared during the early part of the twentieth century and became a popular urban type of music played by groups consisting of strings and percussion. In the Mexican "Sones de Hausteca," the violin player shows the influence of the virtuoso style of concert violinists in the United States. Two of the male singers sing in parallel thirds, which is typical of Mexican music. At times, the harmony and melody don't fit together all that well.

L I S T E N I N G   G U I D E

Mexican Folk Song: "Sones de Hausteca"
CD 3 Track 2

0:00	2 A violin accompanied by a guitar strumming chords begins.
0:15	The violin continues playing many rapidly moving notes.
0:29	One male singer begins singing a melody containing a number of short phrases. Several times he slides his voice up into a falsetto (high false voice).
0:39	Two other men join in, singing in parallel thirds.
0:48	The soloist sings the melody again.
0:57	The violin begins playing many rapidly moving notes.
1:41	The violin and guitar play a rhythmic pattern with short repeated notes.
1:51	The soloist sings the melody again.
2:00	Two males take the melody, singing in parallel thirds.
2:09	The soloist sings the melody again.
2:20	The violin plays many rapidly moving notes.
2:39	The music concludes with a few short chords.

C o d a

Is there a type of folk music that is clearly American?
The answer to that question is not clear. Yes, there are aspects of folk
music in the United States that are found nowhere else in the world. This is
especially true of African American music. But no, much of the folk music
of this country was adopted and adapted from other peoples and nations.
It is both old and new, both an imitation and an original. And this is what
makes it a musically and culturally fascinating type of music.

Music of Africa and the Middle East

9

The continent of Africa is a huge land mass about a fourth larger than all of North America. The Sahara Desert extends for thousands of miles across its upper half. To the south of the Sahara are the black peoples whom we usually associate with that continent. For the remainder of this book, the word *African* refers to the music from the southern part of the continent.

To the north of the Sahara, and especially to the east extending from Egypt in the northeast corner to Iran and Pakistan north of India, lies what is often referred to as the Middle East. These peoples are largely Muslim, with Turks and Arabs being the largest ethnic groups. Sitting in the middle among these countries is Israel, with its unique heritage.

The music of sub-Saharan Africa and that of the Middle East contain many differences within them, and this discussion can offer only a small sample of each overall type of music.

AFRICAN MUSIC

What are the main characteristics of the music of the peoples who live south of the Sahara? Many of the features of folk music mentioned in chapter 7 are found in African music, but several are particularly important.

Relationship with Language

African languages are tonal in character. As pointed out earlier, in such languages the meaning of sound varies depending on the pitch and manner in which it is said. Because they are tonal, African languages have a musical quality about them. There is a strong similarity between the singsong speech of a language and the music of

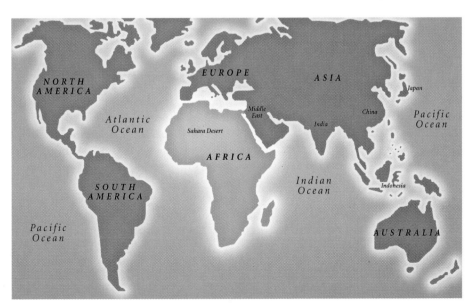

Africa and the world

Actually, the drums do not "talk" so much as they signal. The process is similar to how bugle calls functioned at one time in an army.

the people who speak it. Even the drums used in some African music attempt to imitate the pitches and inflections of the language. These "talking drums" are capable of sending messages that are clearly understood by the people who speak that particular language.

Here is an example of how the pitches of a language influence the rhythm and pitches found in the music:

Text: "Wo ho te sen?" ("How do you do?")

Tone levels: Low high, low high

Rhythm: Short long, short long

Melody:

At best, rendering non-Western music in notation can only approximate the actual sounds.

Association with Dance

Just as language is closely related to African music, so is dance. Dance is used in rituals, worship, celebrations, and for recreation and is considered a natural accompaniment to the music. Some dances are for just the men, and women participate in others. Much of the time, anyone can join in the dancing, often to be observed and rewarded with coins if the dancer was judged to be good by the onlookers. Few people are passive when African music is being performed.

The coins are given to the musicians as payment for their efforts.

Rhythm

The music played by groups of percussion instruments best illustrates the complexity of rhythm in African music. The music starts out simply with a basic rhythm, or "timeline," which might be compared with the role of the bass drum in a marching band in keeping the group together. Soon other percussion instruments are added over the timeline part until as many as five distinct rhythm patterns are sounding at the same time—*polyrhythm*. Then enters the master drummer, who plays the rhythm of a particular piece of music. After a while he gives a rhythmic signal to change to another piece. This process continues until the performance is completed.

Polyrhythm occurs when two or more rhythm patterns are sounded at the same time.

Several other points should be mentioned about African instrumental ensembles, especially as found in Ghana and other West African countries.

♦ Rarely do African drummers tap their feet; they do not think following a beat as do Western musicians.

♦ Not only do the rhythm patterns of the various instruments differ, they also do not begin at exactly the same moment, as is usually true in Western music. In fact, they would lose some of their rhythmic flavor if they did.

♦ Often the meter is unclear as to whether it is in two or three beats. At one moment the pattern seems to be clearly two beats to the measure, but a little while later a three-beat pattern may be perceived. This metric ambiguity makes the music more fascinating.

Improvisation

There is less improvising in African percussion ensembles than is generally supposed; the musicians are often playing preexisting music that has been passed on by oral tradition. Performers, especially master drummers, are allowed to make small changes and alterations in the music, partly to relieve tedium. African musicians do not, however, play whatever they happen to feel like playing; they perform within certain clearly understood guidelines.

Functional Music

Music is very much a part of the daily lives of Africans. For example, it is called on to cure illnesses, appease gods, and celebrate the births of babies. There are songs praising cattle, telling about animal hunts, and paddling a canoe. There is also some music that is simply for entertainment, and a small amount that is played for ceremonies involving a king or chief.

African drum ensemble

A few African men earn their livelihood from their music making, especially drummers. These musicians learn their trade from infancy. They are carefully taught, often by their fathers, and they do not perform publicly until they become truly competent as young adults.

Because most African music is functional, it does not take place in a performer/audience situation. Musical performances are truly participatory events in which there is little distinction between performer and audience. Because African music is functional, its musicians want their work to have an impact. They do not care whether it is considered "beautiful" in the sense that Western musicians often think about music.

Lack of Uniformity

It has been estimated that sub-Saharan Africa contains between five hundred and seven hundred languages or dialects. Such diversity of languages is significant in that continent's music because its music and languages are virtually inseparable. Therefore, the music of one tribe may differ a lot from that of another tribe only a short distance away. And the music that is so vital to one tribe often makes little sense to other tribes, even though they both sound like African music to us.

Four major languages exist just in the small nation of Zambia. These languages are so different that commerce and government are conducted in English, which was used when Zambia was Northern Rhodesia and under British control.

Form

African music features what is termed *call-and-response* form. In this form a leader sings or plays a phrase, and then the group responds with its rendition of the phrase. The pattern is something like a game of musical tennis. Sometimes the response is not identical because members of the group will make small alterations in what they have heard. At other times the response begins before the original phrase is completed, and the result is a brief period of simple counterpoint or harmony.

Some African songs follow a pattern in which the original melody returns or is set in a two-part form.

Melodic Characteristics

African melodies are often altered and ornamented with slight changes of pitch, trills, slides, and other decorative notes. Some of the scales on which the music is based are not very different from those found in Western music, but the style in which they are used is quite different.

Beliefs About Music and Instruments

The practice of attributing human qualities to inanimate objects is termed *animism*.

African have strong beliefs about the spirit of an instrument. For example, a drum is not just a drum; instead, it has an almost human quality. The maker of a drum wants to make sure the drum "speaks" as it should. So he may unobtrusively pick up pebbles to put in the drum from the yard of a woman known to be a gossip. In addition, he may add a piece of lion skin so that the drum will roar, a piece of frog skin to help the drum remain supple, and pieces of metal so that it will rattle. Other musical instruments are similarly "doctored" to achieve a more interesting sound.

Instruments

Mbira

Drums hold the dominant position among African musical instruments. They are constructed of various materials and are made in a variety of sizes. Some are played with the hands; others are played with sticks. An especially interesting drum has an hourglass shape with strings connecting its two heads. The player holds it under the arm and squeezes the strings against his body to change the tension of the heads, which affects the pitch of the drum. In this way, the drum can "talk."

The *mbira,* or thumb piano, is a feature of African music. It usually has about eighteen short strips of metal or cane that sound against a resonating box. Simple flutes are also found in African music, as is a single string instrument called a *gonje,* which is played with a bow.

Other African instruments include a gourd with beads strung around it. It is shaken in performance, often by a woman. A double bell that looks like a cowbell is also heard, as are various rattles. Hand claps and a whistle are also used, as can be heard on "Safari Ya Msanga-Tifu," which is included on the CD. It is an excerpt from a dance song of the Giriyama tribe near Mombasa in Kenya. The text of the song is: "I was so much in love that I found myself in Msanga-Tifu, where my girl lives, without knowing how I got there."

L I S T E N I N G *G* U I D E

African Dance Song: "Safari Ya Msanga-Tifu"
CD **3** Track **3**

0:00	**3** The lead singer begins, as the rattles are heard prominently.
0:12	The group responds in the call-and-response form typical of African music.
0:25	The lead singer continues.
0:28	The group responds briefly. Whoops are sounded and notes a fifth apart can be heard for a moment.
0:30	The lead singer continues.
0:35	The group responds.
0:42	The lead singer takes up the song again.
0:52	The group responds as hand claps are added.
1:02	The lead singer and group make four short exchanges.
1:15	The lead singer continues with the song as a whistle is heard more prominently.
1:22	The group responds.
1:29	The group sings the phrase again at a higher pitch.
1:38	The recording fades.

MIDDLE EASTERN MUSIC

As mentioned earlier, the term *Middle East* usually refers to the Arab world that extends thousands of miles from the northwest coast of Africa from Casablanca on the Atlantic Ocean to the eastern borders of Pakistan north of India. The people who inhabit this vast stretch of land are more united in their religious faith—Islam—than by their culture or language. The people of Iran, for example, consider themselves Persian and speak Parsi, not Arabic, and feel little kinship for the people of neighboring Iraq. The Turks constitute another major segment of the Middle East, while another large segment is centered in Egypt and yet another stretches across North Africa.

The Medes (the people who live in present-day Iraq) and the Persians have a history of conflict that goes back almost two thousand years.

Although the land encompassed by the Middle East is large, the population is not, at least in comparison with Africa, Europe, or the Far East. The people tend to be spread along the shores of the Mediterranean Sea and the Indian Ocean. They are no more homogeneous than are the peoples of sub-Saharan Africa.

Music is in an especially difficult situation because Mohammed, the prophet of Islam, did not approve of music in the mosque. A few restrained prayers and chants are performed in a singsong style, but these are not officially considered music.

In addition to Mohammed's views, music in the Middle East is based on complex and often confusing theories that vary from one area to another. To make matters more complicated, musicians in this part of the world often do not follow these theories and guidelines when they perform.

The Middle East

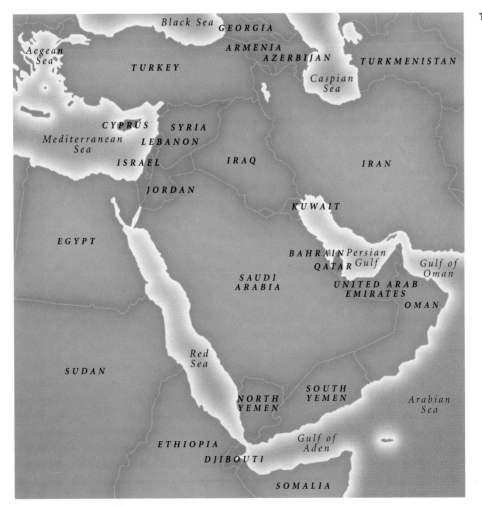

Arabian musicians

In general singers, who are usually men, produce a tense, nasal tone quality. They also add many ornaments to the basic melodic line. Rhythm is treated very freely, which permits singers and instrumentalists to add their particular decorative parts to the music.

A number of instruments are associated with music from the Middle East. One is the *ud,* which is a string instrument with a pear-shaped body. Another string instrument is the *rebab,* which is generally considered the direct ancestor of the violin. The *tombak* is a drum in the shape of an hourglass that is played with the fingers.

There are few concerts in the Middle East. Most performances are informal, many times in cafés. In that setting one may sip a drink while listening. As an added attraction, some pieces featuring gyrating female dancers for which the Arab world is noted may be interspersed among the more thoughtful works. Musical quality is hard to maintain when faced with such competition.

Jewish Music

Israel is situated in the middle of the Arab world, which over the centuries has created many political tensions and wars. Modern Israel is very different from its neighbors. Not only is it the only true democracy in the region, but it is also much more Western and up-to-date. It is a nation with a fascinating history.

Over the centuries Jewish religious music has remained rather well unified in spite of the Diaspora in the Middle Ages and subsequent centuries. Judaism was much less evangelistic than Christianity. It tended to keep its faith within the group, and it seldom incorporated regional music into its worship.

The traditional religious music of Judaism consisted of prayers and invocations, not anthems and other ensemble music. Today its religious music varies according to the degree of orthodoxy. The more-orthodox congregations permit only unaccompanied chanting by cantors; the more-liberal congregations (at least in the United States) often employ Gentile instrumentalists and singers and allow them to perform adaptations of music written for Christian worship. The orthodox chants are similar to some of the chants adopted by the early Christian Church (see chapter 12). A few Jewish melodies have been adapted for use as hymn tunes in Christian churches.

The Diaspora was the scattering of the Jewish people from Palestine to many different parts of the world.

Jewish music and worship practices were very influential in the early Christian Church.

A cantor chanting

The modern nation of Israel was founded in 1948, and most of its population immigrated there from other countries—Poland, Ethiopia, and many other nations and in recent years, especially Russia. These immigrants have retained some of the musical influences of their former lands, so it is not unusual, for example, for German Jews to sing German or Yiddish songs or for Armenian Russian Jews to sing songs of their former homeland. In addition, the influence of the Middle East and its Arab culture has also been felt. When Israelis sing Arab songs, however, they sing them in a Jewish style.

Because the common bond among the people of Israel is religious, not ethnic, attempts have been made to create a new and unifying folk music tradition. New popular songs have been composed with texts on economic and political topics. Folk songs in Israel today are accompanied by tambourines, accordions, and guitars—instruments that represent Israel's diverse musical heritage.

C o d a

African music is not only fascinating in its own right,
it is especially significant because of the enormous role it has played
in Latin American and North American music. Jazz and several other types
of American music reveal a close kinship with the music that
came to the Western Hemisphere with the African slaves.

The music of the Middle East is no less interesting, but its influence in Western
music has not been nearly as great as that of African music. The reason for
this is very likely the fact that until recently there has been little contact and
few immigrants to the United States from that part of the world.

10 *Music of Asia*

What do the three-note songs of the Aborigines of Australia, the ragas of India, and the gamelan music of Bali have in common? In many ways they are different, but each comes from that vast portion of the world called Asia and its related countries along the Indian and Pacific Oceans.

*I*NDIAN MUSIC

India is overwhelming. About 13 percent of the world's people live there. Somewhat protected from outside influences by the giant Himalayan Mountains to the north and the vast Indian Ocean to the south, India developed its own unique and fascinating civilization. Where else does one encounter snake charmers, wandering holy men (some of whom wear no clothes), the ritual bathing in the Ganges River, opulent wealth alongside unbelievable poverty, and the superb Taj Mahal?

And where else does one find music like Indian classical music? Its roots reach back at least two thousand years, and it has existed largely unchanged since then. Today Indian classical music still thrives, but along with it is heard popular music from movies, some rock music from England and America, traditional hymns as well as other Christian music, and even some wind band music that is a carryover from the more than 250 years of English rule.

In a country as large as India, it is not surprising to find sizable differences and diversity. And so its classical music tends to divide into two major types: the *karnataka* music of southern India and the *Hindustani* music of northern India. The music of the north was influenced by Persia and the culture of the Middle East as the result of invasions from those countries over the centuries. It contains more improvisation and showy music. The music of the south is more traditional and is based on composed songs. It also sounds busy and contains more ornamented melodic lines.

What makes Indian music, from both the south and the north, special?

Ragas

It would be easy to describe a raga as a scale or melodic formula, but that would neglect its important affective and philosophical overtones. *Ragas* are intended to express and generate feelings—"colors of the mind." Each raga is thought to have a personality of its own with its own rules. Usually, ragas are associated with particular human emotions, Hindu deities, seasons of the year, and so on.

India and its neighbors

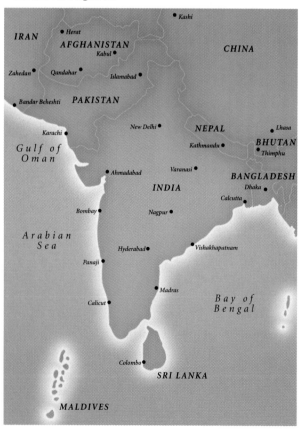

Theoretically, thousands of ragas exist, but only about fifty are performed today. They vary in length, but the average is about twenty to twenty-five notes. Two tones tend to stand out in each raga, one being four or five notes higher than the other. The basic raga is treated to many alterations, including slides, pitch bending, and other figures.

The word *raga* comes from a Sanskrit word meaning "coloring."

The following is a raga from northern India. The small noteheads indicate slides or zigzag figures, and the brackets mark off the phrases.

Talas

Instead of the metrical rhythms found in Western music, both art and popular, Indian musicians use rhythmic cycles of anywhere from 5 to 128 beats, called *talas*. Most talas are 5 to 8 beats long. Below is an example of a 14-beat tala. The / marks in this example indicate how the beats are organized into subgroups.

/ • • • • • / • • / • • • / • • • • /   (5 + 2 + 3 + 4)

Musical Instruments

Indian scholars have grouped musical instruments into three classes, based on how the sound is produced.

Indian musicians have no cases for their instruments. When they take them someplace, they simply wrap them in newspaper for protection.

String instruments The first category includes instruments that produce sound by plucked or bowed strings. The instrument that is most associated with Indian classical music is the *sitar*. It is a large, complicated instrument with five strings for playing the melody and 13 more strings that ring in sympathy with the melodic strings. It has a bowl-shaped body made from wood and a row of pegs along the neck. A similar instrument found in southern India is the *veena*, which has fewer strings and a gourd or papier-mâché jug-shaped resonator attached to the neck.

Wind instruments These include bamboo flutes and the clarinetlike *pungi*, which is the instrument of choice among snake charmers.

Percussion instruments These are instruments on which the sound is produced by striking. These consist mostly of a wide variety of drums. The most important of these is the double-headed *tabla*, which consist of two small drums played with the hands and fingers. There are also percussion instruments that produce sound by striking a solid object such as a gong.

Tamboura and sitar

Performances

Concerts of Indian music are informal. Although people in the audience sometimes sit on chairs, traditionally they sit on mats. They may count time with their hands, converse with one another, or offer comments and encouragement to the players. There is no printed program, because the entire performance is not planned out. In fact, Indian musicians do not rehearse together before a concert. A concert consists partly of existing songs and partly of improvised music. Performances may last as long as three to four hours without an intermission. They are often held at cultural clubs that offer a series of programs that include music, dance, drama, and movies.

Western musicians would find the lack of applause very unnerving, to say the least.

The performers sit on the floor and do not play from notation. The group is usually small, consisting of one singer and several instrumentalists. There is little or no applause at the conclusion of the concert; the audience simply leaves, except for a few persons who hang around to chat with the performers.

Texture

The tamboura is a large string instrument that sounds a few pitches almost continuously throughout the music.

Indian music has a layered texture. The top layer consists of the singer or solo instrument. The second layer is the drone that is a part of most Indian classical music. It is played by one or more tambouras or a simple reed organ. The lowest layer consists of percussion. This layer is performed by the tabla player and sometimes other instruments like the tambourine. Ten musicians constitute a large ensemble by Indian standards; the number is usually fewer than that.

Form

Indian music is balanced between composed music and music that is improvised by the performers. Performances normally contain four types of improvisation.

- ◆ The performance begins with an opening—a free-sounding improvised section based on the raga. It is performed without the tala.

- ◆ The next portion is quite rhythmic and works through variations and combinations of groups of notes.

- ◆ A third section consists of improvisation on one melodic line. The music of this section gradually becomes more elaborate and showy.

- ◆ The fourth section fits both the raga and tala of the composition. If sung, no words are used. Instead, the performer sings the Indian note names— *sa, ri, ga,* and so on. The section grows more complex as it moves along.

Today in India a prospective musician studies either Western or Indian music; few musicians know both types. Indian music is usually learned from a religious teacher, a *guru,* who traditionally receives no pay for his lessons. The guru's purpose is to guide his disciple spiritually and musically.

Cultural Outlook

All music is interwoven with its cultural setting. In the case of India, that setting is highly otherworldly and laced with religious belief. Indian musicians see music as the mystical transfer of human emotion into sound. They even have a special word for it—*bhava.* They believe that without *bhava* the music lacks feeling and "soul."

One Indian musician told a European musicologist, "You in the West play love music when there is no love and winter music in the summer. No wonder you have had several large wars in this century."

Traditions and beliefs seem unchangeable in India. One of these beliefs involves the obligation of a musician to preserve the music and pass on to the next generation what the guru taught. There is also the belief, at least among some musicians, that performing a raga apart from its nonmusical association violates cosmic laws and may cause some natural calamity.

CHINESE MUSIC

China and India have a number of things in common. Both possess very large populations; one out of every five human beings is Chinese. Both also have music traditions that reach back thousands of years. And in both countries music is very much interwoven with philosophy. In fact, one early Chinese emperor ordered musicians and astrologers to work together in calculating the length of pipe to be the standard pitch for music during his reign, because he wanted it to be in harmony with the universe.

Much Chinese music is built on the five-note pentatonic scale. It consists mostly of melody; harmony is largely absent. The most distinctive feature of Chinese music is the instruments used to play it and the resulting timbres. String instruments are especially important. One such instrument is the *pipa*, which is like a four-string lute with its pear-shaped body. Another is the *erhu*, which is a two-string fiddle with strings made of silk. An instrument that is strummed like an autoharp is also used. In addition, several types of flutes are played, as are double-reed instruments.

The lute is discussed in chapter 13.

Southeast Asia

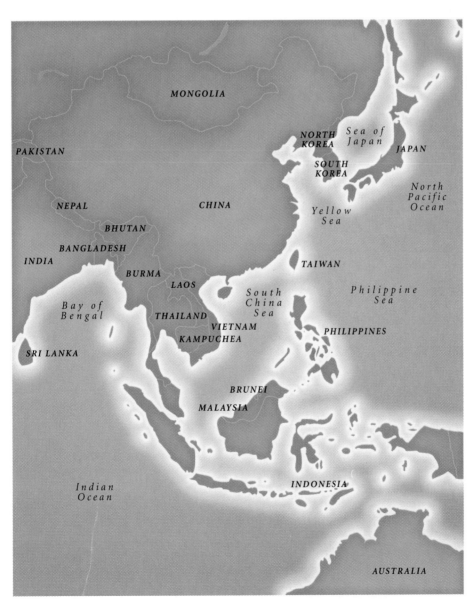

The percussion section includes cymbals and of course a gong. No brasses are found in traditional Chinese music. A few large orchestras existed in China, which was rare outside of the West.

The Chinese developed a unique type of opera. Heroic roles are sung with a rasping sound; heroines sing with a high, thin, "little girl" sound. The lines of opera consist of short phrases separated by instrumental interludes. A drum maintains a steady rhythm, and the sections of the music are concluded with a cymbal crash. It requires years of training to perform Chinese opera correctly.

Chinese music has a spotty history. At times it thrived; at other times it barely survived. After the fall of the last dynasty in 1911, China was declared a republic and the old music of the court went out of fashion. Since 1949 the Communist Party has ruled the mainland, and the traditional, sophisticated music was definitely discouraged. Some of the Chinese musical tradition is being preserved on Taiwan, but that country has rushed to adopt Western culture, including its music.

JAPANESE MUSIC

Much of the classical music of Japan was transported there by Chinese and Korean musicians around the eighth century. For many years it was mainly performed by court musicians, Buddhist priests, and scholars. It reached its peak in the seventeenth and eighteenth centuries, when by orders of its emperors Japan isolated itself from contact with foreign nations. Today Western-style music, both art and popular, dominate the musical scene in Japan.

One of the features of Japanese music is the *koto*, which is a large instrument with thirteen strings. The strings are stretched over a soundboard about six feet long

The koto produces gentle, soft sounds.

Shamisen, koto, and shakuhachi

and are plucked and manipulated by the player. The bridge that holds the strings up off the body can be moved for different tunings.

Much music has been composed for the koto, both solo and in combination with voices or other instruments, such as the *shakuhachi* (a simple bamboo flute) and the *shamisen* (a three-string instrument). Even though a small group of musicians may perform koto music, they play the same basic melody but with different ornamentation and little or no harmony. Generally, Japanese music uses the five-note pentatonic scale. It is subtle and refined, and much attention is devoted to the tone color, pitch, ornamentation, and nuance of the sounds.

BALINESE MUSIC

Bali is one of the islands in the large series that make up the country of Indonesia. The cultural level of this island of less than 3 million people, who live in an area about the size of Delaware, has rightfully earned it a special place in the world of music and dance. Each village on Bali—and there are about fifteen hundred of them—has at least one instrumental group called a *gamelan.* Traditionally, these instrumental ensembles played in courts. Their performances presented musical dramas on life and death, good and evil, justice and injustice, and other philosophical topics.

Gamelans can range in size from four to thirty players. Several instruments are featured, one of which is the bamboo flute. Like some of the bamboo flutes in China and Japan, the Balinese flute is played by blowing on the end, not sideways. Small drums are also used. The larger drum is considered the male, the smaller one, the female. Drummers direct the ensemble by setting the tempo and signaling changes in dynamic levels and transitions between sections of the music.

An instrument that is particularly associated with Balinese music is the *kajar,* which looks like a small metal pot and lid with a knob. Sounds are produced by hitting the knob or striking the lid. Several gongs are also featured, as are cymbals.

Balinese music uses the pentatonic scale found in so much Asian music. Several melodic figures that follow a musical formula are played again and again. The rhythm is free-sounding, and there is little harmony in the music.

"Gender Wajang" is typical of Balinese music. It uses many cymbals, gongs, and xylophonelike instruments playing short melodic figures. Each player in a gamelan contributes bits of music that combine to form a colorful array of sounds. It's somewhat like what the players in a handbell choir do; each player is responsible for

Balinese musicians Some of the practices of gamelan music have been adapted by Minimalist composers in the twentieth century, who are discussed in chapter 42.

Only a small amount of
"Gender Wajang" is included
on the recording.

two bells and contributes those pitches when they are called for. The music is very much ensemble music, with little attention to individuals or particular parts.

To people unaccustomed to Balinese music, it may sound simply like a rain of pretty sounds. Not so. The music is sophisticated and subtle, and it is carefully planned.

L I S T E N I N G   G U I D E

Balinese Gamelan Music: "Gender Wajang"
CD 3 Track 4

0:00	4	A melodic figure containing the rapid alternation between two pitches is featured.
0:06		The music gets softer, but the two-note figure continues.
0:17		The pitch level is lower, but the two-note figure continues to be heard.
0:35		The music becomes louder again.
0:42		A new melody begins. It is built on the five-note pentatonic scale.
0:49		Splashes of notes are heard in the pentatonic scale pattern.
0:54		Twice the music seems to pause as the same note is rapidly repeated.
1:03		The music seems to pause again as the same note is played repeatedly.
1:09		The music speeds up, but soon slows down again.
1:35		Again the music seems to pause as the same note is played repeatedly.
1:48		Splashes of notes in the pentatonic scale pattern are heard again.
2:05		The music comes to a short pause.

C o d a

*This chapter has presented several types of music that are
very different from what we usually hear in the United States today.
Indian, Chinese, Japanese, and Balinese music are evidence of
the inventiveness and diversity of the human race.*

Part III

Western Music Before 1750

Musical Styles and Periods

The music created and performed before 1750 is vital
to the stream of music in Western civilization. Like the headwaters
of a mighty waterway, the music of the Middle Ages leads to the larger
stream of the Renaissance and on to the river of Baroque music.
The music of these earlier times is of much more than historical
interest to musicians and to listeners, because it is an essential part
of knowing what Western music is and how it developed.

To help think about the more than two thousand years of music in Western civilization, scholars have divided music history into style periods. In spite of some drawbacks, the concept of styles is a useful and valid way to understand music better. The manner in which musical sounds are treated in the various styles is basic. Furthermore, knowing about styles helps in listening to music. For example, knowing that the Renaissance ideal for church music was reverence and restraint, listeners will not be surprised or disappointed by the lack of loudness and brilliance in the church music in that style.

Terms such as *Renaissance* and *Baroque,* when applied to music, describe styles of music rather than periods of time. Even after the years in which a style was in fashion have passed, composers occasionally return to it, sometimes centuries later.

Although a style of music is not confined to a particular time and place, it is named for the historical period it is most associated with. These designations can be made only *after* the actual years have passed, because generalizations about a style require some perspective. The dates of their beginnings and endings can never be exact; such dates can only be approximate.

Literature, art, and music are generally given the same style period names, and the arts of a particular style do contain similar viewpoints and artistic goals. The dates of the Renaissance and several other periods for the visual arts and literature are not identical with those for music, however. Each art is affected by technical considerations and conditions peculiar to it. Until about 200 years ago, art and literature tended to be more developed than music. Technical factors such as an inadequate system of notation, uncertainty about systems of tuning instruments, and the lack of a way of recording and thereby preserving music slowed music's development.

ANCIENT GREEK AND ROMAN TIMES

From about 800 B.C. to the fall of the Roman Empire in A.D. 476, Western civilization was dominated by various city states around the Mediterranean Sea. First it was the cities of Greece, especially Athens. Then came the Roman Empire, which dominated most of the known world from the Middle East to England. Although both Greece and Rome were replaced, they left their imprint in architecture, literature, and ways of thinking. In fact, about fifteen hundred years in the future these civilizations would be considered by educated persons as a high point to be greatly admired and copied.

Greek civilization reached its acme in Athens in the fifth century B.C. It produced astounding accomplishments for its time. Its architecture can be seen in countless buildings even today. Great works of sculpture were created. Philosophy flourished with Socrates, Plato, and Aristotle, who also is often credited with starting scientific

The Parthenon The Greeks built this celebrated temple for the goddess Athena in the fifth century B.C. It defines the classic style still seen in architecture today.

thinking. Great poets like Homer and dramatists like Sophocles were active. The ancient Athenians were far ahead of their contemporaries in their type of government, which had the citizens meet and vote in civic matters. Greek religious beliefs revolved around a pantheon of gods and goddesses.

The word *democracy* comes from the Greek word *demos.*

The Roman Republic followed, and the Romans simply took over much of what the earlier Greeks had done. They even adopted and expanded on their religious beliefs, but renamed the gods. Unlike the Athenians, the Romans were militarily strong. They managed an empire that stretched for a thousand or more miles around the Mediterranean Sea. Holding such a huge empire together was quite an accomplishment when there was no communication faster than a man on a horse. But the character and quality of the Roman Empire deteriorated over the centuries, and it collapsed more than it fell to the invading Vandals and Visigoths from the north.

Zeus, king of the gods, became Jupiter, and Athena, goddess of the arts, became Minerva.

THE MIDDLE AGES

With the fall of the Roman Empire in A.D. 476, Western civilization slipped into what some historians call the "Dark Ages." For more than five hundred years following the fall of Rome, life in the *Middle Ages* centered around the manor and the monasteries. A system of feudalism bound peasants to the land and to the lord of the manor. People did not place a great emphasis on life, because they thought that either Jesus would come again and bring a new era or they would soon have a better life after they died. It is hard for us living in America today to understand the hold that otherworldly concerns had on many people during that time, but the impact of this

A monastery in Meteora, Greece

Music and the arts during the Middle Ages were devoted to the worship of God. Books were hand-lettered and decorated by monks, as shown in this capital *C* for *Contate Domino* ("Sing to the Lord").

The use of the word *Gothic* to designate a particular artistic or musical style has little to do with its use in describing a mystery or horror story.

Chivalry perhaps existed more as an ideal in literary works than in real life.

attitude was profound. It is difficult for us to imagine how different and arduous life was for people in the Middle Ages. In short, for most people it was grim.

Monasteries dotted the countryside throughout Europe and England. These monasteries preserved the writings and culture of the ancient world. But there was little interest in the civilizations of the Greeks and Romans, which were considered pagan and to be avoided.

THE GOTHIC PERIOD

About A.D. 800 Western civilization began a long, slow climb toward a more enlightened outlook. There were several catalysts for this trend: increased contacts with the Byzantine civilization to the east, better economic conditions and trade, and the influence of education in the monasteries. Although the Middle Ages would end without fully breaking out of their earlier doldrums, the directions for the future had been pointed out.

The period from about 1100 to 1450 has come to be known as the *Gothic period*. These centuries were marked by continued progress away from the otherworldly outlook that was so strong during the preceding thousand years. The major intellectual movement of the time was Scholasticism, a highly organized and systematic philosophy culminating in the *Summary of Theology* by Saint Thomas Aquinas (1225–1274).

The Gothic age rejected the absolute power of kings, a rejection that encouraged the signing of the Magna Carta in England in 1215.

Another feature of the Gothic period was chivalry, which glorified women and idealized kindness and refined manners. There was an emphasis on the community—the guild, the Church, or the feudal manor; individualism was not encouraged. Many works of art and music were created by artists who did not attach their names to their creations and whose identities are not known.

The Gothic period saw the founding of universities. It was also the time when many of the great cathedrals were built. Literary accomplishments were achieved in the Gothic period with the poems of the troubadours, the romantic legends of a Celtic chieftain named Arthur, and *The Divine Comedy* by Dante Alighieri.

C o d a

It is difficult to remember the details of more than two thousand years of history. For this reason, scholars and students have found it useful to put large portions of history into categories. Remembering the main features of a period or style aids in learning and understanding the arts and other aspects of history. Styles and periods are convenient hooks on which to hang information.

Early Western Music

As far as can be determined, there has been music in every age and place since the dawn of civilization fifteen thousand or more years ago. That's an impressive fact. The problem is that we have very little idea of what any of that music sounded like. No system of notation existed that provides more than a few general clues, and certainly no recordings were possible until the twentieth century.

Attempts to learn about early music are confined largely to verbal descriptions *about* the music and a few pictures of people singing or playing instruments. Words are better than nothing when learning about music, but not much. Words alone are woefully inadequate in describing music.

It is different with art and architecture. Many of the original works in those media can still be seen today.

The Greeks, especially those living in Athens during the Golden Age of Pericles, valued music very much. The philosopher Plato (c. 427–347 B.C.) considered music an essential part of the education of all citizens. One reason for his advocacy of music was his belief that music influenced moral character.

Unfortunately, the development of good character cannot be achieved that easily!

About 555 B.C. Pythagoras found that the vibrations of certain intervals—the distances from one pitch to another—can be represented in mathematical ratios. As was characteristic of the Greeks at the time, he ascribed philosophical qualities to the ratios, calling those with simple ratios like 2:1 and 3:2 "perfect." The ancient Greeks also developed several musical instruments. One of these was the harplike lyre, which is often seen as a musical emblem today.

Pythagoras is well known for his contributions to geometry and the theorem named for him.

Music was found in many Greek dramas too. The chorus did not sing, however; instead it chanted in a singsong style. Poets like Homer sang their epic tales in singsong fashion, perhaps accompanied by a simple harplike instrument.

The Romans had music, too. Probably, most of it was taken over from the Greeks. The Romans emphasized military music more than the Greeks did.

MUSIC IN THE MIDDLE AGES

Christianity had no standard musical practices for its first three centuries. It adopted some aspects of Judaism, including daily prayer hours and the reciting of psalms between the leader and congregation. As the Church expanded throughout Asia Minor into Europe, it adopted other musical practices.

The fact that the early Church included singing in its worship is recorded in Matthew (26:30) and Mark (14:26) and other, nonbiblical writings.

Slowly, the Church at Rome became predominant, and the bishop of Rome became the Pope. In an effort to bring order to worship practices, about the sixth century Pope Gregory I directed that the Church's worship and music be codified. Although Gregory I was not a musician himself, the music that resulted is known as Gregorian chant. The Church now had a *liturgy*—a body of rites prescribed for worship. The most important and frequent service is the *Mass,* which is described in the enrichment box on the following page.

Gregorian chant is also known as *plainsong* or *plainchant.*

The Mass and Its Music

The Mass is central in the Roman Catholic Church. It is a ceremony that reaffirms in a symbolic way the connection between the believers and Jesus Christ through the reenactment of the Last Supper (Eucharist, or Holy Communion) with the sharing of bread and wine and the miracle of that event.

The term Mass *comes from the Latin phrase that ends the service: "Ite missa est." The Mass may be spoken or sung, but in the United States today it is largely spoken.*

The Mass contains several parts. Some portions vary according to the particular day in the Church year. These parts are called the Proper, *because they are proper for a certain day in the Church calendar. Some parts are repeated in each Mass; these are called the* Ordinary, *because they are ordinarily included. The sections of the Ordinary are as follows.*

Kyrie *This is a short prayer using Greek words instead of the usual Latin. The text means, "Lord, have mercy on us; Christ, have mercy on us."*

Gloria *This section offers praise to God in Latin with the words, "Glory to God on high."*

Credo *This rather long statement of belief in Latin ("I believe in one God, . . .") is recited or sung in a reciting style.*

Sanctus *This follows the consecration of the elements when the priest raises the bread and wine for everyone to see. The Sanctus begins with the words, "Holy, holy, holy."*

Agnus Dei *This section is based on the Latin words that mean "Lamb of God, who takes away the sins of the world, have mercy on us and grant us peace."*

Because the Ordinary appears in all Masses, it has been selected by many composers over the centuries as the text for musical works. Ludwig van Beethoven, Wolfgang Amadeus Mozart, and Franz Joseph Haydn—and Igor Stravinsky in the twentieth century—have composed "concert" Masses not intended for use in worship services. Giovanni Pierluigi da Palestrina and other composers of the sixteenth century composed shorter Masses for worship purposes.

A Requiem *is a Mass for the dead. It omits the Gloria and Credo but adds a section called Dies irae ("Day of wrath"), referring to the day of final Judgment.*

Until Vatican Council II (1964–1967), the Roman Catholic Church specified the content and words for every service, which are in Latin. Since then more freedom has been permitted, however, and vernacular (non-Latin) languages are now used. Unfortunately, most chants and music for Masses lose their impact when translated, so much of the inspiring traditional music is no longer heard today.

GREGORIAN CHANT

Gregorian chant is very different from the music you usually hear today. Its features include:

♦ Nonmetrical rhythm: Although there are groups of notes, you will have no inclination to tap your foot as you hear it.

♦ Monophonic texture: There is no harmony.

♦ Smooth contour: Its notes generally move by step to the next note.

♦ *Modal* scales: The melodies generally do not follow the familiar major or minor scale patterns.

♦ A reverent and restrained mood: No attempt is made to reach out and grab the listener.

♦ The texts are in Church Latin, not English.

♦ They are sung only by monks and priests.

In 1994 a recording of chant by the monks at the monastery of Santo Domingo de Silos in Spain became the fastest-selling classical record in history. It sold more than 2 million copies and reached number five on the U.S. pop charts. The monks used the royalties to help the needy in Third World countries and for badly needed repairs to the twelfth-century monastery.

Gregorian chant is not concert music. Its goal is to contribute to worship. This it does for persons who understand its properties in a subtle but moving way.

The music example on these pages is the Dies irae from the funeral or Requiem Mass. It is probably the best-known line of chant, especially its first several notes, because of its use to represent death or evil by many composers in the nineteenth century. The music is shown in two versions. One is the traditional four-line staff and square notes of the Roman Catholic Church in medieval times. The other shows the pitches of the chant on a five-line staff.

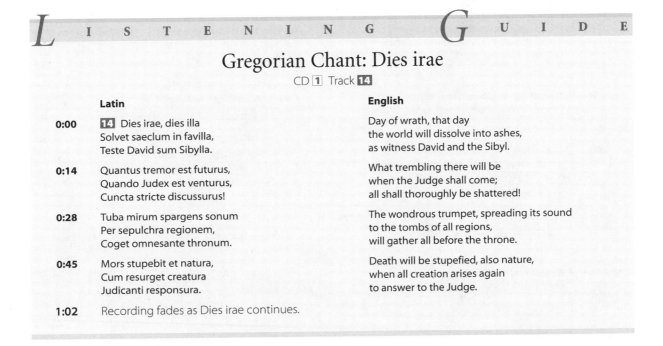

Gregorian musical notation of the Middle Ages   The same phrase in modern musical notation

LISTENING GUIDE

Gregorian Chant: Dies irae
CD 1 Track 14

	Latin	**English**
0:00	**14** Dies irae, dies illa Solvet saeclum in favilla, Teste David sum Sibylla.	Day of wrath, that day the world will dissolve into ashes, as witness David and the Sibyl.
0:14	Quantus tremor est futurus, Quando Judex est venturus, Cuncta stricte discussurus!	What trembling there will be when the Judge shall come; all shall thoroughly be shattered!
0:28	Tuba mirum spargens sonum Per sepulchra regionem, Coget omnesante thronum.	The wondrous trumpet, spreading its sound to the tombs of all regions, will gather all before the throne.
0:45	Mors stupebit et natura, Cum resurget creatura Judicanti responsura.	Death will be stupefied, also nature, when all creation arises again to answer to the Judge.
1:02	Recording fades as Dies irae continues.	

Hildegard's Ordo virtutum

The Virtues are: Knowledge of God, Humility, Discipline, Compassion, Mercy, Victory, Discretion, Patience, Charity, Obedience, Faith, Hope, Chastity, Innocence, World Rejection, and Heavenly Love.

The Devil does not get to sing. Instead, he talks in a raspy voice.

Most of the creators of Gregorian chant are anonymous. Humility was a virtue in the Middle Ages, especially among the religious men and women. One composer of chant who is known was a remarkable woman named Hildegard of Bingen.

Hildegard's *Ordo virtutum (Play of the Virtues)* is a morality play, probably written for the dedication of a convent church. In the play, a soul gives in to the temptations of the devil. The soul is saved through the intervention of the sixteen virtues.

The work contains about eighty chantlike melodies. All the parts were sung by nuns, except the role of the devil, which was played by a priest. Little except the vocal music has survived from most of these medieval plays. Performances today require some creativity in terms of the instruments and staging used.

L I S T E N I N G G U I D E

Hildegard of Bingen: *Ordo virtutum*
excerpt from scene 4
CD 3 Track 5

	Latin	**English**
	Devil	
0:00	**5** Que es, aut unde venis? Tu amplexata es me, et ego foras eduxi te. Sed nunc inreversione tua confundis me— ego autem pugna mea deician te!	Who are you, where do you come from? You were in my embrace, I led you out. Yet now you are going back, defying me— But I shall fight you and defeat you!
	Penitent Soul	

0:22	Ego omnes vias meas malas esse cognovi,
	  et ideo fugi a te.
	Modo autem, o illusor, pugno contra te.
	Ine tu, o regina Humilitas, tua medicamine
	adiuva me!
		I realize that all my ways were wicked,
		  so I fled from you.
		But now, you fraud, I'll fight you face to face.
		Come, Queen Humility, with your medicine
		  give me aid!

	Humility (to Victory)	
1:23	O Victoria, que istum in celo superasti, curre cum militibus tuis et omnes ligate. Diabolum hunc!	O Victory, you who once bested this in the heavens. run now, with all your military manner, and all of you, tie up this fiend!
	Victory (to the Virtues)	
1:54	O fortissimi et gloriosissimi milites, venite, et adiuvate me istum fallacem vincere.	Most brave and glorious warriors, come, and help me to eliminate this false one.
	The Virtues	
2:22	O dulcissima bellatrix, in torrente fonte qui absorbuit lupum rapacem— o gloriosa coronata, nos libenter militamus tecum contra illusorem hunc.	O sweetest warrior, in the scorching torrent that swallowed up the rapacious wolf— o glorious crowned one, how freely we will fight at your side against the faker.
	Humility (to the Virtues)	
2:56	Ligate ergo istum, o Virtutes preclare!	Tie him up then, you shining virtues!
	The Virtues	
3:14	O regina nostra, tibi parebimus, et precepta tua in omnibus adimplebimus.	O our queen, we obey you, and we will follow your orders completely.
3:36	Excerpt concludes.	

Hildegard of Bingen

HILDEGARDIS *a Virgin Prophetefs, Abbefs of*
St Ruperts Nunnerye. She died at Bingen Aº Dºr
1180 Aged 82 yeares.

Hildegard of Bingen (1098–1179) was a powerful abbess; she was also a theologian, naturalist, healer, poet, and musician, and she wrote extensively in these fields. She considered herself an instrument through which God spoke in visions. She was born the tenth child of a noble German family. At the age of eight, she was given to a group of nuns and raised in a Benedictine monastery. During her adult life, she led

Giving a son or daughter to the Church was a common practice at that time.

religious communities for women, first at Disibodenberg and later at Rupertsberg near present-day Bingen. Hildegard used her prominent position with the Church to improve both her own position and that of the women in her charge.

SECULAR MUSIC

Because there were no recordings and only a limited system of notation that was confined to the monasteries and church music, most of the music of the Gothic period was lost. In addition to Gregorian chant, there was other music, probably a great deal of it, in the form of songs and dances. Usually, this secular music was in a vernacular language—French, German, English, Italian, or Spanish—rather than the Latin used in the worship services.

Initially, secular music was largely performed by wandering musicians who traveled from place to place singing songs, reciting poems, and even exhibiting trained animals. (These entertainers also carried news about what was happening in neighboring areas.) Later, about the twelfth and thirteenth centuries, troubadours and trouvères dominated secular music in France. They were noblemen who were poets and composers, but usually not performers; they hired minstrels to sing their songs.

These songs were for solo voice and may have been sung accompanied by a mandola or similar instrument shown in the *Goddess of Music* painting at right, taken from a medieval manuscript. Most of the poems and songs were about an idealized, chivalrous type of love, with a passion more of the spirit than of the flesh. About four thousand such poems and sixteen hundred such melodies have been preserved. Unlike Gregorian chant, they have regular rhythmic patterns and resemble folk melodies.

The goddess Music, seated at center, plays a portable organ accompanied by (clockwise from top center) the "pig snout" psaltery, a mandola, clappers, long trumpets, kettledrums tied around the waist, bagpipe and shawm (both reed instruments), a tambourinelike jingle drum, and a vielle (viol).

POLYPHONY

Polyphony is an important concept in music. Listening to the combinations of two lines of nearly equal melodic interest might be compared to watching two or three television sets tuned to different channels simultaneously. Although it is not easy to follow what is happening on all the sets at once, there are almost no moments during which nothing is happening.

Until about A.D. 1000, music consisted mostly of a line of melody with an occasional improvised accompaniment. The amount of music with combinations of sounds was very small. Notation of Western music from the eleventh century indicates that other pitches were being added to the melody. Medieval musicians, many of whom were anonymous monks, accomplished this in a simple way: They took the lines of Gregorian chant and added an additional line that was exactly parallel to it at an interval of four or five notes below.

The development of music is closely related to the development of a system of music notation. Before a system of preserving musical sounds evolved, music was very limited in its length and amount of sophistication. At first the Greeks and Romans added marks above words to indicate the direction the pitches were to move. Later the signs, which were called *neumes,* were made much more fully. Still they couldn't indicate pitch. The first attempt to do so consisted of one line across the page and placing neumes above and below it. Later more lines were added, and the music staff was developed around A.D. 1000.

Fixed pitch relationships became possible because of Guido d'Arezzo (995–1050), who composed a famous chant in which each phrase began a step higher than the preceding one. The first syllable of each line became the basis for the *do-re-mi-fa-sol-la-ti* syllables that are used today. The notation of rhythm utilized the proportional system that is still used today, although the notes in the Gothic period looked different from today's notation.

In 1163 the construction of the Cathedral of Nôtre Dame in Paris was begun. A few years after that, a composer named Leonin (fl. 1169–1201), who was a musician there, began to put the lines of chant in longer note values and composed another more active line above the original. He was succeeded by Perotin (fl. 1198–1236), who added a third and sometimes a fourth line. Leonin's and Perotin's accomplishments introduced polyphony into Western music.

In these early versions of polyphony, pitches an octave apart and four and five notes apart were considered to be consonant. The interval of a third, which has been the basis for most harmony for the past several hundred years, was regarded as dissonant. That interval was, however, found in the secular music of the time, especially in England. It would be nearly 350 years after Leonin before chords containing thirds would be considered consonant enough to appear in the important final chord of a musical work.

These early types of polyphony are called *organum.*

These intervals are the same ones Pythagoras considered as consonant and they are the most prominent ones in the overtone series.

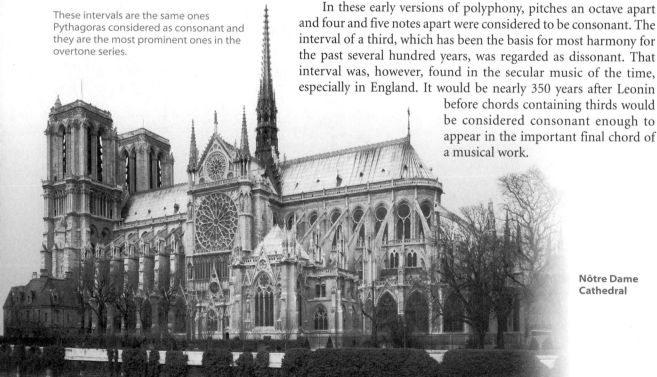

Nôtre Dame Cathedral

THE GOTHIC MOTET

Gothic religious music, at least as it existed in France, contained a complicated type of polyphony. The *Gothic motet* was a musical curiosity. It often contained various languages as well as sacred and secular texts. For example, one motet has two different sets of words for the higher parts: one in Latin, praising the Virgin Mary, and another in French which, translated is, "When I see the summer season returning and all the little birds make the woods resound, then I weep and sigh for the great desire I have for fair Marion, who holds my heart imprisoned."

The words are typical of the chivalric writings of the time.

The lower line typically uses a phrase of Gregorian chant, called the *cantus firmus*, or fixed melody. The length of a motet was determined by the length of this phrase, which usually was not very long.

Composers tended to work out each line, but they were not very concerned about how each line might sound when combined with the other parts. Some harsh dissonances were often the result.

Many composers of the Gothic period were fascinated with concealed meanings and relationships in their music. They delighted in hiding a phrase of chant in a higher part. Or they set up a complex scheme of rhythmic and melodic patterns, so that a rhythmic pattern might appear three times for every two times the melodic pattern was repeated. These intellectual puzzles interested musicians of the time, but they were usually lost on the listeners. Interest in intricate patterns and tricks is revived every so often and can be found in some of the music composed in the twentieth century.

These puzzles can be comprehended only by examining the notation, not by hearing the music.

MUSIC IN THE REST OF EUROPE

While the Gothic motet was reaching its acme with the compositions of Guillaume de Machaut ("Mah-*show*," c. 1304–1377), interest was waning in this style of music. Gothic motets were largely developed in France; composers in other parts of Europe evidently didn't care much for the style or were not advanced enough to attempt composing in it. A blind Italian musician named Francesco Landini ("Lahn-*dee*-nee," 1325–1397) and an English composer named John Dunstable (c. 1385–1453) were writing music that was simpler and more listenable. Both men and their successors often used the same text for all parts, which made it possible for the words to be sung about the same time so that they could be understood by listeners.

These composers also avoided harsh dissonances. A significant contribution of Dunstable and other English composers was the use of simultaneous pitches three and six notes apart. These intervals gave the music a richer sound than the fourths and fifths of Leonin and Perotin. In fact, the music of Landini and Dunstable are a pleasure to listen to today, more than six centuries later.

The interval of a sixth is the inversion of a third; for example, C up to A is inversion of A up to C. The musical effect of both is similar.

C o d a

As the 1450s approached, the Gothic motet was rapidly disappearing. Gregorian chant still continued to play an important role and it could be found in various other types of music as well. Drawing to a close, however, was that long stretch of history called the Middle Ages. This period had not always been "dark," as it has sometimes been described. The years leading up to 1450 laid the foundation for a new age—the Renaissance— which provided some great literature and architecture as well as beautiful, intricate, and interesting music.

Music of the Renaissance

The word *Renaissance* means rebirth. Historically, it referred to a revival of interest in the philosophy and arts of ancient Greece and Rome, although there was much more to it than just the admiration of an earlier civilization. Because music had no ancient models to resurrect, for music the term *Renaissance* refers only to the style that predominated from about 1450 to 1600.

The intense interest of Renaissance artists and scholars in the earlier Greek and Roman civilizations led to a curious mixture of Greek and Christian belief. Michelangelo expressed this union of the pagan and Christian by decorating the ceiling of the Sistine Chapel in the Vatican in Rome with alternating figures of prophets (Christian) and sibyls (pagan). Erasmus, the great philosopher, regarded the ancient Athenian Socrates as a pre-Christian saint.

During the Renaissance certain intellectual viewpoints emerged that are still common in Western civilization today. Among them are optimism, worldliness, hedonism, naturalism, and individualism. But the most important of these is *humanism,* which is an emphasis on the human and natural as opposed to the otherworldly or divine. For example, pride, which was considered a sin in the Middle Ages, was elevated to a virtue.

The humanistic view can be seen by comparing the two treatments of the human body shown on the facing page. One is a sculpture from the great Gothic cathedral at Chartres in France. This figure has a spiritual, otherworldly quality; the head and eyes seem serene, and the position of the body is erect and formal. The proportions of the body are exaggerated to make the figure appear longer; the feet seem to dangle as though they were merely attached to the robes. As with most artworks of the Gothic period, the artist is unknown.

Michelangelo's *David,* on the other hand, looks like a magnificent Greek god. Standing about 13½ feet in height, the sculpture suggests confidence and an admiration of the human body. David looks natural, almost casual, and free.

With increasing interest in the value of life on earth, there was a corresponding interest in the fine arts. Art was valued for its own sake, not just as a means of religious devotion. The result of this new interest in the arts was a long list of outstanding sculptors and painters: Botticelli, da Vinci, Michelangelo, Dürer, Raphael, Titian, Brueghel, and Tintoretto, to name but a few.

Not only were works of art being enjoyed in a new climate of acceptance, but increasing economic conditions meant that money was available to hire artists and musicians. The Church sought rich adornment for its buildings, which was one of the practices that led to the Reformation started by Martin Luther in 1517.

An event that affected education, commerce, and religion was Johann Gutenberg's invention of printing from movable type. Printing made possible the wide dissemination of music, beginning with the appearance of the first printed music books in 1501.

The spirit of the time was one of optimism and discovery. The voyages of Columbus, Cabot, Balboa, and Magellan took place during the Renaissance. Copernicus was announcing his discoveries about the universe.

Hedonism is the belief in the importance of pleasure, especially physical pleasure, for its own sake.

Naturalism is the belief that what is natural is right.

A sketch from Leonardo's notebooks As can be seen here, da Vinci wrote so that the words read from right to left with the letters reversed. His writing is most easily read using a mirror.

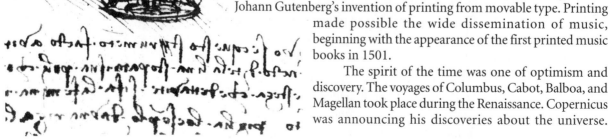

Gothic and Renaissance interpretations of the human form illustrate the advent of *Humanism,* a philosophy that asserts the dignity and worth of mankind and emphasizes secular rather than spiritual concerns.

Rabelais, Machiavelli, Boccaccio, Montaigne, Moore, Bacon, and Erasmus were exploring new ideas in literature and philosophy.

Perhaps the Renaissance is best epitomized by Leonardo da Vinci (1452–1519). It seems there was little that this genius did not do extremely well: design weapons and other devices, recite stories, paint, depict human anatomy, plan cities, make maps, and analyze proportions and things mathematical. He was interested in everything and left 7,000 pages of notebooks!

Da Vinci's most famous painting is the *Mona Lisa.*

FEATURES AND TYPES OF RENAISSANCE MUSIC

Musically, the Renaissance started in the Netherlands. The composers there had reached a level of achievement that was the envy of Europe. Many were eventually lured away from their homeland to better-paying jobs in Spain, Bohemia, Austria, Germany, and especially the cities of northern Italy.

At that time the Netherlands included Holland, northern Belgium, and part of northern France.

The style and techniques of the Netherlanders became internationally known and imitated. Many composers became so cosmopolitan that they thought of themselves as musicians first and citizens of a particular country second.

One composer who shaped the period known as the High Renaissance was Josquin Des Prez. Like composers before him, Des Prez used the device of *imitation,* in which one line of melody appears in another part a measure or two later, somewhat like a round. But instead of having all parts singing continuously, as composers before him did, he had each voice enter one after another. This emphasized the imitation and made the words sung by each entering part easier to hear. The music became clearer to listeners.

For example, Orlando di Lasso (the name he used in Italy), alias Roland de Lassus (the name he used in Germany), composed music in German, French, and Italian idioms as well as the Netherlands style.

THE RENAISSANCE MASS

It was the custom among composers during the Renaissance to compose music for the Ordinary of the Mass using a phrase from a chant as a cantus firmus. The Mass usually acquired the name of the phrase or chant. For example, Josquin wrote eighteen different settings of the Mass. His *Pange lingua Mass* has many melodies from a Gregorian hymn called "Pange lingua." A portion of both the hymn and the Kyrie section of Josquin's Mass are shown here:

Plainsong hymn, "Pange lingua"

Pan - ge lin - gua glorio - - - - si

TENORS Ky - ri - e e - le - - i - son

The Kyrie has three sections based on the text, and each section contains several points of imitation.

More than any previous composer, Josquin was aware of a consistent organization of harmonies. Closely related to more-sophisticated harmony was the development of the bass line. Before Josquin, composers started adding melodies to chant; they placed the chant around middle C and put the additional melodies above it. But this did not provide a convincing sense of chord movement. Therefore, around the year 1450, composers began to add another line *below* the chant to give the music a more solid foundation. Even today this arrangement of voice parts remains the standard for a choral group containing men's and women's voices. At the time, the sections were called *superius, altus, tenor,* and *bassus;* today they are called soprano, alto, tenor, and bass.

The most esteemed composer of the late Renaissance was Giovanni Pierluigi da Palestrina. Historical circumstances encouraged him to be a conservative reformer, musically speaking. The Council of Trent was held intermittently between 1545 and 1563. The Church felt threatened by the Protestant Reformation, so the council met to respond to that situation and to acknowledge the need for some reform within the Church.

One aspect that was under attack was its music, which over the centuries had strayed far from the ideals of Gregorian chant. Complaints were voiced about the use of secular tunes, the complicated polyphony that made the words nearly

Josquin Des Prez

The most esteemed composer of the middle Renaissance was **Josquin Des Prez** ("*Jzhoss-can-deh Pray*"), who lived from about 1440 to 1521. Born in Flanders (now part of Belgium), Josquin was a choir singer in Milan, a musician in the service of the Sforza family, a member of the Papal Choir, a choirmaster, and finally a musician in the service of Louis XII of France. His composing skill was much admired by his contemporaries, including Martin Luther. Josquin composed what and when he wanted, not what his patron wanted, and was known for his chansons and motets.

A *chanson* was a French polyphonic song of the Renaissance.

He also demanded a salary much higher than that of most of his contemporaries, which could explain why he changed jobs rather often. He was also very particular about his music and would become angry if singers tried to make any changes in it.

IOSQVINVS PRATENSIS.

Best-Known Works
Choral:
☐ *Missa Ave Maria Stella*
☐ *Missa de Beata Virgine*

LISTENING GUIDE

Josquin Des Prez: Kyrie from *Pange lingua Mass*
CD 3 Track 6

0:00   **6** The tenor voice enters singing "Kyrie . . ."

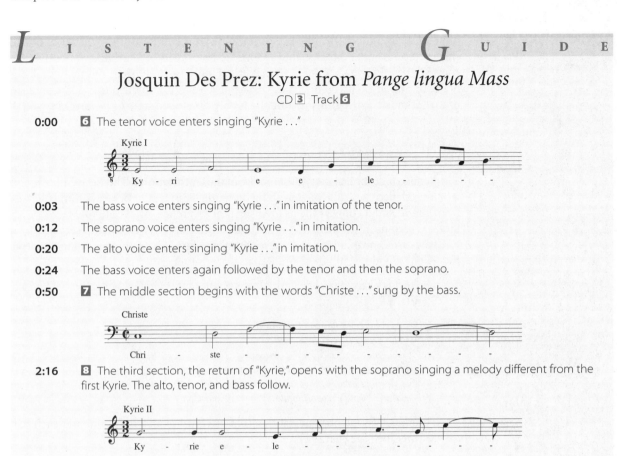

Kyrie I

Ky - ri - e   e - le - - - - - - -

0:03   The bass voice enters singing "Kyrie . . ." in imitation of the tenor.

0:12   The soprano voice enters singing "Kyrie . . ." in imitation.

0:20   The alto voice enters singing "Kyrie . . ." in imitation.

0:24   The bass voice enters again followed by the tenor and then the soprano.

0:50   **7** The middle section begins with the words "Christe . . ." sung by the bass.

Christe

Chri - - ste - - - - - - - - - -

2:16   **8** The third section, the return of "Kyrie," opens with the soprano singing a melody different from the first Kyrie. The alto, tenor, and bass follow.

Kyrie II

Ky - rie e - le - - - - - - - -

3:15   After an extended cadence, the Kyrie concludes.

Singing angels, from the *Cantoria,* or singers' pulpit, by the Renaissance sculptor Luca della Robbia

Renaissance instruments would not seem noisy to people today!

impossible to understand, the use of noisy instruments, and the irreverence of the singers. The council directed that the music be purged of "barbarism, obscurities, contrarieties, and superfluities" so that "the House of God might rightly be called a house of prayer." To his credit, Palestrina achieved a return to the purity and reverence of earlier music without discarding the highly developed style of his predecessors.

THE RENAISSANCE MOTET

The Renaissance motet is very different from the Gothic motet. The *Renaissance motet* is a unified piece with all voices singing the same Latin text. It borrows some phrases from chant, and it conveys the desired spirit of reverence. Above all, the Renaissance motet is serious, restrained, and designed for inclusion in the worship service.

Palestrina's works have a pure, celestial quality. His *Sicut cervus*, included on the CD, is a good example of the Renaissance motet:

◆ The text is in ecclesiastical Latin. It is a portion of Psalm 42, which in the Revised Standard Version reads:

The word *hart* means a male red deer, a stag.

> *As a hart longs for flowing streams,*
> *So longs my soul for Thee, O God.*
> *My soul thirsts for God, for the living God.*
> *When shall I come and behold the face of God?*
> *My tears have been my food day and night,*
> *While men say to me continually, "Where is your God""*

◆ The music is polyphonic. All the lines are given equal attention, and each has distinct melodic character.

◆ Each voice usually enters in imitation of another when new text is introduced.

◆ The music does not have a strong feeling of chord progression.

Giovanni Pierluigi da Palestrina

Palestrina (c. 1526–1594) was born in the small town of Palestrina outside of Rome, which provided him with the name by which he is known today. He began his career as chorister at Santa Maria Maggiore in 1537 in Rome. He returned to his native town in 1544 as organist and choirmaster, where he married and had two sons.

In 1550 the bishop of Palestrina was elected Pope, assuming the name Julius III. A year and half later, he summoned Palestrina back to Rome to become choirmaster of the Cappella Giulia in the Vatican. Soon he was to publish his first book of Masses.

Pope Julius III died and was succeeded by Pope Paul IV, who was determined to reform what he considered the excesses in

church music. In 1555 Palestrina was dismissed from his job because he was married. He was soon appointed choirmaster at the Church of Saint John Lateran in Rome, where he stayed for five years. He then returned to Santa Maria Maggiore and published his first book of motets. In 1571 he returned to Cappella Giulia, but misfortune struck when his two eldest sons and wife died of various diseases.

Palestrina married again and entered the fur business, and he proved to be a highly successful businessman. His more than adequate funds allowed him to publish about sixteen collections of music. He died in 1594, leaving a wealth of beautiful and finely crafted music and the distinction of creating the finest church music of his time.

Best-Known Works
Choral:
◻ *Pope Marcellus Mass*
◻ *Sicut cervus*

♦ *Sicut cervus* does not have a strong meter or beat. Although it moves along steadily, it certainly is not toe-tapping music. Today's versions of the music have bar lines, but these have been added by modern editors so singers can more easily keep their place. The bar lines do not imply a metrical pattern.

♦ Motets today are almost always sung without accompaniment. During the Renaissance, however, the voices were sometimes doubled by a few instruments. But the ideal was a purity of sound, which implies no accompaniment or, in musical terms, *a cappella*.

> The term *a cappella* literally means "for the chapel."

♦ A small group of singers is the authentic performance medium for Renaissance motets. Probably no more than three singers were originally assigned to each part. Boys, or men singing in falsetto, sang the high voice parts.

> Women were not permitted to celebrate the Mass or to sing in choirs in the church.

♦ The lines of melody are very singable. The range for any one voice part does not exceed an octave, except for the bass. Furthermore, the lines do not move far from one pitch to the next. The melodies are quite smooth and conjunct.

♦ The form of a motet is usually based on the structure of the text, which in this case is a psalm, so each verse has its own polyphonic setting.

♦ The music has a restrained quality. Bombast and showmanship were considered not in keeping with the attitude of reverence and awe that should prevail in worship. Even though the text speaks of "longing for flowing streams," the music does not suggest sentimental yearning or pleading.

♦ The melodic lines are woven together with great skill and beauty. That is the main reason Palestrina's music is so highly esteemed and still sung today.

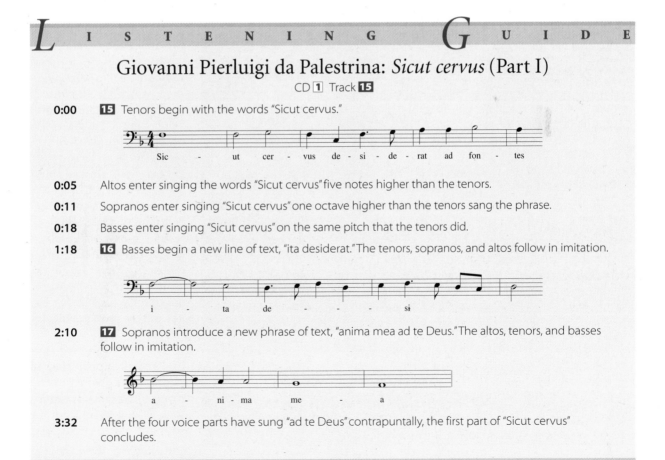

L I S T E N I N G G U I D E

Giovanni Pierluigi da Palestrina: *Sicut cervus* (Part I)
CD 1 Track 15

0:00 15 Tenors begin with the words "Sicut cervus."

Sic - ut cer - vus de - si - de - rat ad fon - tes

0:05 Altos enter singing the words "Sicut cervus" five notes higher than the tenors.

0:11 Sopranos enter singing "Sicut cervus" one octave higher than the tenors sang the phrase.

0:18 Basses enter singing "Sicut cervus" on the same pitch that the tenors did.

1:18 16 Basses begin a new line of text, "ita desiderat." The tenors, sopranos, and altos follow in imitation.

i - ta de - - - si

2:10 17 Sopranos introduce a new phrase of text, "anima mea ad te Deus." The altos, tenors, and basses follow in imitation.

a - ni - ma me - a

3:32 After the four voice parts have sung "ad te Deus" contrapuntally, the first part of "Sicut cervus" concludes.

THE MADRIGAL

The Renaissance also had a distinctly worldly side, as was noted earlier. Many types of secular music were composed and performed, and some of this music contained features of the musical style of a particular country. The most significant type of secular music at this time was the madrigal.

Madrigals are both similar to and different from motets. They are similar in that they were written for a small group of singers. They also have some imitative entrances of new phrases of text, contain singable vocal lines, and are generally more polyphonic than homophonic. But there are some major differences. Madrigals are in vernacular languages, and their texts often deal with sentimental and sometimes erotic love. They tend to have stronger and more regular rhythm, and most of them are composed to be performed at a faster tempo.

Madrigals were sung at courtly social gatherings and meetings of learned and artistic societies, so they were not the popular or folk music of the day. They were very popular, however, among the aristocratic, educated class, and an enormous number of them were composed. In England madrigal singing—with its implied requirement of music reading—was expected of educated persons.

Because madrigals were written for secular situations, they were not limited by religious traditions. They therefore contained more-innovative musical ideas. For instance, many madrigal composers were fond of *word painting* or *text painting,* in which the music attempts to depict the words being sung. This practice is especially evident in the madrigal "As Vesta Was from Latmos Hill Descending," included on the CD.

Instruments often accompanied the singing of secular music, especially a lute or harpsichord. Instrumentalists simplified the written parts by reducing the polyphony to chords. The lute was the most popular instrument of the Renaissance. As can be seen in the painting, it has a pear-shaped body, frets, and several strings. Its pegbox is slanted back sharply away from the body. It is played by plucking, and intricate music can be performed on it.

A Girl with a Lute, an oil painting on wood by Bartolomeo Veneto

The madrigal was originally an Italian development associated with such composers as Cipriano de Rore and Luca Marenzio. By the mid-1500s madrigals had spread to other countries. Interest in madrigals reached England late in that century. English madrigals are especially enjoyable to listeners today for three reasons:

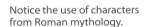

Frets are metal strips placed across the fingerboard to help the player in accurate finger placement.

♦ Their texts are in English, so no translation is necessary for English-speaking people.

♦ English composers had a knack for making the lines of music tuneful and singable.

♦ The English had the delightful trait of not taking themselves too seriously. No matter how sad a song may be, the listener senses a detached quality.

Thomas Weelkes was one of England's finest composers of madrigals. "As Vesta Was from Latmos Hill Descending" is from an anthology of madrigals, *The Triumphs of Oriana*. It was composed in honor of Queen Elizabeth I, who was often called "Oriana." This madrigal is written for six voice parts instead of the usual four. Vesta is the Roman goddess of the hearth and home, and Diana is the goddess of the hunt, chastity, and the moon. The text tells about Vesta coming down a hill with her attendants, who are referred to as "Diana's darlings." At the same time, Oriana, the "maiden queen," climbs the hill with her shepherd attendants. Vesta's attendants leave her and hurry down to join Oriana.

Notice the use of characters from Roman mythology.

Queen Elizabeth never married and was often referred to as the "maiden" or "virgin" queen.

Weelkes's madrigal makes much use of word painting. The words *ascending* and *descending* are each set with scales that move in the direction implied by the words.

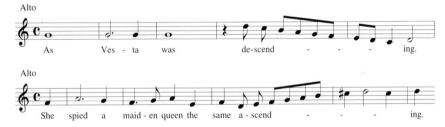

When the text tells about Vesta's attendants leaving her to run down the hill, Weelkes has the appropriate number of singers singing—two, then three, and then one. Later in the piece, the word *long* is the longest note in that portion of the madrigal.

Thomas Weelkes

Thomas Weelkes (c. 1576–1623) was one of several excellent composers of choral music who flourished at the end of the sixteenth century and the early part of the seventeenth. His contemporaries included William Byrd (1543–1623), John Dowland (1562–1626), Thomas Morley (c. 1557–1603), Thomas Tallis (c. 1501–1585), and John Wilbye (1574–1638). Although madrigals were slow in coming to England, interest in them seemed to explode once they finally arrived.

Weelkes was organist first at Winchester College, but spent most of his career in

Chichester. There he married the daughter of a wealthy merchant, and they had three children. His most musically productive years were the early ones in Chichester. As the years

went by, he became more negligent in his church music duties and drank heavily. He was reported to the bishop as being "noted and famed for a common drunkard and notorious swearer and blasphemer." By 1617 he was fired from his job and apparently was employed only sporadically after that.

Whatever Weelkes's personal foibles, he composed some of the finest church music and madrigals during that period of English history. Typical of most of his contemporary composers, his madrigals were lighter and more experimental than his church music.

L I S T E N I N G G U I D E

Thomas Weelkes: "As Vesta Was from Latmos Hill Descending"

CD 3 Track 9

0:00	9 As Vesta was from Latmos hill descending,	Descending scales.	
0:12	she spied a maiden queen the same ascending,	Ascending scales.	Examples of word painting.
0:33	attended on by all the shepherds swain,		The word *swain* in the text refers to male admirers.
0:48	to whom Diana's darlings came running down amain.		
1:12	10 First two by two, then three by three together,	Rapid descending notes. Two voices, three voices, then all voices.	
1:23	leaving their goddess all alone, hasten thither,	One voice.	
1:31	and mingling with the shepherd of her train		
1:41	with mirthful tunes her presence entertain.		
1:55	Then sang the shepherds and nymphs of Diana,	Short, happy phrase in imitation.	
2:07	Long live fair Oriana!		
3:07	Madrigal concludes with long notes in the bass part.		

Weelkes also fits the words and rhythm of the music together in a way that would be natural if they were spoken. Often the rhythmic setting of the words contributes to their expressiveness.

RENAISSANCE INSTRUMENTAL MUSIC

A number of composers during the Renaissance wrote music for the lute, which was the most popular instrument of the day.

Composers during the Renaissance devoted almost all of their efforts to vocal music. The lute reached its peak of popularity during this time. The violin and harpsichord were in the early stages of development.

Dances were often paired: a slow dance followed by a fast one.

Instruments were used extensively for dance music. One of the most popular dances of the time was the *pavane* ("pa-*vahn*"), a solemn dance in two beats to the measure with the dancers moving in a formal way. The pavane was often paired with the *galliard*, which had three beats to the measure. These and other dances are made up of clearly identifiable sections that produced forms such *A A B B* and *A A B B C C*.

C o d a

Renaissance music was not intended for the concert stage; its subtle qualities are lost in an auditorium. It is not massive and colorful. Instead, it has other virtues. The centuries since that time have seen the development of new forms and media. The world of music has grown much larger, which makes it more difficult to give each musical style the attention it deserves.

That's too bad, because Renaissance composers achieved a quality in their motets and madrigals that has never been surpassed. Different works in different styles have been written since then, but subsequent efforts have not diminished the quality of the music of the sixteenth century.

Renaissance and Baroque Art

The restrained quality of Renaissance motets can be sensed in the artworks of the time. Madonna and Child *by Giotto di Bondone has a planned, posed look. This work from the fourteenth century was originally part of a polyptych, or series, of paintings. Several points are worth noting about this painting.*

First, it was part of a polyptych, which contains the same stem word as polyphony, *which is a feature of Renaissance music. Second, it has a flat, two-dimensional look; only a little shading was used to outline the figures. Third, the outline of the Madonna and Child are in a three-quarter position and create an elegant Gothic shape broken only by the almost geometric figure. Fourth, the hands and faces are not very lifelike. The Madonna's hand looks as though it could be attached to a mannequin. Fifth, the painting is not very realistic: The Child has a mature face and body for an infant; he is also far too big to be held with one arm. Sixth, the gold background shows the influence of Byzantine or eastern European art. But whatever its limitations, it is nevertheless a compelling work of art.*

Another example of Renaissance art is Sandro Botticelli's Adoration of the Magi. *It depicts the three wise men or kings paying homage to the infant Jesus. It was painted about 150 years after Giotto's* Madonna and Child, *and it shows the more mature Renaissance characteristics. It reveals the fondness of artists of the time for order and balance. A group of figures at the left of the painting is balanced by a group on the right, with the Madonna and Child in the center. The painting has a "staged" look. Like the sacred music of the time, it has a restrained quality.*

The converging lines of the Greek and Roman ruins add linear perspective to the painting and indicate a renewed interest in these ancient civilizations. In contrast to the golden quality of Giotto's painting, Botticelli gives many of his figures brightly colored clothing. In addition, the sky is bright and clear.

Baroque artworks *are very different from those of the Renaissance. Consider Peter Paul Rubens's* The Meeting of Abraham and Melchizedek, *which was painted about 1625. Originally designed for a tapestry, this work is the opposite of the calm, posed quality of Giotto's* Madonna and Child. *A similar change can be observed in Baroque music, with its development of opera and oratorio. The painting looks as though a movie director had shouted "Action!" to the figures; even the horse on the left side of the picture appears to have responded to the command. The bodies of the figures are often twisted to add to the dramatic effect. Abraham and Melchizedek lean actively toward each other. The men on each side are set in a tight design of profiles and frontal poses. Their bodies look natural and robust. The edges of the painting show a luxurious carpet piled up on a ledge, and the scene is anchored by the columns on the right and clamped into place by the servants in the foreground.*

Rembrandt van Rijn's Descent from the Cross *shows another side of Baroque painting. It features the dramatic treatment of light on the faces of people, much like a spotlight in a stage production centers attention on a particular character. The light focuses on two parts of the painting. One is the body of Jesus and the face of the man helping lower His body. The other, weaker spotlight is on the woman, presumably Mary, on the right-hand side. The light in this painting seems to be coming from the candle shielded by a man's hand, which gives the scene an eerie pall. To increase the spotlight effect, Rembrandt painted an almost black background.*

Another Baroque characteristic of Rembrandt's painting is the twisted, almost corkscrew design. Notice that Jesus' body is turned, as are most of the other figures in the painting; none is facing straight forward or sideways. And the cross is not in the center of the painting, as it would have been if this were a Renaissance work. As if the spotlighting and twisted figures were not enough, you can also seen the tenderness and grief in the faces of the people. It's a very dramatic painting.

The Baroque love of size and grandeur is evident in the ceiling painting Apotheosis of Saint Ignatius *by Andrea Pozzo, which adorns the San Ignazio (St. Ignatius) Church in Rome. The work is a fresco; that is, it was painted right into the ceiling plaster while it was still fresh. It is one of a sizable number of ceiling paintings completed during the Baroque period, the most famous of which are Michelangelo's frescos for the Sistine Chapel in the Vatican in Rome. It seems that Baroque artists (and/or their patrons) thought that bigger was better. Works of music became much longer and involved more performers, and artwork became larger, both in concept and in actual size. This fresco tries to exceed its physical limits by creating the illusion that the viewer is gazing into heaven. The scene depicts saints, angels, and sinners all overwhelmed by what they see.*

The cornetts of that time used a brass mouthpiece but were made of wood and had six holes for the player's fingers.

Viols are string instruments that look something like those of today, but viols have frets, flatter and less curving bodies, and more strings.

in all of Italy. Over the years the distinguished musicians who held that post composed more and more for two choruses placed with the two organs on each side of the church. And not only were there singers and pipe organs, there were also trombones, cornetts, and viols.

The result was a powerful and exciting stereophonic sound with one group of performers answering the other. This technique was known as *polychoral* or *antiphonal*. Giovanni Gabrieli (1555–1612) brought antiphonal music to a peak in the early years of the seventeenth century. He was also the first composer to specify particular instruments for a part and the first to indicate dynamics in music notation.

RECITATIVE

The practice of singing in a singsong or reciting style started long before the years of the Baroque. In ancient Greece, two thousand years earlier, Homer related his epic poems in this style, as countless poets did before and after him. The reciting style of singing, which is called *recitative* ("*reh*-si-tah-*teev*"), was refined and used in music throughout the Baroque. Recitatives have the following characteristics.

Expressive Text

Like the artists, musicians in the Baroque were fond of drama. This interest fostered a desire to make vocal music express the feelings or moods of the words. The polyphonic lines of Renaissance choral music with several different words being sung at the same time restricted expression—or so Baroque composers thought.

In early attempts at recitative, the singers went so far as to grimace, act, and imitate inflections of crying and gasping.

A group of amateur musicians living in Florence, Italy, about 1600 wanted to revive the ancient Greek practice of having musical declamations in dramas. They reasoned that a single line of melody would be freer to express the words than several different lines being sung at the same time.

Whatever the merits of such attempts at expression, they did open up a new dimension in vocal music. The single melody could have a wider range, more movement by half-steps, and more rhythmic freedom than a line of a traditional Renaissance motet.

Doctrine of Affections

As used in the doctrine of affections, the word *affections* refers to all feelings, not just love.

The distinctive treatment of the words in recitatives and other vocal music illustrates the belief of Baroque composers in projecting the ideas of the text in the music. Called the *doctrine of affections* or *doctrine of affects*, this belief is often evident in Baroque music. Because the type of music associated with particular moods or ideas is often not known by listeners today, this doctrine is largely of historical interest; however, the concept of music expressing the text certainly is not. The doctrine of affections is also reflected in the consistent mood that is maintained throughout an entire section of a work.

Homophony

The type of homophony consisting of a solo vocal line with instrumental accompaniment that flourished in the early seventeenth century is often called *monody*.

Recitatives are clearly homophonic. All of the attention is focused on the melody; the orchestra merely sounds some short chords as a background for the singer's efforts.

Homophony existed long before the Baroque, but composers had not devoted much attention to it. Around the year 1600, composers wanted a change from the refined polyphonic style of the Renaissance. This change can be seen in the books of madrigals by Monteverdi. Between 1587 and 1603, he published four books of

Claudio Monteverdi   Henry Purcell

Two Early Baroque Masters

Best-Known Works of Monteverdi
Opera:
- *Combattimento di Tancredi et Clorinda*
- *L'incoronazione di Poppea*
- *L'Orfeo*

The most influential composer of the early Baroque was **Claudio Monteverdi** (1567–1643). He was born in Cremona, Italy, which was famous for its violin makers, and his early musical training included learning to play the violin. His father was a chemist/physician, who wanted his son to have a good education in music. Monteverdi was first employed as a court musician at Mantova and later was appointed to be in charge of the music there. He left when the duke failed to pay him some of the wages due him. At the age of forty-

five, he was awarded the coveted position as music master at Saint Mark's in Venice.

Monteverdi began writing madrigals in the Renaissance, but slowly his madrigals began to change. Instrumental parts were added, and they became more homophonic in texture. In a real sense, he bridged the Renaissance and Baroque periods and helped bring about a major change in music.

Although his position in Venice was to produce music for the church, he never stopped composing operas. *L'Orfeo (Orpheus)*, written in 1607, was his first successful opera and one of the most important in the development of Western music. *L'incoronazione di Poppea (The Coronation of Poppea)*, composed in 1642, was his last. He was very effective in injecting emotional qualities into his music. He was also probably the first composer to ask the violinists for effects like *tremolo* (rapidly moving the bow back and forth on the string) and vibrato to add warmth to the tone quality.

Henry Purcell (c. 1659–1695) was born and lived in England. Despite his short life, he composed an enormous amount of excellent music. Trained as a choirboy, he began composing when he was eight. His voice changed early, so he worked as an assistant in caring for the king's keyboard and wind

Best-Known Works of Purcell
Opera and stage works:
- *Dido and Aeneas*
- *The Fairy Queen*

instruments. Later he was appointed organist at Westminster Abbey and composed much music. He probably died of pneumonia and was buried in Westminster Abbey in recognition of his great contributions to English music.

Purcell was especially adept at writing music for the stage. Although *Dido and Aeneas* was his only true opera, he composed a number of works that combined spoken words with music, as well as music for royal occasions, including the funeral of Queen Mary the year before he died.

polyphonic madrigals in Renaissance style. In 1605, however, he published a book of homophonic pieces, some of which have accompaniments. By the eighth book, in 1638, Monteverdi's music also contained works for small vocal and string ensembles.

Melodic Qualities

Because a recitative was supposed to convey the feeling of the words being sung, the quality of its melody is a secondary consideration. When you listen to the lines of recitative between Nero and Poppea in Monteverdi's *Coronation of Poppea,* you will notice that they are not the kind of tune you whistle as you walk along; they are not beautiful songs. Instead, the emphasis was on the dramatic rendition of the words. Although sung in Italian, you can sense Poppea's impatience with Nero's leaving and his attempts to reassure her of his return.

The reciting style presents its text as economically as possible. Often each note is set to just one syllable or word. For this reason, recitatives are sometimes short—often less than one minute.

Flexible Rhythm

Composers wrote recitatives so that they appear to be metrical. It is understood by the performers, however, that much liberty is permitted in performance.

Because adhering to a regular rhythm pattern can get in the way of expression, Baroque composers and singers followed the inflections of the speaking voice and the expression of the words instead of a metrical pattern in performing recitatives. Singers were permitted to speed up or slow down if they thought the music called for it. The accompanying performers understood this, and they became adept at following the soloist.

Tonal Center

Tonality and cadences are discussed in chapter 3.

The Baroque period saw the establishment of music with a *tonal center,* or *key center,* and the systematic use of harmony. Prior to that time, composers concentrated on fitting the lines of music together well. Now composers began to think much more about how the progression of chords affected the music. They based their use of chords around the "magnetic pull" of the tonal center.

Modulation

Music with no modulations is like a room with beige carpeting, beige draperies, beige walls and ceiling, and beige furniture.

Having established a key center, Baroque composers then devised ways of changing it during a recitative or other musical work. Today listeners are so used to hearing music modulation that they are not aware of how monotonous music would sound without it. Changes of key center make music more interesting.

MONTEVERDI'S *CORONATION OF POPPEA*

Many characteristics of recitative can be heard in a portion of Monteverdi's *Coronation of Poppea.* In the excerpt presented here, dawn has just broken, and the scheming Poppea had enticed Nero to spend the night with her. She tries to delay his departure as long as possible and make him promise to return. Several times she sings the word "Tornerai?" ("Won't you return?") in a seductive way. Notice how the singers' lines follow the natural rise and fall and changes of speed and inflection as the words would if spoken. The recitative style is broken only by a short solo in which Nero sings passionately that he cannot live without her.

Is Poppea able to work her charms on Nero? Check out the Listening Guide.

Types of Recitatives

Handel's *Messiah* is presented in chapter 15.

Because each recitative is built around its unique text, no two are exactly alike. In fact, they can vary a great deal. For example, in *Messiah* by George Frideric Handel, four recitatives for the soprano soloist appear in a row.

♦ In the first she sings, "There were shepherds abiding in the field, keeping watch over their flocks by night." This recitative is accompanied by simple chords.

♦ The text of the next recitative is, "And lo! the angel of the Lord came upon them, and the glory of the Lord shone round about them, and they were sore afraid." These words are sung to a bright-sounding accompaniment by the orchestra.

♦ "And the angel said unto them, Fear not" follows, accompanied with a minimum of chords and giving an impression of steadfastness.

♦ The fourth recitative in the series begins, "And suddenly there was with the angel a heavenly host . . ." It projects the idea of excitement as the strings play many short notes derived from the chords.

Claudio Monteverdi: Recitative from act I, scene 1, of
The Coronation of Poppea
CD **3** Track **11**

0:00	**11** **Poppea:** Tornerai?		Won't you return?
	Nero: Se ben io vò		I leave you only
	Pur teco io stò, pur teco stò . . .		to be with you all the more . . .
	Poppea: Tornerai?		Won't you return?
	Nero: Il cor dalle tue stella		My heart can never be torn away
	Mai mai non se divelle . . .		from your beautiful eyes . . .
	Poppea: Tornerai?		Won't you return?
0:33	**Nero:** Io non posso da te, non posso da te		I can never really live away from you
	da te viver disgiunto		
	Se non si smembra la unità del punto . . .		no more than a soul can be severed from itself . . .

(Line repeated)

1:04	**Poppea:** Tornerai?		Won't you return?
	Nero: Torrnerò.		I will return.
	Poppea: Quando?		When?
	Nero: Ben tosto.		Very soon . . .
	Poppea: Ben tosto, me'l prometti?		Very soon, you promise?
	Nero: Te'l guiro.		I swear it.
1:17	**Poppea:** E me l'osserverai?		Very soon, you promise?
	Nero: E s'a te no verrò, tu a me verrai!		If I do not come, you'll come to me!
	Poppea: Addio . . .		Good-bye . . .
	Nero: Addio . . .		Good-bye . . .
	Poppea: . . . Nerone, Nerone, addio . . .		. . . Nero, Nero, good-bye . . .
	Nero: . . . Poppea, Poppea, addio . . .		. . . Poppea, Poppea, good-bye . . .
	Poppea: Addio, Nerone, addio!		Good-bye, Nero, good-bye!
	Nero: Addio, Poppea, addio!		Good-bye, Poppea, good-bye!
2:37	Scene 1 closes.		

ARIA

A second type of homophonic vocal music that developed during the Baroque was the *aria* ("*ar-ee-ah*"). Arias are very different from recitatives in a number of ways.

♦ Arias are much longer than recitatives. "Dido's Lament" from Henry Purcell's *Dido and Aeneas* requires about five minutes, which is much longer than the recitative in Monteverdi's *Coronation of Poppea*, even with its short melodic section.

The term for the short, "mini" aria like the one Nero sings is *arioso*.

◆ The accompanying orchestra has a much larger and more important role in the aria. The accompaniments usually have some musically interesting passages, which they often perform without the soloist. It may also reiterate a figure that the soloist has sung, or it may play musical material of its own. In "Dido's Lament" the orchestra plays a repeated bass line called a *basso ostinato,* or *ground bass,* a line that descends by half-steps for several measures, which adds to the sorrowful character of the music.

◆ In arias the soloists often sing rapidly moving notes or perform long phrases on one word or syllable.

◆ Although most arias are much longer than recitatives, often their texts are shorter. Arias are usually longer because they often repeat words and phrases, as well as contain passages for the accompanying instruments.

◆ The texts of arias dwell on a single idea. Sometimes they are like sung soliloquies that offer reactions to situations. Usually, they do not advance the story by describing an event. The mood of "Dido's Lament" is one of tragedy and despair.

◆ Arias often have a formal pattern, and sections of them are frequently repeated. In the case of "Dido's Lament," it is a rather short, slow-moving bass line that is repeated eleven times in descending half-steps. Even if the words were not in English, you could easily sense the overall mournful mood projected by the music.

◆ Arias follow the strict metrical rhythm and steady beat found in most Baroque music. Except for unmetered recitatives, Baroque rhythm is very straight-forward. Changes of tempo in arias and other works are permitted only near the ends of sections in a long work. In fact, the rhythm of Baroque music is so structured that it can be performed without a conductor.

◆ Composers intended arias to stand on their own musical merits to a much greater extent than recitatives, which often serve mainly to advance the story or to be a bridge between sections. For this reason, they gave arias more memorable melodic and vocal qualities.

PURCELL'S *DIDO AND AENEAS*

The story of *Dido and Aeneas* comes from Virgil's *Aeneid,* one of the masterpieces of classical Latin literature.

Dido and Aeneas was written for a private girls' school in Chelsea outside of London. Aeneas, the hero of Troy, is fleeing from his conquered homeland. He sets sail to found the city of Rome, but is blown off course onto the shores of Carthage, where Dido is the widowed queen. They meet and fall in love, but soon the gods order Aeneas to continue on to found Rome. Feeling very alone and betrayed, Dido expresses her feelings in the tender and beautiful aria, "When I am laid in earth," which is often called "Dido's Lament." Dido and her servant, Belinda, are alone onstage, and only Dido sings. The ostinato is a distinctive feature of this aria.

The term *ostinato* comes from the Italian word for stubborn, and indeed ostinatos are persistently repeated musical phrases. Dido sings her moving melody over the ostinato, and the combination gives the aria the qualities of both unity and variety.

Notice that Dido's phrases are incomplete, as though she were consumed in her thoughts. The exclamation "ah" is sung four times in the aria on a major chord, but is followed by a minor chord, as if it cannot shake the shadow of death. Six times she asks to be remembered. In most stage versions, she stabs herself and dies as the orchestra plays its closing appearances of the ground bass.

Henry Purcell: "Dido's Lament" from *Dido and Aeneas*
CD 1 Track 18

0:00   **18** The music opens with a short recitative accompanied by the harpsichord and low strings. Dido sings, "Thy hand, Belinda! Darkness shades me; on thy bosom let me rest. More I would—but Death invades me: Death is now a welcome guest."

0:50   **19** The basso ostinato (ground bass) is played by the low strings.

1:03   The ostinato is played again with harmony added as Dido begins her aria. She sings, "When I am laid in earth, may my wrongs create no trouble in thy breast. Remember me, but ah! forget my fate."

1:20   Third appearance of the ground bass.

1:36   Fourth appearance of the ground bass.

1:53   Fifth appearance of the ground bass.

2:11   Sixth appearance of the ground bass.

2:29   Seventh appearance of the ground bass.

2:48   Eighth appearance of the ground bass.

3:07   Ninth appearance of the ground bass as Dido's melody reaches a climactic point.

3:29   The tenth appearance of the ground bass is played by the strings alone.

3:52   The eleventh appearance is played by the strings alone.

4:08   The aria concludes, and the music continues to a section for the chorus.

C o d a

*Baroque music is rarely flashy or overwhelming. Instead
it is quite predictable as it moves along through its somewhat
standardized style. Yet there is something about it that is so logical,
so satisfying, so comfortable, so moving, so right!*

Oratorio and Cantata

Three dramatic genres of music were developed
during the Baroque period: oratorio, cantata, and opera.
This chapter concentrates on the oratorio and the cantata.

Opera is presented
in chapter 21.

ORATORIO

An *oratorio* is a lengthy musical work for voices and orchestra. Oratorios consist of many arias, recitatives, and choruses, plus a few sections for the accompanying orchestra. When oratorios first appeared on the musical scene early in the Baroque, they were more like operas on religious topics, complete with scenery, costumes, and actions. Long before the end of the Baroque, however, the stage elements had been discarded, but the idea of drama remained. Soloists still represented specific characters, the text related a story, and the music exploited the dramatic situation.

Although oratorios are on religious topics, they are not intended for use in worship services. They are too long and require too many performers. Instead they were created for performance in concert halls or special occasions in churches.

Because of the cost of hiring an orchestra, oratorios are usually performed with organ.

The Old Testament with its dramatic stories is an especially rich source for oratorio texts.

Handel's Messiah

Probably the most famous oratorio of all time is *Messiah* by George Frideric Handel. It consists of 53 sections: 19 choruses, 16 arias, 16 recitatives, and 2 sections for orchestra alone. It is typical in terms of its length and distribution of sections. It is not so typical, however, in that its text is taken entirely from the Bible. Although based on biblical stories, oratorios normally were not confined to scripture. *Messiah* also lacks a role for a narrator, usually a tenor, who relates the story. It is primarily a contemplation on Christian belief in three parts: The prophecy and Christ's birth, His suffering and death, and the Resurrection and Redemption.

Messiah is also atypical in terms of its success with audiences over the more than 250 years since it was written, as well as its many translations into other languages and a multitude of recordings. Its "Hallelujah Chorus" is familiar to most people and is traditionally performed at Christmas. In fact, at the first performance of *Messiah* in London, King George II was so impressed when he heard "Hallelujah Chorus" that he stood up. In those days, when the king stood, everyone stood. King George's spontaneous action started a tradition that is still honored today.

Nearly three hours are required to perform all the music in *Messiah*. Today conductors usually select which sections they wish to perform.

Word of the new work spread before the premiere. Because only seven hundred people could be squeezed into the hall—even though they stood because the hall had no seats—advertisements requested that ladies avoid wearing dresses with hoops and men come without swords.

The "Hallelujah Chorus" concludes the middle section on Jesus' suffering and death.

CHORUS

The word *chorus* has two meanings in music. One is a group that sings choral music. The other meaning refers to the choral sections of a large choral work such as an oratorio or opera. So a chorus sings a chorus.

Choruses can vary a lot in size. They can have as few as sixteen singers, although that is unusual, or they can have several hundred singers, but that also is unusual. More typical is the fact that unless specifically limited to men or women, they contain approximately an equal number of men and women. The choruses that sang Handel's *Messiah* during his lifetime were definitely on the small side; only eighteen singers made up the chorus at its premiere performance.

This is logical, albeit a bit confusing.

A hundred years later at a festival honoring Handel, a chorus of four thousand and an orchestra of five hundred performed his music!

Chorus sections of oratorios are similar to arias in several ways:

♦ They are somewhat lengthy, with about the same amount of text, and often repeat words.

♦ The rhythm is strictly adhered to, unlike what happens in recitatives.

♦ The accompanying part plays an important role.

♦ The music for choruses normally requires more than average singing skill. In fact, some of them are quite challenging and contain virtuoso-like passages.

But there is one major difference: The music of a chorus in an oratorio is often contrapuntal. The various sections often enter in imitation, somewhat like what happens in a round.

"Hallelujah Chorus" from Messiah

As you listen using the Listening Guide, notice how skillfully Handel has placed the words in terms of their rhythmic emphasis. The word *Hallelujah* is written as one

George Frideric Handel

George Frideric Handel (1685–1759) was a German by birth, the son of a well-to-do barber-surgeon in the city of Halle in Saxony, who never wanted his son to pursue music as a career. Young George showed much talent in composing and playing the harpsichord and organ. His father's early death removed the obstacle to pursuing a career in music. After a year of college, he went to Hamburg, where he got a job playing in an orchestra.

Handel soon moved to Italy, which was the center for music at that time. He studied composition and cultivated friendships with music patrons. At the age of twenty-five, he returned to Germany as music director of the Electoral Court at Hanover. In two years he managed to take two leaves of absence to go to London, where his operas (in Italian) were very successful. He was in London when the elector of Hanover was proclaimed King George I of England.

> It was not uncommon in Handel's day for a king or queen of one country to be from another country. Royal blood was considered more important than nationality. A monarch from another country would be appointed when the previous ruler had no heir apparent or because of political turmoil.

Handel stayed in London for the remainder of his life. For eight years he held an important position as director of the Royal Academy of Music, which was founded to present Italian opera. The job was not an easy one. The musicians were temperamental and engaged in much infighting, and the situation was

> One hair-pulling and shouting fight between singers took place at a performance when Princess Caroline (for whom North and South Carolina were named) was in the audience.

not helped by Handel's stubborn and overbearing personality.

In time another type of musical theater became fashionable with English audiences. Called *beggar's opera*, it was more like a play with politically satirical songs inserted. Handel refused to abandon his Italian operas, however. After nine more years of writing and losing money in that endeavor, his health broke and he was heavily in debt. He went abroad to recover.

And recover he did. After a few more futile tries at reviving Italian opera, he turned to oratorios. Within a few years, he was again at the top of the English musical world. He wrote more than twenty-six oratorios, but none is heard as often today as *Messiah*. Handel composed this monumental work in 1741 in a little more than three weeks! He worked at it almost constantly and paid little attention to the meals servants left at his door. Its first performance was a benefit concert in Dublin, Ireland. It was a tremendous success, although

Best-Known Works
Oratorios:
▪ *Messiah*
▪ *Israel in Egypt*
▪ *Samson*
▪ *Saul*
Opera:
▪ *Acis and Galatea*
▪ *Giulio Cesare (Julius Caesar)*
▪ *Semele*
▪ *Hercules*
Instrumental suites:
▪ *Water Music*
▪ *Fireworks Music*

later performances in London were received more coolly.

In 1759 Handel collapsed after conducting a performance of *Messiah*. He died eight days later and was interred with state honors in Westminster Abbey.

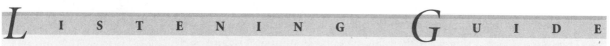

George Frideric Handel: "Hallelujah Chorus" from *Messiah*
CD 1 Track 20

0:00   **20** A short introduction is played by the orchestra.

0:06   The chorus sings together the word "Hallelujah" five times, and then five more times at a different pitch level.

0:24   The chorus sings in unison "for the Lord God Omnipotent reigneth," which is followed by four "Hallelujahs."

0:34   The altos, tenors, and basses repeat the "for the Lord God . . ." phrase, which is followed by four more "Hallelujahs."

0:46   The sopranos sing the "for the Lord God . . ." phrase, with the rest of the chorus singing "Hallelujah" in counterpoint.

0:52   The tenors and basses take up the phrase "for the Lord God . . ." while the sopranos and altos sing contrasting "Hallelujahs."

1:01   The altos and tenors sing "for the Lord God . . ." while the sopranos and basses sing contrapuntal "Hallelujahs."

1:11   **21** The chorus sings together with no counterpoint, "The kingdom of this world is become the Kingdom of our Lord and of His Christ."

1:29   **22** The basses begin a new melodic phrase and text, "and He shall reign forever and ever."

1:34   The tenors follow, singing "and He shall reign . . ." as the basses sing free contrapuntal material.

1:40   The altos sing "and He shall reign . . . " as the tenors and basses continue singing contrasting lines.

1:46   The sopranos sing "and He shall reign . . ." as the other three voice parts continue singing contrasting lines.

1:52   The sopranos and altos sing "King of Kings," with the second "Kings" held. The basses and tenors sing "forever and ever, Hallelujah," and alternate with "Lord of Lords."

2:06   The same basic pattern is repeated four more times, each time at a higher pitch level.

2:28   The sopranos reach the highest pitch level to sing "and Lord of Lords." They are joined by the other sections of the chorus.

2:33   The basses begin "and He shall reign . . ." again as the other sections sing contrasting material.

2:44   The tenors sing "King of Kings," and the other sections respond with "forever and ever" and "Hallelujah."

2:53   The chorus sings together, with the basses having the melody, "and He shall reign . . ." followed by "King of Kings." The same basic pattern is repeated, except that the sopranos sing "King of Kings."

3:37   The chorus concludes after four "Hallelujahs" and one long final "Hallelujah."

would say it when really pleased. In phrases such as "and He shall reign forever and ever," the important words in the phrase land on the important beats and parts of the beats in the rhythm pattern. The important words in the phrase are *He, reign,* and *ev-* of *forever,* because it is the emphasized syllable in that word. It would be much more difficult to sing the phrase, "*and* he *shall* reign *for-*ev-*er,*" and it would sound awkward and unmusical.

To realize how important the placement of emphasis in words is, try saying "Hallelujah" in different ways: "*HAL-* le-*lu-*jah," "Ha-*le-*lu- *JAH,*" and so on.

Handel did a lot of things right in "Hallelujah Chorus" in addition to matching words and music so well. In the first part, he contrasts quick "Hallelujahs" with the steady, solid-sounding "For the Lord God Omnipotent reigneth." He uses text painting when he has the first four notes of that phrase ascend by step up to the word "God." In the middle section, the words "The Kingdom of the world" are sung softly at a low pitch level. Then they become much louder and higher as the words progress: "is become of the Kingdom of our Lord . . ." At one point in the third section, he builds on the words "King of Kings, and Lord of Lords" by repeating them several times in succession, each time at a higher level of pitch. Finally, the trumpets enter to bolster the dramatic impact of the music at that point. Especially important is the sense of power and grandeur that this chorus conveys.

Handel's success in matching words and music is especially interesting because he never learned to speak English well after emigrating from Germany in his late twenties.

"Every Valley Shall Be Exalted" from Messiah

"Every Valley Shall Be Exalted" and "Dido's Lament" (discussed in chapter 14) are both arias, but they are very different in several significant ways. It is clear that the texts seem at opposite poles of emotion, which logically affects the kind of music used. One is slow and serious; the other is full of wonder and praise.

The upbeat mood of "Every Valley" allowed Handel to write music that shows off the singer's vocal prowess through long series (called *runs* by musicians) of sixteenth notes on the word "exalted":

These runs are examples of the Baroque practice of *virtuoso singing.* A *virtuoso* is someone who has outstanding skill in performing.

The word *virtuoso* is not restricted to music. It can also describe performances by very skilled athletes, dancers, and others.

Much attention was given to soloists in the Baroque. Vocalists competed with one another for the favor of audiences by adding flashy runs and ornaments to the music. This custom grew until the music became merely a framework for soloists to build on as they wished. Some astonishing singing skill was the result, but the quality of the music often suffered. Although the situation had been somewhat moderated by Handel's time, the virtuoso style was still very much alive, and audiences expected to hear some vocal displays.

In "Every Valley" the runs do more than show off the skill of the singer. Handel integrates them into the overall musical fabric so that they enhance the effect of the music and emphasize the message of the words.

The text of "Every Valley" says basically that things are going to be turned upside down when the Messiah comes. The valleys will be raised up—they will be exalted. By having the soloist sing long runs on "exalted," Handel emphasizes that thought.

Virtuoso passages in Baroque vocal music are sometimes baffling to people who are not familiar with it. At first glance it is difficult to understand why one syllable or

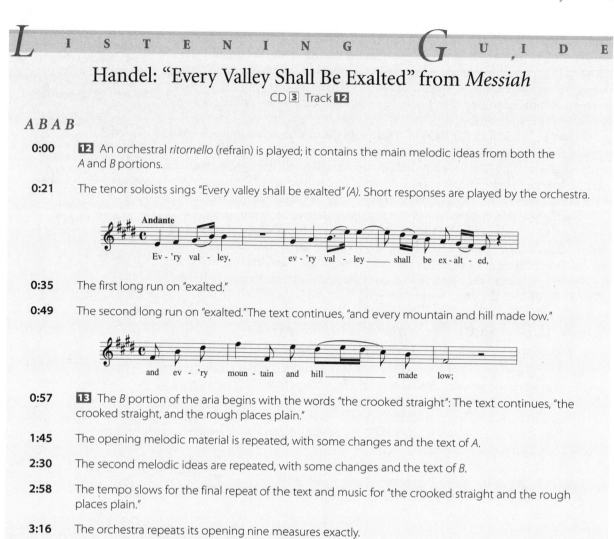

Handel: "Every Valley Shall Be Exalted" from *Messiah*

CD **3** Track **12**

A B A B

0:00   **12** An orchestral *ritornello* (refrain) is played; it contains the main melodic ideas from both the *A* and *B* portions.

0:21   The tenor soloists sings "Every valley shall be exalted" *(A)*. Short responses are played by the orchestra.

Andante

Ev - 'ry val - ley,   ev - 'ry val - ley____ shall   be ex - alt - ed,

0:35   The first long run on "exalted."

0:49   The second long run on "exalted." The text continues, "and every mountain and hill made low."

and ev - 'ry   moun - tain and hill____   made   low;

0:57   **13** The *B* portion of the aria begins with the words "the crooked straight": The text continues, "the crooked straight, and the rough places plain."

1:45   The opening melodic material is repeated, with some changes and the text of *A*.

2:30   The second melodic ideas are repeated, with some changes and the text of *B*.

2:58   The tempo slows for the final repeat of the text and music for "the crooked straight and the rough places plain."

3:16   The orchestra repeats its opening nine measures exactly.

3:39   "Every Valley" concludes with a solid ending.

word is stretched out over forty or more notes. "Exalted" could be sung with just three notes, of course. In everyday practical terms, it seems pointless to use forty notes to sing one syllable or word. But the music would not have nearly so much impact and interest. It is impressive to hear a skilled singer execute long runs, and to hear them fit so well into the music.

Handel follows the doctrine of affections in the aria as well as the chorus. The words "The crooked straight" are set to pitches that rock back and forth one step apart, except for the word "straight," which is a steady long note. The word "mountain" is high and the word "valley" is low. The word "plain" is set in a sequence of smooth planes.

What is it about the arias from Handel's *Messiah* that motivates people to listen to them more than 250 years after they were written? They feature several exceptional qualities:

♦ They demonstrate the expressive impact when words and music are combined so skillfully. When a sensitive recitative or a tender aria is sung well, the music has much expressive power.

◆ They exhibit the virtuoso techniques of a good singer. Hearing a virtuoso singer executing the difficult or showy passages of an aria is similar to watching a champion figure skater flawlessly execute a difficult routine.

◆ They contain the qualities of Baroque music that help it to "wear well" with listeners.

Handel established a standard for the oratorio in England and America, a standard that has lasted.

CHORALE

The chorale was a product of early Protestant belief and practice. In the sixteenth century, when Martin Luther's break with the Roman Catholic Church became final, Luther and some of his colleagues set about providing music suitable for worship in the newly developed services. They wanted the members of the congregation to be participants in the service, not just observers.

One way to involve them was to have them sing. But what should they sing? Chant was associated too strongly with the rejected Roman Catholic Church. Also, its style and subtleties are difficult for untrained singers to perform properly. The answer was to create a new body of religious music that had strong, simple melodies. So from German religious songs, from adaptations of chant and secular tunes, and from the pen of Luther himself and others came the *chorale,* which is basically a German Lutheran hymn.

Luther believed not only that worshipers should sing, but also that their music should encourage the proper religious attitude. So one purpose of the chorale was to proclaim beliefs and contribute to the spirit of worship. The Protestant attitudes of that time are clearly expressed in "A Mighty Fortress Is Our God." Here is a translation of one verse:

It is very likely that Luther himself composed the words and music for "A Mighty Fortress Is Our God."

> *Though devils all the world should fill,*
> *All eager to devour us;*
> *We tremble not, we fear no ill,*
> *They shall not overpower us.*

As his metaphor for God, Luther chose the German word *Burg,* a medieval stone fortress, a symbol of austere strength. The chorale reflects the serious religious outlook of the early Protestants. Each note in its melody stands like a block of stone in a fortress.

Musically, a chorale-hymn is very different from Gregorian chant:

◆ A hymn has a regular rhythm.

◆ It is in German or other vernacular language.

◆ It has several verses of words for the same melody.

◆ It can be accompanied by organ or other instrument.

On first hearing, a chorale, like Gregorian chant, may seem uninteresting. It's true; both lack novelty and flashiness. But religious music seeks to express what the faithful believe to be the ultimate and eternal. Theological beliefs and the music need to be congruent, with one reflecting the other. Furthermore, both the chorale and the chant provide devout worshipers with a sense of communion with believers who have gone before, as well as suggest the timeless nature of their beliefs.

CANTATA

Because of their strong, simple qualities, chorale melodies are well suited for use as themes for other musical works. These melodies are often found in cantatas. Originally, the word *cantata* meant any sizable work, sacred or secular, that was sung. By the time of Johann Sebastian Bach (1685–1750), the cantata had become a short oratorio, with an instrumental accompaniment, arias, recitatives, and choruses. Not only is a cantata much shorter than an oratorio, it is also written to be performed in a worship service. A *cantata* typically has between five and eight sections and incorporates a chorale melody into some of its sections. It often ends with the chorale on which it is based being sung by the congregation and choir.

There was plenty of time in the worship service at Bach's church in Leipzig, Germany, for a twenty-minute cantata. The main service began at 7 A.M. and could last until noon! There were also three other short services on Sunday, as well as daily services and special religious celebrations. Altogether, Leipzig's Lutheran churches required fifty-eight cantatas each year, as well as other types of music for special occasions. Bach composed about one cantata per month during most of his career in Leipzig.

Bach's Cantata No. 140

One of Bach's best-known cantatas is *Wachet auf, ruft uns die Stimme (Wake Up, Call the Voices)*. It was written for the Sunday before Advent, which is four Sundays before Christmas. The text, based on Matthew 25:1–13, tells the parable of the five wise and five foolish maidens. The message of the cantata for the congregation was: Be prepared and vigilant, because you never know when you will be called to be with God.

Cantata No. 140 is divided into seven sections. The chorale melody appears in the first, fourth, and seventh sections. The first section is the longest and most complex. It is a chorus that features the driving, uneven rhythm of dotted-eighths and sixteenths played against a contrasting part. The chorale melody appears in long notes in the soprano part. As these notes are sung, the alto, tenor, and bass parts sing contrasting musical lines.

The chorus illustrates the interest of Baroque composers in the doctrine of affections, which can be seen in many Baroque vocal works. For example, in Bach's cantata the words *wach' auf* (wake up), *wohl auf* (cheer up), and *steht auf* (get up or arise) are sung to notes that move from lower to higher pitches.

The second section of Cantata No. 140 is a recitative for tenor. It sets forth the image of Christ as the Heavenly Bridegroom and tells about His coming.

The third section is a duet between an anxious soul (sung by the soprano soloist) and Jesus (sung by the bass soloist). This section also features a florid violin solo.

The fourth section appears in the next Listening Guide. A gentle melody is played by the strings while the tenor section in unison sings the chorale melody.

The fifth section is a recitative for bass in which Jesus tenderly greets the bride.

The sixth section is a duet between the soprano (the soul) and the bass (Jesus).

The seventh and final section of Cantata No. 140 is a harmonization of the chorale melody in which the worshipers praise God and rejoice. It was customary for the congregation to join in singing the final chorale. The chorales were familiar to the congregation and were sung in their native language. The chorale melody appears in the soprano (top part in the treble clef). Bach did not compose the melody. He added the alto, tenor, and bass parts to complete the harmony.

The idea of chorale singing by the congregation was also influenced by the educational level of the worshipers. Many people in the Baroque could not read or write, so pictures, statues, and music in churches were intended to be educational as well as beautiful. A text for a chorale was selected for reasons of instruction as well as worship.

Several types of organ works that use chorale melodies are discussed in chapter 16.

About two hundred of the three hundred cantatas Bach composed have been preserved.

Bach did not number his cantatas. Editors did that years after they were composed.

Life expectancy was much shorter in the eighteenth century.

Many cantatas use the analogy of Christ as the groom and the Church as His bride.

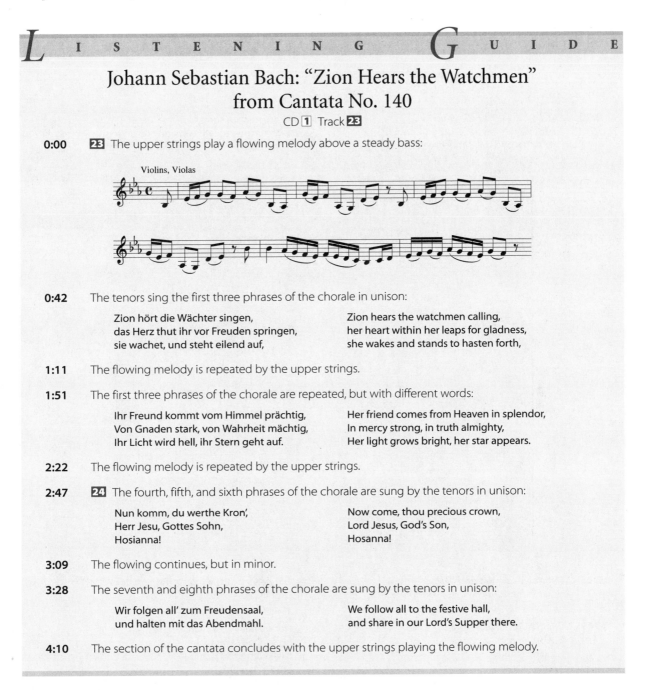

L I S T E N I N G   G U I D E

Johann Sebastian Bach: "Zion Hears the Watchmen" from Cantata No. 140

CD 1 Track 23

0:00 23 The upper strings play a flowing melody above a steady bass:

Violins, Violas

0:42 The tenors sing the first three phrases of the chorale in unison:

Zion hört die Wächter singen,
das Herz thut ihr vor Freuden springen,
sie wachet, und steht eilend auf,

Zion hears the watchmen calling,
her heart within her leaps for gladness,
she wakes and stands to hasten forth,

1:11 The flowing melody is repeated by the upper strings.

1:51 The first three phrases of the chorale are repeated, but with different words:

Ihr Freund kommt vom Himmel prächtig,
Von Gnaden stark, von Wahrheit mächtig,
Ihr Licht wird hell, ihr Stern geht auf.

Her friend comes from Heaven in splendor,
In mercy strong, in truth almighty,
Her light grows bright, her star appears.

2:22 The flowing melody is repeated by the upper strings.

2:47 24 The fourth, fifth, and sixth phrases of the chorale are sung by the tenors in unison:

Nun komm, du werthe Kron',
Herr Jesu, Gottes Sohn,
Hosianna!

Now come, thou precious crown,
Lord Jesus, God's Son,
Hosanna!

3:09 The flowing continues, but in minor.

3:28 The seventh and eighth phrases of the chorale are sung by the tenors in unison:

Wir folgen all' zum Freudensaal,
und halten mit das Abendmahl.

We follow all to the festive hall,
and share in our Lord's Supper there.

4:10 The section of the cantata concludes with the upper strings playing the flowing melody.

OTHER TYPES OF BAROQUE VOCAL MUSIC

The cantata is only one of several types of vocal music composed for Protestant worship services in the Baroque period. Another type is the *Passion*, which is like an oratorio except that its subject is the suffering of Christ on the cross. Bach's *St. Matthew Passion* was rediscovered and performed seventy-nine years after his death, and that performance renewed interest in other music by Bach. Like the cantatas, the *St. Matthew Passion* gives a prominent place to a chorale, "O Sacred Head Now Wounded."

Felix Mendelssohn, an important composer in the nineteenth century, was responsible for this performance. He is discussed in chapter 26.

There is also a Baroque motet. It is an unaccompanied, religious, and polyphonic work. In the Baroque, however, the music had a strong sense of metrical rhythm and systematic harmony. It was also written in a vernacular language.

L I S T E N I N G   G U I D E

Bach: Chorale from Cantata No. 140

CD 3 Track 14

| 0:00 | **14** Gloria sei dir gesungen
it Menschen und englischen Zungen,
it Harfen und mit Zimbeln schon. | Glory now be sung to praise Thee
with tongues of all mankind and angels,
with harps and cymbals sounding forth. |

0:23	Von zwölf Perlen sind die Pforten an deiner Stadt; wir sind Konsorten der Engel hoch um deinen Thron.	Of twelve pearls are built the portals of thy fair city, we have joined hosts of angels high around thy throne.
0:47	Kein Aug' hat je gespürt, kein Ohr hat je gehört solche Freude. Dess sind wir froh, io, io! ewig in dulci jublio.	No eye hath ever seen, no ear hath ever heard such wondrous joy. Thus we rejoice, io, io! for evermore in sweetest praise.
1:22	Chorale concludes.	

C o d a

*The idea of fitting text and music together to achieve a dramatic
impact was born during the Baroque period. Cantatas and oratorios with
their recitatives, arias, and choruses added a new dimension to music.*

BAROQUE INSTRUMENTAL MUSIC:

The Fugue

Some important differences existed between
instrumental and vocal music during the Baroque period.
That fact alone makes the Baroque different from earlier periods.
Until the Baroque, a piece of music was not composed specifically
for a particular instrument, with the exception of works for lute
or keyboard instruments. In fact, many works could be
performed by instruments or voices or both.

The eventual distinction between vocal and instrumental styles was probably inevitable. Instruments and voices do not produce music in the same ways; certain types of music are more suitable for the voice, and others lend themselves better to instruments. For example, a violin or flute can easily produce sounds that are higher than the upper limits of the human voice. Performers on most instruments can also play notes with a speed and clarity that is impossible for a singer to achieve.

The human voice has an expressive capability that cannot be achieved on an instrument.

In spite of the characteristic styles that emerged, the Baroque saw quite a bit of interchange between vocal and instrumental music. After an aria was written, for instance, it was not unusual for the composer to make a *transcription* of that aria for harpsichord or violin. The musical success of a transcription depends on the composer, who must first choose an appropriate piece and then be skilled in making the necessary adjustments for the new medium.

A transcription involves adapting a piece written for an instrument or voice to another instrument or voice, or to a group of either.

In general, Baroque instrumental music tended to be more contrapuntal than homophonic, while the opposite tended to be true for vocal music. There is a logical explanation for this. In vocal music composers tried to project a message; recitatives and arias were developed as a means of giving expression to the ideas contained in the text. Instrumental music was, of course, not affected by a text.

BAROQUE INSTRUMENTS

Two keyboard instruments were important in the Baroque period: the organ and the harpsichord (described in chapter 6). The organ had existed in a rudimentary form for fifteen hundred years, but it reached its height of development during the Baroque. In fact, many organs built in the twentieth century attempt to replicate those of the eighteenth century. During the late-nineteenth and early-twentieth centuries, several ranks of pipes were added to organs, especially those built for use in theaters, to imitate the sound of trombones and other instruments. But these synthesized sounds were seldom musically satisfying.

The harpsichord was frequently played during the Renaissance, and it became even more important in the Baroque. When the Baroque period ended, the harpsichord receded in significance, and was not heard

The organ and choir loft of St. Thomas Church in Leipzig, Germany, where J. S. Bach served for many years

Harpsichords date from
the fourteenth century,
but the oldest ones still
existing come from the
sixteenth century.

from much until the twentieth century. In the past several decades, there has been a revival of interest in the harpsichord, and new ones are being constructed.

Several orchestral instruments are featured prominently in Baroque music. One is the "whistle" flute, or *recorder,* which is played straight forward from the player's mouth, rather than sideways as flutes are today. This flute was made of wood and had a lighter, less brilliant tone quality.

The trumpet too was given important roles during that period. It had no valves, so pitches had to be controlled entirely by the player's lips. Many Baroque trumpets were smaller and had narrower bores, which made it easier for players to reach the high notes found in some Baroque compositions.

Gut strings are really made
from dried and treated
animal intestines.

The violin also played a major role in the Baroque. It looked a little different from the violins of today. The fingerboard was shorter because the players did not play very high notes. The bow curved slightly away from the hair, with a shape somewhat resembling an archer's bow, from which it got its name. The tension on the bow hair was looser, too, and the strings of the instrument were set on a flatter plane, making it easier for violinists to play more than one string at a time. Gut strings were used instead of the metal strings generally in use today.

FEATURES OF BAROQUE INSTRUMENTAL MUSIC

Tuning

A significant breakthrough was made during the Baroque in how instruments were tuned, a problem that had plagued musicians since the time of Pythagoras around 555 B.C. Pythagoras's discovery of certain basic intervals did not solve the problem of precisely where the intervening notes should be placed. The situation was made much more difficult by a caprice of nature. Theoretically, if you play a series of intervals of a fifth, ascending or descending from a given note, the thirteenth note should duplicate the original pitch. But if the Pythagorean ratio for the fifth is used, and if the fifths are computed upward, the thirteenth note is noticeably higher than the original!

This phenomenon is known
as the *Pythagorean comma.*

This pitch problem did not bother singers or string players, because they could easily make slight pitch adjustments to account for it. But it was quite different for keyboard instruments, which have fixed pitches. To get perfect tuning in some keys, people who tuned keyboard instruments had to sacrifice the pitch accuracy in others. Keys with several sharps or flats were therefore usually avoided, because keys with few sharps or flats were normally favored in the tuning process. These tuning complications meant that modulations only to nearly related keys were possible on keyboard instruments.

Bach's two-volume (forty-
eight piece) work known as
the *Well-Tempered Clavier* is
a musical landmark.

The problem was resolved through a compromise: Make all the intervals slightly off so that the distance between all half-steps is equal. The term for this tuning practice is *equal temperament,* and it is the system of tuning still used today. To promote better systems of tuning, and to help develop a player's technique for playing in all keys, a few composers, including Bach, wrote a series of pieces in all twenty-four major and minor keys.

Terraced Dynamics

A gradual increase or decrease in dynamic levels was not common in Baroque music. Renaissance composers placed no dynamic markings in their music at all, and Baroque composers wrote very few. Often composers rehearsed and performed their own music, so extensive markings were not necessary. The few indications that are present, however, call for abrupt changes of dynamic level. A *forte,* or loud level, changed suddenly to a *piano,* or soft level, and vice versa. These abrupt changes are called *terraced dynamics.* Probably, they were made in this way because Baroque artists and musicians were interested in dramatic contrasts. Also, the keyboard instruments of the time could not make gradual changes; they could be made only abruptly or not at all.

There is another reason for the lack of detail in directions that Baroque composers placed in their compositions. It is hard for us today to appreciate the demand for new music during the eighteenth century. There were no established "classics" from which performers could draw. Instead there was a prodigious output from many composers. Because they were under pressure to turn out large amounts of music, composers in those days did not or could not fuss over details.

Continuo

The harmonies in Baroque music became so well standardized that musicians devised a shorthand system called *figured bass* to notate chords. The composer provided a bass line that contained cues in the form of numbers and an occasional sharp, flat, or natural to indicate the parts between the highest and lowest notes. Keyboard players were expected to read these symbols while performing the music, a process called *realization*.

The highest and lowest parts became the two important lines, with the melody being the most important. The bass part provided a foundation to the music. Because it sounded nearly all the time, it came to be known as the *basso continuo* (continuous bass), which for convenience is usually shortened to *continuo*.

PERFORMANCE OF BAROQUE MUSIC

No professional orchestras existed during the Baroque. The only orchestras were associated with the courts and used only part-time musicians. The orchestras were also small—about twenty players. No conductor stood before the group with a baton. The leader was usually the harpsichord player or first violinist, who started the group with a nod of the head. There were few public concerts. Instead, performances were held in churches or palaces of the nobility.

The quality of performance on most orchestral instruments was probably not impressive compared with performers today. Most players held other jobs, often not associated with music, and the technical development of playing skills including the instruments themselves was limited. One exception to this general situation were the trumpeters; they were known to have performed brilliantly. Some organists and harpsichord players were virtuoso performers as well.

Improvisation was an important aspect of the performance of Baroque music. The fact that figured bass had to be realized by the keyboard player was mentioned earlier. A church organist was expected to improvise intricate and complex music. The abilities of Bach, Handel, and some other Baroque composer-performers made them legends in their own time. Singers and instrumentalists frequently added ornaments to a melody. In summary, what is seen in the notation of Baroque music was sometimes only a skeleton of what was actually performed.

THE FUGUE

Because a pipe organ can produce a wide variety of tone colors with tremendous power and range, Baroque composers began to write music specifically for it. In the process they developed several forms of organ compositions. The *fugue* ("fewg") is the most important of these forms.

The fugue, as is true of most musical forms, did not appear fully developed. It evolved from less complex types of keyboard music. The fugue and its predecessors have one thing in common: They are contrapuntal, with the lines of music often imitating one another.

Sidebar notes:

The organ and harpsichord could change dynamic levels only by coupling manuals, adding pedals, or pulling out stops.

Bach, Handel, and other Baroque composers thought of themselves as highly skilled craftsmen. They would probably be amazed (and pleased) if by some time warp they were able to attend concerts today and hear their music being performed.

A cello, gamba, or bassoon usually played the continuo line along with the keyboard player.

Woodwinds had few keys, and brasses had no valves with which to produce pitches not in their basic overtone series.

Handel continued to give organ concerts at which he improvised even after he became blind.

The word *fugue* comes from the Italian word *fuga*, meaning flight.

Bach's "Little" Fugue in G Minor

J. S. Bach's Fugue in G Minor carries the designation "Little" to distinguish it from a larger fugue that he wrote in the same key.

What makes this and other fugues interesting to listen to? At least three things:

◆ Fugues are built around one main theme, which helps to give the work a strong sense of unity. This theme is featured alone at the beginning and then repeated often during the work.

◆ Contrasting lines of counterpoint give the work variety and make it more interesting. These lines fit together with the theme and with one another.

Johann Sebastian Bach

The name **Johann Sebastian Bach** (1685–1750) seems to appear in nearly every discussion of Baroque music. And well it should! He ranks as one of the musical giants of all time.

Bach lived an uneventful life, not very different from that of many gifted musicians of his time. The most notable feature about him was his lineage. Over a period of about six generations, from 1580 to 1845, more than sixty Bachs were musicians of some repute,

> Bach had more than twenty children. Only half of them lived to adulthood, and only four outlived him.

and at least thirty-eight of them attained eminence as musicians. Included among the latter were Johann Christoph (1642–1703), who was a cousin of Johann Sebastian's father, and several of J. S. Bach's own sons: Wilhelm Friedemann (1710–1784), Carl Phillipp Emanuel (1714–1788), Johann Christoph Friedrich (1732–1795), and Johann Christian (1735–1782).

J. S. Bach was born in Eisenach, Germany, the son of a town musician. When he was ten, his father died. Johann's musical training was taken over by his elder brother, Johann Christoph, who was an organist. During his early career, Bach was known more as an organist than as a composer. After two brief positions as organist, Bach was appointed to his first important post as court organist and musician to the Duke of Weimar. He stayed nine years, during which he concentrated on organ, both as a composer and a performer.

When the duke failed to advance him, Bach accepted a position at Cöthen. The prince there wanted music for instrumental groups,

> Bach's music is catalogued by the initals *BWV*, which stand for *Bach Werke Verzeichnis*—itself an abbreviation of a longer title.

so the versatile Bach turned to composing for instruments other than organ. During this time he wrote the Brandenburg Concertos. After the sudden death of his wife, Maria Barbara, he married Anna Magdalena and immortalized her by writing a book of keyboard music for her. Piano students today often play pieces from this book.

The third and final portion of Bach's life began with his appointment in 1723 as organist-teacher at Saint Thomas Church in Leipzig. The position called for him to compose, teach the boys in the choir school,

> His contract also required him to walk with the boys at funerals, not to leave town without permission, and to "chastise them with moderation" if the boys disobeyed. His salary was low, and he had to pay for a substitute in case he couldn't perform a duty.

and prepare the music for worship services. Ironically, Bach was not the first choice for the position. In spite of the annoyances of the position and tragedy in his personal life (six of his eight children born in Leipzig died), Bach continued his vast stream of great music. Later in life he suffered a stroke and became blind. In 1750 he died, with his true stature still unknown.

Except for a few brief journeys in Germany, Bach knew little of the world beyond where he lived and worked. He created no new musical forms and instituted no new compositional techniques. His music was

Best-Known Works
Choral:
- *St. Matthew Passion*
- *Christmas Oratorio*
- Mass in B Minor
- *Magnificat*
- Cantatas Nos. 4, 84, and 140

Keyboard:
- French Suites (6)
- English Suites (6)
- *The Well-Tempered Clavier*
- *Goldberg Variations*

Orchestra:
- Brandenburg Concertos (6)
- Suites for Orchestra (4)

seldom heard outside of Leipzig during his lifetime, and even there it was probably not performed well.

Why, then, is Bach so dominating a figure in music? The answer is that he wrote with such skill and effectiveness. Especially remarkable was his ability to write counterpoint. Words are inadequate to describe his genius. Perhaps the late Dag Hammarskjöld, secretary general of the United Nations, expressed it best. In speaking of Bach and Vivaldi, another great Baroque composer, he said, "Both have a beautiful way of creating order in the brain."

◆ The entire work is crafted so that it evolves in a wonderfully logical manner. The musical process of a fugue is somewhat like a complicated mathematical formula working itself out to a beautifully correct conclusion.

Fugues have their own vocabulary. The various lines are called *voices,* even though they are actually played on an instrument, not sung. The main theme is called the *subject,* and the contrasting theme is called the *countersubject.* The opening section that presents the subject in each voice is termed the *exposition;* the remainder of the fugue is known as the *development.* Sections of the fugue following the exposition in which the subject does not appear are called *episodes.*

The term *sequence* is used several times in the Listening Guide. It means that a pattern of notes is repeated several times in succession, *each time at a different pitch level.* Sequence is a staple of Baroque music, especially its instrumental music. The basic design of the "Little" Fugue in G Minor is as follows:

The use of sequence makes a portion of the music predictable. But the new level of pitch also makes it fresh and interesting.

	Exposition			Development	
Voice I	S	CS	FM		
Voice II		S	CS	FM	
Voice III			S	CS	Return and development of subject and countersubject
Voice IV				S	Close with subject

S = subject   CS = countersubject   FM = free contrapuntal material

This fugue has four voices, which is the usual number, but it could have had two, three, or five. The order in which the voices enter is a matter of choice for the composer. Each fugue is structured somewhat differently.

LISTENING GUIDE

Johann Sebastian Bach: "Little" Fugue in G Minor
CD 1 Track 25

Exposition

0:00 25 The subject is presented in the first voice:

0:18 The subject is presented in the second voice (four notes lower than the first voice); the countersubject begins in the first voice; it is a more rapidly moving and ornamented melody than the subject.

0:41 The subject is presented in the third voice (five notes lower than the second voice); the second voice takes up the countersubject as the first voice begins free material.

0:59 The subject begins in the fourth voice (four notes lower than the third voice). It is played on the pedalboard. The third voice sounds the countersubject as the second voice begins free material.

Development

1:14   **26** An episode begins with the upper voices alternating a four-note figure in sequence.

1:24   After a one-measure fragment of the subject in the third voice, the entire subject appears in the first voice, with the countersubject appearing in the third voice.

1:52   The subject appears in the third voice, and the countersubject in the first voice.

2:20   The subject is played in the fourth voice on the pedalboard, with the countersubject played in the second voice.

2:36   The four-note figure is alternated in sequence by the second and third voices.

2:54   The subject is played in the first voice, while portions of the countersubject appear somewhat later in the fourth voice.

3:10   The four-note figure appears in inversion alternately in sequence between the second and third voices, with a running pattern based on the notes of the chords in the first voice.

3:40   The subject is sounded in the fourth voice, with the countersubject in the first voice.

4:00   The "Little" Fugue in G Minor closes with a major chord.

OTHER KEYBOARD FORMS

The fugue was not the only musical form composed for keyboard instruments during the Baroque. Two forms based on the chorale are chorale variations and chorale prelude. In *chorale variations* a chorale melody is repeated several times in succession but with changes each time. The *chorale prelude* is usually a contrapuntal piece for organ built on a chorale melody.

A third type of keyboard music, one that is especially suited to the organ, is the *passacaglia* ("pah-sah-*cahl*-ya"). It begins with a statement of the theme in the bass. In a passacaglia this melody is repeated over and over in its original form, but variations are added in other voices each time. The melody usually remains in the bass throughout. Continuous repetition combined with continuous variation provides both unity and variety in the music. One of Bach's greatest organ works is his Passacaglia in C Minor.

Another form often used for the harpsichord as well as the organ was the *toccata*, a flashy work with many rapid scale passages. The *prelude* was another common work for keyboard instruments. In the Baroque period, this title simply meant a short piece of instrumental music

The pedals are ideal for maintaining the rather slow-moving melody, leaving the player's hands free to play the faster, higher-pitched lines.

Composers from Purcell to Bach to Elton John (in his song "Sorry Seems to Be the Hardest Word") have composed music using persistently repeated bass lines.

C*o d a*

The features of instrumental music presented in this chapter
are additions to several of those described for Baroque vocal music:
systematic harmony, metrical rhythm, and modulations.

The Suite and Concerto Grosso

Although fugues have been written for instrumental groups and voices, they are strongly associated with keyboard instruments and Baroque music. A large body of Baroque instrumental was written in addition to the types mentioned in chapter 16. This chapter examines two of these: the suite and the concerto grosso.

THE SUITE

The word *suite* ("*sweet*") as used in music is a series or set of musical works that belong together. During the Baroque, a suite referred to a collection of dances that were intended for performance as a group. Suites were usually written for keyboard instruments.

The dances included in the suites of Bach and other composers of the time were *stylized;* that is, they were "dressed up" to make them interesting pieces for listening. Composers wrote their own music for them, but the meter, tempo, and other characteristics were derived from various types of dances that had previously been in fashion.

Many different dances were incorporated into suites during the Baroque. The four most frequently used ones were the allemande, courante, sarabande, and gigue. The *allemande* ("*ah*-leh-mahnd") probably came from Germany. It has a moderate tempo and a continuous pattern of eighth or sixteenth notes. The *courante* ("koo-*rahnt*") was French in origin. It moves a little more rapidly than the suballemande. The *sarabande* ("*sah*-ra-bahnd") is a slow dance, probably imported by the Spaniards from Mexico. The *gigue* ("*zheeg*") originated in England, where it was called a *jig.* It is lively and is usually placed as the final dance in a suite.

Other dances found less often in suites include the bourrée, minuet, gavotte, loure, polonaise, and passepied. These optional dances were usually placed before the concluding gigue. Often a composer wrote a *double*—a variation of the dance preceding it. Many times a suite is preceded by a prelude or an overture.

It is customary for all the dances in a suite to be written in the same key, with the double in the parallel major or minor key (e.g., C major is the parallel major to C minor, and vice versa). Composers achieved variety by arranging the movements so that the faster dances contrast the slower ones. Most of the dances in a suite are in two-part, or *binary,* form, with each part repeated.

Baroque composers sometimes did not specify which keyboard instrument they intended. In Bach's famous *Well-Tempered Clavier,* the word *clavier* does not refer to a specific kind of keyboard instrument; instead it simply means keyboard. The pieces in that collection can appropriately be played on the clavichord, harpsichord, or piano.

The word *suite* also refers to a grouping of rooms or pieces of furniture.

A contemporary composer might do the same thing by taking a popular dance of a generation or more ago and writing similar music with more-interesting harmonies while retaining the essential rhythm and style of the original.

Allemande is the French word for "German."

Popular dances of the Baroque period were musically embellished and grouped into suites for performance.

Bach's French Suite No. 5

Bach may not have named the six French Suites himself. The name may have been attached later because of the French origin of some of the dances in these suites.

The French Suites were written for keyboard, and today are often played on the piano as well as the harpsichord. Bach also composed a parallel set of six English Suites. In addition, he composed six suites for solo cello and four for orchestra.

French Suite No. 5 has seven dances. Each one is in typical binary form, with each half repeated. The two halves of each dance are rather similar. The first half begins in the home key of G major and modulates to the dominant key, which is D major. The second half does the opposite. The seven dances of the French Suite No. 5 are allemande, courante, sarabande, gavotte, bourrée, loure, and gigue.

The gigue is a lively work. Its notation looks different because it is in the somewhat unusual meter of 12/16 instead of the typical 6/8 for a gigue. (Because in both meters the beats subdivide into threes, the different meter does not affect the sound of the music.) This gigue is actually two short, three-voice fugues, one in each half. The subject of the second fugue is an inversion of the subject of the first fugue. But it is not only the technical aspects of the work that listeners can enjoy. The music itself is exhilarating and provides a lively conclusion to the suite.

The tones of the piano and harpsichord begin to decay once the note is sounded. Composers compensate for this by having these instruments sound a more continuous stream of notes than they do with winds, strings, or voices. This gigue is an example of such writing.

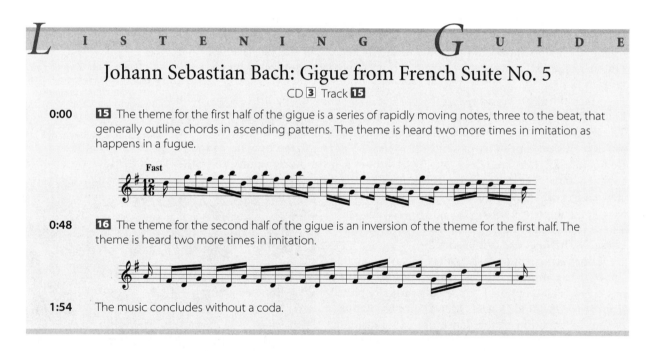

L I S T E N I N G   G U I D E

Johann Sebastian Bach: Gigue from French Suite No. 5
CD **3** Track **15**

0:00   **15** The theme for the first half of the gigue is a series of rapidly moving notes, three to the beat, that generally outline chords in ascending patterns. The theme is heard two more times in imitation as happens in a fugue.

0:48   **16** The theme for the second half of the gigue is an inversion of the theme for the first half. The theme is heard two more times in imitation.

1:54   The music concludes without a coda.

THE CONCERTO GROSSO

A favorite musical effect during the Baroque was the contrast between groups of instruments, or what is called *concerted style*. This style took two forms. One emphasized the contrast between different types of instruments, such as woodwinds versus strings. The other and more common of the two contrasted a large group of instruments with a smaller group or an individual player.

The type of concerto most associated with the Baroque style is the *concerto grosso*, in which a small group is contrasted with a large group *(tutti)*. There is little difference in the difficulty of the music each group performs. No attempt was made to have one group show off, as is true in later concertos. The small group remains seated and often plays along in unison with the large group. Usually, concerti grossi are composed for strings, with a harpsichord filling in the harmonies. A few wind instruments are sometimes included in the small group.

Players in the small group were generally the first-chair players in their respective sections.

The fact that the same or similar instruments play the same music sometimes makes it difficult to distinguish which group is playing at a particular moment. Orchestras during the Baroque were small, so the larger group really wasn't large by today's standards. Also, three or four good string players can produce a quite vigorous sound. Recordings tend to make the groups less distinguishable by taking away most of the physical distance of live performances.

Concerti grossi typically exchange themes between the two groups. Usually, the main theme, called the *ritornelli*, is played by the large group and returns frequently during the movement.

Vivaldi's Concerto *"Spring" from* The Four Seasons

Antonio Vivaldi's "Spring" from Concerto for Violin and String Orchestra, Op. 8, No. 1 is from a collection of four concertos often called *The Four Seasons*. Each concerto is basically a concerto grosso, but the principal violinist is given a virtuoso part to play. The four concertos each have three movements arranged in a fast-slow-fast order of tempos.

The Listening Guide is for only the first movement of "Spring."

The title of the work comes from the fact that Vivaldi associated each concerto with a different season of the year by its title and by inserting lines of poetry in the orchestral score. Such nonmusical associations were not typical of instrumental works during the Baroque, although they are encountered occasionally. Instrumental works associated by the composer with nonmusical ideas are known as *program music* and were very popular during the nineteenth century.

Antonio Vivaldi

Antonio Vivaldi (c. 1675–1741) is much admired by musicians today, but not so well known to the general public. He was born in Venice, Italy, the son of a violinist. As a young man, he was ordained a priest, but his life was not typical of a cleric. He concertized throughout Europe, wrote and produced almost fifty operas, made a good deal of money, and lived with a French soprano for many years.

From 1703–1740 he taught at the Ospedale della Pietà in Venice. It was an orphanage for about four hundred young women, probably most of them illegitimate. According to accounts written at the time, each Sunday the girls offered public performances of an exceptionally high quality. His lifestyle got him in trouble with Church authorities, however, and he was forbidden to continue his music-making activities in areas controlled by the Pope. The ban

drastically reduced his income and seemed to drain him of his creative juices. He died in Vienna, poor and virtually unknown.

Vivaldi was a prolific composer who wrote an enormous amount of music of practically every kind. He wrote many works for the girls at the school to play or sing, including concertos for violin (about three hundred of them!), flute, bassoon, guitar, mandolin, and piccolo—more than 450 in all. His music was much admired during his lifetime but had fallen from favor by the time he died.

> Appropriately, The Weather Channel sometimes uses a recording of *The Four Seasons.*

It has enjoyed a rebirth of interest in the past fifty years. For example, more than 150 recordings have been made of *The Four Seasons* alone.

Best-Known Works
Concertos:
- Concerto for Two Violins, Strings and Continuo (*L'Estro armonica*)
- Concertos for Violin, Strings and Continuo (*The Four Seasons*)

Choral:
- *Gloria*

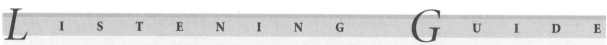

Antonio Vivaldi: "Spring" from *The Four Seasons*
First Movement
CD **1** Track **27**

0:00   **27** The main theme (ritornello) is played by the large group (tutti).

0:07   The ritornello is repeated softly.

0:14   The second section of the ritornello is played by the tutti.

0:25   The second section of the ritornello is repeated softly.

0:33   **28** The solo violin (with notes added by two violins from the tutti) play chirping, birdlike sounds. At this point the words in the score can be translated: "Spring with all its happiness is here. And the birds welcome it with happy songs."

1:10   The second part of the ritornello is played again.

1:18   **29** The large group softly plays many sixteenth notes in runs. The poetry can be translated: "And the brooks, touched by the breezes, flow with sweet murmurings."

1:43   The second part of the ritornello is played again.

1:51   **30** The tutti plays rustling, nervous sounds (tremolos), and the violins zip up notes of the scale. The poetry can be translated: "Dark clouds fill the sky announced by lightening and thunder."

1:59   The solo violin plays agitated music while the tremolos continue in the tutti.

2:19   The second part of the ritornello is played again.

2:28   **31** The solo violin plays chirping, birdlike sounds. The poetry continues: "But when everything is quiet, the birds begin to sing again their enchanting song."

2:45   The first part of the ritornello returns, with a few changes.

2:57   The solo violin plays ascending sixteenth notes.

3:11   The second part of the ritornello is played again by the tutti.

3:35   "Spring" concludes.

The Baroque Sonata

The term *sonata* came from an Italian word meaning "to sound."

During the time of the Baroque, the word *sonata* referred to an instrumental piece, which is a very broad definition. Early Baroque sonatas involved several instruments, but the form evolved in two different directions. One became like a suite.

The other, the sonata as it is known today, exists in several different forms. A *trio sonata* had three instrumental parts, two melodic and the continuo. Another type involved a piano plus another instrument. It is discussed in chapter 22. The third type of sonata figured prominently in the music of Bach and other Baroque composers; it is the sonata for one unaccompanied instrument.

A Baroque instrumental ensemble might include recorder, violin, harpsichord, and viola da gamba.

Sonatas were generally made up of three or four movements that alternate between fast and slow. A three-movement sonata had a fast-slow-fast pattern of movements; a four-movement sonata was likely to be arranged in a slow-fast-slow-fast order.

MUSIC FOR ORCHESTRAL INSTRUMENTS

The Baroque witnessed the beginning of music for instruments other than keyboard instruments. Until this period composers did not designate which instrument should play which part; apparently, whatever was available at the time was acceptable. One leader in the use of instruments was Giovanni Gabrieli.

Gabrieli's Canzona per Sonare No. 4 is a short work for four brass instruments that contains much imitation of melodic figures. Some of the harmonies are not yet as fully complete as they were by the end of the Baroque.

Giovanni Gabrieli

Giovanni Gabrieli (1557–1612) studied music with his uncle Andrea in Venice; later he probably studied with Orlando di Lasso in Munich. In 1585 he succeeded his uncle as organist at Saint Mark's, a position that he held until his death twenty-seven years later. Prior to around 1600, his compositions were in the Renaissance style. His later compositions were in the new Baroque style.

Although an organist and master at writing choral music, today he is remembered more for his use of instruments, especially brasses. They included trombones (which were puny instruments compared with the modern versions) and cornetto. His Sonata pian'e forte is recognized as probably the first work to specific dynamic levels.

The *cornetto* was a wooden instrument that bears little resemblance to the present-day cornet.

Best-Known Works
Motet:
■ *In eccelisiis*
Brass chorus:
■ *Canzoni* (7)
Orchestra and voice:
■ *Symphoniae Sacrae*

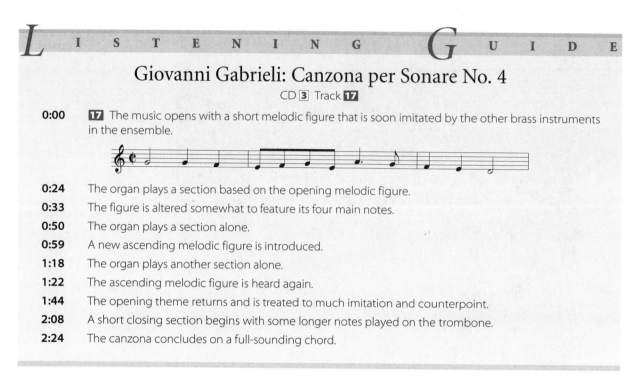

LISTENING GUIDE

Giovanni Gabrieli: Canzona per Sonare No. 4

CD [3] Track [17]

0:00 [17] The music opens with a short melodic figure that is soon imitated by the other brass instruments in the ensemble.

0:24 The organ plays a section based on the opening melodic figure.

0:33 The figure is altered somewhat to feature its four main notes.

0:50 The organ plays a section alone.

0:59 A new ascending melodic figure is introduced.

1:18 The organ plays another section alone.

1:22 The ascending melodic figure is heard again.

1:44 The opening theme returns and is treated to much imitation and counterpoint.

2:08 A short closing section begins with some longer notes played on the trombone.

2:24 The canzona concludes on a full-sounding chord.

OTHER BAROQUE COMPOSERS

Arcangelo Corelli   The leading exponent of Italian violin playing, Arcangelo Corelli (1653–1713) was educated in Bologna, but spent most of his life in Rome, where he was much admired as a violinist and composer. In his music he promoted the technical and tonal capabilities of the violin. He is known only for his sonatas and concerti grossi.

Jean-Baptiste Lully   Though Italian by birth, Jean-Baptiste Lully (1632–1687) made his way into the court of French kings by wit and luck. He changed his name from the Italian *Lulli* to the French version by which he has been known throughout history. Lully was a supreme entertainer in what was the most sumptuous court in Europe. There he staged dance spectaculars and other performances. He developed the *French overture*. It had a slow introduction with many dotted rhythms, a fast middle section with imitation of a short melody, and usually a third section in a slow tempo like the first.

The story of Lully's death is probably true. To keep the performers together, he would mark the beat by pounding a stick on the floor. One day he hit his toe, which later became infected. He died from the infection.

Georg Phillip Telemann   One of the best-known composers of the first half of the eighteenth century, Georg Phillip Telemann (1685–1767) spent most of his life near Hamburg, Germany. He left a huge amount of music—40 operas, 44 Passions, 12 Lutheran services, and more than 3,000 works of other types! He was adept at composing instrumental music, especially for the flute.

Coda

Baroque instrumental music had both a serious and a cheerful side.
The serious music is found in the fugues and slow movements. The more
upbeat works exist in the suites and the faster movements. There is also
a logical side to Baroque instrumental music. This is evident in the
frequent use of sequence, as well as the doctrine of affections
and the overall unity of mood throughout a movement.

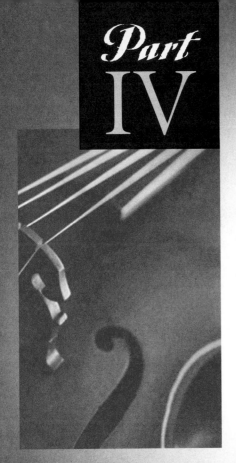

Part IV

Classical Music

18 Classicism and Classical Music

When most people use the word *classic* to describe
something, they mean that it has an enduring quality of excellence.
The Wizard of Oz is a classic motion picture and *Moby Dick* is a classic
novel, to give two examples. That use of the word is close to the
original Latin *classicus,* meaning "something of highest quality."

When most people use *classical* with regard to music,
they mean concert or art music, music that is not popular or folk.
On the other hand, when musicians use the word *Classical* (written
with a capital *C*), they are talking about the musical style
that was dominant from about 1750 to around 1820.

CULTURAL SETTING

Although the approximate dates of the Classical period give it a life span of only
seventy or eighty years, it produced much wonderful and enjoyable music.
Instrumental music developed and equalled or exceeded vocal music in importance.
The symphony, solo concerto, and chamber music and musical forms associated with
them were developed. Opera also continued to flourish.

The center of music moved from the cities of Italy to Vienna, the capital of the
Austrian Empire. Four master composers lived there—Mozart and Haydn during
the Classical period and then Beethoven and Schubert, whose music bridged into
the nineteenth-century style.

During the eighteenth century, there was a widespread interest among the
educated population in intellectual accomplishments in the philosophy, science, and
arts of the ancient Greeks. Because of this, these years are often referred to as the Age
of Enlightenment or the Age of Reason. This interest can be seen in the publication
of Denis Diderot's *Encylopédie* in France and the *Encyclopædia Britannica* in England.
These books sought to break away from the religious restrictions of the past and
promote reason and scientific thinking.

*Haydn, Mozart, Beethoven,
and Schubert are often
referred to as the "Viennese
Classicists."*

*The intellectual and artistic
accomplishments described
here were associated with
the upper classes of society.*

The word encyclopædia *(the
traditional English spelling)
is from two Greek words
meaning "general education."
The ligature* œ *also reveals
the word's Greek heritage.*

Four Leaders

Four persons are especially representative of the spirit of the time. One was Frenchman
François Marie Arouet (1694–1778), who called himself Voltaire. His writings spoke
out for justice and challenged the government and religion of France at that time,
even to the point where he spent a year in prison for his beliefs. But he had his weak
and inconsistent side too. He was shrewd at business and lived comfortably, and
some of his writings were published anonymously. Later when questioned about
them, he continued to deny writing them. But in the end, his influence toward an
enlightened outlook was enormous.

The Swiss-French Jean-Jacques Rousseau (1712–1778), like Voltaire, sought to
reform the moral climate and governmental policies. In his writings he strongly urged
a less dogmatic, formal system of government. He believed that people were naturally
good and that they had been corrupted by civilization, education, and governments.
Rousseau was a skilled musician who advocated a new system of music notation. He
composed music and wrote comedies. His music was simple and folklike in
comparison to the highly decorated style of the other French composers of the time.
He has sometimes been inaccurately credited as being composer of the melody of
"The Marine's Hymn."

*This was the time of the
House of Bourbon, and its
kings were very repressive
and self-indulgent.*

*Elements of Rousseau's
beliefs are still very
much alive in the United
States today in some
militant groups.*

A third person representative of the spirit of the Age of Enlightenment was the American Benjamin Franklin (1706–1790). In spite of his rather unkempt appearance, he was a brilliant and well-read man who published books and magazines, promoted education, was pivotal in bringing about the Constitution of the United States, contributed much to the understanding of electricity, invented the Franklin stove and bifocal glasses, and developed a musical instrument called the "glass harmonica."

Thomas Jefferson (1743–1826), the fourth representative of the outlook of the period, was not only author of the Declaration of Independence and third president of the United States, but was also an outstanding scholar and architect. His ideas can be seen in his home (which he named Monticello) at Charlottesville, Virginia; the University of Virginia (which he founded); and the Library of Congress (which he also founded and whose books served as the nucleus of its original holdings). He was also a competent violinist and singer. The music stand he used for string quartet playing is on display today in Monticello.

Architecture

Admiration for the ancient Greeks and Romans can also be seen in architecture and art. Greek pillars and symmetrical, balanced designs are found in many public and private buildings in America today. The west front of the U.S. Capitol in Washington, D.C., is very much in the Roman tradition. Note the sensible proportions of the triangle above the pillars; it is neither too tall nor too low from the baseline to the peak. Notice also the symmetry of the four columns to each side of the center of the roof.

Classical painting is described in chapter 25.

Philosophy

The philosophical approach of eighteenth-century thinkers was founded on three basic propositions:

1. Reason and logic are the way to truth. Emotions are false and misleading.

2. The universe is governed by permanent laws that people cannot alter. What is true is true throughout the world and for all time. It is universal and eternal.

3. Therefore, the intellect should control people's activities, including art and music.

These philosophical ideas began with Socrates and Plato in ancient Athens, but they were refined and applied to many areas of culture and scholarship by thinkers in the eighteenth century. One of the many areas affected by the Classical outlook was music, which is explored later in this chapter.

*T*OWARD CLASSICISM: THE ROCOCO STYLE

A forerunner of sorts of the more typical Classical style in the arts was the *Rococo* or *galant style,* which was popular mainly in France during the first half of the eighteenth century. Coming from the French word *rocaille,* meaning "shell-work," the Rococo style marked the acme of the highly decorative, almost frivolous French style of the Court of Versailles. It can be seen in the paintings of François Boucher (1703–1770), Antonie Watteau (1684–1721), and Jean Honoré Fragonard (1732–1806). Boucher's "Venus Consoling Love" is discussed in chapter 25.

Two Rococo composers who merit mention are François Couperin (1688–1733) and Jean-Philippe Rameau (1683–1764). The happy tunes and almost frilly quality in Rameau's music seem perfectly suited for the powder-and-wig world of the Court of Versailles at the time of Louis XIV. Rameau is also important in music history for a book he wrote on harmony. In it he outlined principles of chord structure and progressions that prevailed for hundreds of years.

The glass *armonica,* as Franklin called it, was a rank of glasses set perpendicular to the player like a series of grindstones. The player used a pedal to spin the glasses as his or her wetted fingers rubbed the rims of the glasses, causing eerie, ethereal sounds.

Notice that three of the four leaders mentioned here were very active in music

U.S. Capitol The cornerstone of the Capitol was laid in 1793, but the dome was not finished until 1863.

As used in this sense, *galant* is much closer in meaning to *elegant* than to *gallant.* It is pronounced "gah-*lahnt.*"

Much of Rameau's and Couperin's music is for a French version of the harpsichord called the *clavecin.*

CHARACTERISTICS OF CLASSICAL MUSIC

The overall impression of Classical music is that it is light, airy, elegant, and well thought out. It is music in which reason prevails over feelings. Composers thought more about creating beautiful and interesting works of music rather than pouting out their personal feelings in their music.

Much music of the time was written under an arrangement called *patronage*. In the patronage system, a composer accepted exclusive employment with a noble family or the church. The composer was probably thought of much as we consider a skilled craftsman today: a person with a highly developed skill but no extraordinary status. People who use or view the craftsman's product do not know (and perhaps do not care) about any personal feelings of the maker of the product, because any such conditions should have no effect on the product's quality.

The social situation during the Classical period, therefore, produced a quite homogeneous style of music. For example, although there are subtle differences between the music of Haydn and Mozart, their works tend to sound quite similar. In fact, using themes of other composers was an accepted practice at the time. The original composer of the theme considered its appropriation by another composer a compliment, not a case of plagiarism. One theme called the "Mannheim rocket," for example, was used by Mozart, Beethoven, and many other composers.

People in the Classical period, including composers, seemed to attribute little mystery to the act of creating music, an attitude that would change radically in the nineteenth century. For example, Mozart prepared a booklet with which anyone with a pair of dice could "compose" a piece of music. The booklet contained a short work for two violins, flute, and bass with each measure numbered. A chart indicated which measure of the work should be used for each of the 11 numbers that could appear on the dice. Whatever one's luck with the dice, a pleasant piece of music was certain. The style of Classical music could be systematized to that extent.

> Patronage had its good and bad points. Although it provided composers with steady employment, they had to please their patrons, or else they might have to look for another job. Therefore, composers were not encouraged to try new ideas.

> The "rocket" is discussed further in chapter 23.

> Mozart's booklet went through six or seven editions. It was published in London under the title *Mozart's Musical Game*, fitted in an elegant box, showing by an *Easy System* how to compose an unlimited number of *Waltzes, Rondos, Hornpipes, and Reels.*

FEATURES TO LISTEN FOR IN CLASSICAL MUSIC

Melody

For the most part, the themes are pleasant and tuneful. Most of them can be sung, if put in the right range. These melodies are made up of short phrases of two and four measures in length. And the phrases often are arranged in a statement/answer pattern. They form a musical equivalent of "How do you do?" and "Very well, thank you." Such paired patterns are balanced and symmetrical and they contribute to the clear, logical quality of the music.

Counterpoint

The music of the Classical period was usually homophonic—melody plus accompaniment. There is some counterpoint in Classical music, but it is more the exception than the rule.

Harmony

Classical composers used essentially the same system of harmony as Baroque composers, but they made two important changes: (1) They abandoned the continuo part and the filling in of chords from figured bass, and (2) they changed chords less frequently. Sometimes Classical composers would keep the same chord for a measure or two before making a change, and then may change chords several times in a rather short span of time. Classical harmony has the role of providing a backdrop for the melodies and does not draw attention to itself.

Rhythm

Classical music follows regular metrical patterns with little fluctuations in steadiness of the beat, except for recitatives in operas and oratorios. But it lacks the persistent driving quality of the rhythm of many Baroque works. Part of the reason for this difference is the result of abandoning the continuo and its steady stream of notes.

Dynamic Levels

The gradual crescendo and decrescendo developed during the Classical period. These gradual changes in dynamic level were considered quite dramatic at the time. They were an important contribution of that period to the development of music.

Performance

The orchestras of the Classical period grew somewhat, but did not reach the size of the symphony orchestras of today. When orchestras today perform a symphony by Haydn or Mozart, they often reduce the size of the string section by about one-fourth. Orchestras during the Classical period used only pairs of woodwinds and brasses. No trombones or tubas were included, and the percussion section usually consisted of the timpani player.

Orchestra players were part-time musicians who also held other jobs, so the level of performance was probably not high by today's standards.

There were no permanent orchestras in the Classical period.

Public concerts began during this time in the sense that performances were not always closed to all except invited guests in a palace. Public concerts were available in a few large cities such as Paris, London, and Leipzig, and they were within the financial means of the prosperous merchant class.

Forms

Probably the most noteworthy feature of Classical music is the development and refinement of various forms of instrumental music. Such music is referred to as *absolute music.* The rational outlook of the time encouraged the creation of music that was well ordered and planned, as well as in good taste. Writing music (especially instrumental music with its lack of a story and text) that spans more than a few minutes generally requires some means of organization, some plan. Classical composers continued to use the sectional forms of the Baroque, but they also developed and expanded sonata, rondo, and theme-and-variation forms. These forms contributed to the creation of symphonies, concertos, and chamber works.

Absolute music has no association with any object, idea, or event outside of itself. It is the opposite of *program music,* which is presented in part V.

C o d a

It is easy to understand why the rational, intellectual outlook
of the Enlightenment and its goal of beauty and good taste encouraged
the kind of music that was composed during the Classical period.
Loud, crass music would have been as out of place as wearing
a clown suit and red rubber nose to a formal banquet.

Sonata Form

The most important form developed during the Classical period was *sonata form*, which is also called *first movement form* or *sonata-allegro form*. It became the expected form for the first movements of symphonies, concertos, and chamber music works in the last part of the eighteenth century and, with modifications, in the nineteenth century as well. And it is still used in compositions today. Sonata form was also found in other movements of multimovement works as well.

Sonata form and a *sonata* are different. One is a form, but a sonata is a genre of instrumental music.

DEVELOPMENT IN MUSICAL WORKS

As the word is used in music, *development* does not mean "building up" or "finishing," but rather "working with."

Sonata form is more than just a plan or schema, however. It features a fundamental idea in art music: *the development of themes*. True, sonata form contains themes, which are of interest, but what a composer does with the themes makes the music even more interesting and enjoyable to listen to. The themes are at best only half of what music in sonata form has to offer. The other half is the way the themes are developed.

Several years ago people in a small town in Ohio realized that zucchini grew abundantly in their gardens and farms. In fact, the conditions one summer were so good that they could never use all of it, and a lot of zucchini would rot unused on the vine. What to do? They decided to hold a "Zucchini Festival," complete with crafts, dancing, music, and, of course, zucchini. Sure enough, it was chopped, sliced, and ground up and incorporated in all sorts of vegetable dishes, made into preserves and pickles, and blended in bread and muffins. Even the arts were included as many fine pieces of zucchini sculpture were carved.

It's a bit like that with the development of themes in sonata form. Composers take a theme and work with it in all sorts of ways. The themes—or at least parts of them—are still there, but they have been given a variety of treatments.

MOZART'S SYMPHONY NO. 40, K. 550

Actually, it is not Mozart's fortieth symphony. That number is the order of its publication among his symphonies. He wrote about fifty symphonies in all.

The *K.* by the title comes from the name of a person—Ludwig Köchel—who catalogued Mozart's music.

As the biographical sketch on the facing page points out, Mozart was perhaps the greatest musical genius of all time. He wrote a huge amount of music, much of which is still performed today. His Fortieth Symphony was composed in 1788. Why he composed it and two other symphonies that year is not known. It is unlikely that he ever heard them performed.

The score calls for the typical orchestra of the time: violins, violas, cellos (doubled by string basses in performance), a flute, two oboes, two bassoons, and two French horns. Later Mozart revised the score to include two clarinets.

The first movement is in sonata form, which is explored in depth here. It has three other movements. The second has a slow tempo and features beautifully crafted melodies. The third is a stylized minuet. The fourth provides a lively conclusion to the symphony. Not typical of symphonies of the Classical period is the fact that three of its four movements use sonata form.

Wolfgang Amadeus Mozart

Wolfgang Amadeus Mozart ("*Mo*-tzart," 1756–1791) is certainly one of the greatest musical geniuses of all time. He was born in Salzburg, Austria, where his father was a recognized violinist and composer in the court of the archbishop. The elder Mozart was quick to realize that his son was a musical prodigy, and he set out to have him bring the family extra income. By the age of five, young Mozart composed his first pieces; at the age of six, he and his sister, who was four years older, toured Europe. By the age of thirteen, he had composed concertos, symphonies, sonatas, religious music, and an opera. At fourteen he was knighted by the Pope.

Mozart had a phenomenal memory for music and the ability to work out entire pieces in his head. When he committed the music in his mind to paper, he said that it rarely differed from what he had imagined. He was an excellent pianist and a competent violinist.

His great talent did not bring him financial success, however. He never had a steady appointment as a composer to a patron. He tried to work for the prince-archbishop at Salzburg, but the archbishop was a difficult man to please. Mozart did not get along with him, and so he was dismissed.

At the age of twenty-five, he moved to Vienna, where he spent the last ten years of his life. There he married, but had trouble supporting himself and his wife. As he put

> The motion picture *Amadeus* contained many inaccuracies about Mozart's life and death. The probability of being poisoned by his competitor Antonio Salieri was one such inaccuracy.

it, his existence consisted of "hovering between hope and anxiety." He managed by teaching, giving concerts, composing, and borrowing from friends. During some of those years, he was able to earn a reasonable income, but he was overly generous and not good at managing money.

At the age of thirty-five, Mozart died, probably of complications from rheumatic fever. He was buried on a cold, rainy December day in a common grave, which was customary in those days.

During his short life, he was able to compose more than six hundred works, including many sizable compositions such as symphonies, concertos, and operas. He never assigned opus numbers to his music, but some were added by publishers. All his works were later catalogued by a Viennese botanist and amateur musician named Ludwig Köchel.

> The word *opus* (abbreviated *Op.*) means "work" in Latin and is traditionally the way most composers' works have been catalogued.

Best-Known Works
Chamber music:
- Clarinet Quintet
- String Quartet No. 17

Choral:
- Requiem

Orchestra:
- *Eine kleine Nachtmusik*
- Symphonies Nos. 39, 40, and 41 ("Jupiter")
- Clarinet Concerto
- French Horn Concerto No. 3
- Piano Concertos Nos. 20, 21, 24, and 26
- Violin Concertos Nos. 3, 4, and 5

Opera:
- *Don Giovanni*
- *The Magic Flute*
- *The Marriage of Figaro*

THE PLAN OF SONATA FORM

Sonata form itself is divided into three large sections: exposition, development, and recapitulation. Each section has a number of characteristics and features.

Exposition

In the *exposition* of sonata form, the composer presents or exposes the themes for the movement. The first theme is heard immediately:

Several features can be pointed out about these eight measures:

- The theme is divided into two equal halves, with the second being nearly identical to the first, but one note lower. Each half is further divided in half, with the first portion sounding like a melodic statement and the second like its musical answer.

- The theme is actually simpler than it seems. The same rhythmic pattern appears on each of the four pitches. The quarter notes (♩) suggest chords: D D D B-flat (G minor) and C E-flat C (C minor) in the first four measures, and so on. To this uncomplicated basic structure Mozart adds some musical spice—a little dissonance. The eighth notes marked with an × in the example are not in the harmony of the chord. Because they are short and do not occur on the beat, the effect is not harsh. Instead, it is more like a quick nudge.

- The repeated three-note figure that leans upward creates a sense of forward movement, a necessary quality in concert music.

- The theme is in a minor key, which is unusual among Mozart's symphonies. The minor mode adds its own particular mood to the music. Many composers in the nineteenth century used the minor mode to suggest gloomy music, but not Mozart. His use of minor in this symphony adds only a tinge of color; never does the music become sticky or sentimental.

- In a sense, the theme is a collection of several melodic fragments. It is not a sweeping, arching series of pitches, but instead contains neat and concise phrases that are clearly delineated from each other. This quality makes it easier to develop.

After a few closing chords, the theme starts to repeat. But this time, halfway through, the music shifts to some solid-sounding chords and rapidly moving scales. A transition has begun. *Transitions* act as bridges to the next theme and its new key. They may or may not have much musical character of their own. Two chords followed by a rest mark the end of the transition. Such clear-cut points marking out the form are typical of music in the Classical period.

The second theme is divided between the violins and the woodwinds:

It differs from the first theme in several ways:

- It has longer note values.

- It has no frequently repeated rhythm pattern.

- It contains few skips up or down to other notes.

- It is more difficult to remember than the first because of its chromatic movement.

- It is in a different key from the first theme, which is true of the themes in the exposition. If a movement begins in a minor key, the second theme is generally in the relative major key. If the movement is in major, the second theme often is in the major key five notes higher.

It's somewhat like saying words several times for emphasis.

Composers in the Classical period did not let their personal feelings show through in their music.

Transitions can: (1) help the music modulate smoothly, (2) make a gradual change to a new theme, and (3) provide new musical ideas.

Chromatic movement is movement by half-steps. Usually it can be seen in the added sharps and flats.

Following the second theme, another transition appears. Fragments of the first theme are interspersed in it. At this point in sonata form, composers have some options. They can introduce a third theme (sometimes called the *closing theme*), they may write an extended transition, or they may borrow a fragment from one of the themes, which is what Mozart did here.

The transition concludes with a *codetta,* which is a short concluding section. Sometimes codettas have a brief melody of their own.

So far, only the first of the three sections that sonata form comprises has been presented. The exposition can be depicted:

Exposition

First theme	Transition	Second theme	Transition	Codetta
In tonic key		*In dominant key or relative major*		

Classical composers usually indicated that the entire exposition was to be repeated. In performances today the repeat sign is sometimes ignored, and the music moves right into the next section.

Development

Logically, the *development* section is where much of the development of themes described earlier in this chapter takes place. What does Mozart do in the development section of the first movement of Symphony No. 40? Essentially, he treats the first theme in three ways:

1. The first half of the first theme is played three times, each time in a different key.

2. Counterpoint is introduced. While the lower strings play the first theme in a different key, the violins begin a countermelody of rapidly moving notes:

   When the lower strings finish the first half of the first theme, they take up the countermelody while the violins play the theme. A similar exchange occurs two more times, each time one note lower than its preceding phrase.

3. The first theme is fragmented even more. The first few notes are tossed back and forth among the flute, clarinet, and violins. The music modulates often, but this section is quiet compared with the busy, vigorous exchanges between low and high strings that preceded it. Soon the answer in the woodwinds is shortened again to include only its first three notes. Several times the melodic figure is inverted, so it ascends in pitch rather than descends:

   Fragments of the first theme appear in *all but the first two measures* of the development section. Fragments of the theme also appear in the transition leading from the development into the next main section of sonata form.

In this particular development, Mozart works with only the first theme. He breaks it apart, modulates frequently, adds countermelodies, and inverts it. Such treatments of the theme are typical of development sections in sonata form. He could have done other things as well. He could have developed the second theme, or he could have introduced a new theme. He might have altered the rhythm, written different chords for it, or combined two themes in a contrapuntal manner. The means of development are endless.

Recapitulation

The word *recapitulation* literally means "return to the top."

The term for the third section of sonata form is *recapitulation*. The first five letters of the word *recapitulation* form the word *recap*. And, sure enough, Mozart comes back to the first theme. It is played by the same instruments and with the same accompanying music. This literal repetition doesn't last long, however. Changes are introduced gradually as the bassoon adds a few notes in contrast.

More changes occur as the music moves into the transition heading toward the second theme. The transition is longer than it was in the exposition. In fact, for a short time it sounds almost like another development section has begun. While the second violins play rapidly moving notes, the short fragment heard just briefly in the exposition is exchanged between the first violins and the low strings:

There is another difference. The second theme is not in a new key; it stays in the tonic. If the second theme were in a different key, the composer would have to have the music modulate quickly back to the tonic before the movement ends and sound convincing about it. That is not an easy thing to do. Following the second theme, the transition uses music similar to what was played at the comparable place in the exposition.

Coda means "tail" in Italian.

The movement ends with a *coda*. The coda is like the codetta, except that it is longer so that it can provide a convincing conclusion to the entire movement. In this coda Mozart again uses a fragment from the first theme. Dominant (V7) and tonic (I) chords alternate in typical Classical style to give the movement a solid ending.

No two movements in sonata form are exactly alike; each is unique. In general, however, sonata form can be diagrammed as shown here.

Sonata Form

Exposition

Introduction (optional)	First theme	Transition	Second theme	Transition	Codetta
	In tonic key		*In dominant key or relative major*		

Development

Working over of musical ideas; sometimes new melodies introduced

Recapitulation

First theme	Transition	Second theme	Transition	Coda
		In tonic key		

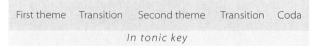

Wolfgang Amadeus Mozart: Symphony No. 40
First Movement

CD 1 Track 32

SONATA FORM

Exposition

0:00   **32**   The first theme begins almost immediately played by the violins. (Repeats at 2:04.)

0:24   The first theme is repeated by the violins. (Repeats at 2:27.)

0:33   The transition begins in the violins; it contains a short motive and many scalewise passages. (Repeats at 2:54.)

0:52   **33**   The second theme is presented by the violins and woodwinds. (Repeats at 2:54.)

1:02   The second theme is repeated by the woodwinds and violins before the music moves on to some transitional material. (Repeats at 3:07.)

1:28   A motive from the first theme is played by the clarinet and bassoon. (Repeats at 3:30.)

1:48   The codetta begins with rapidly moving notes played by the violins. (Repeats at 3:49.)

2:00   The codetta concludes with a solid chord. (Repeats at 4:02.)

Development

4:04   **34**   The development section begins with two short chords and notes played by the woodwinds.

4:08   A portion of the first theme is played by the violins three times in sequence, each time one note lower than before.

4:21   A portion of the first theme is alternated between the upper and lower strings, as is a contrasting line of rapidly moving notes.

4:49   The motive from the first theme alternates quietly several times between the violins and the flute.

Recapitulation

5:21	36	The first theme returns, played by the violins in the tonic key.
5:44		The first theme is repeated by the violins.
5:55		The transition begins. It is longer and more complex that the transition in the exposition.
6:36		The second theme is played by the woodwinds and strings.
6:47		The second theme is repeated by the woodwinds and strings before the music moves to some transitional material.
7:19		The motive from the first theme is played by the clarinet and bassoon.
7:38	37	The coda begins with rapidly moving scalewise passages.
7:50		The first of several appearances of the motive from the first theme is played by the second violins, first violins, violas, and woodwinds.
8:09		The first movement close with three solid chords.

OTHER ASPECTS OF SONATA FORM

The key of the music was important in the Classical period. The key is usually provided along with the title of the work: Symphony No. 40 in G Minor by Mozart. Sometimes a work is referred to by its key, for example, "Mozart's G Minor Symphony." Today, however, the key of a work is not particularly important to listeners. Music of the nineteenth century modulated so often and so far from the tonic that the impact of key change has been greatly reduced. And music in the twentieth century continued this trend, even to the point where some music has no key center at all.

You need to keep in mind that *everything* in a movement matters. It is not that the themes are the really good stuff and the transitions are just filler around them. As in doing a puzzle, every piece of it is needed for the complete picture.

Many movements in sonata form have introductions. They are usually in a slow tempo and seldom have much musical relationship with the rest of the movement in terms of their themes.

C o d a

A simplified line score of the first movement of Mozart's Symphony No. 40 is included in the *Study Guide* that accompanies this book.

What makes sonata form and the first movement of Mozart's Symphony No. 40 musically satisfying and enjoyable to listen to?

❖ *Sonata form is a plan that, when fulfilled by a composer of Mozart's capabilities, results in a balanced, symmetrical, and beautifully logical piece of music.*

❖ *The themes demonstrate the composer's skill in developing musical ideas. Development answers the question:* When is a theme more than a theme? *The answer:* When it is developed by a talented composer.

❖ *The music of the Classical period has a bright, sunny quality to it.*

❖ *The music demonstrates the craftsmanship and imagination. Listening to Mozart's music is like admiring the delicate beauty of a fine piece of china or the subtle perfection of a prize rose. His music is so—musical!*

The Concerto

20

Neil Simon, the highly successful contemporary playwright, has written two plays consisting of three short plays that take place in the same location. But each play has characters and stories not found in the other plays. The location of *Plaza Suite* is New York's Plaza Hotel; *California Suite* utilizes a hotel setting in California. The only connection among the acts of each play is the suite of rooms.

It is somewhat like that with the multimovement works composed during the Classical period. Instead of a single location, however, Classical composers related the movements only in terms of tempos and keys. They planned for contrast among the movements in terms of forms, melodic character, amount of development, tempo, and so on. In this chapter we look at how composers during the Classical period achieved contrast in the solo concerto.

THE SOLO CONCERTO

The word *concerto* is hardly a new one to you. First it appeared in Rodrigo's *Concierto de Aranjuez* for guitar and orchestra in chapter 4. Then it appeared in chapter 17 in Vivaldi's *Four Seasons*, which pitted both a solo part and a part for a small group in contrast to a larger group. The difference between these two concertos involved not only the solo versus the small group. The solo part in Rodrigo's concerto also plays a part that is quite different and more showy than that of the small group in the Baroque concerto grosso.

The concerto grosso of the Baroque period with its continuo part and contrast in size of groups went of out fashion in the Classical period and was replaced by the solo concerto. Since that time, the word *concerto* refers only to a solo concerto.

The solo concerto can largely be attributed to two sons of J. S. Bach—Carl Philip Emanuel Bach and Johann Christian Bach. Carl Philip lived in Berlin, where he accompanied the king of Prussia, Frederick the Great, as he played his flute. Carl Philip composed a number of flute concertos for his patron.

The advent of the solo concerto also parallels to some degree the beginning of public concerts, for which the composer organized and managed most of the administrative details. Audiences were then, as today, attracted by the opportunity to hear an outstanding performer. The small group was not the best means of presenting the talents of virtuoso performers; it is difficult to write music that really shows off two or more performers.

Mozart and Haydn composed many concertos and brought the solo concerto to new level of musical sophistication. It is through their works that the solo concerto of the Classical period is examined here.

Most concertos are for the piano or violin, which are the most frequently featured instruments in concertos. Both Haydn and Mozart also composed concertos for less typical instruments such as clarinet, trumpet, bassoon, and French horn. These works are of such high quality that they are still performed often today.

Frederick the Great was a strong military leader who also loved music. He composed some works and played the flute very capably.

In the nineteenth century, Johannes Brahms composed a double concerto for violin and cello, and Beethoven a triple concerto, but such works are rare.

The concertos for these instruments are amazing in terms of overcoming or working around the technical limitations of wind instruments at the time.

MOZART'S VIOLIN CONCERTO NO. 5

Mozart must have liked, or thought his listeners would like, solo concertos, because he certainly wrote a lot of them: about 27 for piano, 7 for violin, 4 for French horn, 2 for flute, and 1 each for bassoon, clarinet, and oboe. In addition, he composed a number of concertos for two violins and other combinations of instruments.

Mozart composed his Violin Concerto No. 5 when he was nineteen years old. He probably composed it for himself to play as first violinist of the orchestra at Salzburg. In any case, its first movement serves as the exemplar here for the initial movements of almost all concertos of that time.

Mozart's principal instrument, however, was the piano.

Three features characterize the first movements of Classical concertos.

Double exposition   Although the movement is in sonata form, a second or *double exposition* incorporated in the form. The first exposition is played by the orchestra; the second by the orchestra and the soloist. Because the second exposition usually includes music that shows off the soloist's prowess on the instrument, it tends to be longer than the first exposition.

Cadenza   The movement usually specifies a cadenza just before the coda. The difference between the cadenza in Classical concertos and the cadenza in Rodrigo's *Concierto de Aranjuez* is the fact that Rodrigo wrote out every note for the performer to play. In the Classical period, composers just wrote the word *cadenza* or its abbreviation *Cad.* at the appropriate place in the music. The performer was expected to make up a technically impressive paraphrase of the themes in the movement.

At some of his performances, Mozart would accept themes handed to him by members of the audience and make up music based on them.

Whether soloists actually did so on stage is open to question. Improvisation was a far more common practice during the Baroque and Classical periods than it is today. Performers at that time probably worked at being good improvisors. One wonders about doing so before an audience without prior preparation, however. For this reason concerto programs today will sometimes indicate who wrote the cadenza for a particular Classical concerto, and the cadenzas will differ depending on the preferences of the soloist.

Length   Movements written in sonata form tend to be longer than the movements in the typical concerto grosso. Not only does it take more time to perform the various parts of the sonata form, but more time is also needed to show off the soloist's abilities.

No two movements in sonata form are exactly alike. And Mozart adds a few unique features to the first movement of his Violin Concerto No. 5. The orchestra plays the usual two themes in its exposition.

♦ When the soloist enters, an expressive interlude is inserted before the soloist and orchestra take up the first theme together.

♦ When the first theme does appear in the second exposition, the solo violin plays a brilliant countermelody above the theme in the orchestra.

♦ The development section is not particularly complex. The attention in this work is on melodies and the soloist's playing abilities; it is not on the development of themes.

THE SECOND MOVEMENT OF CONCERTOS

The second movement of almost all concertos composed in the Classical period features beautiful melodies and a slow tempo. This practice has continued into the twentieth century. As you will recall, the second movement of Rodrigo's *Concierto de Aranjuez* has these qualities, so in that regard it can be an exemplar for the second movement of most concertos, even those composed two centuries earlier.

Wolfgang Amadeus Mozart: Violin Concerto No. 5
First Movement
CD **3** Track **18**

Exposition 1

0:00   **18** The strings play the first theme, which is built around the notes of a major chord.

0:36   The strings play the second theme, which contrasts two measures of short notes with two with longer and smoother notes.

1:18   **19** The solo violin enters, playing an interlude with a flowing, calm quality.

Exposition 2

2:17   **20** The second exposition begins with the strings in the orchestra playing the first theme while the solo violin plays a brilliant countermelody above the theme.

2:45   A transitional theme is played by the orchestra and soloist.

3:27   The second theme is played by the solo violin.

Development

4:41   **21** The rather short development section begins with an exchange of thematic material between the soloist and the orchestra as the music modulates several times.

Recapitulation

5:34   **22** The first theme returns played by the solo violin.

5:54   The transitional theme is played by the orchestra and soloist.

6:49   The second theme is played by the soloist and orchestra.

8:09   **23** The cadenza begins.

9:43   The movement concludes quietly.

RONDO FORM

The word *rondo* comes from the French *rondeau,* meaning "to come around again."

Most third movements of concertos are written in rondo form. The basic idea of a *rondo* is the return of the same themes several times after other themes have been interjected among its various appearances. A rondo can be represented *ABACADA,* and so on. Theoretically, there is no limit to the number of sections possible in a rondo, but five is the minimum number of sections. The pattern does not need to alternate as indicated by the foregoing example. They can be juggled *ABACABA,* or *ABACDA,* or the shorter *ABACA,* and so on, so long as the principle of the return of the *A* theme is followed.

The themes used in rondos tend to be shorter, less complicated, and happier than those in the first or second movements. Because the sections of a rondo are not usually long, composers do not have much room in which to develop themes or complex musical ideas. Movements in rondo form seem especially suited to the final movements of concertos and symphonies, because they leave the listeners in an upbeat mood. The principle of the rondo is found in the final movement of most multimovement works composed during the Classical period and many such works since then.

HAYDN'S TRUMPET CONCERTO

Valves, which are clearly superior, supplanted keys on the trumpet about 1813.

Haydn composed his Trumpet Concerto in E-flat in 1796 for a keyed (not a valve) trumpet. Keys were added to the sides of the instrument somewhat like keys on a clarinet or saxophone. The work was written for the trumpet virtuoso of the time, Anton Weidinger. He must have been quite a performer, because Haydn did not hesitate to write difficult passages for him to play.

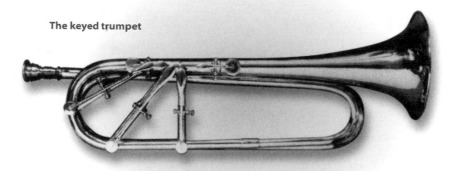

The keyed trumpet

What makes Haydn's trumpet concerto a pleasure to listen to?

♦ The trumpet has a brilliant, full sound.

♦ The music has a truly happy quality to it, with its bubbling personality.

♦ Rondo form gives listeners the expectation that the main theme will return. When it does, they have the satisfied feeling of being right.

♦ Rondo form contains both something old and something new. The main theme appears a number of times with new material interspersed.

Often the contrasting sections in a rondo do not have memorable themes. Also, occasionally the composer works the material into a short development section, as Haydn does in this concerto. The movement concludes with a coda that contains two brief statements of the main theme.

Franz Joseph Haydn

Franz Joseph Haydn (1732–1809) was born the same year as George Washington, in eastern Austria. An uncle with whom Haydn went to live at the age of six gave him his first instruction in music. At eight he became a choirboy at the Cathedral of Saint Stephen in Vienna. When his voice changed, he was dismissed. For the next few years, he managed to exist doing odd jobs and teaching, as well as studying music theory. At the age of twenty-nine, he was taken into the service of Prince Paul Anton Esterházy, head of one of the richest and most powerful noble families in Hungary.

The next year Nicholas Esterházy succeeded his brother Paul. Nicholas was a connoisseur of music. Most of the time, the Esterházys lived at a country estate that rivaled the French court at Versailles. On the estate were two concert halls and two theaters, one for opera and one for marionette plays. Prince Nicholas was also an amateur performer on a string instrument called a baryton that looks something like a cello.

As was typical of the time, Haydn not only composed but also conducted the performances, trained the musicians, and kept the instruments in repair. Fortunately, he had twenty-five good instrumentalists and a dozen or so fine singers. His contract was typical in that it required him "to produce at once any composition called for" and to smooth out all difficulties among the musicians. He was expected to present himself twice daily to await orders.

After Haydn had been with the Esterházys for thirty years, Prince Nicholas died. Haydn

> For the most part, Haydn's experience with the Esterházy family represented the patronage system at its best.

subsequently made two visits to London in the 1790s. For each trip he composed six symphonies. After the London visits, he returned to work for a while for Nicholas Esterházy II, who was not as interested in music as his father had been. He gradually retired from composing and died in 1809, the same year Abraham Lincoln was born.

Haydn is sometimes referred to as the "father" of the symphony, the string quartet, the modern orchestra, and instrumental music in general. Although such claims are exaggerated, they give an indication of his importance. What Haydn actually did was work out a better balance for the new forms. For example, he developed the finale of the symphony. Before him, the fourth movement had been no more than a light little section.

Best-Known Works
Chamber music:
- String Quartets (6) Op. 76
- Piano Trios Nos. 27, 28, and 29

Concertos:
- Concerto No. 1 for Cello
- Concerto for Trumpet

Choral:
- *The Creation*
- *Lord Nelson Mass*
- *The Seasons*

Orchestra:
- Symphony Nos. 92 ("Oxford"), 94 ("Surprise"), 100 ("Military"), 101 ("Clock"), and 104 ("London")

Esterházy Palace, the "Hungarian Versailles," where Haydn was court musician for thirty years

Franz Joseph Haydn: Concerto for Trumpet in E-flat
Third Movement, Rondo
CD 1 Track 38

0:00   **38** The main theme *(A)* is played by the violins rather softly and at a rather fast tempo.

0:21   **39** The first contrasting theme *(B)* is played by the violins.

0:36   The solo trumpet enters playing the *A* theme.

1:05   The trumpet and violins alternate playing the *B* theme in a new key.

1:23   **40** The second contrasting theme *(C)* is played by the violins and the trumpet. It is in minor.

1:44   The trumpet plays the *A* theme again.

1:54   A short development of the *A* theme is played by the trumpet and the orchestra; the key changes several times.

2:30   The trumpet plays the *A* theme; some imitation of the theme is played by the violins.

2:45   The trumpet and the violins play the *B* theme again.

3:17   The trumpet plays the first portion of the *A* theme.

3:26   A portion of the *C* theme is played by the violins and the trumpet with trilled notes.

3:53   The coda begins with the trumpet playing a portion of the *A* theme softly.

4:08   The rondo movement closes after a crescendo and a full-sounding chord.

Coda

*The music of the Classical period seems so—civilized. It presents neatly
organized themes in balanced, sensible formal plans. In addition, those
themes are developed and varied in interesting ways.*

Opera

21

Although *opera* was founded almost a century and a half before the Classical period, and many operas were composed and performed, these earlier operas are seldom part of the standard repertoire of opera companies today. It's not that earlier operas are inferior; rather, it's a matter of the number of operas a company can produce each season, and which ones draw sizable audiences. Operas written by Mozart and later composers have found greater favor than earlier ones. Therefore, the Classical period is a logical place to start when learning about opera.

The operas written during the Classical period share much in common with operas of other centuries. All operas include several artistic elements in addition to the music. Because they take place onstage, operas are a form of theater, requiring eye appeal and action. As drama they must present a story, delineate the various characters, and project their feelings. Dancing is sometimes integrated into operas, as well. Opera is the great amalgamation of the arts.

OPERATIC CONVENTIONS

All forms of theater have conventions and customs that audiences accept. For example, in films an orchestra is heard in the background, adding to the suspense as an actor is about to be attacked in a dark, deserted house. What's an orchestra doing there? No one wonders about that, because viewers are accustomed to the convention of background music. Nor is anyone bothered when a scene changes in a few seconds to one that supposedly occurs hours or even years later, or that the stage in a theater is like a room with one wall removed so that the audience can see what's going on.

The reason people are not bothered by these conventions is simple: They are used to them. On the other hand, most people are not familiar with operatic customs, and so such customs often hinder their enjoyment.

What are the more obvious conventions associated with opera? One is the replacement of speaking with singing. In everyday life a phrase such as "Robert will be here at three o'clock" is spoken. Furthermore, sometimes rather robust singing takes place when logically it does not make a lot of sense—like when a character is dying or very sick.

Not only are all the words sung, but they are sung in a highly trained style, which is another operatic convention. Most operas have a "bigger than life" quality about them, and that is one of their attractive features. The style of singing, therefore, needs to be bigger than life. It must have enough power to be heard over an orchestra in a large hall, and it should have a quality that moves listeners emotionally. Folk singers can sing their ballads in a simple, unaffected style because they usually perform in a small room accompanied by a guitar. On the other hand, opera singers must sing in a vibrant and dramatic way.

Another convention concerns the words. Even when sung in English, they are not easily understood. The problem is increased by the large number of operas in foreign languages. These operas can be translated and sung in English, but should they be? Although translations are not easy, involving correct numbers of syllables, natural accents, shades of meaning, and rhyme schemes, the answer is probably yes,

Music for films is discussed in chapter 45.

Neither singing style is more musical than the other, because each is appropriate for a particular type of music and setting.

It is almost impossible to translate the lines of an opera without losing some of their original meaning.

at least for people who are not familiar with opera. When operas are sung in languages other than English, listeners need to follow a translation or a good synopsis of the opera.

A fourth convention involves the element of time. In addition to the usual flexibility in the treatment of time in films and dramas, operas have to deal with the impact of singing on the amount of time available. If the words, "Robert will be here at three o'clock" are spoken, they don't require much time. If those words were set to a nice melody, however, they would take much more time. The difference would be some pleasant music, but an interruption of the story. If the words were to be sung in about the same amount of time as when spoken, they would not be of much musical interest. Operagoers accept the distortions of time caused by the addition of the music, because of the heightened overall musical and dramatic impact.

> The increased impact of music on words can be demonstrated by reading the words of an aria or a chorus aloud, and then hearing those same words as they have been set to music by a great composer.

ENJOYING OPERA

When the conventions of opera are accepted, most people find that they enjoy attending an opera. This is true for several reasons:

♦ The music is often stunning and beautiful. Operas offer listeners a rich source of flowing melodies, impressive tonal effects, and sensuous harmonies. And, of course, there is a great deal of outstanding singing.

♦ The combined expressiveness of words and music is a pleasure to hear. Opera sets up situations in which the combination of the two can have even greater emotional impact than music apart from the dramatic situation. While the singing of the text may slow down the action on stage, it adds much to the overall drama. Some operatic *I-love-you*s, for example, can cause chills to run up one's spine.

♦ Opera appeals to both the ears and the eyes. Looking at an opera without hearing the music is an incomplete experience, just as it would be when listening to the music without seeing what takes place onstage.

♦ Opera lets people see and hear experiences that are beyond ordinary life. For some rather deep-seated psychological reasons, people enjoy stories, films, television shows, and the like that take them temporarily out of their own everyday existence. In soap operas, for example, the actors undergo traumatic experiences with a frequency and an intensity that far exceed what most people encounter in their lives. Good opera is good theater.

> Soap operas were given that name because originally they were often sponsored by soap companies, and also because the characters' lives are much more crisis-ridden than those of ordinary people.

THE ELEMENTS OF OPERA

Each element in the amalgam that is opera makes a particular contribution, and each merits further discussion, beginning with singers and their voice ranges and types.

Voices and Roles

Opera has acquired a number of traditions regarding the types of voices and characters portrayed. The heroine is almost always a soprano. In most operas she is young and beautiful, so a high, light voice is appropriate. Often the heroine's part calls for virtuoso singing. Some female parts are written for lower or heavier voices such as mezzo-soprano or contralto. These roles often portray older women, servants, rivals, or villainesses.

> In Western civilization there seems to be an association in people's minds between age and the pitch level of the voice: the older a person is, the lower the voice.

Opera can be lighthearted as well as dramatic. Mozart's *The Marriage of Figaro* features a fast-moving plot full of double entendres, mistaken identities, and dialogue more reminiscent of a situation comedy than a soap opera.

The leading male role is often for a tenor. He is young and frequently sings duets with the leading soprano, often doubling her pitches one octave lower. This puts his notes near the top of the male voice range and gives the singing more intensity. Other male parts may be sung by a baritone, a voice that is lower and heavier than the tenor. The bass, which is the lowest and heaviest male voice, is often used to portray villains, older men, or authority figures such as kings.

The vocal and dramatic demands for singing operatic roles are great. Almost all roles require extensive training in the use of the voice to achieve the necessary breath control, endurance, wide pitch range, richness of tone quality, control of dynamic levels, and technical know-how, not to mention the ability to project the singing over an orchestra all the way to the last row of the balcony. Not only do opera singers sing, they must also be actors in a drama. They must make their efforts sound and look convincing.

Operas are usually sung without amplification.

Ensembles

Most operas have parts for small ensembles and choruses. Ensembles frequently consist of several characters singing different words and music expressing their particular feelings, creating a kind of musical and emotional counterpoint.

Operatic choruses usually appear in scenes with many people—a wedding, a coronation, a crowded tavern. To a degree, the chorus participates in the stage action, but usually from behind the soloists. Often the words the chorus sings are a commentary on the situation.

The final scene of Mozart's *Don Giovanni,* presented later in this chapter, is an excellent example of such counterpoint.

The Orchestra

The orchestra is placed largely out of sight in a pit in front of the stage. Although unseen, it has an important role in opera. Not only does the orchestra accompany the singers, it also sets moods, enhances the actions onstage, and performs overtures and preludes while the curtain is closed. The orchestral music written for operas by some nineteenth-century composers is so complete that today portions of it are frequently performed as concert works without any singing at all.

The Libretto

Libretto means "little book" in Italian.

The script or text of an opera is called the *libretto*. The composer of the music usually does not write the libretto for the opera. Instead, a librettist generally creates a version of a play, historical event, or story. Often the libretto is set in poetic form, especially the portions that are likely places for arias or choruses. Once the libretto has been written, the composer takes over and sets the words to music.

Staging

Visual elements are an integral part of opera. The quality of acting, costumes, scenic design, lighting, and dancing makes a great difference in the success of an opera. The lighting and stage effects that can be achieved in a first-rate opera house are truly amazing and at times dazzling. If a character is to be demolished in smoke and fire, this can be done in quite a convincing and dramatic way.

Smoke and fire finish off Don Giovanni in Mozart's opera.

The technicians and stagehands often are paid more than the dancers or members of the chorus.

The need for set designers, costumers, electricians, and stagehands in addition to singers, orchestral musicians, and sometimes dancers is one of opera's greatest obstacles: It is a very expensive art form. A large opera can require the services of several hundred highly skilled technicians and musicians, and this need is usually reflected in the high ticket prices and the chronic financial problems of opera companies. A lack of funds also discourages touring by opera companies and presentations of new operas. The fact that opera is still active and vital in American musical life, in spite of its high costs and lack of familiarity to much of the population, is eloquent testimony to its musical and dramatic value.

THE DEVELOPMENT OF OPERA

Opera began in Florence, Italy, shortly before 1600 as an attempt to re-create ancient Greek drama. At first it consisted almost entirely of recitative, but opera composers soon became more concerned with melody and less with dramatic declaration. By the time the first public opera house opened in Venice in 1637, the artistic ideals of a resurrected version of Greek drama had been largely forgotten. The stories were burdened by the addition of irrelevant incidents, spectacular scenes, and incongruous comedy episodes. But other changes were more constructive. Arias, duets, and ensembles evolved, and the orchestra took on more importance.

Gluck's operas were based on characters from Greek mythology, which was typical at that time.

"The War of the Buffoons" occurred about the middle of the eighteenth century in Paris between those who favored buffa opera and those who favored the more serious court opera. The word *buffoon* is derived from *buffa*.

As opera spread throughout Europe, its dramatic element became less and less important. The singers reigned supreme. In their desire to hold center stage, soloists added all kinds of embellishments to the melody to show off their virtuosity. The situation deteriorated so much that German composer Christoph Willibald Gluck (1714–1787) felt compelled to lead a reform movement. Gluck had composed many operas himself, so he knew the genre well. He tried to bring back its dramatic integrity by making the music serve the text. Everything in opera, including ballet, was to be an integral part of the drama. Gluck wrote several operas that demonstrated his reforms.

In the decades following the opening of the first opera house in Venice, opera evolved into two rather distinct styles. *Opera seria* had a serious nature and was somewhat close to the original dramatic intent of the first operas. *Opera buffa* ("*boo*-fah") was a light style of opera and was often comic. Mozart wrote both kinds, but his greatest public successes were of the *buffa* type.

MOZART'S *DON GIOVANNI*

The title of the opera *Don Giovanni (Don Juan)* indicates that it is in Italian. The libretto was written by the Italian Lorenzo da Ponte, the most recognized librettist of his day. The selection of an Italian text was a happy choice for the reason that opera was a thoroughly Italian product, and Viennese audiences were more accustomed to hearing opera in Italian than in their own language.

Mozart's native language was German, but he had made several journeys to Italy and knew that language well.

For the most part, *Don Giovanni* is opera seria. It contains some humorous moments, but its outlook is serious. Because of the opera's length, the discussion here is limited mainly to the last portion. The plot is intricate, so the opera should be listened to with the aid of the Listening Guide.

Don Giovanni opens with a typical overture. The stage action starts as Don Giovanni begins his adventures with Ottavio's fiancée, Donna Anna. She refuses his advances, and her father, the Commendatore (the Commandant), is killed by Don Giovanni in a duel while defending his daughter's honor. At an engagement party, Don Giovanni attempts to seduce Zerlina, the bride of the peasant Masetto.

It is claimed that Mozart composed the overture only one day before its performance.

Later Don Giovanni plays a cruel trick on Donna Elvira, whom he had seduced long ago and then deserted, and pursues other amorous adventures and pleasures. During one of his escapades, he takes refuge in a cemetery, where he discovers the statue of the Commandant and mockingly invites it to dinner. The statue nods its head to accept the invitation.

The final scene is set in the banquet hall in Don Giovanni's palace. The light and bouncy music lets the audience know immediately that the Don isn't worried. In fact, he seems to have forgotten all about the graveyard and the statue. He commands his private orchestra to play some dinner music. A wind ensemble plays a song from a popular opera of the day:

Leporello serves the table and looks hungrily at the food. "What a greedy appetite," he complains as he watches Don Giovanni down one mouthful after another.

A second piece is heard from the wind ensemble:

Leporello pours the Don some wine and, thinking that he won't be seen, stuffs some food in his mouth. As the third number begins—"Non più andrai" from Mozart's own *Marriage of Figaro*—Leporello helps himself to more food.

The Don, realizing that Leporello's mouth is full, asks him to whistle along with the music from *Figaro*. Poor Leporello is forced to admit that he has been snitching. The whole scene bubbles along like champagne.

Donna Elvira breaks the mood as she rushes in and throws herself at Don Giovanni's feet. She begs her former lover to give up his immoral ways. Leporello is moved, but not Don Giovanni. He mocks Donna Elvira by proposing a toast to her ("Long live women and good wine!"). Angered and humiliated, she turns and runs out the door. As she is leaving, she screams as she sees the statue of the Commandant.

The Listening Guide presents the words in both Italian and English. The music reflects the lines of the characters—the sternness of the Commandant, the cowardice of Leporello, and the cockiness of Don Giovanni. At several points in the music, Mozart has the singers repeat words or phrases. In this book those repetitions appear only the first time they are sung, which makes the libretto less cluttered.

Notice how the story and music build to a climactic movement.

L I S T E N I N G   G U I D E

Wolfgang Amadeus Mozart: *Don Giovanni*
excerpt from act II, scene 5

CD 1 Track 41

Indicates two or more lines are sung at the same time

0:00 | **41** **Don Giovanni:** Che grido è questo mai? | **Don Giovanni:** What's that scream about?

Leporello: Che grido è questo mai? | **Leporello:** What's that scream about?

Don Giovanni: Va a veder che cosa è stato. | **Don Giovanni:** *(to Leporello)* Go and see what's happened.

Leporello goes to the first door, looks out, screams, and returns.

Leporello: Ah! | **Leporello:** *(screaming)* Ah!

Don Giovanni: Che grido indiavolato! Leporello, che cos'è? | **Don Giovanni:** What a devilish scream! Leporello, what is it?

Leporello: Ah! Signor! per carità! non andate fuor di quà! l'uom di sasso, l'uomo bianco, ah! padrone! io gelo, io manco. Se vedeste che figura, se sentiste come fa ta, ta, ta, ta! | **Leporello:** Ah! Sir, for pete's sake don't go out there! The man of stone, the white man. Ah! Master! I'm cold; I'm shaking. If you had seen that form; if you had heard how it goes—ta, ta, ta, ta!

Don Giovanni: Non capisco niente affatto. | **Don Giovanni:** I don't understand this.

Leporello: Ta, ta, ta, ta! | **Leporello:** *(imitating the statue)* Ta, ta, ta, ta!

Don Giovanni: Tu sei matto in verità, in verità, in verità! | **Don Giovanni:** Really, you're crazy!

A knock is heard.

Leporello: Ah! sentite! | **Leporello:** Ah! Do you hear!

Don Giovanni: Qualcun batte! Apri! | **Don Giovanni:** *(impatiently)* Someone's knocking! Open it!

Leporello: Io tremo! | **Leporello:** I'm trembling!

Don Giovanni: Apri, dico! | **Don Giovanni:** Open it, I say!

Leporello: Ah! | **Leporello:** *(pleading and terrified)* Ah!

Don Giovanni: Apri! | **Don Giovanni:** Open it!

Leporello: Ah! | **Leporello:** Ah!

Don Giovanni: Matto! Per togliermi d'intrico ad aprir io stesso andrò. | **Don Giovanni:** Madman! In order to clear this up, I'll open the door myself!

Don Giovanni takes one of the candle stands from the table and goes to the door.
Leporello crawls underneath the table.

Leporello: Non vo' più veder l'amico, plan, pianin, m'asconderò! | **Leporello:** I don't want to see my friend again. Quietly, very quietly, I'll hide!

With a rumbling of timpani, the marble statue of the Commandant enters the room.

1:30 | **42** **Statue:** Don Giovanni! a cenar teco m'invitasti! e son venuto! | **Statue:** Don Giovanni! You invited me to dine with you! And I have arrived!

Don Giovanni is somewhat startled but conceals his surprise under an air of cockiness.

Don Giovanni: No l'avrei giammai creduto; ma farò quel che potrò. Leporello! un'altra centa! fa che subito si porti!

Don Giovanni: I can hardly believe this. But I'll do what I can. Leporello, another dinner! Bring it immediately!

Leporello peers out from under the table with a bewildered look on his face.

Leporello: Ah, padron! slam tutti morti!

Leporello: Ah, master! We're as good as dead!

Don Giovanni: Vanne, dico!

Don Giovanni: Get to it, I say!

Leporello begins to crawl out.

Statue: Ferma un po'! non si pasce di cibo mortale, chi si pasce di cibo celeste! Altre cure più gravi di queste, altra brama quaggiù mi guidò.

Statue: Wait a minute! One who partakes of heavenly food does not partake of mortal food. Things more serious than these brought me down here.

Leporello crawls back under the table.

Leporello: La terzana d'avere mi sembra, e le membra fermar più non sò.

Leporello: I have the chills and I can't stop shaking.

Don Giovanni: Parla dunque! che chiedi? che vuoi?

Don Giovanni: *(to the Statue)* Speak, then! What do you want?

Statue: Parlo: ascolta! più tempo non ho.

Statue: I speak—listen! I don't have much time.

Don Giovanni: Parla, ascoltando ti sto.

Don Giovanni: Speak! I am listening.

Leporello: Ah le membra fermar più non sò. la terzana d'avere mi sembra, e le membra fermar più non sò!

Leporello: Ah! I can't stop shaking. I have the chills.

Statue: Parlo: ascolta! più tempo non ho.

Statue: I speak—listen! I don't have much time!

Don Giovanni becomes more defiant.

Don Giovanni: Parla, ascoltando ti sto.

Don Giovanni: Speak! I am listening!

Statue: Tu m'invitasti a cena, il tuo dover or sai, rispondimi, verrai tu a cenar meco?

Statue: You invited me to dinner. Do you know your obligation? Answer me! Will you come to dine with me?

Leporello shakes with fear beneath the table.

Leporello: Oibò, tempo no ha, scusate.

Leporello: Oh! He doesn't have time, sorry.

Don Giovanni: A torto di viltate tacciato mai sarò.

Don Giovanni: *(coolly)* I will never be accused of being a coward.

Statue: Risolvi!

Statue: Decide!

Don Giovanni: Ho già risolto!

Don Giovanni: I have already decided!

Statue: Verrai?

Statue: You will come?

Leporello: Dite di no! dite di no!

Leporello: Say no. Just say no!

Don Giovanni: Ho fermo il core in petto, non ho timor, verrò!

Don Giovanni: My heartbeat is steady. I am not afraid! I will come!

The statue extends a hand toward Don Giovanni.

6:10 **43 Statue:** Dammi la mano in pegno!

Statue: Give me your hand as a pledge!

Still defiant, Don Giovanni gives the statue his hand.

Don Giovanni: Eccola! Ohime!

Don Giovanni: Here it is! Ah!

Statue: Cos'hai!

Statue: What's the matter?

Don Giovanni: Che gelo è questo mai?

Don Giovanni: It's freezing cold!

Statue: Pentiti, cangia vita, è l'ultimo momento!

Statue: Repent! Change your life! It's your last chance!

Don Giovanni tries to withdraw his hand.

Don Giovanni: No, no, ch'io non mi pento, vanne lontan da me!

Don Giovanni: No, no. I will not repent! Get away from me!

Statue: Pentiti, scellerato!

Don Giovanni: No, vecchio infatuato!

Statue: Pentiti!

Don Giovanni: No!

Statue: Pentiti!

Don Giovanni: No!

Statue: Sì!

Don Giovanni: No!

Statue: Sì!

Don Giovanni: No!

With a desperate effort, he wrests his hand away from the statue.

Statue: Sì! Sì!

Don Giovanni: No! No!

The Commandant's statue begins to move toward the door.
Roaring flames begin to surround Don Giovanni.

Statue: Ah! tempo più non v'è!

Don Giovanni: Da qual tremore insolito sento assalir gli spiriti! dond'escono quei vortici di foco pien d'orror?

A chorus of ghostly demon voices sounds from below.

7:40   **44** **Demon Voices:** Tutto a tue colpe è poco! vieni! c'è un mal peggior!

Don Giovanni: Chi l'anima mi lacera? Chi m'agita le viscere? Che strazio, ohimè, che smania! Che inferno, che terror!

Leporello: Che ceffo disperato! Che gesti da dannato! che gridi! che lamenti! come mi fa terror!

Demon Voices: Tutto a tue colpe è poco!

Don Giovanni: Chi l'anima mi lacera?

Leporello: Che ceffo disperato!

Demon Voices: Vieni! c'è un mal peggior!

Don Giovanni: Chi m'agita le viscere? che strazio, ohimè, che smania! Ah! che inferno! che terror!

Leporello: Che gesti da dannato! che gridi! che lamenti! Come mi fa terror!

Demon Voices: Vieni! vieni! vieni! c'è un mal peggior!

Don Giovanni: Ah!

Don Giovanni utters his final sound, is enveloped by flames, and sinks to hell.
Leporello echoes the Don's shout.

Leporello: Ah!

8:52   Recording fades.

Statue: Repent, villain!

Don Giovanni: No, you stupid old man!

Statue: Repent!

Don Giovanni: No!

Statue: Repent!

Don Giovanni: No!

Statue: Yes!

Don Giovanni: No!

Statue: Yes!

Don Giovanni: No!

Statue: Yes! Yes!

Don Giovanni: No! No!

Statue: Ah! There is no more time!

Don Giovanni: I feel my strength afflicted by really unusual trembling! Where are those horrible whirlpools of fire coming from?

Demon Voices: This is nothing compared to your crimes! Worse things await you!

Don Giovanni: Who rips my spirit? Who shakes my innards? What twisting, alas, what frenzy! What hell! What terror!

Leporello: What a terrible look on his face! What gestures of a damned soul! What shouts! What wailing! It terrifies me!

Demon Voices: All this is nothing compared to your crimes!

Don Giovanni: Who rips my spirit?

Leporello: What a terrible look on his face!

Demon Voices: Come! Worse things await you!

Don Giovanni: Who shakes my innards? What twisting, alas, what frenzy! Ah! What hell! What terror!

Leporello: What gestures of a damned soul! What shouts! What wailing! It terrifies me!

Demon Voices: Come! Worse things await you!

Don Giovanni: *(screaming)* Ah!

Leporello: Ah!

Following the immolation of Don Giovanni, the mood suddenly changes to something more lighthearted. Donna Anna, Donna Elvira, and Zerlina rush in, followed by Ottavio and Masetto. They find Leporello crawling about on the floor and demand to know what has happened. Leporello stammers out the story of what he just witnessed.

The music is again filled with wit and sparkle. Don Giovanni is already just a memory. In a brief duet, Donna Anna and Ottavio tell of their plans to marry after her year of mourning for her father is over. Donna Elvira pledges to end her days in a cloister. Zerlina and Masetto are anxious to be off so they can have dinner. And Leporello sets about finding himself a new master. As the six singers face the audience, they deliver the moral of the opera. The whole scene is so mischievous that one wonders whether Mozart was not really attempting to have the last laugh with the moralizing. The sextet sings:

> *Such is the end*
> *Of those who do evil.*
> *The death of the wicked*
> *Always matches their life.*

This last scene containing moralizing by the sextet has often been omitted from the opera. In the nineteenth century, it was thought out of place after the damnation of Don Giovanni. Mozart himself approved the deletion the second time it was staged.

Don Giovanni is escorted by demons into the inferno and is quickly forgotten.

C o d a

The music of Mozart's opera represents its eighteenth-century outlook in its good taste and controlled emotions. True, the librettos of his comic operas are sometimes spiced with double entendres, and the singers' emotions are exaggerated for comic effect, but the situations in his serious operas often contain strong emotions and drama. And the music is always handled with a restraint that contrasts nicely with any incongruities of text or action. Even in serious moments, he does not allow the music to become too overbearing or sentimental. There is about his operatic writing a light touch, an awareness that music can be worth knowing even when conceived of as entertainment.

Chamber Music

Until the Classical period, most instrumental music (except for keyboard) did not clearly indicate the size of the group for which it was written. As the orchestra became more standardized, composers began to specify the type of group for which they were writing. Apparently, they felt that music for an orchestra was not suitable for music created with a small group in mind, and vice versa. The music they created for small groups is known as *chamber music*.

A symphony orchestra concert is like a banquet; a chamber music performance is like a gourmet dinner with a few close friends.

Musicians to this day have continued to value chamber music, primarily because it permits a refinement and intimacy of expression that cannot be derived from a large musical organization. An orchestra has power and color; a string quartet provides a sense of involvement and clarity. One medium can be as musically satisfying as the other in the hands of skilled composers and performers.

CHAMBER MUSIC IN THE CLASSICAL PERIOD

Chamber music thrived in the Classical period, because the social setting encouraged its creation and performance. Most performances of music were still for private audiences of the rich and noble. When a host wished to provide after-dinner music for guests in his palatial home, he often thought of a chamber group.

Haydn's experience with chamber music indicates its use during the Classical period. As mentioned earlier, his patron, Prince Nicholas Esterházy, happened to enjoy playing the baryton. The instrument looks something like a cello, but has sloping shoulders and more strings that vibrate sympathetically. Haydn composed a great deal of music for his patron to play: 125 trios, 12 short divertimentos, and 2 duets. But he wrote much more chamber music than those involving the baryton.

The baryton is a very different instrument from the baritone horn. It is a member of the viol family.

THE NATURE OF CHAMBER MUSIC

The chief characteristic of chamber music is one player on each part. This definition refers to parts, not instruments. For instance, a string quartet consists of two violins, one viola, and one cello, but there are two *different* violin parts. So long as each has a different part, there could be three or more violins, and the work would still be considered chamber music.

Voices are not usually involved in chamber music, although early chamber works were influenced by vocal style. In fact, during the Renaissance madrigals could be either sung or played on string instruments. In the twentieth century, Igor Stravinsky, Arnold Schoenberg, and others have written for voices in chamber compositions. Since the Renaissance, however, and particularly during the Classical period, chamber music has consisted of instrumental music.

The players perform chamber music while looking at their music notation; only soloists play from memory. In chamber music the individual must be subordinate to the group, so memorizing is not called for. Furthermore, the undistinguished quality of the parts when providing harmony and the number of players involved make the memorized performance more susceptible to error.

The formal patterns found in chamber music in the Classical period are the same as those presented in earlier chapters in conjunction with the symphony and the concerto. Not only are the same forms used for individual movements, but the pattern of movements is also the same. The first movements of sonatas, string quartets, and other chamber works are in sonata form. The second movements have slow tempos and emphasize melody; often they are in a three-part form. The third movements of four-movement works are usually in the form of a minuet and trio. The fourth or last movements generally have a fast tempo and often are rondos. This arrangement of forms and movements tends to be true regardless of the particular combination of instruments used in a work.

LISTENING TO CHAMBER MUSIC

The methods for listening to chamber music are essentially the same as those for listening carefully and thoughtfully to music of any type. But because chamber music is performed by a small group, it lacks the tonal power and the lush, colorful sounds of a full orchestra or chorus. Listeners must therefore concentrate on what is happening in the music itself. The composer's musical ideas and treatment of them in a composition are the heart of chamber music.

> The appeal of chamber music lies in its refined and intimate musical qualities, not its sensuous sounds.

The fewer players there are, the easier it is to hear small errors in playing, so the performers must execute their parts with accuracy and unity. This feeling of oneness in musical performance is called *ensemble*. Chamber music is usually performed without a conductor, so the sensing of tempos, phrasing, and dynamics is the responsibility of each player.

> The word *ensemble* means "together" in French.

Although one person is acknowledged to be the leader, the cues and nods that start and stop the group are so subtle that the audience sees only by watching carefully. That is why the word *ensemble* refers not only to the sense of unified performance by the players, but also to the chamber music group itself.

> The person who plays the first violin part is usually considered the leader.

When a chamber music group is heard live in a home or small recital hall, something is added to the listeners' enjoyment. Perhaps the closeness of the performers provides a sense of involvement that makes listening to chamber music enjoyable. In any case, chamber music is best heard in a live performance in small recital halls or the living room of large homes.

Music for orchestra is generally far better known than chamber music, probably because more knowledge and attention are required for successful chamber music listening. Because there is a limited audience, few chamber groups can earn a living solely from performing. Today, chamber ensembles are found in residence at a number of universities.

THE SONATA

From the Classical period forward, the *sonata* became a sizable instrumental work in three or four movements. Classical sonatas are divided into two categories. The *ensemble sonata* is usually a composition for two instruments: piano and one other instrument. The *solo sonata* is for a single instrument, usually piano.

> A sonata frequently has one or more of its movements in sonata form. It's logical but confusing.

The two parts are considered to be of equal importance in the ensemble sonata. In no sense is the piano accompanying the other instrument. As a matter of fact, some of the time the piano part contains a more important musical idea, while the other instrument plays accompanying material. Because the presence of the piano is assumed, the sonata is called by the name of the other instrument. So a violin sonata is for violin and piano.

Unlike other ensemble works, a solo sonata is usually played from memory. Although a few solo sonatas have been written for violin or other instruments, the solo sonata is most associated with the piano.

The piano sonata is presented in chapter 24.

THE STRING QUARTET

With its instrumentation of two violins, a viola, and a cello, the *string quartet* is probably the most significant chamber ensemble. Early in the eighteenth century, compositions called *divertimentos* were common. As the name implies, they were diversionary, innocuous little pieces. They could be played by either a quartet or a string orchestra. Haydn took the divertimento, deleted one of its two minuets, and gave it more musical substance. He called these new works *quartets* rather than divertimentos. The change did not occur quickly; it was stretched out over much of Haydn's adult life.

OTHER TYPES OF CHAMBER MUSIC GROUPS

Almost every conceivable combination of instruments has had chamber music written for it, but certain types of chamber groups are more common, including the sonata and the string quartet. Another likely string group is the *string quintet* (two violins, two violas, and one cello). The *woodwind quintet* (flute, oboe, clarinet, French horn, and bassoon) was not common in Haydn's time, but it has become a standard chamber ensemble in this century. Brass ensembles have the least standardized instrumentation. Perhaps the *brass quintet* (two trumpets, a French horn, a trombone, and a tuba) has most frequently drawn the attention of composers.

It is not unusual to find one nonstring instrument added to a string quartet. For example, Mozart's work for clarinet and string quartet has the title Clarinet Quintet in A Major, although only one clarinet is present. If a piano plus a string quartet is called for, the work is a piano quintet. Apparently, the presence of strings is taken for granted in such ensembles, so the added instrument is cited in the name of the group.

MOZART'S CLARINET QUINTET

The Clarinet Quintet in A Major, K. 581, is a relatively late work by Mozart, written after his Symphony No. 40. It is in the best polished style of the eighteenth century. The form is clearly delineated, the instrumental parts are well balanced, and everything is neat and enjoyable.

First movement   The first movement is in sonata form. Its first theme consists of a simple, songlike portion played by the four string instruments. The clarinet follows playing a florid passage containing many rapidly moving notes.

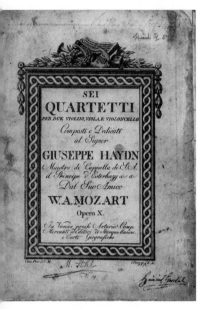

The cover for six string quartets by Haydn that he dedicated to his "friend W. A. Mozart." The language here is Italian, not the native German of Haydn and Mozart.

A *piano trio* is for a piano plus a violin and a cello. Many composers have written music for this chamber ensemble.

The Clarinet Quintet by Mozart is for clarinet in A, not B-flat, the key of most clarinets today. There is a subtle difference in timbre between the two clarinets, and this quintet is a bit easier for the A clarinet because it is in the key of A major. This means that the clarinet is looking at notes in C major, but, of course, sounding pitches a third lower.

The development begins quietly with the first theme presented in a different key. Other figures from the exposition are also heard.

The recapitulation is very similar to the exposition, except for small changes.

The movement closes, as did the exposition, with a statement of the opening theme.

Second movement   In the second movement, the clarinet plays a beautiful melody that could easily be an aria in a Mozart opera. The *B* portion of the movement contains contrasting melodic material played by the violin, with the clarinet adding decorative melodic comments from time to time, which are later taken up by the violin. The opening melody returns, again played by the clarinet.

Third movement   The third movement is an elegant-sounding minuet and trio. This minuet is unusual because it has two trios, one for the strings and a second one giving the clarinet a chance to show off its capabilities at playing notes over a wide range along with its varied timbre.

Wide changes of pitch are quite easy on the clarinet because of its register key, which is operated by the player's left thumb.

Fourth movement   The fourth movement is both a form and a musical process: *theme and variations.* The basic idea of theme and variations is simple: Take a melody and cast it in different settings. The process is something like taking a number of pictures of a house, but each time under different conditions and from different angles. One picture might be at daybreak, another during a rainstorm, another from ground level, another from a ladder at a 45-degree angle, and so on.

The idea is, of course, best understood by listening carefully to an example by a master composer like Mozart.

The meter signature indicates that the half note (♩) gets the beat. Therefore, the music moves more quickly than it appears to in the notation.

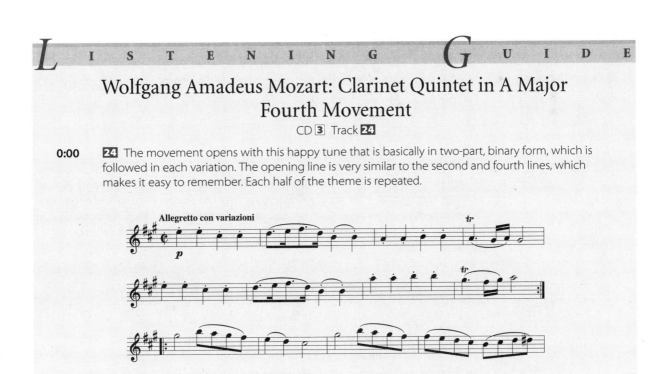

Wolfgang Amadeus Mozart: Clarinet Quintet in A Major
Fourth Movement
CD 3 Track 24

0:00   **24** The movement opens with this happy tune that is basically in two-part, binary form, which is followed in each variation. The opening line is very similar to the second and fourth lines, which makes it easy to remember. Each half of the theme is repeated.

Allegretto con variazioni

1:00   **25** The first variation begins. It presents some of the melody played by the violin, but it gives the clarinet a freewheeling countermelody.

1:58   **26** The second variation begins. In it the violin plays an ornamented version of the melody, while the violins play contrasting melodic material.

3:03   **27** The third variation has a different mood from the previous variations partly because the music changes to a minor key as the viola "sobs" out the melody. The second half of the variation contains many chromatic notes.

4:16   **28** The fourth variation begins as the music returns to a major key. The clarinet and then the violin play many rapidly moving notes.

5:15   A link to the next variation is played.

5:35   **29** A very slow-moving variation begins, featuring the same figure played by the violins in the second variation. The harmony of the theme is preserved, but the original melody is only implied.

8:40   The theme returns as the coda begins while the tempo becomes much quicker.

9:35   The movement ends after fragments from the first theme are played, followed by two short chords.

The difference between varying and developing a theme can be made clearer by thinking about what Mozart did in developing themes in his Symphony No. 40 and contrasting that with what he did in varying the theme in his clarinet quintet. *Development* involves fragmenting and remolding a theme. *Variation* consists of placing the theme in a new setting or giving it a new harmonic, rhythmic, or melodic costume.

Coda

In one sense, opera and chamber music represent the extremes on the continuum running from operatic to symphonic to chamber music. Both Mozart and Haydn, who were successful in each of these areas, display in their music a similar sense of taste and proportion and the high regard for musical craftsmanship that permeated the Classical period.

Beethoven and the Symphony

23

Our discussion of the symphony is presented in
conjunction with one of the biggest names in all of art music:
Ludwig van Beethoven. He did not develop the genre,
but he certainly changed it in a massive way.

With Beethoven the symphony became the most important and
largest musical genre during his lifetime and for nearly a hundred
years afterward. Beethoven composed just nine symphonies, and
most of them take about forty minutes or more to perform. Haydn
wrote more than a hundred symphonies and Mozart about fifty,
some as short as fifteen minutes. And number and length were
not the only differences, as this chapter explores.

THE SYMPHONY

A *symphony* is a large work composed for an orchestra that is divided into movements,
usually four. The four movements present a contrast of tempo and mood, which is
discussed here through Beethoven's Symphony No. 5.

BEETHOVEN'S SYMPHONY NO. 5

Beethoven composed his Symphony No. 5 in C Minor, Op. 67, between 1804 and
1808, when it received its premiere performance. Less than twenty years passed
between when Mozart composed his Symphony No. 40 and Beethoven composed
his Symphony No. 5. But what huge changes Beethoven wrought in his symphony!
They are found not so much in the technical features of the music, although he did
make a number of modifications, as in the overall impact of the music.

The difference might best be described by the word *more*. Mozart and Haydn
developed themes and had some contrast, but Beethoven presents much more
development and more contrast of mood and character. In some of Beethoven's music,
including his Fifth Symphony, he seems to want to burst the limits of musical sound.
Musical ideas are worked and reworked and reworked again. Some chords are almost
hammered into the listeners' ears, and at other times a quiet interlude is suddenly
interrupted with a burst of sound.

Beethoven also increased
the size of the orchestra,
including the addition of
trombones and the piccolo.

First Movement

This movement is a prime example of how Beethoven took what appears to be an
ordinary theme and built something monumental out of it. It begins with a four-
note motive. These four notes are repeated again and again, and they become the
basis for the main theme:

There have been several attempts to explain the origin of this motive.
One is that it is Fate knocking at the door; another claims that the three
dots and a dash stand for the letter *V* in Morse code. Neither of these
theories has been substantiated. The latter is especially doubtful because
Morse code was developed years after the writing of the symphony!

And what happens to that theme? It is treated as a germinal idea. For example, right after the first theme is presented, it is developed somewhat in the transition leading to the second theme:

Notice the extensive use of sequence in this example.

Most of the development section is an outgrowth of the original theme. Beethoven does such things as fill in the interval of the original motive:

Sometimes to the filled-in interval he adds the inversion—the upside-down version—of the motive:

He reiterates a few simple musical ideas based on the theme:

He also fragments themes. The notes circled in the second example in the Listening Guide are the two middle pitches from the transition played by the French horn. The two pitches are echoed between the woodwinds and the strings, and then the segment is fragmented further until just one note is echoed:

The first two-note fragments have boxes around them in the example.

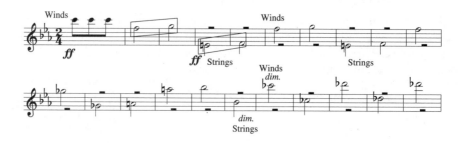

There are also long, gradual crescendos and abrupt changes from loud to soft.

The recapitulation is followed by an extended coda. In fact, the coda in Beethoven's symphonies is almost as important as the other three sections of sonata form. He seemed to regard it as a second development section. A synthesis of the themes of the coda can be seen in this example:

The first theme is circled here.

The pitches of the first theme and the rhythm pattern of the transition are combined. The two-pitch fragment emphasized in the development appears again, this time in a downward sequence.

The outline of the first movement is presented in the following Listening Guide.

The Listening Guide is not an easy one to follow. Events occur rapidly and many melodic ideas are repeated. Several hearings using it are suggested.

L I S T E N I N G   G U I D E

Ludwig van Beethoven: Symphony No. 5 in C Minor
First Movement

CD 2 Track 1

Sonata Form

Exposition

0:00   **1** The first theme (form *A* of the theme) is played loudly by the orchestra, with the fourth note held by the violins. (Repeats at 1:23. **3**)

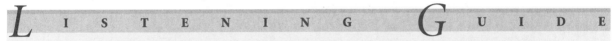

0:06   The first theme is played quietly and repeatedly by the strings; the theme leads to a note held by the strings. (Repeats at 1:34.)

0:19   The first theme is played loudly by the orchestra, and the fourth note is held again. (Repeats at 1:47.)

0:21   A transition begins with repeated soundings of the first theme. The music grows in loudness and rises in general pitch level. (Repeats at 1:49.)

0:44   The French horn sets the stage for the second theme with a vigorous short solo based on the first theme (form *B* of the theme). (Repeats at 2:12.)

0:46   **2** The second theme, which is in a major key, is played softly by the violins and is followed by other instruments. The first theme can be heard very softly every four measures in inversion in the cellos and basses. (Repeats at 2:15.)

| 1:07 | The codetta begins as the violins take up chord outlines in a pattern from the first theme; the music leads to the motive sounded loudly by the orchestra. (Repeats at 2:34.) |
| 1:18 | A version of the first theme reappears. (Repeats at 2:45.) |

Development

2:55	**4** The first theme is played loudly by the French horns, then the strings. The first theme, sometimes inverted, is passed softly among sections of the orchestra while the music slowly grows louder.
3:23	The winds play full-sounding chords. This is followed by repeated notes and the first theme played by the strings, which in turn are followed by silences.
3:31	The strings play the *B* form of the first theme as fragments of the first theme are passed among the woodwinds.
3:41	The two-note motive derived from the *B* form of the first theme predominates. Later it is reduced to only one note that is exchanged between the winds and strings.
4:03	Loud, vigorous appearances of the *B* form of the theme are played. These are contrasted with softly played single notes.
4:12	A sudden, loud appearance of the first theme, form *A*, is played.

Recapitulation

4:17	**5** The first theme is played loudly by the orchestra, and the fourth note of the motive is held.
4:37	The oboe plays a short cadenza.
4:51	A transition begins that grows out of the first theme. The music gradually increases in loudness and rises in pitch.
5:12	The French horns play the *B* form of the first theme.
5:15	The second theme, this time in minor, is played softly by the violins. A transition follows based on a portion of the second theme, and again the first theme is played every so often by the low strings in inversion.

Coda

5:41	**6** The coda begins as smooth phrases of the second theme. The violins soon take up chord outlines in the pattern of the first theme.
5:59	The rhythm pattern of the first theme is alternated between the winds and strings. Many notes are repeated and followed by rests.
6:14	The *B* form of the first theme is played by the low strings. The two-note motive is expanded and extended.
6:30	The four-note melodic figure derived from the second theme is played in ascending sequence by the violins, sometimes in inversion.
6:40	The woodwinds and strings alternate playing the four-note idea, which is fragmented to two notes as the music progresses.
7:06	The first theme's rhythm pattern is played loudly by the orchestra. Twice this leads up to held notes.
7:15	The first theme is played quietly, but this is followed by a sudden loud version of it.
7:29	The movement closes with a series of brusque chords.

Second Movement

The second movements of almost all symphonies created in the eighteenth and nineteenth centuries are slow and melodic in character. In addition to the contrast in character, second movements also differ in their home key. If the symphony is in a major key, the tonic of the second movement is usually in the major key four notes higher. For example, a symphony in G major would have a second movement in C major, a key that has one less sharp than G. If the key is in minor, the second movement is in the major key three steps higher. In the case of Beethoven's Symphony No. 5 in C Minor, the second movement is in E-flat major. Its signature is the same as the signature of C minor. The main point to remember is that the second movement is in a *different* key from the rest of the symphony.

Keys are considered closely related if their key signatures are no more than one sharp or flat different.

Several forms can be found in second movements of symphonies. The most common is the large three-part form, *A B A*. Theme and variations are also encountered some of the time, and even sonata form with a shortened development section is used.

The second movement of Beethoven's Fifth Symphony reveals his ability to write beautiful melodies. He is so often thought of in terms of the brusque, forceful qualities in some of his music that it is easy to forget he could write lovely lyric melodies as well.

The second movement of the Fifth Symphony is a theme and variations built on two melodic ideas. The first one contains three shorter melodic sections. During the course of the second movement, these ideas are varied by changing the melody and ornamenting it, and by altering the harmony, rhythm, dynamics, tempo, and type of accompaniment.

The eighth note (♪) receives the beat in 3/8 meter. Therefore, the music moves much more slowly than it looks like it should.

LISTENING GUIDE

Beethoven: Symphony No. 5 in C Minor
Second Movement
CD **3** Track **30**

Themes

0:00 **30** The violas and cellos open with the first part of the first theme.

0:24 The woodwinds continue with the second part of the first theme.

0:36 The violins play the third part of the first theme.

0:53 The violins and woodwinds play the second theme.

dolce

1:14 The brasses play the second theme in an expansive style.

1:31 The music becomes quiet and mysterious.

Variation 1

1:58 **31** The strings play the middle part of the first theme.

2:31 The strings play the third part of the first theme.

2:49 The woodwinds and violins play the second theme.

3:10 The brasses play the second theme in an expansive manner.

3:24 The music again becomes quiet and mysterious.

Variation 2

3:52 **32** The upper strings play rapidly moving notes over the first theme.

4:48 Running scale passages lead to a held note.

5:05 The woodwinds play fragments from the first part of the first theme.

5:50 The full orchestra plays the second theme in an expansive style.

6:36 The woodwinds play the first part of the first theme in short notes and in minor.

Variation 3

7:18 **33** The violins play the first part of the first theme loudly.

7:43 The woodwinds play the second part of the first theme.

7:53 The strings play the third part of the first theme.

Coda

8:08 **34** The tempo picks up as the bassoons play the beginning of the first theme.

8:24 The violins play fragments of the second theme.

8:35 The woodwinds play the second part of the first theme.

8:48 The strings play the third part of the first theme.

9:57 The movement concludes with the same rhythm with which it began.

Third Movement

The third movement of the symphonies of Haydn and Mozart was a stylized dance—the minuet. With its graceful 3/4 meter, it provided a nice contrast to the lyrical, melodious second movement. Even the three-part form of the minuet was followed, with the middle section being called the *trio*. This movement was in the home key of the symphony.

The trio got its name from the fact that originally it was written for two instruments plus continuo.

Beethoven made a couple of important changes in the minuet of his predecessors:

◆ He called for a faster tempo, which gave the movement a more lively, energetic, jovial character. No longer was 3/4 felt in three beats per measure; rather, the music is felt in one strong beat per measure.

◆ He named the movement "Scherzo," a word that means "joke" in Italian. Accordingly, the movement did not just fulfill a formal pattern; it could—and often did—contain surprises for its listeners.

The main theme of the third movement is one that several other composers of the time had also used. In fact, the theme had acquired a name—the "Mannheim rocket." The *Mannheim* part of the name comes from the southern German city that figured prominently in the development of the symphony, and the *rocket* probably came from the fact that it is the ascending notes of a chord.

The trio of the movement is interesting in that it starts out sounding like a lively fugue, but Beethoven does not follow through with a full-blown fugue. In musical terms, he wrote a *fugato*—a fuguelike passage.

Another feature of the movement is its attachment to the fourth movement. A movement normally comes to an end, and a few moments of silence are observed before the next movement begins. Beethoven and composers who followed sometimes connected two movements together.

This was not the first time Beethoven had composed a scherzo for a symphony. The first one appears in his Third Symphony.

L I S T E N I N G   G U I D E

Beethoven: Symphony No. 5 in C Minor
Third Movement
CD 3 Track 35

Scherzo

0:00   35   The low strings play the theme soft and low. The music has an "eerie" character.

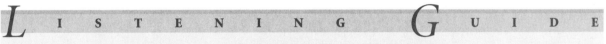

0:19   The character of music changes dramatically when the French horns enter playing the second theme in a raucous manner.

0:40   The low strings return playing softly the "Mannheim rocket" theme.

1:03   After a long crescendo, the orchestra plays the second theme loudly.

1:52   After the second theme is played loudly again, the scherzo ends softly.

Trio

1:58   36   The key changes to major. The cellos and basses present a dancelike theme in imitation. Soon the violas and bassoons enter, then the second violins, and finally the first violins.

2:13   The imitative section is repeated.

2:30   A short link leads to a repeat of the imitative music played by the strings.

2:58   The short link is heard and the imitation continued, but it is extended as it leads back the opening theme of the movement.

Scherzo

3:29   **37** The cellos and basses almost sneak back in, playing the first theme of the scherzo.

3:40   The first theme is repeated by the strings playing pizzicato (plucking).

3:50   The second theme is played very softly.

Bridge to the Fourth Movement

4:46   **38** A long note is held very quietly by the strings as the timpani quietly beat out a slow, steady stream of notes.

4:59   The violins begin playing a three-note pattern that is repeated many times as the music grows louder. A long crescendo leads without a break to the fourth movement.

Fourth Movement

The fourth movements of Classical symphonies are lively and filled with happy melodies. Apparently, the hope was to have the listeners leave feeling good. Often fourth movements are rondos. They were almost always in the home key of the symphony.

But Beethoven seems to have been more interested in leaving a serious but positive impression on his audiences. His optimism had deeper roots than just pleasant, cheery music.

The fourth movement of Beethoven's Fifth Symphony is in sonata form. A rondo would not have accommodated the monumental concept of this movement, which is the longest of the symphony. The themes, especially the first one, contribute to the massive quality of the movement.

An unusual feature of this fourth movement is the brief appearance of a theme from the third movement. The appearances of themes from other movements would become more common later in the nineteenth century, but it was very rare at the time the Fifth Symphony was composed.

L I S T E N I N G   G U I D E

Beethoven: Symphony No. 5 in C Minor
Fourth Movement
CD **3** Track **39**

Exposition

0:00   **39** The orchestra plays the first theme forcefully.

0:33   The French horns play a transitional theme.

0:59   The strings play the second theme.

1:25   The orchestra plays a theme for the codetta.

Development

2:00   **40** The strings play a loud tremolo (trembling sound with the bow on the string).

2:09   A four-note motive from the second theme is introduced. It becomes more prominent later in the development as the brasses play it.

2:22   The string basses play a line of counterpoint as the fragment of the second theme continues.

3:00   The music reaches a climactic moment that is followed by a pause.

3:38   A short portion of the theme from the scherzo suddenly appears.

Recapitulation

4:09   **41** The orchestra plays the first theme vigorously.

4:42   The French horns play the transition theme.

5:13   The strings play the second theme.

5:39   The woodwind plays the theme for the codetta.

Coda

6:09   **42** The violins play the second theme.

6:40   The woodwinds and French horns continue with the transitional theme.

7:23   The tempo suddenly becomes very fast and many repeated notes are heard.

7:48   The brasses play the first theme, which is now twice as fast as it was originally.

8:26   The movement concludes with a series of V-I cadences and several successive soundings of the final chord.

Coda

*Art music and the symphony were never the same after Beethoven.
Now they had become something to be taken seriously. No longer
was music just a pleasure to hear and something to be enjoyed.
Music had moved to a deeper and more profound level.*

Beethoven and the Piano

The change from the classical style of Mozart and Haydn to the romantic style of the nineteenth century took place over a period of years. Several composers made the transition from one style to the next, but Beethoven is undoubtedly the name most associated with it. This chapter examines the changes that he brought about in piano music.

THE PIANO

In Mozart's time, only one generation before Beethoven, the piano was essentially a drawing-room instrument. Its tone was light and delicate, and composers wrote for it accordingly. During Beethoven's lifetime many improvements were made in the piano, probably the most important of which was the addition of metal braces to the frame across which the strings were strung. These braces permitted heavier strings, because the frame could now withstand the greater tension required to bring such strings up to pitch. In turn, the greater tension and heavier strings gave the piano more power. The combination of Beethoven's forceful music and a more powerful instrument inevitably enabled the piano to gain a prominent place in the concert hall.

The piano of today has changed only slightly since the beginning of the nineteenth century. The key action has been made a bit more responsive, and a pedal has been added to permit certain sustaining effects, but these improvements are minor.

The type of piano construction affects the musical results. The grand piano is superior to the upright in structural design. In order to fit inside the case of an upright, the low strings have to be shortened and tuned with less tension. So the upright or spinet lacks the volume and consistency of tone found in the grand piano. The smaller the instrument, the more serious the loss of tone quality. Concert music such as a Beethoven sonata understandably is shown off to best advantage when performed on a high-quality grand piano.

The piano had an especially important role in the days before recordings and radio, because it was the chief means of hearing instrumental music. You either heard a work in a live performance, or you didn't hear it at all. This included orchestral, chamber, *and* piano music. For this reason, publishers usually published piano versions of well-liked orchestral works.

Later the entire frame was made of cast iron, which is an absolutely rigid material.

The piano was also the chief means of music in the home.

BEETHOVEN'S PIANO SONATA, OP. 53 ("WALDSTEIN")

Beethoven's instrument was the piano, and his compositions for the instrument constitute some of his greatest contributions to music. He composed thirty-two solo piano sonatas, and often they are known by their number, as well as their key or nickname. In 1804 he wrote a piano sonata dedicated to Count Ferdinand von Waldstein, a friend and benefactor. This sonata, No. 21, reveals many elements of Beethoven's musical style, especially for the piano.

The numbers of the thirty-two sonatas are in the order in which they were published.

First Movement

The first movement is typically in sonata form, as can be seen in the Listening Guide. But there is much more to the movement than its form. To begin with, the first theme is not like anyone's before him (and possibly since). It begins with a soft thumping chord that is repeated thirteen times before any note is changed! And when the pattern does end, it leads into two short, motivelike figures (circled in the example).

The same idea is repeated immediately, but this time the chords are "broken" so that pitches are sounded one after another instead of simultaneously.

Several points merit comment about the first theme:

♦ It is not melodious. Its musical value lies in its potential for development.

♦ It does not contain notes of much length. Rather, it relies on the sounding of many tones to maintain the intensity that Beethoven wanted here.

♦ It starts softly, and works up to—or, rather, erupts into—the short melodic figures. This sense of eruption is typical of Beethoven's music.

♦ It is highly suitable for the piano, but would fail as a vocal melody.

A sense of drama is one of the characteristics of the Romantic style of the nineteenth century.

The transition to the second theme illustrates another of Beethoven's techniques when writing for piano: the use of broken chord patterns. He likes to have the patterns and scales come toward or move away from each other. The simultaneous contrast of pitch direction is called *contrary motion:*

The second theme is in the remote key of E major. The practice of Classical composers was to write the second theme in the key that centered five notes above the original key center. Beethoven is more harmonically daring and moves to the key *three* notes higher. The traditional adherence to key schemes was breaking down even by the early 1800s.

Following the second theme, the *triplets* (three notes to the beat) take over and become the main thought leading to the codetta:

In a work such as this sonata, the pianist plays an enormous number of notes.

The coda is greatly expanded. Instead of stopping after the closing theme, the first theme starts up again. Soon its two motives are treated to another development. This second development is much like the first, with the addition of rapidly moving scale passages.

LISTENING GUIDE

Ludwig van Beethoven: "Waldstein" Sonata No. 21, Op. 53
First Movement
CD 4 Track 1

Exposition

0:00   **1** The movement begins immediately with the first theme. (Repeats at 2:24.)

0:22   The first theme is repeated with a different accompanying pattern. (Repeats at 2:46.)

0:56   **2** The second theme is played, and then repeated with some changes. (Repeats at 3:20.)

1:25   Triplets take over and are exchanged between right and left hands. Then sixteenth notes take over. (Repeats at 3:48.)

2:01   The codetta, complete with its own theme, begins. (Repeats at 4:25.)

Development

4:56   **3** The development begins. Figures from the first theme are heard, often with many changes of key.

5:34   The triplet figure is heard frequently.

6:22   The music becomes quiet, but soon it builds slowly back to the recapitulation.

Recapitulation

6:45   **4** The first theme returns in the recapitulation.

7:15   A short interlude is inserted before the first theme is repeated.

7:20   The first theme is repeated with a different accompanying pattern.

7:54   The second theme is played.

8:02   The second theme is repeated in minor, and then again in major.

Coda

9:00	**5**	The coda begins.
9:29		The first theme is played again.
10:19		Several pauses follow held chords.
10:28		The second theme is played again. Several pauses follow, and the music becomes softer.
10:59		The first theme is played vigorously.
11:11		The movement ends after several short, abrupt chords.

Second Movement

The second movement is hardly a movement at all. Instead, it is a short section that Beethoven labeled "Introduzione." It sounds like an introspective introduction to the third movement.

There is an unconfirmed story that Beethoven wrote a lengthy second movement but was persuaded by a friend to exchange it for the present short version.

Third Movement

The third movement is a rondo—but what a rondo! Unlike the rondo in Haydn's Concerto for Trumpet in E-flat, with its short, happy melodies and four-minute length, this rondo has those monumental qualities that we observed in Beethoven's Fifth Symphony. As a result it is twice as long as Haydn's rondo. Its theme is presented several times, as happens in rondos, but several times it is treated like a theme in a symphony as it appears three times in a row, each time more magnificent than before.

APPRECIATING BEETHOVEN'S MUSIC

The "Waldstein" sonata and the Fifth Symphony have provided a good idea of what Beethoven's music is like. What is it about his music that causes people to continue to listen to it today? What about it has contributed to continuing interest in the man himself? Among the many potential reasons, four stand out:

♦ *Contrast.* Beethoven's music is filled with dramatic contrasts. His themes often seem to be paired by opposites that can be thought of as male/female, rough/smooth, loud/soft, brusque/tender, and so on. A placid passage can be suddenly broken as a *sforzando* chord is sounded, or a raging section can abruptly cease and change to a gentle melody.

♦ *Motive development.* Beethoven's music is a showcase of developing musical ideas, especially short simple ones. A theme becomes a seed that grows and takes many shapes, and it is fascinating to follow that musical process.

♦ *Sense of drive.* Beethoven's music contains a wonderful drive or what has been described as "inevitability." This quality is difficult to put into words, but his music seems always to be heading toward its final destination. Even though it has many changes and stops, the sense of inevitability is still there. Listeners sense that though the music is quiet at a particular moment, that situation will not last. The musical journey will resume and continue on to its inevitable conclusion.

Ludwig van Beethoven

Ludwig van Beethoven ("*Bay*-toe-ven", 1770–1827) was born in Bonn, Germany. His father was an alcoholic musician who hoped that young Ludwig would be a prodigy like Mozart and bring in lots of money. Although talented, young Beethoven never became the prodigy his father hoped for. At the age of twenty-two, he set off for Vienna, which was to be his home for the remainder of his life.

Beethoven had little formal schooling. He studied composition with several teachers, including a few lessons with Haydn, and made a name for himself as a pianist. He was able to win the support and admiration of the aristocracy, and in ten years established himself as a composer and performer. Although trained in the formal style of the Classical period, other events left a lasting impression on Beethoven. One was the revolutionary spirit that was awakening in Europe, which erupted in the French Revolution in 1789.

> Beethoven originally dedicated his Symphony No. 3 to Napoleon. He tore up the dedication, however, after Napoleon had himself declared emperor, and wrote a new dedication: "To the memory of a great man."

Then there was Beethoven's own personality. Were he alive today, he would probably identify himself with humanitarian causes and social protest groups. For example, as early as 1792 he had thought of setting German dramatist-poet Friedrich von Schiller's "Ode to Joy" to music. The ethical ideals of the universal human race and its basis in the love of a heavenly Father expressed in the poem appealed to Beethoven. Schiller's "Ode to Joy" became the text for the last movement

> Beethoven's high ideals did not carry over to his dealings with publishers. He was sometimes unscrupulous with them.

of Beethoven's Ninth Symphony. He was probably the first composer in history to be considered a "personality." His mature works sound like no one else's music.

Beethoven's personality was also affected by a gradual loss of hearing that eventually led to complete deafness. The condition was evident by the time he was twenty-eight, and it caused him to lose contact with others and to withdraw into himself. His final compositions were products of this time in his life, and they tend to be more personal, meditative, and abstract.

How was it possible for Beethoven to write entire symphonies when he was completely deaf? The process can be understood if you think about your own experience. You can recall melodies and the sounds of people's voices in your memory, even though you aren't actually hearing them. Trained musicians can think out a large amount of music in their minds. And Beethoven was clearly a well-trained musician with outstanding abilities!

There is a second reason for his ability to compose while deaf. It was his custom to write down themes in a sketchbook. Then he would work over these themes, revising and rewriting them, and trying them out to determine their suitability for the piece he had in mind. This process went on over a period of years, so the themes for many of his later compositions had actually been worked out when he was still able to hear fairly well.

Best-Known Works
Chamber music:
- String Quartets Nos. 7 and 14
Choral:
- *Missa solemnis*
Orchestra:
- Piano Concertos Nos. 3, 4, and 5 ("Emperor")
- Violin Concerto
- *Egmont Overture*
- *Overture to Leonore No. 3*
- Symphonies Nos. 3 ("Eroica"), 5, 6 ("Pastoral"), 7, 8, and 9 ("Choral")
Opera:
- *Fidelio*
Piano:
- Sonatas Nos. 8 ("Pathétique"), 14 ("Moonlight"), 21 ("Waldstein"), and 23 ("Appassionata")

Beethoven was not a "natural" composer like Mozart. He poured much effort into each measure he wrote, as is evident from the manuscript on the facing page. As someone once said, his manuscripts look "like a bloody record of a tremendous inner battle."

Beethoven's death from jaundice and cholera occurred during a thunderstorm, a coincidence that seems appropriate to the man and his life.

One of Beethoven's ear trumpets, an early type of hearing aid. The mechanist J. N. Mälzel, inventor of the metronome, made a variety of ear trumpets for the increasingly deaf composer.

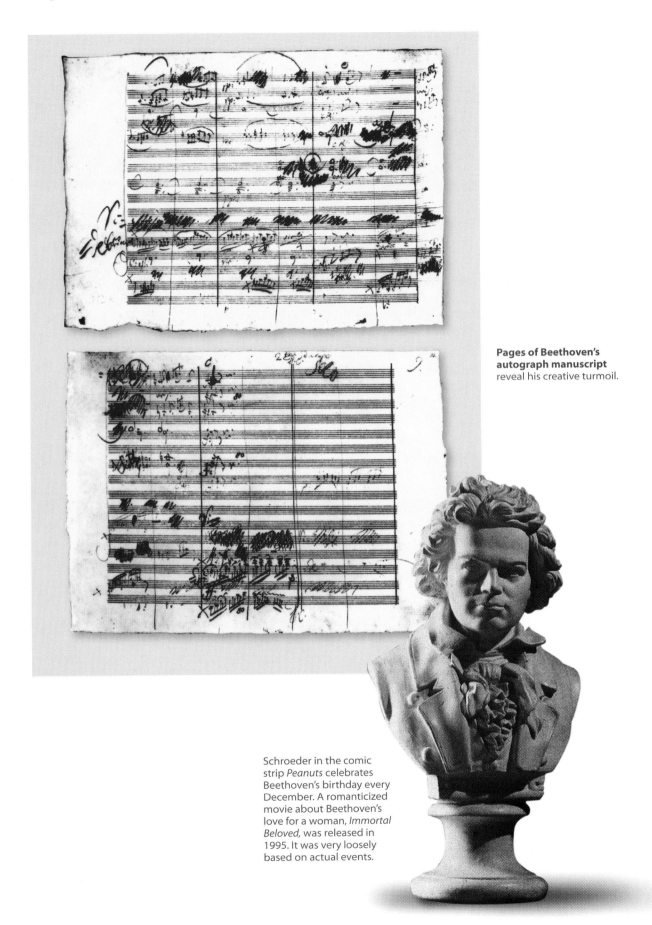

Pages of Beethoven's autograph manuscript reveal his creative turmoil.

Schroeder in the comic strip *Peanuts* celebrates Beethoven's birthday every December. A romanticized movie about Beethoven's love for a woman, *Immortal Beloved,* was released in 1995. It was very loosely based on actual events.

♦ *Personality.* Beethoven's music has a personality all its own. His mature works don't sound like those of Mozart, Haydn, or any other composer. A person does not need to be familiar with a lot of concert music to sense that there is something unique about Beethoven's music. It presents listeners with dramatic contrasts, a fiery spirit, huge amounts of thematic development, and an inner sense of musical logic.

OTHER MUSIC BY BEETHOVEN

Piano and symphonic music were not the only types Beethoven composed that merit attention.

The first three *Leonore* overtures were Beethoven's unsuccessful attempts to write an overture that would not overwhelm *Fidelio.* He finally settled for the fourth overture, which he titled *Fidelio.*

Overtures   Traditionally, overtures were written to be played before the curtain went up on an opera or, especially in Beethoven's day, a play. Beethoven composed a number of such works that have survived long after the original play. His overtures include *Egmont, Prometheus, Coriolan, Leonore No. 1, Leonore No. 2, Leonore No. 3,* and *Fidelio.*

Chamber music   Beethoven composed much excellent chamber music. The sixteen string quartets he wrote are among the finest ever created for that ensemble. In addition to his thirty-two piano sonatas, he composed ten violin sonatas and six cello sonatas. His ten piano trios are among that ensemble's premier works.

Vocal music   Beethoven was not as at ease with vocal music as he was with instrumental. He composed only one opera, *Fidelio,* and he compared its writing to bearing a child. He also composed some songs and religious music. His *Missa Solemnis* is a monumental work. His last symphony, No. 9, includes soloists and a choral group in its fourth movement, singing Schiller's "Ode to Joy."

Concertos   All five of Beethoven's piano concertos are among the most often performed works for that instrument. His violin concerto holds a similar position in the violin repertoire.

C o d a

If a person of Beethoven's complexity can be summarized at all, it might be said that he lived at a favorable moment in history. He inherited the objective, logical style of the Classical period, but his personality and the emerging revolutionary spirit of the times provided him with strong Romantic inclinations. Beethoven stands in the musical world with one foot firmly planted in Classicism and the other in Romanticism, bringing together the best of both artistic perspectives.

Part V

Romantic Music

25 Romance and Romanticism

To most people, the word *romantic* refers to the
emotion of love. To scholars, however, it means much more.
It comes from *romance,* which originally referred to a medieval
poem written in one of the Romance languages (those that
developed from Latin) and dealing with a heroic person or event.
Later the word took on the connotation of something far away
and strange or something imaginative and full of wonder.
Yes, it also includes the idea of love—romantic love.

Romanticism came of age during the nineteenth century. It began in some of the music of Beethoven and Schubert, and it continued into the early years of the twentieth century. In fact, elements of romanticism are still encountered in some music being written today. The Romantic outlook affected every type of music and it brought some kinds of music to their high point of development.

CHARACTERISTICS OF ROMANTICISM

Romanticism was an artistic viewpoint that also predominated in dance, theater, the visual arts, and music throughout the nineteenth century. What were the features of this outlook?

The love of mystery and the unknown is evident in the song "The Erl King," discussed in chapter 27.

♦ Romanticists were fascinated by the unknown and stood in awe of the world. They were impressed by the mystery, not the clarity, of the world and its inhabitants. At times, they were almost mystic. They seemed especially fascinated by the mystery and power of evil.

♦ Romanticists also tended to rely on emotion and imagination rather than rational intellect, which had been central to the Classical outlook. Feelings replaced reason. Truth became what a person *felt* to be true, so it was wrong to deny one's feelings. Poet John Keats wrote in one of his letters: "I am certain of nothing but the holiness of the heart's affections, and the truth of the imagination. What the imagination seizes as beauty must be truth." Inevitably, Romanticism grew to distrust reason and science. To quote Keats again, this time from his poem "Lamia":

During Keats's lifetime the word *philosophy* was a synonym for *science.*

> *Do not all charms fly*
> *At the mere touch of cold philosophy?*

♦ Romanticists were fascinated by the long ago and far away. During the Classical era, intellectuals had thought of medieval times as the "Dark Ages"; the Romanticists considered them heroic. Literature is filled with examples of this attitude, including Alfred, Lord Tennyson's *Idylls of the King,* John Keats's "Eve of St. Agnes," Samuel Taylor Coleridge's "Christabel," and Sir Walter Scott's *Ivanhoe.*

♦ Not only were the Romanticists impressed by the unknown forces of the world, they also reveled in the struggle against those forces. In Coleridge's poem "The Rhyme of the Ancient Mariner," the sailor is "alone on a wide, wide sea."

Rococo, Classical, and Romantic Art

François Boucher's Venus and Cupid *is a good example of Rococo art, which was strongly associated with the court of the French kings at Versailles. Boucher was trained as a decorator by his father, who designed embroideries. That influence can be seen in the exquisite lightness and decorative qualities of his paintings. The aristocracy of the time demanded a type of art and music that was pretty and decorative, even if it was superficial. A wide range of colors was used. Often the subjects of Rococo art were mythological or allegorical. The protagonist almost always appears as a young, elegant, and sensually abandoned woman. Cupids, nymphs, and doves are found in many paintings, which are frequently set in beautiful gardens or forests.*

The Death of Socrates *by Jacques-Louis David has a very different character from that of Boucher's painting. The painting depicts the great philosopher of ancient Greece just about to drink the poisonous cup of hemlock. His students grieve while he remains composed and upright. In spite of the anguish of the scene, the figures seem almost frozen or posed. There is a detached quality about the picture.*

The admiration of the culture of ancient Greece and Rome can be seen in its symmetrical, balanced design—a symmetry that can be heard in the sonata and other forms used by Haydn and Mozart. Groups of men are placed on each side of Socrates, who is the focus of attention. The colors are somewhat muted in keeping with the overall nature of the scene. The arches of the building add a linear perspective to the painting.

Romantic characteristics fill Eugène Delacroix's The Bark of Dante. *The painting depicts the struggling souls of the wicked people of Florence, Italy, trying to escape from Hell by climbing into the boat with ancient Roman poet Virgil and the fourteenth-century poet Dante Alighieri, whose best-known work was* Inferno *from* The Divine Comedy. *It demonstrates the interest of Romantic artists in subjects from the past and their fascination with evil and its consequences. In the painting the sea and clouds swirl around ominously. The twisted and pained bodies of the Florentines are very much involved in the scene, unlike the characters in David's* The Death of Socrates. *Instead, they struggle hopelessly. There is little symmetry; Dante (in the green cloak) stands about a third of the way to the left. The straight angles are gone, too, as the bodies of the sinners writhe throughout the picture.*

A Traveler Looking over a Sea of Fog *by Caspar David Friedrich shows another aspect of Romanticism: its the-individual-against-all-the-elements attitude, its self-centered outlook. Friedrich's belief was that the artist's feeling is his law. The erect, determined posture of the man viewing the fog and mountains is expressed well in the famous nineteenth-century poem "Invictus" by William Ernest Henley, which begins, "I am the master of my fate, the captain of my soul." A similar heroic outlook is evident in many Romantic works of music, including the tone poem* Ein Heldenleben (A Hero's Life) *by Richard Strauss.*

The Romanticists' love of nature can be seen in Jean-Baptiste-Camille Corot's Villa D'Avray *as it can heard in many Romantic musical works ranging from Beethoven's Sixth Symphony ("Pastorale") and Smetana's* The Moldau. *The painting is of a peaceful rural scene filled with flowers, beautiful trees, and a lake. The two figures in the foreground blend in with the scene. The lake is calm and it reflects the villa on the other side. The message of the picture could easily be* Nature is good and beautiful.

◆ Many Romanticists resented rules and restraints. They regarded the Classical period as cold and formal and were unimpressed by its rational deductions and universal laws. They felt perfectly capable of making their own rules—and proceeded to do so in their artworks. They cherished freedom, limitless expression, passion, and the pursuit of the unattainable. After all, what more glorious struggle could there be than seeking the impossible? This search is perhaps best represented in the legend of the Holy Grail.

The Holy Grail was the cup that Jesus used at the Last Supper. It was believed to have special powers.

The virtues of rural life were celebrated by artists of the Romantic period, as shown in *Potato Planters* by Jean François Millet.

Beethoven intended the music of Symphony No. 6 to convey the moods evoked during his visits to the countryside around Vienna.

◆ Romanticists were enthralled by nature. They had a rural outlook instead of the urban outlook of the Classical period. In Mozart's day the cities—London, Paris, Vienna—were the centers of artistic activity and so they attracted people with creative and artistic interests. To Romanticists, however, nature had more appeal because it represented a world untainted by humans. Sometimes nature was extolled to the point of pantheism—the belief that God and nature are one. The rural interest of the time led to landscape painting, poems on natural phenomena, and works such as Beethoven's Symphony No. 6 (*Pastoral*).

JEAN FRANÇOIS MILLET, FRENCH, 1814–1875. *POTATO PLANTERS*, OIL ON CANVAS, ABOUT 1861, (17.1505). GIFT OF QUINCY ADAMS SHAW THROUGH QUINCY A. SHAW, JR., AND MRS. MARIAN SHAW HAUGHTON. COURTESY, THE MUSEUM OF FINE ARTS, BOSTON.

◆ Beginning with Jean-Jacques Rousseau and the Earl of Shaftesbury (A. A. Cooper) and continuing through the American Henry David Thoreau in the nineteenth century to the present time, a group of philosophers have expounded the idea of natural goodness. The "artificialities" of civilization are rejected because they corrupt people. William Wordsworth summed up the Romanticists' thinking on nature when he wrote in his poem "The Tables Turned":

> *One impulse from vernal wood*
> *May teach you more of man,*
> *Of moral evil and of good,*
> *Than all the sages can.*

Vernal means springtime, and *sages* refers to wise men.

◆ Because Romanticists were highly subjective and individualistic, it is not surprising that they tended to be self-centered. Works of art were no longer objective examples of a person's skill. Instead they were considered a projection of the person who created them. Romantic artists felt that a bit of their psyche had been given to the world in their poems and preludes. Their works were now created for posterity, for an audience that someday, somewhere, would appreciate their true value.

◆ Some Romanticists were nonsocial, if not antisocial. They withdrew into a world of their own, surrounded by a close circle of friends and admirers. Yet the Romantic era saw the establishment of the concert hall with its large audiences, and some Romantic musicians thoroughly enjoyed the adulation of the public.

◆ Romantic musicians were often concerned with the other fine arts as well as with philosophy. They were familiar with the writings of Johann Wolfgang von Goethe and Alphonse Lamartine, and many times they knew the writers personally. Franz Liszt wrote a number of literary works, including a book on gypsy music and another entitled *Life of Chopin*. Robert Schumann's literary interests led him to edit a music magazine. Richard Wagner wrote lengthy treatises on music, art, and philosophy. Romantic composers believed strongly in a unity of the arts. This attitude is epitomized in the music dramas of Wagner.

Unfortunately, Liszt's book contains many inaccuracies.

Wagner's music dramas are presented in chapter 30.

C o d a

In the arts one style tends to replace another over time.
But that does not mean that the new style is better. *Instead, it means*
only that the new style is different *and that the new style is currently in*
vogue. Perhaps Mozart and Haydn had done all that could be done at the
time with the Classical outlook. The Romantic style offered composers and
artists venues that had never before been explored. And explore they did!
The result was a huge body of beautiful and exciting music.

Early Romantic Music

The Romantic attitude and outlook had a massive
impact on music. Changes happened not so much in new
forms or techniques of composing, although some changes
occurred in those areas, but more in what composers tried to
accomplish in their works. Their music tended to be much more
personal and expressive. They reveled in the qualities of mystery,
emotional release, love of nature, and inner feelings that
were fashionable during the nineteenth century.

In their music, Romantic composers favored the following characteristics:

♦ Flowing melodies accompanied by rich harmonies, with frequent use of
chromatic notes

♦ A freer use of rhythm, often speeding up or slowing down in the tempo

♦ Lengthy symphonies, concertos, and operas

♦ A rich, warm, often passionate quality

♦ The infusion of drama and contrast

These characteristics made music in the Romantic style very different from what
had preceded it.

THE ART SONG

Lied ("leed") is the
German word for "song";
Lieder is its plural.

The songs Schubert wrote are called art songs. An *art song*, or *Lied*, is a musical
setting of a poem. The order is important here. Composers of art songs first select a
suitable poem and *then* compose music that will best project the mood and thought
of the text. The idea of preserving and building on the message of the words is
fundamental to the art song.

Because the setting of the words was so vital, composers were not primarily
concerned with writing a lovely melody. They wanted a good melody, of course, but
more than that they wanted the melody to express the
words. The idea of expression also carried over to the
piano part, which evokes a mood, paints a picture, or
enriches ideas beyond what a singer can achieve. For
example, through rapidly moving notes and changes of
dynamic level, the piano can suggest wind blowing
through the trees.

Singers of art songs must project the idea of the
song. Sometimes they are called on to convey different
roles in the same song. Any mood can prevail in an art
song—anger, sadness, anxiety, joy, pity, contentment.

The demands on singers of art songs are, therefore,
somewhat different from those required of opera

The art song combines poetry, melody, the expressiveness of
the human voice, and the tonal power of the piano.

singers. In fact, singers tend to specialize in one type of vocal music or another. The art song is less demanding in a technical sense; the vocal range is narrower and there are few virtuoso passages. But singers of art songs must be versatile and able to project the essence of a character or situation. Because art songs are sung in small recital halls, singers must establish a rapport with the audience while maintaining a balance between good taste and expressiveness. In some ways, art songs and chamber music have several musical similarities. Both are intended to produce a sense of intimacy, refinement, and listener involvement.

A sense of involvement is not achieved if the listener does not understand the words. Most art songs are in languages other than English. As was pointed out earlier, word placement in vocal music is crucial, so translations are difficult. In fact, strictly speaking, something is lost in translation, no matter how carefully it is done. Many words have shades of meaning that cannot be translated. For these reasons, art songs are usually sung in their original languages.

Translation difficulties are only part of the language problem. Many of the poems that Schubert and other composers set to music are not of high literary merit. Some of them seem overly sentimental to people today who have grown up with down-to-earth (if not downright earthy) popular songs.

Art songs are a type of music well worth knowing, however.

♦ They reveal much sensitivity and skill in combining words and music.

♦ They are very expressive of their texts. For example, when the singer of "Der Erlkönig" sings "My father, my father, can't you see . . . ," listeners can really sense the child's frustration and fear.

The different roles for the singer are crucial in "The Erl King."

♦ The human voice can be a very expressive and beautiful musical instrument. When coupled with the tonal power of the piano in the infinite variety of the art song, the result can be very moving.

Franz Schubert

Franz Schubert (1797–1828) is often considered along with Beethoven to be a composer who marked the beginning of the Romantic style in music. And there is much about his life to justify his reputation as the prototype of the Romantic artist. Born into the family of a schoolteacher in a Vienna suburb, young Schubert's creative talent was evident while he was still a boy. After completing school, he tried to follow in his father's footsteps, but he could not accept the routine involved in teaching. He preferred to spend his time composing music.

Schubert did not adjust well to adult life. He never held a real job, and made only halfhearted attempts to find one. He had a small circle of friends, who appreciated his talents. They housed and fed him when he was in need, which he was often. He was not good at dealing with publishers, who made hefty profits from his music.

As the years passed, Schubert became lonelier and more discouraged. He was even unlucky in love and once contracted venereal disease. He was not in good health the last five years of his short life, but his compositions kept on coming. He died from typhus at the age of thirty-one, leaving almost no worldly goods—except for a vast store of beautiful music.

Schubert was a versatile composer. He wrote piano works, chamber music, and symphonies. But it is his vocal music, especially his six hundred songs, that ensured his place in the world of music.

Schubert's Symphony No. 8 ("Unfinished") was not left incomplete because he was heartbroken over a failed romance, as is sometimes claimed. He simply never got around to finishing it.

Best-Known Works
Chamber music:
  ▪ Piano Quintet ("Trout")
  ▪ *Arpeggione* Sonata
Orchestra:
  ▪ *Rosamunde* (incidental music)
  ▪ Symphonies Nos. 8 ("Unfinished") and 9 ("The Great")
Songs (more than 600) including:
  ▪ "Der Erlkönig"
  ▪ "Gretchen am Spinnrade"
Song cycles:
  ▪ *Die schöne Müllerin*
  ▪ *Winterreise*

The Split Personality of Romanticism

Every era in history seems to carry its contradictions. In the case of the Romantic period, those contradictions are massive. On the one hand, it produced much extremely beautiful and tender music and works of art. On the other hand, it showed a fascination with evil and misery. Song after song and opera after opera ends unhappily, often with the hero or heroine (or both) dying. For example, in Schubert's "Der Erlkönig" ("The Erl King") the son dies in his father's arms; in Wagner's Götterdämmerung *after Brünnhilde rides her horse into the funeral pyre of her beloved Siegfried, flames and then a flood engulf the home of the gods, Valhalla.*

The fascination with evil led to the inclusion of the Dies irae chant in several musical works, and compositions such as Mephisto Waltz (Mephisto *being another name for the devil*), Danse Macabre, *and* Totentanz (Dance of Death). *The disasters of the nineteenth century certainly did not reach the heights of mayhem that can be seen in films or described in books over the past few decades. They did, however, reveal a side of Romanticism that seemed to enjoy being miserable.*

Romanticists also had their optimistic and happy side that loved beauty. The music of Brahms, Mendelssohn, Tchaikovsky, Grieg, Schumann, and many others contains rich harmonies and luscious melodies. Such music is difficult to top in terms of sheer beauty. Many paintings also reveal a love of beauty; Corot's Villa D'Avray is one example. Beauty of motion and movement was (and still is) one of the main goals of ballet. Often its stories are pure and lovely fantasy, and present beauty that seems to exceed anything in ordinary life. The scene of the Snow Maidens dancing gracefully in The Nutcracker to Tchaikovsky's beautiful music as snow falls gently around them seems to be as total an experience of loveliness and beauty as can be conceived.

SCHUBERT'S "DER ERLKÖNIG"

Schubert wrote "Der Erlkönig" ("The Erl King") when he was only eighteen. He chose a text from the great German writer Goethe. The overall mood of the song is one of fear and suspense because of the mythical king of the elves. According to legend, whoever is touched by him must die. The singer is required to represent the narrator, the father, the son, and the Erl King—quite an assignment.

Before listening to the song, read over the text to determine which of the four roles the singer is presenting. As you listen, notice how Schubert, the singer, and the pianist treat the different roles. For example, be aware of how "My son, it's only a misty cloud" differs from "You lovely child, come . . ." and how "My father, my father, now don't you hear . . ." differs from "My son, my son, all I can see . . ." Notice not only the difference in the tone quality of the singer's voice for each role, but also how the entire mood changes when the Erl King speaks.

The piano sets the mood and helps delineate the characters in the song, as well as playing the role of the horse.

LISTENING GUIDE

Franz Schubert: "Der Erlkönig"
CD 1 Track 45

0:00	**45** Wer reitet so spät durch Nacht und Wind? Es ist der Vater mit seinem Kind;	Who rides so late through the night and wind? It is a father with his child.
	Er hat den Knaben wohl in dem Arm, Er fasst ihn sicher, er hält ihn warm.	He holds the boy within his arm, He clasps him tightly, he keeps him warm.
	"Mein Sohn, was birgst du so bang dein Gesicht?" "Siehst, Vater, du den Erlkönig nicht?	"My son, why do you hide your face in fear?" "See, father, isn't the Erl King near?
	Den Erlenkönig mit Kron' und Schweif?" "Mein Sohn, es ist ein Nebelstreif. "	The Erl King with crown and shroud? " "My son, it's only a misty cloud."
1:29	**46** "Du liebes Kind, komm, geh' mit mir! Gar schöne Spiele spiel' ich mit dir;	"You lovely child, come, go with me! Such pleasant games I'll play with thee!
	Manch' bunte Blumen sind an dem Strand, Meine Mutter hat manch' gülden Gewand."	The fields have flowers bright to behold, My mother has many a robe of gold."
	"Mein Vater, mein Vater, und hörest du nicht, Was Erlenkönig mir leise verspricht?"	"My father, my father, now don't you hear What the Erl King whispers in my ear?"
	"Sei ruhig, bleibe ruhig, mein Kind; In dürren Blättern säuselt der Wind."	"Be calm, be calm and still, my child; The dry leaves rustle when wind blows wild."
	"Willst, feiner Knabe, du mit mir geh'n? Meine Töchter sollen dich warten schön;	"My lovely boy, won't you go with me? My daughters all shall wait on thee,
	Meine Töchter führen den nächtlichen Reih'n Und wiegen und tanzen und singen dich ein."	My daughters nightly revels keep, They'll sing and dance and rock thee to sleep."
	"Mein Vater, mein Vater, und siehst du nicht dort Erlkönigs Töchter am düstern Ort?"	"My father, my father, can't you see the face Of Erl King's daughters in that dark place?"
	"Mein Sohn, mein Sohn, ich seh' es genau, Es scheinen die alten Weiden so grau."	"My son, my son, all I can see Is just the old gray willow tree."
	"Ich liebe dich, mich reizt deine schöne Gestalt, Und bist du nicht willig, so brauch' ich Gewalt."	"I love thee, thy form enflames my sense; Since thou art not willing, I'll take thee hence!"
3:15	**47** "Mein Vater, mein Vater, jetzt fasst er mich an! Erlkonig hat mir ein Leid's gethan!"	"My father, my father, he's grabbing my arm, The Erl King wants to do me harm!"
	Dem Vater grauset's, er reitet geschwind, Er hält in Armen das ächzende Kind,	The father shudders, he speeds through the cold, His arms the moaning child enfold,
	Erreicht den Hof mit Müh' und Noth: In seinen Armen das Kind war tot!	He reaches home with pain and dread: In his arms the child was dead!
4:05	The song ends with two solid-sounding chords.	

None of the music is repeated in "Der Erlkönig." New lines of melody follow one another until the song ends. The term for this type of song is *through-composed*. The accompaniment adds to the mood with an agitated triplet figure and a foreboding bass pattern, which depicts the urgency of the scene.

Dissonance is heard as the child expresses fear, and the father's music has a reassuring quality. Notice how effectively Schubert ends the song. The piano stops, and the singer declaims, "In his arms, the child"—a pause to allow anticipation to build up—"was dead."

Art songs provide a kind of music that is not duplicated in arias or folk songs; those forms of vocal music have other qualities and functions.

Felix Mendelssohn
Fanny Mendelssohn Hensel

As caring a brother as Felix was, that did not keep him from discouraging Fanny's efforts at composing.

Best-Known Works of Mendelssohn
Orchestra:
- Incidental Music for *A Midsummer Night's Dream*
- Symphonies Nos. 3 ("Italian") and 4 ("Scottish")
- Violin Concerto
Oratorio:
- *Elijah*

It is appropriate to couple **Felix Mendelssohn** (1809–1847) and his older sister, **Fanny** (1805–1847) together in the same biographical sketch. The two were very close during their childhood and remained so throughout their lives. They took music lessons and read Shakespeare's

plays together, and their young lives were certainly idyllic ones. Their father was a wealthy banker who hired musicians to come to the Mendelssohn home in Berlin to give concerts and later to play music that one of his children had composed.

In his adult life, Felix became a very successful pianist, composer, conductor, and organizer of concerts. He was one of the first conductors to stand in front of the orchestra, and he was very influential in stimulating an interest in the music of Bach with his performance of the *St. Matthew Passion*. He made ten journeys to England to conduct and perform, and was warmly received by Queen Victoria at Buckingham Palace.

And what about Fanny's musical career? She too was a gifted composer and pianist, but her father insisted that a lady of her social standing should not become a professional musician. Eventually, she married the painter Wilhelm Hensel. She did not completely give up her interest in music, but she refrained from pursuing it as a career. She performed occasionally as a piano soloist and composed more than two hundred works, mostly songs,

Best-Known Works of Hensel
Choral:
- *Gartenlieder*
Songs:
- Op. 7

chamber music, and short piano pieces. Only a few of her compositions have been published.

In May 1847 Fanny died of a stroke during a rehearsal for one of the family concerts. Felix was crushed. Although his own health was failing, he composed a string quartet in her memory. He also journeyed to visit her grave, which was especially hard on him and hastened his death about six months later. He was buried near his sister.

MENDELSSOHN'S *ELIJAH*

Ever since the days of Handel nearly a century before, the English had been fond of oratorios. So it was not unreasonable to expect that Felix Mendelssohn would compose oratorios for some of his visits to England. His most successful oratorio was *Elijah*.

Elijah was an Old Testament prophet who attempts to turn Israel away from the false prophets of Baal. He revives a widow's son and is able to bring about the end of a three-year drought. But his most dramatic accomplishment was his challenge to the prophets of Baal: Place a slain bullock on the altar at Mount Carmel—but do not light a fire under it. Instead, Elijah and the prophets of Baal will call upon their God or gods to ignite the fire. The prophets of Baal try their best, but nothing happens. Their gods remain silent.

Elijah offers a prayer to God that ends with these words: "Thou, whose ministers are flaming fires, let them now descend." Soon the flames consume the offering. The price of defeat is high for the prophets of Baal: They are all taken to Kishon's Brook and killed.

Understandably, this upsets the Baalite King Ahab and his equally evil Queen Jezebel. They order Elijah killed, and he has to flee for his life into the wilderness. Exhausted, he falls asleep under a juniper bush, and angels gather round to watch over him. Mendelssohn uses this setting to write two very reassuring, comforting, and beautiful pieces of music. The first is a trio that is often sung by boy sopranos, "Lift thine eyes." The other is sung by the chorus, "He watching over Israel."

A biblical prophet was not so much one who predicted the future as a social critic who pointed out the wrongs of society.

Baal was a deity of storms and rain from the land of Canaan.

Mount Carmel is in the city of Haifa in Israel.

Religious tolerance was not an Old Testament virtue!

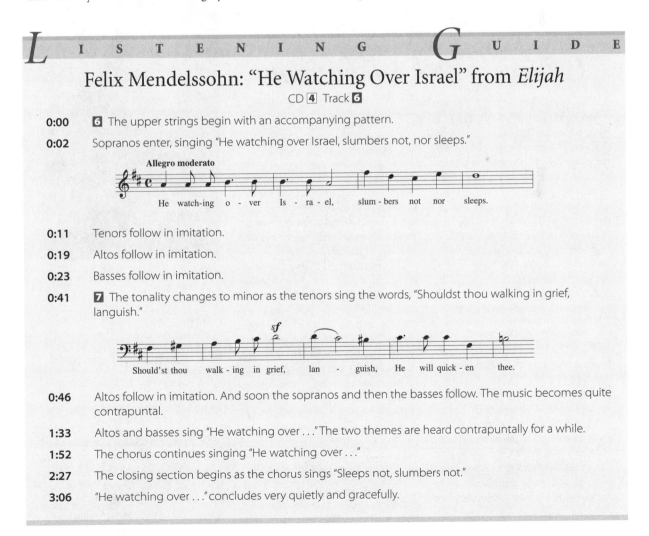

L I S T E N I N G   G U I D E

Felix Mendelssohn: "He Watching Over Israel" from *Elijah*

CD 4 Track 6

0:00	6	The upper strings begin with an accompanying pattern.
0:02		Sopranos enter, singing "He watching over Israel, slumbers not, nor sleeps."

Allegro moderato

He watch-ing o - ver Is - ra - el, slum - bers not nor sleeps.

0:11		Tenors follow in imitation.
0:19		Altos follow in imitation.
0:23		Basses follow in imitation.
0:41	7	The tonality changes to minor as the tenors sing the words, "Shouldst thou walking in grief, languish."

sf

Should'st thou walk - ing in grief, lan - guish, He will quick - en thee.

0:46	Altos follow in imitation. And soon the sopranos and then the basses follow. The music becomes quite contrapuntal.
1:33	Altos and basses sing "He watching over . . ." The two themes are heard contrapuntally for a while.
1:52	The chorus continues singing "He watching over . . ."
2:27	The closing section begins as the chorus sings "Sleeps not, slumbers not."
3:06	"He watching over . . ." concludes very quietly and gracefully.

The text of "He watching over Israel" comes from two Psalms. Some of the words in the chorus are not used as they are today. In more contemporary English, its text "He watching over Israel, slumbers not, nor sleeps" might be "He who watches over Israel is vigilant." "Shouldst thou walking in grief, languish, He will quicken thee" might be expressed, "If you encounter hardship and lose heart, He will give you strength."

While in the wilderness, God speaks to Elijah and commands him to return to Israel, where "mighty kings by him were overthrown." The people's hearts were finally changed from their former false gods back to Jehovah. At the end of his life, Elijah is taken up to heaven in a fiery chariot.

Solo and Chamber Music

This type of piece is often called a "character piece." It is discussed in chapter 27.

Although the Romantic era is noted for large compositions, its composers continued to produce many excellent works for small groups and solo works other than concertos. Schubert composed an enormous amount of chamber music, as did Mendelssohn. Two other early Romantic composers merit mentioning: Carl Maria von Weber (1786–1826) and Robert Schumann. Weber is especially recognized for his operas, but he also composed a number of chamber works. Schumann is a major name in the world of music.

Robert Schumann
Clara Wieck Schumann

Robert Alexander (1813–1856) and Clara Wieck Schumann (1819–1896) were husband and wife. Robert's father was a bookseller and writer, who encouraged his son's musical interests. Robert entered law school at the University of Leipzig in Germany, but gave it up to pursue his ambitions to become a piano virtuoso. However, he permanently injured his hands in an attempt to develop finger strength with a mechanical device. His interests moved on to the founding of an important music magazine and to composing.

> Robert's magazine was very influential in promoting Romantic music and its composers.

Besides a great deal of piano music, he wrote chamber music, concertos, and symphonies. He composed about 150 songs, many of them written the year after he married Clara.

Clara Wieck was the daughter of Robert's piano teacher, and he fell in love with her when she was sixteen. At that time she was already well on her way to becoming an outstanding concert pianist. Her father strongly opposed their marriage, so the couple had to wait until she was twenty-one (minus

> In nineteenth-century Germany, children seldom could or would go against their father's wishes.

one day) before getting married. Their marriage was a happy one and they had eight children. In spite of Robert's bouts with mental illness, Clara continued her career as a concert pianist, although her family demanded more and more of her time.

Two years before his death, tormented by hallucinations, Robert leaped into the Rhine River. He was saved, but spent the remainder of his life in an asylum. Those were difficult years for Clara. At the age of thirty-seven, she lost her husband, to whom she was devoted. She later found herself attracted to the twenty-two-year-old protégé of her husband, Johannes Brahms. Brahms remained a bachelor and Clara never remarried, but they did remain close friends and admirers.

For the last forty years of her life, Clara continued to teach and give concerts. Although

> Clara went on tour again after Robert's death. She gave the last of her thirteen hundred public concerts at the age of seventy-two.

Best-Known Works of Robert Schumann
Chamber music:
- Piano Quintet
Orchestra:
- Piano Concerto
- Cello Concerto
Piano, many character pieces, plus:
- *Carnaval*
- *Fantasia in C*
- *Kinderscenen*
Song cycle:
- *Frauenliebe und-leben*

she was a promising composer, she was not able to devote much time to this aspect of her great talent. She did write a few works for piano and a piano trio, however. Throughout her adult life, she promoted Robert's music through her performances.

Where Are the Women Composers?

You have probably noticed by now a distinct absence of women's names among composers. Shouldn't there be a nearly equal number of men and women? Why such a preponderance of males? Granted, a few women have been successful composers: Hildegard of Bingen and Péronne d'Armentières in early music, Fanny Mendelssohn Hensel and Clara Schumann in the nineteenth century, and others. But the number of women composers and their compositions are few.

As is true of most things in life, there is no single, simple explanation for the paucity of women composers. Several factors very likely contribute to the situation. A major one was the fact that it was a "man's world" until only the past couple of decades. Women usually could not own property, vote in the few democratic countries that had elections, engage in enterprises outside the home, or travel overnight without an escort. They were generally treated as the property of their husbands. They were often discouraged by their fathers or husbands from composing, which happened in the case of Fanny Mendelssohn. Such circumstances hardly encouraged women to have the fortitude to compose music and hope to have it published.

An additional impediment to women composers is the fact that it has seldom been easy for anyone to have compositions published. Until a composer had achieved a certain degree of name recognition, which made a publisher more confident of sufficient sales, getting a work published was no easy matter, a situation that is still true today. There are a number of works now well regarded for which composers had difficulty finding a publisher. And yet a publisher's cautious approach is understandable.

After all, how many sales of a symphony could be anticipated at a time when there were no permanent orchestras or residuals from the sale of recordings?

Another reason for the lack of women composers was the prejudice they faced in pursuing instruction in harmony, counterpoint, orchestration, and similar subjects. For example, the Paris Conservatory did not permit women in advanced theory classes until the late 1800s.

A few women authors, such as George Sand and George Elliot, were able to break the male dominance by writing under a male pseudonym. An undetermined number of Fanny Mendelssohn Hensel's songs were published under Felix's name! Are there other works by women published under a man's name? We don't know, but if it happened once with Fanny Mendelssohn, it probably happened with other women too.

Has the situation changed for women in the world of musical composition? Fortunately, in at least two important ways it has. Much research has recently been conducted on locating compositions by women, and a considerable body of music has been uncovered. The other change is in the acceptance of women composers. Whether the playing field is level between men and women today in terms of recognition for their compositions is difficult to determine. However, Ellen Taafe Zwilich, Joan Tower, Pauline Oliveros, and others are rightfully being recognized for their works. Perhaps in another hundred years the question about the lack of women composers will no longer be a logical one to raise.

CLARA SCHUMANN'S ROMANCE FOR VIOLIN AND PIANO

Romance for Violin and Piano is a short, intimate work. It does not seek to impress listeners with powerful, showy music. Instead it seeks to charm listeners with its unpretentious beauty.

The work contains two themes. The first theme is heard four times and the second theme twice. But each time they contain subtle changes.

LISTENING GUIDE

Clara Schumann: Romance for Violin and Piano, Op. 22, No. 3
CD 4 Track 8

Ternary Form: ABA

0:00   8 The violin opens with the first theme. It is accompanied by rippling notes on the piano that outline chords.

0:36   The piano joins in, playing the first theme.

0:58   The first theme is extended.

1:45   9 The *B* section begins as the second theme is played by the violin. The piano plays short chords.

2:06   The piano plays the *B* theme as the violin plucks a harmony part.

2:27   The *B* section is extended.

2:49   The piano plays the second theme again.

3:22   The *A* section returns as the violin plays the first theme.

4:23   The piano plays the first theme as the violin adds counterpoint.

4:48   Fragments of the first theme are heard.

5:09   Rich harmonies are heard as the work concludes.

Coda

The Romantic period began geographically close to where the Classical period had ended: in the cities of central Europe, especially Vienna. In fact, Vienna and the Germanic style were to dominate the musical scene for the remainder of the nineteenth century. In was not that other kinds of music were lacking. Rather, German Romanticism was the pacesetter.

Romantic Piano Music

The Romantic period tended to exhibit two different viewpoints regarding piano music. One outlook exploited the power and brilliance of the instrument; the other treated the piano in a more intimate, sensitive way. These two approaches were by no means mutually exclusive, but they were distinctive enough to be noticeable. For example, Liszt composed piano music that dazzled his audiences with technical display and forceful sounds. Chopin, on the other hand, usually wrote piano pieces that sought to enchant listeners with their beauty and tonal quality.

One type of piano music might be thought of as extroverted and the other as introverted.

The Romantic period featured piano music. An enormous amount of music was written for the instrument, not only at concert level but for amateur players as well. The piano was the most popular instrument in the home during the nineteenth century.

Piano recitals became important during this time. Many composers were also pianists themselves and introduced their own works to the public; Liszt, Beethoven, Frédéric Chopin are among the composers who did this. But gradually a class of virtuoso performers emerged who were known for their interpretative abilities as well as their stunning technical virtuosity.

CHARACTER PIECES

Romantic composers did not want to be confined to the carefully balanced forms that Mozart and Haydn had used so well. To replace the rondo, sonata, and other forms, composers in the nineteenth century created many free, short forms that are often referred to as *character pieces,* such as the ballade, berceuse, étude, prelude, impromptu, fantasia, scherzo, and nocturne.

The *ballade* ("bah-*lahd*") and *berceuse* ("bair-*soos*") are songlike pieces. The ballade is the longer and more complex of the two and is supposed to hark back to the ballad poems of the Middle Ages. An *étude* ("*ay*-tood") is an instrumental piece that develops a particular technique. Études were written for all instruments, but were especially popular for the piano. In the hands of Chopin, Liszt, or similarly gifted composers, an étude is transformed into an exciting concert work. A *prelude* is a short work for piano.

Étude comes from the French for study.

An *impromptu* is supposed to convey the spontaneity its name suggests. A *fantasia* or *fantasie* is a free and imaginative work. The *scherzos* by Chopin are not as playful as those by Beethoven. Instead, they are longer and more serious, although the typical triple meter and fast tempo of the scherzo are retained. *Nocturne* was the name given by the Irish composer John Field to his piano pieces with a songlike melody. Chopin adopted the title from Field and wrote many beautiful, lyrical nocturnes.

The word nocturne refers to night song.

Another type of character piece consisted of stylized dance forms such as the mazurka, polonaise, and waltz. What Romantic composers did was essentially the same as what Bach had done with his Baroque keyboard suites. The Romantic composers, however, used different dances and wrote in a very different style from their Baroque and Classical predecessors. They expanded the forms so that each dance became a separate piece, rather than just one part of a larger suite.

These character pieces were often intended to convey an air of improvisation as if they were an inspiration—a momentary feeling that had been rendered in sound. The impression of improvisation is an illusion, however, because Chopin and his

Chopin was known to spend as much as six weeks on a single page of music, changing note after note, stomping around in frustration, and breaking pens. Sometimes he would return to exactly what he started with in the first place.

Rubato originally meant "robbed" in Italian.

contemporaries labored carefully over each measure they wrote. They worked hard at sounding spontaneous.

There is a feature of Romantic music that cannot be seen in music notation but is used frequently in performing the music. It is known as *rubato* ("roo-*bah*-toh"). Rubato is a style of performance in which the performer deviates slightly from the exact execution of the rhythm. A fraction of time is borrowed from one note to lengthen another. Chopin was occasionally criticized as a performer for his use of rubato. Some listeners charged that he could not keep a steady beat. Undoubtedly, he could, but he sometimes chose not to. He wanted the music to have the free expression that the Romanticists admired.

CHOPIN'S NOCTURNE IN D-FLAT

Broken style means that the notes of a chord are neither sounded together nor in succession.

Chopin composed about twenty nocturnes. Most of them have an introspective, delicate, lyric quality. The Nocturne in D-flat, Op. 27, No. 2, is one the most voluptuous and passionate of these works. It contains rich harmonies and many musical "sighs" consisting of descending intervals and delayed resolutions of phrases and harmonic progressions. The left-hand part is made up of six continuously moving notes for each beat. The notes are actually chords that are sounded in a broken style. The right hand plays a songlike melody that is decorated with grace notes and other

Frédéric Chopin

Frédéric Chopin ("*Show*-pan," 1810–1849) was the son of a French father and a Polish mother. He exhibited much talent at an early age and received his musical education at the Conservatory in Warsaw. Before he was twenty, he was on his own in the world. He left Poland and traveled awhile before settling in Paris. Shortly after his departure from Poland, the Poles revolted against the Russians and their czar. In time the Russians crushed the revolt, which caused Chopin much anguish.

> Chopin's loyalty to Poland remained strong throughout his life.

His abilities as a composer and pianist made him a sought-after musician in Paris. Soon he acquired a circle of artistic friends—the painter Eugène Delacroix, musicians Franz Liszt and Hector Berlioz, writers Victor Hugo, Honoré de Balzac, Alphonse de Larmartine, Alexandre Dumas (père), and Heinrich Heine. Through this group of friends, Chopin met George Sand, and they lived together for nine years.

George Sand was the pen name of Amandine Aurore Lucie Dupin, Baroness

> She took her pen name from an earlier lover, writer Jules Sandeau.

Dudevant, who was one of the outstanding writers of the time with more than a hundred books to her credit. She favored novels in which love transcended the obstacles of convention and social class. She had liaisons with a number of famous men, but her most lasting relationship was with Chopin.

When they first met, Chopin, who had always been drawn to beautiful women and loved the polished and elegant life, was repelled by her: She had adopted a number of masculine attitudes and habits, including wearing men's clothes and smoking cigars. And she was not physically attractive. Yet in time he was drawn to her. Her fame as a writer and her strong personality seemed to be a good balance for his not very forceful ways. When they separated, she did not seem

> Liszt wrote of the separation: "In the breaking of this long affection, this powerful bond, he had broken his life."

to be affected. But Chopin lived only another two years before his death from tuberculosis.

Most composers before Chopin wrote well in a variety of types of music. Chopin was different. He was one of the first composers to limit his writing to one or two areas. He wrote almost exclusively for the piano, and

Best-Known Works
Orchestra:
■ Piano Concertos Nos. 1 and 2
Piano—character pieces:
■ Études (24), including "Black Key," "Winter Wind," and "Revolutionary"
■ Fantasies, including *Fantasie-Impromptu*, Op. 66
■ Nocturnes (21)
■ Preludes (24, one in each major and minor key)
■ Scherzos (4)
Piano—stylized dances:
■ Polonaises, including Op. 53
■ Mazurkas
■ Waltzes, including "Minute Waltz"
Piano—sonatas (3)

it is this music that made a place for him in the world of music. He is often referred to as "the poet of the piano."

melodic figures. Although the music notation makes the rhythm look steady and regular, pianists almost always take liberties with the rhythm, as Chopin himself did in his own playing.

Grace notes are printed in half the size of other notes and have no prescribed rhythmic value.

Pianists also use the pedals a great deal in playing romantic music. The *Ped.* marking in the notation tells the pianist to depress the damper pedal, which lifts the dampers and allows the strings to resonate freely. Richness is added to the music when the dampers are raised. Proper pedaling also contributes to smooth, lyrical phrasing. The composer and performer must plan carefully for the use of the pedals, because unwanted notes that are allowed to sound create a blurring effect.

The various features of Chopin's piano music can be heard in this nocturne in the Listening Guide.

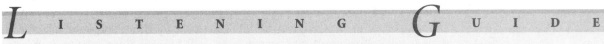

Frédéric Chopin: Nocturne in D-flat Major, Op. 27, No. 2

CD 4 Track 10

0:00 10 The accompaniment figure begins in the left-hand part but is soon followed by a tender melody *(A)* by the right hand:

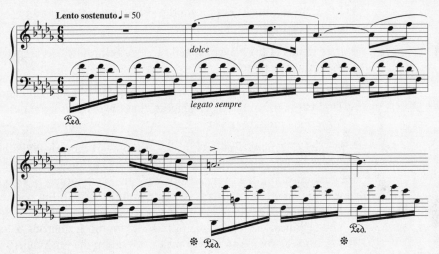

0:42 11 The melodic line changes character somewhat with contrasting material *(B)*. The melodic figure is repeated and varied several times.

1:56 The *A* melody returns.

2:37 The *B* portion of the melodic line resumes and is treated to more-extensive melodic variation, which leads to a climactic moment.

3:25 The *A* melody returns more intensely and is changed somewhat as it progresses. Much use is made of decorative figures.

3:59 The *B* portion of the melody is heard. The music grows more passionate as it leads to a conclusion of the main portion of the nocturne.

4:32 The coda begins that consists of a descending, "sighing" interval.

4:57 The sighing figure is heard again as the music slowly fades away.

5:44 The nocturne closes with a simple cadence after an ascending, fading scale.

Virtuoso Music

Another type of piano music was for the virtuoso performer. Audiences during the nineteenth century were fond of dazzling, showy music and stunning performances by musical idols such as the pianist Franz Liszt and the violin virtuoso Niccolò Paganini.

Liszt's *La Campanella*

Liszt admired the virtuoso skills of Paganini on the violin. This admiration led to Liszt's transcribing six of Paganini's violin works for piano under the title *Transcendental Études After Paganini. La Campanella (The Little Bell)* is the third of these pieces. Liszt retains the bell effect by sounding a high D-sharp repeatedly throughout the piece.

Transcriptions were popular in the Romantic era. They offered the new public audience the opportunity of hearing technically stunning variations on operatic melodies and other works not originally written for piano. Because there were no recordings and few orchestras, a piano recital was often a listener's only contact with art music.

La Campanella is a typically Romantic composition, for several reasons:

♦ It is virtuoso music; even a good professional pianist does not undertake it lightly.

♦ It demands of the player the full range of techniques developed in the Romantic period.

♦ It is an attempt to make the piano more orchestral in sound and concept. The very name of the piece suggests that the piano is to be descriptive of something more than itself.

While *La Campanella* is technically awesome, it is musically rather simple. It is a set of scintillating variations on a simple melody in which the opening two-measure phrase is stated and then repeated twice with a concluding phrase. After the main theme is presented again, there is a contrasting section. It too is composed of short, repeated phrases. The piece has a form of *a a b*.

The technical devices of piano playing are too numerous to cover fully here. A few examples provide an idea of what Liszt did in the way of virtuoso display. One involves rapidly repeated notes, which Liszt used often. It may seem that the pianist is simply rapping his or her finger repeatedly on the key with tremendous speed. Not so. It is much easier to play notes rapidly in succession if the key is struck with a different finger for each sound. Here is an example of where that technique is used:

Liszt arranged many of the transcriptions in the form of duets for two persons playing at the same keyboard.

There were no orchestras that toured in those days.

Liszt also calls for very fast playing of the chromatic scale:

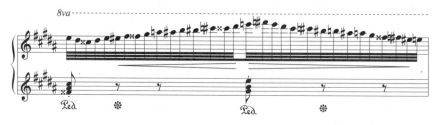

A contemporary caricature of Lizst lampoons his extraordinary virtuosity.

Alternating hands gives the pianist more speed and power:

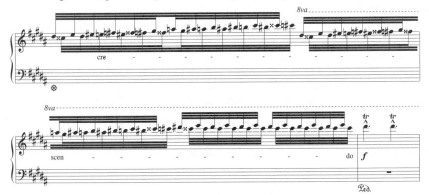

The *8va* sign tells the performer to play the notes one octave higher than written.

Niccolò Paganini

Franz Liszt

Niccolò Paganini (1782–1840) and **Franz Liszt** (1811–1886) had much in common. First, they were the supreme virtuoso performers of the nineteenth century on their respective instruments: Paganini on the violin and Liszt on the piano. Second, they both came from modest circumstances. Third, for what it's worth, both successfully pursued many women over the course of their lives.

Paganini had a more interesting reputation. Part of his fame was the result of his appearance and character. He had a pale, long face with hollow cheeks and thin lips that seemed to curl in an evil smile, and his eyes had a piercing quality. There were also popular suspicions that he was influenced by the devil.

> Paganini was even forced to publish letters from his mother to prove that he had human parents!

His ability to play the violin was legendary, and he added a whole new dimension to the playing of the instrument. He developed a repertoire of violin tricks and technical maneuvers that he guarded jealously, refusing to have much of his music published for fear that others might find out exactly what he was doing.

> One of Paganini's violin pieces is the basis for a work by Rachmaninoff that is presented in chapter 33.

On the night of March 9, 1831, Liszt attended a recital by Paganini. The dazzling virtuoso left an indelible impression on the nineteen-year old Liszt, who became consumed with the idea that he could do for piano technique what Paganini had done for the violin. Liszt canceled all his concerts for two years and began to retrain himself. He spent hours practicing techniques such as octaves, trills, scales, and arpeggios (playing notes of a chord successively rather than simultaneously). He returned again and again to hear Paganini and take notes on what he did. He even imitated some of the visual effects of Paganini's appearance: his black tight-fitting clothes, tossing hair, and facial expressions.

Traditionally, pianists had performed with their backs to the audience and played with the music in front of them. Liszt was one of the first to turn the piano to its familiar sideways position and to memorize his music. His chiseled profile fascinated the audience, especially the women, as he crouched over the keys, alternately caressing and pounding them.

Behind the image of the sensational artist, which Liszt did not discourage, there was a musician of depth and a man of generous

Best-Known Works of Liszt
Orchestra:
- *Hungarian Rhapsodies* Nos. 2 and 14
- *Les Préludes*
- Piano Concertos Nos. 1 and 2
- *Totentanz* for Piano and Orchestra

Piano:
- *Harmonies poétiques et religieuses*
- Sonata in B Minor
- *Transcendental Études* (6)

heart who helped many young musicians. There was also a prolific composer. Although he is especially known for his piano music—and many more piano transcriptions—he also composed many works for orchestra as well as about sixty religious works.

> Toward the end of his life, he took minor religious vows and had the title Abbé Liszt.

Liszt's exploitation of the range of the piano can be heard in the long trill on the high D-sharp, only a few notes from the top of the keyboard.

Perhaps virtuoso compositions may not be as intellectually challenging as other types of musical works. But most of them—and *La Campanella* is certainly one—contain some really imaginative writing. The high notes of the piano are used in a way that is not found in Mozart or Beethoven sonatas or other piano music. And the variations are fresh and attractive. One must be a virtuoso pianist to play these works well. Technical virtuosity, or any artistic endeavor, whether achieved by an Olympic figure skater or a fine pianist, demands exceptional dedication and talent It is a pleasure to observe such performances, especially if the observer has tried some skating or piano playing and therefore can appreciate better the skill demanded.

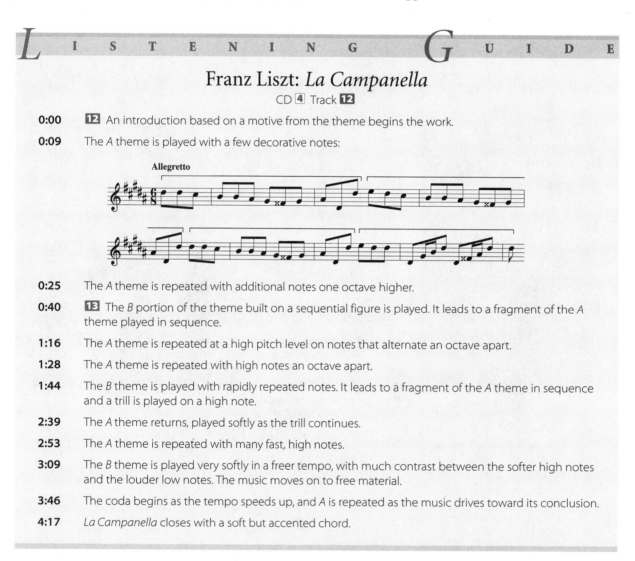

L I S T E N I N G   G U I D E

Franz Liszt: *La Campanella*
CD 4 Track 12

0:00	12 An introduction based on a motive from the theme begins the work.
0:09	The *A* theme is played with a few decorative notes:

0:25	The *A* theme is repeated with additional notes one octave higher.
0:40	13 The *B* portion of the theme built on a sequential figure is played. It leads to a fragment of the *A* theme played in sequence.
1:16	The *A* theme is repeated at a high pitch level on notes that alternate an octave apart.
1:28	The *A* theme is repeated with high notes an octave apart.
1:44	The *B* theme is played with rapidly repeated notes. It leads to a fragment of the *A* theme in sequence and a trill is played on a high note.
2:39	The *A* theme returns, played softly as the trill continues.
2:53	The *A* theme is repeated with many fast, high notes.
3:09	The *B* theme is played very softly in a freer tempo, with much contrast between the softer high notes and the louder low notes. The music moves on to free material.
3:46	The coda begins as the tempo speeds up, and *A* is repeated as the music drives toward its conclusion.
4:17	*La Campanella* closes with a soft but accented chord.

C o d a

*The Romantic composers demonstrated the wide variety of
music written for the piano. But they did more than show off the vast
potential of the instrument. In addition, they created a wealth
of music that has withstood the test of time.*

Program Music 28

Romantic composers in the nineteenth century had a problem: They did not want to continue using the forms of the Classical period, which they thought were too structured and restrictive. But how can you have a musical work of much length without a form such as sonata or rondo? One answer that several Romantic composers developed was to use a story, person, or situation as a stimulus. Such nonmusical associations could replace patterns of themes and development sections.

NATURE OF PROGRAM MUSIC

Instrumental works that composers consciously associate with nonmusical ideas are called *program music*. The particular associations are often indicated in the title, or in some cases by an explanation included in the score—the "program." Works that have been named by a publisher or other person are not really program music.

Program music became especially important in the nineteenth century. It provided one type of "form" for a major work. Some program works, however, actually follow one of the traditional forms, even if the composer does not admit doing so. And the opposite may also be true: A composer may compose a work with a title such as Sonata No. 2 that was sparked by some nonmusical association.

Musical sounds cannot really tell specifically about an event or a person. Only a song and its words can do that in music. Musical sounds can, however, convey an atmosphere, a general feeling. Listeners may hear some massive chords and assume that they signify something great or big—the coronation of a king or a large animal walking. The idea of largeness or importance is there, but not the specifics. It is possible to make up a story to go with a musical work, of course, but that story may not be what the composer had in mind. Furthermore, instrumental music that tries to tell a story in detail becomes almost comic. It loses its value as musical expression and becomes something closer to sound effects.

Identifying the nonmusical association is not really all that important anyway. Good program music has substance in and of itself; it can stand without the story because of its musical qualities.

The term *program music* refers only to instrumental music. Vocal music usually has specific references through its words.

Publishers and others sometimes give a work a name, because names are easier to remember than numbers.

Only the composer knows if there was a nonmusical association.

TYPES OF PROGRAM MUSIC

There are several types of program music: concert overtures, incidental music, tone poems (also called symphonic poems), and program symphonies.

Concert Overture

An *overture* to an opera is an instrumental introduction that incorporates programmatic ideas from the story that follows. A *concert overture* is similar, but it is an independent one-movement work that is not associated with an opera. Sometimes it is in sonata form. Several overtures of this type were composed in the nineteenth century. Examples include Felix Mendelssohn's seascape *Hebrides (Fingal's Cave)* and Piotr Ilich Tchaikovsky's *Festival Overture "1812."*

Tchaikovsky's overture celebrates the victory of the Russians over Napoleon in 1812. The score calls for six cannon, and some performances of it include fireworks.

Incidental Music

Early in the nineteenth century, composers were often asked to write *incidental music* for a drama or play. They would compose an overture and five or six other pieces to be performed during the play or between various acts. Although strictly instrumental music, these works are associated with a particular drama. Beethoven wrote a number of incidental works, including some of his better-known overtures such as *Egmont* and *Coriolan*. Mendelssohn composed incidental music for Shakespeare's *A Midsummer Night's Dream*. Georges Bizet wrote *L'Arlésienne* for a drama, as did Edvard Grieg (1843-1907) for Ibsen's drama *Peer Gynt*.

Today the music composed as incidental music for plays is usually heard in suites extracted from the more complete works.

Tone Poem

The most important type of program music is the *tone poem,* or *symphonic poem.* It is a rather long, complex orchestral work in one movement that develops a poetic idea, creates a mood, or suggests a scene. It differs from the concert overture in that it is much freer in its structure. The symphonic poem was developed by Liszt and Berlioz and expanded by Richard Strauss (1864–1949).

One of the best-known tone poems is *Les Préludes* by Liszt. Its programmatic association is a philosophical poem by Alphonse de Lamartine. The poem begins:

Notice the fascination with the unknown and the heroic sentiments of these lines of Romantic poetry.

> *What else is life but a series of preludes to that unknown song*
> *whose first solemn note is intoned by Death?*
> *Love is the enchanted dawn of all existence;*
> *but what destiny is there whose first delights of love*
> *are not interrupted by some storm?*

In this work Liszt developed the technique of theme transformation, which Berlioz uses so well in his *Symphonie fantastique.*

PROGRAM SYMPHONY

The main difference between a tone poem and *program symphony* is the presence of more than one movement in a program symphony. Some of the themes usually appear in more than one movement.

BERLIOZ'S SYMPHONIE FANTASTIQUE

Berlioz's *Symphonie fantastique (Fantastic Symphony)* is a multimovement tone poem. And what a program it has! Berlioz had become infatuated with the actress Harriet Smithson. To ease his pain and indulge his fantasies, he decided to compose a symphony. He wrote this about the music:

> A young musician of morbid sensibility and ardent imagination in a fit of lovesick despair has poisoned himself with opium. The drug, too weak to kill, plunges him into a heavy sleep accompanied by strange visions. The sensations, feelings, and memories are translated in his sick brain into musical images and ideas. The beloved one herself becomes for him a melody, a recurrent theme that haunts him everywhere.

Listeners may not be aware of the retained pattern of pitches, but they can usually sense its presence.

This recurrent theme is a *fixed idea,* or in French *idée fixe,* that becomes a melodic fragment associated with a particular person or object. The fixed idea, then, is subject to changes in rhythm, harmony, tempo, meter, and elaboration with other tones, but its characteristic pattern of intervals is retained. This technique is called *theme transformation.*

Hector Berlioz

Hector Berlioz (1803–1869) was born in a small town near Grenoble, France. His father was a well-to-do physician who expected his son to follow in his footsteps. Hector was even sent to Paris to attend medical school, but he was much more interested in the musical life of the city, so he gave up medicine for music.

Berlioz soon found himself part of a group of artists and writers, including the painter Delacroix and the writer Hugo. His parents cut off his funds, so he gave music lessons, sang in a theater chorus, and did other odd jobs of a musical nature. He became fascinated with the music of Beethoven and the dramas of Shakespeare. It was in attending one of these plays that he first saw the actress Harriet Smithson and became obsessed with her. He made no attempt to meet her, but was content to visit rehearsals of her plays. He would take solitary midnight walks around Paris and write letters with lines like, "Trust me, Smithson and Berlioz will be reunited in the oblivion of the tomb."

> During a rehearsal Berlioz saw Harriet in the arms of a stage lover. He emitted a loud shriek and ran from the theater.

In 1830 Berlioz was awarded the coveted Prix de Rome, which provided an allowance and an opportunity to work in Rome. It was during that year he composed *Symphonie fantastique*. When he returned to Paris, a hectic courtship of Harriet Smithson followed. Both families objected, but the two married anyway. It was a stormy marriage, and it lasted until Hector left about nine years later to live with an Italian opera singer.

Like several other composers of the nineteenth century, Berlioz also wrote reviews and articles. He was the author of an important book on orchestration. His literary efforts earned him income and allowed him to promote his ideas about music. He tried his hand at several operas and wrote a gigantic requiem, but he was at his best with programmatic works.

Best-Known Works
Choral:
- *Requiem*
Orchestra:
- *Harold in Italy*
- *Roman Carnival Overture*
- *Symphony fantastique*

Theme transformation should not be confused with theme development or theme and variations. Variation involves keeping the theme intact to some extent and arranging the variations so that they contrast with one another. Development involves retaining the theme but manipulating it, often by breaking it into fragments.

Transformation is a looser concept in which a few characteristic intervals are preserved, sometimes with new material interspersed. The retained intervals give the music a sense of unity, and the transformations provide variety. Composers in addition to Liszt and Berlioz exploited this technique; Brahms was masterful in its use.

What are the strengths of Berlioz's music, especially his *Symphonie fantastique*? At least two features stand out:

- His fertile and vivid imagination. Not only is the program associated with the work a bit far out and exaggerated, but the music also builds on those sometimes bizarre scenes into a wonderfully imaginative "soundscape." No one can accuse Berlioz of composing run-of-the-mill music!

- His masterful use of instruments. Berlioz's expertise in orchestration shows in his ability to get the best out of each instrument and combine their sounds to get the effects he wants to achieve.

Symphonie fantastique contains five rather long movements. Berlioz provided descriptive commentary for each movement.

I. Reveries, Passions   "He remembers the weariness of the soul, the indefinable yearning he knew before meeting his beloved. Then, the volcanic love with which she at once inspired him, his delirious suffering."

Audiences of Berlioz's time were sometimes taken aback by the power of his musical vision. This cartoon satirizes Berlioz's willingness to expand the orchestra and experiment with new instruments, such as the saxophone and English horn. The cannon is meant here as an outrageous joke.

A slow introduction establishes a reverent atmosphere. Soon the *idée fixe* is heard:

Brackets have been placed over the fixed idea in the music examples.

The orchestra builds up to mighty climactic moments of sound, which is typical of Berlioz's Romantic style.

II. A Ball   "Amid the tumult and excitement of a brilliant ball, he glimpses the loved one again."

    This movement is a waltz. Its introduction features the harp playing in contrast to rapidly repeated notes in the strings. A waltz is marked to be played sweetly and tenderly. This movement is in a three-part form, with the middle section containing the fixed idea.

The themes from the first and second movements may look different in the examples because they are in different keys, but the pattern of pitch intervals is the same in each.

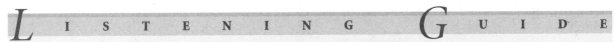

Hector Berlioz: *Symphonie fantastique*, Op. 14
Fifth Movement
CD **2** Track **8**

0:00 **8** The movement opens softly with muted strings playing eerie music. Soon chromatic scales in the various sections of the orchestra give the impression of unearthly sounds.

1:21 A distorted version of the *idée fixe* is played shrilly by the clarinet.

1:38 **9** The woodwinds and then the entire orchestra join in, playing loudly and joyfully a grotesque version of the *idée fixe*.

2:55 Funeral bells are sounded three times, each time with a fragment of the upcoming Witches' Dance interspersed among the tolling of the bells.

Dies irae

3:22 **10** The first phrase of the famous Dies irae chant is played slowly by the low brasses.

3:43 The French horns and trombones play the Dies irae theme with note values cut in half (diminution). Funeral bells are heard occasionally throughout this entire section.

3:54 The woodwinds play a perverted version of the Dies irae at an even faster tempo.

3:59 The second phrase of the Dies irae chant is played. It is followed by repeated appearances of the woodwinds playing dancelike notes and the brasses playing the chant.

Witches' Round Dance (Fugato)

5:15 **11** Four entrances of the same theme are heard as in the exposition of a fugue.

5:43 A short episode begins.

6:02 Three more entrances of the theme are heard, some of which begin before the theme has been completed.

6:19 Another episode, this one containing a rhythmic motive from the theme, begins.

6:58 Fragments of the Dies irae are heard in the low strings, and then the music begins a long buildup based on the Witches' Dance.

7:12 The theme of the Witches' Dance returns and grows to a climactic moment as syncopated chords are clearly heard.

8:01 **12** The witches' theme and the Dies irae are heard together.

9:06 A short section of the Dies irae is played again in the low brass and with the percussion. The music then begins to build.

9:43 The movement ends in a burst of sound.

One of the characteristics of nineteenth-century Romanticism was its interest in nature and rural scenes.

III. Scene in the Fields

"On a summer evening in the country, he hears two shepherds piping. The pastoral duet, the quiet surroundings . . . all unite to fill his heart with a long absent calm. But *she* appears again. His heart contracts. Painful forebodings fill his soul. The sun sets—solitude—silence."

The movement begins slowly. The English horn is featured, which had only recently been included in the orchestra when Berlioz composed the work. The *idée fixe* appears in the middle section of the movement, which is in a three-part form. Before the movement concludes, a distant rumble of thunder can be heard played by the timpani as the English horn plays a melancholy melody.

A *scaffold* is the platform on which criminals were hanged or beheaded.

It is easy to imagine the falling of the ax and the head rolling away when hearing this portion of the music.

IV. March to the Scaffold

"He dreams that he has killed his beloved, that he has been condemned to die and is being led to the scaffold. The procession moves to the sound of a march somber and wild, now brilliant and solemn . . . at the very end the fixed idea appears for an instant like the last thought of love interrupted by the fall of the ax."

The movement is basically a march. Also, in spite of Berlioz's desire to write program music, this movement is essentially in sonata form.

V. Dream of a Witches' Sabbath

"He sees himself at a witches' sabbath surrounded by a host of fearsome specters who have gathered at his funeral. Unearthly sounds, groans, shrieks of laughter . . . the melody of his beloved is heard, but it has lost its noble and reserved character. It has become a vulgar tune, trivial and grotesque. It is *she* who comes to the infernal orgy. A howl of joy greets her arrival. She joins the diabolical dance. Bells toll for the dead. A burlesque of the Dies irae. Dance of the witches. The dance and the Dies irae combined."

The Dies irae appears in many Romantic works, including Rachmaninoff's Rhapsody on a Theme of Paganini, presented in chapter 33. It was also discussed in chapter 12.

The movement opens in a slow tempo. There are flickering scales played softly on muted violins and violas to create an eerie, unearthly quality. In the allegro portion that follows, the theme of the beloved is transformed into a grotesque dance played by the clarinet. It is as if everyone is mocking him. Laughter can be heard in the bassoon part that accompanies the fixed idea. Soon bells toll for the dead (himself), followed by the traditional religious Dies irae ("Day of Wrath") motive, taken from the medieval Mass for the dead, played by the bassoons and tuba.

In the "Ronde du sabbat" ("Witches' Dance") portion of the movement, a driving rhythm first heard in the cellos and basses is taken up by other instruments. The combination of the various lines creates an intricate fabric of sound.

RICHARD STRAUSS

A portion presenting majestic chords from *Also Sprach Zarathustra* achieved popularity from its use in the sound track of the film *2001: Space Odyssey*.

Another major nineteenth-century composer of program music was Richard Strauss. His tone poems are monumental in size and sound. At least four or five are performed frequently: *Don Juan, Death and Transfiguration, Till Eulenspiegel's Merry Pranks, Don Quixote,* and *Also Sprach Zarathustra.*

Strauss also composed three successful operas, plus songs and two concertos for French horn and orchestra, but today he is best remembered for his programmatic works.

Coda

Program music explores the imaginative side of Romanticism in a way that is both entertaining and fascinating. What else can one say about a work based on the images of a young man's beloved dancing around him as a cackling witch and other equally fantastic scenes? But what matters most is the music that such scenes inspired.

Ballet and Ballet Music

Ballet is an art form in which music and the visual aspects of body movement, costumes, and scenery are combined for the psychological and artistic satisfaction they provide. Ballet is to dance as art music is to music—an intellectually and emotionally satisfying creation.

There is no clear distinction between concert music and ballet music. Composers originally wrote music specifically to be danced to. But in the past one hundred years, every style of music has also featured ballets. Some ballet music is heard more often today as concert music than in conjunction with a ballet.

Composers often arrange ballet scores as orchestral suites.

Traditionally, the music for a ballet was the result of a collaboration between a composer and a choreographer. Sometimes the choreographer is quite explicit about the type of music desired; at other times only a vague outline is provided for the composer. In a few instances in this century, the dance has been created first, and then the composer has written the music to fit the dance. But the opposite procedure has probably happened more often, when a ballet was created for an existing piece of music.

Like opera, early ballet stories were based on mythological subjects. During the nineteenth century, many plots of ballets had a fairy-tale quality, which is true of Tchaikovsky's *Swan Lake, Sleeping Beauty,* and *The Nutcracker.*

TCHAIKOVSKY'S *NUTCRACKER*

Tchaikovsky was already a famous composer by the time he composed the music for *The Nutcracker* in 1891, only two years before his death. It is the shortest and best known of his three ballets, consisting of fifteen musical works and an overture. A suite of eight pieces from the ballet was organized and presented in 1892, the same year that the ballet itself was given its premiere performance at the Maryinski Theater before the tsar and his court.

The story is filled with fancy and magic, as are many ballet stories. At a Christmas party, Clara receives a gift of a Nutcracker from the eccentric Drosselmeyer. Her brother Fritz breaks her new gift. Sadly she cradles the broken Nutcracker and puts it to sleep in a toy cradle before she goes to bed.

After everyone has fallen asleep, she sneaks back into the room to look at the Nutcracker. Magically, the Christmas tree begins to grow to enormous size. Large mice appear from the corners of the room and challenge the toy soldiers, who are led by the Nutcracker. The soldiers are about to lose the fight when Clara throws a shoe at the Mouse King, and the invading mice flee. The Nutcracker is then transformed into a handsome Prince. The Prince invites her go with him to his kingdom. On the way, they stop in a snow-covered pine forest, and then go to the Kingdom of the Sweets, where Clara is treated to a lavish banquet, complete with entertainment and dancers from several different lands—Arabia, China, Spain, Russia—as well as by the Reed Flutes.

The Development of Ballet

Classical ballet began in the courts of Europe, especially France, about three hundred years ago. Its main goal was to achieve grace and courtliness, not artistic expression. Deportment and etiquette were supreme virtues among the aristocracy. In the court of Louis XIV of France, for example, everyone took dancing lessons, and this dancing was not a type in which they just shuffled around. One feature of such dancing was proper ballet posture; another was a balance of footwork and elevation—the ability to rise on the toes and to leap gracefully. Ballet posture was based on a straight and quiet spine; a stiffened, straight knee; and a level hip line. The hips were not to lift, thrust out, or rotate, and the shoulders were not to ripple.

From such principles and practices there developed a systematic set of positions and steps that are basic in classical ballet. From these and other movements, which often carry French names, the choreographer *(the designer of dances) plans routines and sequences for a complete scene. The choreography is carefully designed to fit with the music and its story, if there is one. (Not all ballets are developed around a story.)*

The first truly Romantic ballet was La Sylphide *(1832) by Jean Scheitzhöffer. Its story was one of love between a supernatural being and a human. If not remembered for its music, this ballet can make two claims to fame: (1) The female lead wore a tight-fitting costume with a short, flared skirt that became the standard for women in all Romantic ballets. (2) It was the first ballet in which the leading ballerina danced on the points of her slippers, which created the technique for dancing on the toes, referred to as* en pointe.

Other ballets that followed in the Romantic tradition are: Giselle *by Adolphe Adam,* Coppélia *by Leo Délibes, and the three ballets by Tchaikovsky discussed in this chapter.*

The art of ballet remained relatively unchanged until the twentieth century. Ballet is a beautiful art form, but it is also artificial. The first reaction against these artificialities occurred near the turn of the twentieth century, when Isadora Duncan threw off her corset and shoes and danced barefoot throughout Europe. She believed that dancing should be harmonious and simple with no ornaments. Although she devised no new techniques, she gave ballet a more natural look. Her ideas were adopted by Michel Fokine, Ruth St. Denis, Martha Graham, Agnes de Mille, and others. To some extent the separation between classical ballet and modern dance still exists, with dancers often promoting one type or the other.

The music for ballet also changed greatly in the twentieth century. One of the most important landmarks in ballet is The Rite of Spring *with music by Stravinsky, which is presented in chapter 42. Other well-known twentieth-century American ballets are* Rodeo, Appalachian Spring, *and* Billy the Kid, *all with music by Aaron Copland.*

Piotr Ilich Tchaikovsky

Until early adulthood **Piotr Tchaikovsky** ("Chy-*koff*-skee," 1840-1893) seemed destined to follow in his father's footsteps by working in a government position. At the age of twenty-three, however, he decided to become a musician, resigned his job, and entered the newly founded Conservatory of Music in St. Petersburg. He did well, and in three years he had finished his course of study. He was recommended for a teaching position in the new Conservatory in Moscow, where he taught harmony for twelve years.

Throughout his life Tchaikovsky was plagued by the fact that he was a homosexual. He once described his existence as "regretting the past, hoping for the future, without ever being satisfied with the present." He married a Conservatory student, a rather unstable girl who was madly in love with him. The marriage was a disaster. Finally, on the verge of a complete mental breakdown, he went to live with his brothers in St. Petersburg.

Nadezhda von Meck entered his life at this point. She was a wealthy widow who, though a recluse, successfully ran her inherited business empire and the lives of her eleven children. She was impressed by the beauty of Tchaikovsky's music and decided to support him financially. There was, however, one unusual stipulation: So that she could be sure she was supporting a composer, not a personal friend, she required that they should never meet. And so it was. For thirteen years they carried on an intense and devoted relationship—all by letters.

In 1893 while in St. Petersburg to conduct his Sixth Symphony, Tchaikovsky contracted cholera and died. Although he was born and

> Tchaikovsky visited
> New York City in the
> early 1890s and conducted
> at Carnegie Hall.

lived in Russia, his music is not particularly nationalistic, especially in contrast to some of his contemporaries, who are discussed in subsequent chapters.

Best-Known Works
Ballet:
- *The Nutcracker*
- *Sleeping Beauty*
- *Swan Lake*

Opera:
- *Eugene Onegin*

Orchestra:
- Piano Concerto No. 1
- Violin Concerto
- *Romeo and Juliet*
- Overture 1812
- Symphonies Nos. 4, 5, and 6

In the ballet Clara usually wears a diamond-like crown.

The Nutcracker looks like an old-fashioned soldier in dress uniform. A lever in his back caused the jaw to move up and down. It would crack a nut that had been placed in its mouth.

The Nutcracker ends as Clara awakens to find that she has had only a vivid dream.

The music for the ballet is not heavy and serious; that would not be in the character of the story. All of it is beautiful and very listenable. The eight parts of the *Nutcracker Suite* are:

1. Miniature Overture
2. March
3. Dance of the Sugar Plum Fairy
4. Russian Dance, "Trepak"
5. Arab Dance
6. Chinese Dance
7. Dance of Reed Flutes
8. Waltz of the Flowers

The Waltz of the Flowers is danced in tribute to Clara by the Sugar Plum Fairy's attendants.

L I S T E N I N G   G U I D E

Piotr Tchaikovsky: Waltz of the Flowers from *The Nutcracker*
CD **4** Track **14**

0:00 **14** The orchestra opens with a fragment of the first theme, which is followed by a short passage for the harp.

0:20 The harp plays a long cadenza.

1:08 The French horns play the first theme, which is answered by running eighth notes played by the violins.

1:16 The running eighth notes continue to build until the strings reach the high point of the waltz.

1:24 The waltz section is repeated exactly, beginning with the French horns followed by the violins.

1:40 The waltz continues and is repeated.

2:12 The *A* theme returns.

2:43 The *A* theme is repeated.

3:14 **15** A second waltz theme is played by the violins.

3:46 The second waltz theme is played again by the violins.

4:28 The violins play the *B* theme again.

4:40 The first waltz theme returns, played by the French horns, which are then followed by the violins playing running eighth notes.

5:11 The high point of the waltz is reached again as the music glides along.

5:51 The music suddenly becomes softer as the running notes of the violins begin to build. Soon the meter changes for several measures from three beats to two, which increases the intensity of the music.

6:21 The music suddenly becomes soft again and another passage in two-beat meter begins; the music grows in intensity as it pushes to the end.

6:50 The Waltz of the Flowers concludes with a series of full-sounding chords.

C o d a

The goal of ballet in the nineteenth century was to present sheer beauty. The scenery, dancing, and music were rich and enchanting. It was definitely not of this world, but one that transcended it, just as Clara's dream took her away to new and wonderful experiences.

Many Romantic artists and musicians held the view that the arts were not of this world but rather were above it or exceeded it.

Romantic Opera

Italian opera dominated the opera world until the
nineteenth century. But that situation was about to change.
Several other distinct styles of opera developed during the
Romantic period. One was the German style, followed
later in the century by the French and Russian styles.
Italian opera also changed, but less dramatically.

THE ITALIAN STYLE

There are some differences in the two operas. Figaro is a valet in Mozart's opera, not a barber as he is in Rossini's.

At the beginning of the nineteenth century, Italian opera was still in the style of Mozart's *Don Giovanni*, discussed in chapter 21. Gioacchino Rossini (1792–1868) even based his opera *The Barber of Seville* on the same characters found in Mozart's *The Marriage of Figaro*.

With Vincenzo Bellini (1801–1835) Italian opera reached a high point of interest in melody. The arias in his operas such as *Norma* emphasize beautiful singing through technically demanding melodic lines, cadenzas, and ornamentation. This style of opera is termed *bel canto,* which means "beautiful singing" in Italian. Gaetano Donizetti (1797–1848) also contributed to the bel canto style of opera. Although these early operas often lack convincing dramatic qualities, the brilliance of the soloists' lines and the beauty of the melodies make them highly enjoyable listening.

The two most important names in Italian opera in the nineteenth century were Giuseppe Verdi and Giacomo Puccini. Both wrote operas that contained the beauty of bel canto melodies, but they added much more to their music.

VERDI'S *RIGOLETTO*

In Europe, especially Italy, opera was very popular. Its appeal reached well beyond the upper classes.

"La donna è mobile" achieved a popular status in the United States in the 1950s as recorded by a tenor named Mario Lanza.

Rigoletto is hardly the typical hero—handsome and dashing. Instead, he is a hunchbacked court jester. And he isn't even a nice guy. His one redeeming virtue is his love for his daughter, Gilda. Rigoletto's master, the womanizing Duke of Mantua, has been able to get Gilda to fall in love with him while he pretended to be a poor student. He manages to seduce Gilda, which motivates Rigoletto to plot the Duke's murder. But Gilda really loves the Duke, even when she finds out that he is a liar and a cheat. In the end she sacrifices her own life to save his. As often happens in Romantic opera, evil overcomes good.

The Duke's aria "La donna è mobile" ("Woman is fickle") expresses the Duke's pleasure-seeking personality. It also shows Verdi's ability to compose rousing music. He knew that the aria would be a hit, and he didn't want it to leak out of rehearsals and have everyone singing it before the opera opened. Therefore, he waited until as close as possible to the premiere to give the music to the tenor who had the Duke's role.

PUCCINI'S *LA BOHÈME*

A *garret* is an unfurnished space just under the roof.

La bohème (The Bohemian) is a story of the artsy, hippie life on the Left Bank of the Seine in Paris. The curtain rises on the run-down garret where four young men live: the poet Rodolfo, the painter Marcello, the philosopher Colline, and the musician

Giuseppe Verdi

Best-Known Works of Verdi
Opera:
- *Il trovatore*
- *La traviata*
- *Rigoletto*
- *A Masked Ball*
- *Aïda*
- *Otello*
- *Falstaff*

Giuseppe Verdi ("*Vair-dee,*" 1813–1901) was born in a small town in northern Italy, the son of a poor innkeeper. He probably would not have had a musical education had it not been for the support of a prosperous merchant who paid for two years' study in Milan. When Verdi returned, he fell in love with the merchant's daughter. The marriage was a happy one, but misfortune struck. His two children and his young wife died within a three-year span.

Although Verdi's first opera had been moderately successful, the next one was not. That failure, coupled with the tragedies in his family, caused him to give up composing for a year. He was finally persuaded to write another opera on the story of Nebuchadnezzar,

> Verdi shortened the title to *Nabucco.*

the biblical king of Babylon. It was an immediate success and it launched Verdi on a career that spanned more than fifty years. Part of his success lay in his selection of high-quality libretti. He was also an excellent dramatist and sensed what would be effective onstage.

Verdi's career was helped by the strong nationalistic feelings of the Italians, who were attempting to free themselves from the control of Austria. Cries of "Viva Verdi" rang out in Italian opera houses, both in admiration of Verdi and in allegiance to Italy. To many patriots the letters of his name represented "*Victor Emmanuel, Rex d'Italia.*"

> The phrase means "Victor Emmanuel, King of Italy." He was Italy's first king.

In spite of his fame, Verdi remained a simple man who preferred the quiet of his farm to the pressures of society. His second wife was a sensitive and intelligent woman who encouraged him in his work. Verdi was able to produce one masterpiece after another. He wrote his last operas when he was nearly eighty years old.

Giacomo Puccini ("*Poo-chee-nee,*" 1858–1924) was a generation younger than Verdi and perhaps not so sophisticated a composer. He possessed a wonderful gift of melody,

Giacomo Puccini

Best-Known Works of Puccini
Opera:
- *La bohème*
- *Tosca*
- *Madame Butterfly*
- *Turandot*

however, and an instinct for successful theater. These attributes made his operas very popular.

Puccini belonged to a group of opera composers who stressed *verismo* (realism).

> *Verismo* operas have no mythological queens or gods.

Their characters came from everyday life, and they rejected heroic or exalted themes from mythology and history. In *La bohème,* for example, four young men occupy a shabby, cold apartment and have trouble meeting the rent and finding enough to eat.

Schaunard. It's Christmas Eve, and they can't afford fuel for a decent fire. Colline and Schaunard come back and flourish some of that rare item—money. The landlord, who seems to have heard of their good fortune, soon comes to ask for the rent. By the use of a little trickery, they are able to get rid of him. They decide to celebrate at the Café Momus, and everyone except Rodolfo leaves; he is finishing some writing and plans to join them shortly.

The young men's break comes when the landlord brags about his virility with women, and they threaten to tell his wife.

Soon there's a knock at the door. It is Mimi, who has not met Rodolfo before. Her candle has gone out, and she can't see to get up the stairs to her apartment. She is also weak and out of breath, so Rodolfo gives her a little wine and offers her a chair. As he helps her search for the key she has dropped on the floor, a draft of wind blows out their candles. They grope in the dark for her key. He finds it and, thinking quickly, slips it into his pocket without telling her. As they continue feeling along the floor, Rodolfo's hand meets hers and he exclaims, "*Che gelida manina!*" ("How cold

How fortunate for the plot that the wind just happened to come along at that moment!

LISTENING GUIDE

Giuseppe Verdi: "La donna è mobile" from *Rigoletto*

CD [2] Track [13]

0:00   [13] The orchestra plays a short introduction.

0:13

La donna è mobile	Woman is fickle
Qual piuma al vento,	Like a feather in the breeze,
Muta d'accento	She changes her words
E di pensiero.	And her thoughts.

0:21

Sempre un amabile	Always a lovable
Leggiadro viso,	And beautiful face,
In pianto o in riso,	Crying or laughing,
É menzognero	Is lying.

Obviously, the Duke is pretty cynical.

0:31   La donna è mobile, ecc.   Woman is fickle, etc.

1:07   [13]

É sempre misero	The man's always miserable
Chi a lei s'affida,	Who believes in her,
Chi le confida	Who carelessly trusts
Mal cauto il core!	His heart to her!
Pur mai non sentesi	And yet one who never
Felice appieno	Enjoys love on that breast
Chi su quel seno	Never feels
Non libra amore!	Really in love!

1:26   La donna è mobile, ecc.   Woman is fickle, etc.

2:02   Aria concludes with the tenor singing a long high note and decisive chords played by the orchestra.

your little hand is!") Then begins one of those glorious arias and a duet that show off Romantic opera at its best.

First Rodolfo tells Mimi about himself and his lonely life as a poet. Mimi responds with an equally beautiful aria. In it she describes her simple life and the flowers she embroiders.

Rodolfo's friends return to the courtyard outside, urging him to get going. He goes to the window and tells them to return to Momus and reserve a table. As his friends leave, Mimi and Rodolfo break into a duet in which they speak of the newfound love that binds them together. Some of the melodies previously introduced in the arias are heard again.

In good operatic tradition, Mimi and Rodolfo fall in love very quickly. Musically, it all works very well, even if it isn't quite realistic. The scene would not be effective opera if their relationship were allowed to grow more naturally over several hours.

The rest of *La bohème* is equally beautiful and not long, as least by the standards of nineteenth-century opera. Act II is a delightful scene at the Café Momus in which Musetta, Marcello's former love and a notorious flirt, sings a tantalizing waltz. In act III, Mimi and Rodolfo have had a falling out. There is a hint of impending doom because of Mimi's deteriorating health from tuberculosis.

LISTENING GUIDE

Giacomo Puccini: *La bohème*
excerpt from act I
CD 4 Track 16

0:00   **16**   Rodolfo is entranced with the sight of Mirni as she stands in the moonlight.

Indicates that the pitches Rodolfo is to sing are one octave lower than written.

0:39   **17**

1:44

2:30

4:07   The curtain falls and the music for act I ends as Mimi and Rodolfo leave the stage arm-in-arm.

In act IV the setting is again the garret, and there are several musical dramatic parallels to the first act. This time Musetta enters, saying that Mimi is downstairs, too weak to climb up them—an ironic parallel to the events of the earlier act. Mimi is helped into the room, and the friends leave quickly to get medicine and a doctor. Rodolfo and Mimi recall their first meeting. The old themes are heard, but the music is no longer robust. It is weak and shattered. The friends return. They talk quietly among themselves, hoping Mimi can sleep. Suddenly, they realize that she has died. "Mimi! Mimi!" Rodolfo cries out. The orchestra strikes the same chords heard in the love music from act I. This time, however, the music is heavy with grief. The curtain falls.

Romantic operas usually end tragically. It's more dramatic that way.

The final act of *La bohème* ends with the death of Mimi in the arms of Rodolfo, here performed by Luciano Pavarotti. Often the duet is staged so that it is sung with a soft spotlight shining on the couple.

THE FRENCH STYLE

The French did not develop quite as distinct a style of opera as the Italians or the Germans did. Yet their operas do sound different. The more distinctive French quality would flourish at the turn of the century in the impressionistic music of Debussy and Ravel.

Three French opera composers merit attention. One is Charles Gounod ("Goo-*noh*," 1818–1893). His best-known work is *Faust*, in which a man named Faust sells his soul to the devil in exchange for eternal youth. The Faust legend, which exists in a number of different versions, fascinated the Romantic poets and musicians. Another composer of French opera was Jules Massenet ("Mass-en-*nay*," 1842–1912). His best-known operas are *Manon* and *Thaïs;* the "Meditation" from that opera is often heard as a solo for violin or singer.

The opera that nearly everyone has heard about, and most people find very attractive, is *Carmen* by Georges Bizet. Actually, *Carmen* was first presented at the opera comique with spoken lines instead of sung recitatives. It is not as long and serious as the operas usually presented at the Opera House in Paris. Ironically, it was not initially very well received, which broke Bizet's spirit, and he did not live long after its premiere. Today *Carmen* is the most popular opera in the Western world.

Although *Carmen* takes place in Spain and contains much Spanish-sounding music, it is in French and was composed by a Frenchman.

The opera comique was more family theater, and probably the femme fatale role of Carmen was disturbing to its patrons.

THE GERMAN STYLE

German opera differs from Italian opera in a number of ways. To begin with, the languages are very different. Italian words end in one of the five vowel sounds of the language. German words often conclude with consonants, many of them with hard *t*'s and *k*'s. The subjects are no longer ancient Greek gods but rather the Nordic gods of northern Europe. And the music is different, too. German opera tends to sound heavier and less lighthearted than that of Italy or France.

In 1821 the German composer Carl Maria von Weber ("*Vay*-ber," 1786–1826) wrote *Der Freischütz (The Freeshooter)*, an opera based on German folklore. The story involves a marksman who receives from the black huntsman seven magic bullets. Six of the seven do as he wills, but the seventh does as the devil wills. The devil also gets the soul of the one who is hit by the bullet. Besides mysticism, the opera features peasants, rustic scenes, and hunting horns.

The black huntsman is the devil.

Weber completed two more operas before his early death. Although they are seldom performed today, they exerted a significant influence on Richard Wagner, one of the musical giants of the nineteenth century.

Wagner's Music Dramas

More than any previous opera composer, Richard Wagner consciously tackled the dilemma of balance between music and drama. In his lengthy philosophical discourses, he often indicated his belief that poetry and music should be one. To meet his artistic goals, he created a different kind of opera, one that he called *music drama*.

Music dramas required a new and different approach to the concept of libretto, so Wagner wrote his own texts. The topics were mythological, because he felt that such stories appealed best to the emotions. Wagner's favorite libretto themes were also rich with philosophical overtones—the struggle between good and evil, the contest between the physical and the spiritual, and the idea of redemption through love. Because these overarching themes are present, the characters in the music dramas are not personalities but more like symbols or pawns being pushed about by uncontrollable forces. In this respect, Wagner approaches the drama of the ancient Greeks.

Wagner frequently associates a musical motive with a particular character, emotion, or idea. In his music such a motive is called a *leitmotiv,* or leading motive. As soon as various leitmotivs are established, Wagner weaves them in and out of the music at appropriate times to enhance the intrigue of the plot and to provide unity in the work. Such use of motives permits the orchestra to assume a much

Each of his operas has a score the size of a large book.

Richard Wagner

Richard Wagner ("*Ree*-card *Vahg*-ner," 1813–1883) was an artistic phenomenon. Born in Leipzig, Germany, he was the son of a minor police official who died when Richard was still an infant. His mother married an actor and playwright, who encouraged his stepson along similar lines. For most of his career, Wagner was largely self-taught. At the age of twenty, he became a chorus master in a small opera house in Leipzig and produced his first operas.

Success was slow in coming, and for the next ten years it seemed like Wagner would spend his life hovering on the edge of poverty. His first successful opera was *Rienzi,* which earned him a position as conductor for the king of Saxony. Other successful operas followed in the 1840s.

In 1848 Wagner became associated with the political uprisings that were taking place in Europe. He even published two articles in a magazine that advocated anarchy. A revolution broke out in Dresden in 1849, and the king and his court fled. Wagner was forced to escape to the home of his friend Franz Liszt in Weimar. Because there was a warrant out for his arrest, Wagner soon fled over the border into Switzerland. At that point

he seemed a ruined man. But he was helped by some willing patrons, and the years in Switzerland were some of his most productive. It was during this time that he began work on *The Ring of the Nibelung.*

Wagner became estranged from his wife, who had grown unsympathetic to his artistic aims and desires. He became involved with a succession of married women. In 1864 again all seemed lost. At that point fate seemed to step in. A nineteen-year-old admirer of Wagner's music ascended to the throne in Bavaria. He was Ludwig II, known as "Mad Ludwig." He summoned Wagner to Munich, where he resumed work on *The Ring of the Nibelung.*

> Bavaria, now part of Germany, was an independent state at that time.

By 1876 Wagner had reached the top of the operatic world. It was during that year that he opened his first Bayreuth ("*By*-royt") festival. Later he built an opera house there, and the Bayreuth festivals continue today. It is the only theater in the world devoted exclusively to the music of one person. He is buried at Bayreuth, which in a sense is his monument.

Best-Known Works
Opera:
- [ ] *The Flying Dutchman*
- [ ] *Tannhäuser*
- [ ] *Lohengrin*
- [ ] *Tristan and Isolde*
- [ ] *The Meistersingers of Nuremberg*
- [ ] *The Ring of the Nibelung*

more vital role in the music drama, because it can expand on the people and ideas referred to in the text.

Because the division of music into recitatives, arias, and choruses interrupts the forward motion of the drama, Wagner eliminated these forms as independent sections. Instead he created a flowing, melodious line to serve as an unending melody. The vocal line emphasizes the expression of the words being sung. With its continuous interweaving of motives, the orchestra contributes to the impression of never-ending motion.

There are some arias in Wagner's music dramas, but they are carefully woven into the flow of the music.

To increase the impression that a musical work is seamless, Wagner used much chromatic harmony. By making half-step alternations in the chords, he weakened the magnetic pull of the harmony toward the tonic. The absence of a strong tonic means that the music seldom arrives at a cadence point, so the feeling of key is somewhat nebulous.

Wagner did not treat the orchestra as mere accompaniment for the singers onstage. The importance of the orchestra in his works equals, or perhaps exceeds, that of the singers. In a real sense, his orchestra is symphonic, both in size and in its ability to stand almost without the vocal parts.

Portions of his music dramas are often performed as concert pieces without singers.

Wagner's most ambitious achievement was a cycle of four complete operas titled *Der Ring des Nibelungen (The Ring of the Nibelung)*. The four operas in the cycle are *Das Rheingold (The Gold of the Rhine), Die Walküre (The Valkyries), Siegfried,* and *Götterdämmerung (The Twilight of the Gods)*.

The story of the cycle of operas revolves around some gold that had been fashioned into a ring and is guarded by the Rhine maidens in the Rhine River. The gold is stolen and a curse put on it. The curse states that if the possessor will renounce love, he will rule the world. The result is a chain of misfortunes affecting all the characters in the drama.

In Romantic operas the course of events often hinges on curses or magic potions.

WAGNER'S *GÖTTERDÄMMERUNG*

In an earlier opera in *The Ring* cycle, Wotan, king of the gods, made his favorite daughter, Brünnhilde, mortal because she disobeyed him. She falls into a deep sleep, surrounded by a wall of fire. Siegfried passes through the flames and awakens her. Siegfried and Brünnhilde fall in love and become husband and wife.

While on one of his adventures, Siegfried gains possession of the ring. Unfortunately for him, he does not know about the curse. He is subsequently murdered by the evil Hagen, who lusts after the gold.

The immolation scene occurs very late in *Götterdämmerung*. It takes place in front of a castle on the Rhine River. In this scene Brünnhilde sings her farewell before joining Siegfried in death by riding her horse into his funeral pyre. Before ending her life, she takes the ring from Siegfried's finger and puts it on. She also bequeaths it to the Rhine maidens upon her death. After she disappears into the flames, a flood engulfs the stage. The flood is followed by a fire. Valhalla, the home of the gods, is destroyed, along with its inhabitants. *Götterdämmerung* ends in tragedy for all except the Rhine maidens.

The Twilight of the Gods ends with flaming death, flood, and utter destruction. But because of the power of love, a new world will emerge.

The immolation scene is presented in the Listening Guide. The stage actions appear in parenthetical statements. The text is provided in the original German and in an English translation.

As you listen to this scene, pay careful attention to Wagner's use of the leitmotivs. Notice how they not only enhance the text, but continue the story, even after the characters have died.

Although *Götterdämmerung* ends tragically, the final leitmotiv is "Redemption by love." The philosophically minded Wagner was saying through this leitmotiv that the most powerful force of all is love, and that, in spite of all that had happened, a new world will emerge through its power.

Richard Wagner: Immolation scene from *Götterdämmerung*

CD **4** Track **18**

0:00   **18** The trumpets and trombones play the leitmotiv for "Law" at a loud dynamic level.

Brünnhilde, the ring on her finger, takes a torch from one of the men.
She then sings to a pair of ravens, which are Wotan's messengers.

0:14   Fliegt heim, ihr Raben! raunt es eurem Herren,   Fly home, you ravens! Tell your master
        was hier am Rhein ihr gehört!   what you have heard here on the Rhine!

0:27   The orchestra plays the "Magic fire" and "Loge, god of fire" leitmotivs.

Brünnhilde continues singing to the ravens.

An Brünnhildes Felsen fliegt vorbei: Fly past Brünnhilde's rock,
der dort noch lodert,   where Loge is still burning,
weiset Loge nach Walhall!   and tell him to go to Valhalla!
Denn der Götter Ende dämmert nun auf: Because the end of the gods now is dawning.

She throws the torch onto the pyre. The two ravens fly into the background.

so—werf' ich den Brand   See—I throw the torch
in Walhalls prangende Burg.   into Valhalla's glorious fortress!

1:27   The strings play an ascending passage.

The pyre bursts into flames. Brünnhilde turns to her horse.

Grane, mein Ross.   Grane, my steed,
sei mir gegrüsst!   Greetings to you!

1:57   The French horns and other instruments sound the "Ride of the Valkyries" leitmotiv.

Weisst du auch, mein Freund,   My friend, do you know
wohin ich dich führe?   where I am leading you?
Im Feuer leuchtend.   Into the blazing fire.

2:09   **19** The flute and Brünnhilde sound the "Redemption by love" leitmotiv.

liegt dort dein Herr, Siegfried, mein seliger Held.   Your master lies in there, Siegfried, my blessed hero.
Dem Freunde zu folgen,   Are you eager to follow your friend?
wieherst du freudig?   Are you neighing?
Lockt dich zu ihm die lachende Lohe?   Are you attracted by the laughing flames?

2:43   Fühl' mein Brust auch, wie sie entbrennt;   Notice my breast also, how it is burning;
        helles Feuer das Herz mir erfasst.   bright flames consume my heart.
        Ihn zu umschlingen, umschlossen, von ihm,   To hold him, to be held by him,
        in mächtigster Minne vermählt ihm zu sein!   to be united with him by the power of love!

3:16   Hei-a-ja-ho! Grane! Grüss deinen Herren!   Hei-a-yo-ho! Grane! Greet your master!
        Siegfried! Siegfried! Sieh!   Siegfried! Siegfried! See!
        selig grüsst dich dein Weib!   Joyfully your wife greets you!

3:34   The brasses play the "Ride of the Valkyries" leitmotiv.

Brünnhilde mounts her horse and rides it into the flaming pyre.

3:42   The orchestra plays the "Magic fire" leitmotiv at a loud dynamic level.

Flames engulf the area in front of the castle, which also soon catches fire.

The "Magic sleep" leitmotiv is heard.

When everything seems to be burning, the glow is extinguished. Soon only a cloud of smoke is seen.

The Rhine begins to rise, and its waters pour over the fire. Three Rhine maidens ride the waves and appear by the funeral pyre. Hagen, Siegfried's murderer, panics when he sees them. He tosses down his spear and shield, and then plunges into the waters, crying:

Zurück vom Ring!   **Away from the ring!**

Two Rhine maidens grab Hagen and drag him down under the water. Another Rhine maiden triumphantly holds up the recovered ring.

A descending pattern played by the strings suggests Hagen's drowning.

5:03   **20**   The oboes and clarinets play the "Rhine maidens" leitmotiv.

5:12   The brasses sound the solemn "Valhalla" leitmotiv.

The Rhine gradually returns to its banks, and the Rhine maidens play with the ring in its calm waters.

5:23   An interweaving of leitmotivs is heard. The oboes and clarinets play the "Rhine maidens"; the violins play "Redemption by love"; the brasses sound "Valhalla." That leitmotiv grows more prominent as the music progresses.

From the ruins of the burned castle, the men and women see the red glow in the heavens. In that glow appears Valhalla, with gods and heroes sitting together.

6:51   The music grows louder as the brasses sound the "Siegfried" leitmotiv.

Flames overcome Valhalla. The gods disappear in the flames.

7:03   Strings sound "Redemption by love" leitmotiv.

7:56   The curtain falls with a long chord.

$C\ o\ d\ a$

Although the Italian, French, and German styles of opera differed from one another in the nineteenth century, they were similar in their fondness for expansive emotion—especially feelings associated with tragedies—and glorious, sensuous music. Romantic operas reach out over the footlights and capture the emotions of the audience.

Romantic Instrumental Music

The composers of the Romantic period never completely abandoned the forms used by Mozart and Haydn in the Classical period. In fact, some composers, especially in the last half of the nineteenth century, used traditional forms extensively. Most of these compositions were for orchestral instruments, although quite a number of them involved the piano.

The works created in the century after the Classical period do not sound at all like their predecessors. They are noticeably different, even though the same basic form may be the framework for the music.

The music composed between about 1785 and 1910 constitutes the heart of the repertoire for the symphony orchestra.

The music of two important Romantic composers is discussed here. These works can then serve as examples for the very large body of music they represent.

BRAHMS'S SYMPHONY NO. 4

Brahms composed only four symphonies, but each has a prominent place in the repertoire of the symphony orchestra. By the second half of the nineteenth century, composers were treating symphonies as almost monumental efforts. Brahms was so awed by the symphonies of Beethoven that he waited to complete his first symphony until he was forty-three years old. An earlier aborted attempt at writing a symphony became his First Piano Concerto. He completed his Fourth Symphony nine years later in 1885.

Of all the Romantic composers, Brahms liked to use traditional forms the most. In fact, during his lifetime he was considered by many musicians to be an outmoded conservative. But conservative, Romantic, or whatever, he composed much music of extraordinary quality.

First Movement

The first movement is in sonata form. It begins with a theme that has the sweeping, Romantic quality of many of Brahms's melodies:

The term for reducing the note values in half or other smaller proportions is *diminution.* The result is that the notes go by faster.

The theme is worked with and manipulated throughout much of the movement. For instance, in the next few measures the same idea appears at *twice* its original speed. The notes don't follow the theme exactly, but the general idea is present:

At the end of the development section, the same idea appears at *half* its original speed. At this point in the movement, Brahms retains the melodic line but alters the rhythm:

The term for doubling the note values is *augmentation*. The result is that notes last longer and sound slower.

At another place, the theme is varied and exchanged between the first and second violins:

Elsewhere it is exchanged between the strings and woodwinds:

One could go on for pages showing the many ways Brahms fragments, varies, develops, and transforms the theme. Almost from the time the theme appears, he is developing it and blending it into the structure of the music in such a way that throughout the symphony he maintains the warm sounds of the Romantic style. From it he extracts two motives, circled in the Listening Guide, that appear often in the movement.

The second theme combines two melodic ideas. One is played by the horns and a few woodwinds. It sounds somewhat like introductory music—and perhaps it is, because soon a passionate melody starts in the cellos and horns. A portion of the theme, including the triplets, is also used as a unifying motive in the movement. Sometimes it is exchanged with the first motive.

A third theme appears later in the movement, but it is not developed extensively. Four qualities stand out about Brahms's music in general and his Fourth Symphony in particular:

◆ The sheer beauty of the music. Listening to the rich sounds of its melodies and harmonies could be compared to eating a piece of a perfectly baked German chocolate cake.

You can listen to Brahms's music with your heart, or your head, or both, which is the best way.

◆ The skill with which themes are organized and developed. This is much more than sensual pleasure in listening to this symphony. Brahms is masterful in working with themes and utilizing forms.

◆ The quality of optimism and good feeling. This is a subjective element, of course, but there is something about Brahms's music that gives the feeling that things are right and will continue to turn out right. There is no sense of hand-wringing or self-pity in the music.

◆ The noble quality of the music. The word *noble* doesn't do justice to the music of Brahms and many other composers, but it comes as close as any. It means "possessing outstanding or superior qualities." There is something extraordinary about the music of Brahms and many other composers, something that is beyond or better than what we usually encounter in everyday life.

A listener's score for the first movement of Brahms's Symphony No. 4 is provided in the *Study Guide*.

Johannes Brahms: Symphony No. 4 in F Minor
First Movement
CD 4 Track 21

Exposition

0:00   21 The violins play the first theme, which contains two motives.

0:37   The first theme is repeated, accompanied by moving notes.

1:40   22 The second theme is introduced by the woodwinds. It also contains a motive.

1:46   The second part of the second theme is a passionate melody played by the cellos.

1:59   The violins play the second part of the second theme at a high pitch level.

2:13   The first part of the second theme returns in somewhat varied form.

2:51   The third theme is introduced by the French horn and clarinet.

3:18   The first part the second theme is played by the woodwinds in a somewhat varied form.

4:02   The codetta begins with the woodwinds playing fragments of the first theme.

Development

4:20   23 The development section begins with the return of the first theme, but soon a motive from it is heard several times in succession in different keys.

5:06   A fragment from the first theme consisting of three solid, accented notes is played many times in succession, sometimes in inversion.

5:44	The first part of the second theme is played by the woodwinds.
6:19	The first part of the second theme is continued by the strings and is soon answered by the woodwinds.
6:40	Fragments of the first theme are played pizzicato by the violins.
6:54	The motive from the first theme is played many times in succession alternately by the violins and woodwinds.
7:37	The woodwinds play the return of the first theme in augmentation, followed by flowing notes played by the violins.

Recapitulation

8:05	**24** The first theme returns at the original speed.
9:18	The first part of the second theme is played by the woodwinds.
9:24	The cellos and French horns play the second part of the second theme.
10:03	A fragment from the first part of the second theme is played by the woodwinds.
10:27	The third theme is played by the oboe and French horn.
10:55	The opening motive from the first part of the second theme is played softly by the woodwinds.
11:10	The opening motive of the first part of the second theme is played loudly by the strings and is extended by the violins.
11:58	**25** The coda begins with two-note fragments from the first theme being exchanged, and then in imitation between the strings and French horns at a full dynamic level.
12:57	The two-note fragment from the first theme is exchanged more frequently as the intensity of the music increases.
13:19	The movement concludes after five abrupt chords and a final cadence of two long chords.

Second, Third, and Fourth Movements

Brahms is especially gifted in writing melodious second movements, and his Fourth Symphony is no exception. It is built around two themes. The first consists of a short pattern that is immediately followed in inversion and repeated several times. The second theme is a warm, flowing melody first played by the cellos.

The third movement is filled with an optimistic, jovial spirit. Its theme appears in two versions at the same time, with one being the inversion of the other.

The slur marks (⌒) cause the rhythmic emphasis to occur off the beat in the first and third measures. Portions of the melody appear throughout the movement.

The fourth movement is one of the most unusual and musically interesting found in the symphonies of the nineteenth century. It is a massive *chaconne,* which is a set

Johannes Brahms

Johannes Brahms (1833–1897) was the son of a rather shiftless string bass player in Hamburg, Germany. Johannes started his musical career by playing piano in the notorious waterfront area of the city. He was highly talented and by the age of twenty-five became the accompanist for one of the finest violinists of the day. He studied composition with Robert Schumann, and the Schumanns took the shy young man into their home. Brahms grew fond of Clara, and he was much help to the family during Robert's illness.

Brahms was aware that he had extraordinary talent as a composer, and for this reason never accepted a position that made heavy demands on his time. Unlike Beethoven, he left no rejected versions of his music for posterity to find. He wanted the world to know only his best work, so his rough sketches were deliberately destroyed.

One of Brahms's greatest accomplishments is *Ein Deutsches Requiem* (*A German Requiem*). This profound and monumental work consists

> It was said that Brahms burned as many of his works as he allowed to be published.

of seven movements for bass and soprano soloists, chorus, and orchestra. For its text he selected biblical verses from both the Old and New Testaments.

Brahms never composed an opera or a tone poem. His coolness toward opera may be due to the overblown competition between his admirers and those of Wagner. The division concerned artistic philosophy as much as it did personalities. The Wagnerites believed that music was a means for communication of emotions and ideas. The admirers of Brahms viewed music as an end in itself and, therefore, favored absolute music. Brahms ignored the controversy as best he could and went about his composing. Because there is some truth in both views, the dispute has never been resolved.

Best-Known Works
Chamber music:
- Clarinet Quintet
- Trio in E-flat for Horn, Violin, and Piano

Choral:
- *A German Requiem*

Orchestra:
- Concerto for Piano No. 2
- Concerto for Violin
- Symphonies Nos. 1, 2, 3, and 4
- Variations on a Theme by Haydn

of variations on a short theme. The theme for this movement is only eight measures long with only one note per measure. It is very plain and solid.

Thirty-five variations and a coda follow. At the beginning of the thirteenth variation, the speed of the notes of the theme is slowed to one-half their original speed—augmentation. During this middle section of the movement, the theme is only implied in the harmony. It is easy to tell when the theme returns, because it is played forcefully again, as it was at the opening of the movement. The return of the original theme gives the movement an overall three-part form in addition to the variations of the chaconne. The continually repeated pattern provides unity to the music, while the variations provide contrast.

DVOŘÁK'S AMERICAN STRING QUARTET IN F MAJOR

This was the twelfth quartet that Dvořák had published.

The quartet Op. 96 (No. 12) by Antonín Dvořák is often called the *American Quartet* because he wrote it in the town of Spillville, Iowa. For three years in the 1890s, Dvořák was director of the Conservatory of Music in New York City. He was homesick for his native Bohemia, so he spent his summers living among the Czech-Bohemian people of that town. But this quartet is largely Bohemian in character, not American.

The *American Quartet* contains the traditional four movements, with the same pattern of forms and tempos found in most symphonies, concertos, and chamber works of the Classical and Romantic periods. And because the Romantic period is noted for its large works, it is worth remembering that nineteenth-century composers also wrote much excellent chamber music. Dvořák's *American Quartet* is only one example of this type of music.

First Movement

The first movement of this quartet is in the traditional sonata form. The first theme is built around four one-measure phrases. These one-measure phrases become the germinal ideas for much of the movement. Dvořák uses many dotted-note figures in his music.

Several features stand out about Dvořák's music, specifically the first movement of this string quartet:

♦ The energy and vitality of the music

♦ The good-natured quality of the music

♦ The skill with which Dvořák worked with the four melodic ideas that make up the first theme

♦ The songlike beauty of the second theme

This movement is presented in the Listening Guide.

The notation for the viola part in the Listening Guide uses the alto clef, the normal clef for the viola. Middle C is on the middle line of the clef. It eliminates the extensive use of ledger lines.

LISTENING GUIDE

Antonín Dvořák: *American Quartet*
First Movement
CD **2** Track **15**

Exposition

0:04　**15**　The first theme is played by the viola:

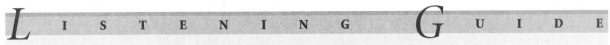

0:12　The first theme is repeated by the first violin.

0:20　The transition, which is based on measures 3 and 4, begins; it is exchanged among the other instruments.

1:32　**16**　The second theme is played softly by the first violin.

2:20　The first three notes of the second theme are used to move into a transition.

2:27　The codetta, which is based on measures 1 and 2 of the first theme, is played softly. The tempo becomes slower just before the development begins.

Development

2:37   **17** The first theme is played by the viola in a somewhat changed version.

3:15   The first measure of the first theme is played by the first viola.

3:48   **18** A new melodic idea is introduced and is soon treated in fugal style by the second violin, with the first violin, viola, and cello following.

Recapitulation

4:22   **19** The first theme is played by the viola.

4:30   The first theme is repeated by the violin.

4:40   A transition begins based on measure 4 of the first theme. The music modulates, and the transition is longer than it was in the exposition.

4:45   A short countermelody is played by the cello.

5:59   The second theme is played by the first violin.

6:12   The second theme is repeated by the cello as the dynamic level begins to build.

6:55   The coda begins with melodic figures from measures 3 and 4 of the first theme.

7:09   The movement closes with loud chords.

Antonín Dvořák

Antonín Dvořák (1841–1904) was born into the family of a Bohemian innkeeper and amateur musician. He grew up listening to the folk music of his native land. After several years of conflict between Dvořák's music teacher and his father, an uncle provided him with the funds needed for a year of music study in Prague. When the money ran out, he earned his living playing in café bands and the National Opera Orchestra.

When Dvořák was about forty, his fortunes changed. He submitted a composition to the Austrian Commission. Although the prize he won was small in monetary terms, it gained for him the devoted friendship and unsparing help of committee member Johannes Brahms. Brahms opened many doors to publishers and conductors for Dvořák, who was genuinely grateful.

By 1885 Dvořák was recognized throughout the world. A few years later, he accepted

> Dvořák once expressed his gratitude in a letter to Brahms: "All my life [I] owe you the deepest gratitude for your good and noble intentions toward me, which are worthy of a truly great artist and man."

the directorship of the Conservatory of Music in New York at a salary twenty times what he was earning in Prague. While in America he was introduced to African American music by his pupil Harry T. Burleigh. He also became acquainted with the music of the Native Americans. He was the first composer, native- or foreign-born, to recognize these musical treasures.

After three years in the United States, Dvořák returned to Bohemia, where he became director of the Prague Conservatory. When he died, a national day of mourning was declared in his honor.

Best-Known Works
Chamber music:
  ☐ String Quartets Nos. 10, 11, and 12
Orchestra:
  ☐ Concerto for Cello
  ☐ Concerto for Violin
  ☐ *Slavonic Dances*
  ☐ Serenade for String Orchestra
  ☐ Symphonies Nos. 8 and 9

Second, Third, and Fourth Movements

The second movement is in a three-part form. The main melody is flowing and sentimental. The middle section of the movement is also melodious, with the first and second violins playing three notes apart.

The third movement has a scherzolike quality. It contains five brief sections in a *ABABA* pattern.

The scherzo is discussed in conjunction with Beethoven's music in chapter 23.

The fourth movement is a rondo, with the pattern of *ABACABA*, which is sometimes termed *sonata rondo*. It has a lively character. It also contains many dotted-note patterns, which Dvořák was fond of using.

THREE ROMANTIC COMPOSERS

The nineteenth century produced so many excellent composers that is it difficult to refrain from discussing many more; however, three French composers merit mention here.

Gabriel Fauré ("For-ray," 1845–1924) was for many years not fully appreciated outside his native France. He was masterful in his handling of harmony, and his music is subtle and melodious. He wrote many songs and a requiem that is often performed, as well as music for piano, orchestra, and chamber ensembles.

César Franck (1822–1890) was born in Belgium but lived most of his life in Paris. He was a quiet, unassuming man who was organist at Saint Clotilde Cathedral. At the age of fifty, he was appointed organ professor at the Paris Conservatory, but his music received only modest acclaim until the last few years of his life. In addition to organ works, he composed a highly successful symphony, a set of variations for piano and orchestra, and a violin sonata. Several of his techniques influenced later composers, especially Claude Debussy.

Camille Saint-Saëns ("Sahn-*sahwns*," 1835–1921) was a gifted, well-read man who could converse with authority on many subjects other than music. He was more conservative than many of his contemporaries. Some of his best-known works are programmatic. One of these is *Danse Macabre*. Its nonmusical association is a postmidnight dance of the skeletons and spirits in a graveyard; the event ends with a rooster's crow. Other works include the *Carnival of the Animals*, an opera *Samson and Delilah*, and several symphonies and piano concertos.

For some reason, Saint-Saëns did not allow public performances of *Carnival of the Animals* during his lifetime.

Coda

As Brahms and Dvořák demonstrate, much of the instrumental music of the nineteenth century retained many of the formal practices of the eighteenth century. Sonata form with its development of themes continued, as well as techniques such as theme and variations. What these composers poured into the forms of the Classical period was very different, however. The flowing melodies, rich harmonies, and expansive character are attributes that mark Romantic instrumental music.

32 *Nationalism*

Romanticism exalted the inherent goodness of humankind in its natural condition. Eighteenth-century intellectuals had considered common folk to be untutored and rough; the Romantics admired them. They thought the life of the simple folk to be good and right because it was largely uncorrupted by society. Furthermore, the life of the common people was a source of subject matter that composers and artists had seldom tapped before.

It should be noted that almost no Romantic composers lived *as peasants. They admired the simple life from a distance.*

CHARACTERISTICS OF NATIONALISM

When associated with the arts, *nationalism* refers to a deliberate, conscious attempt to develop artworks that are characteristic of a particular country or region. Often nationalism involves specific subject matter, such as a painting of a national event or an opera about a historical character.

During the nineteenth century, this search for nationalistic expression was mainly an attempt to break away from the prevailing German-Austrian style. Bach, Mozart, Beethoven, Schubert, Liszt, Schumann, Brahms, and Wagner had long ruled the musical world. To men like Modest Mussorgsky in Russia, Bedřich Smetana in Bohemia, and Edvard Grieg in Norway, it was time for something different. They knew that Russians and Bohemians and Norwegians were as capable of composing music as were the Germans! And they set about proving it.

There was an additional reason for nationalism in the arts during the nineteenth century: It was a time of rising patriotism. Italy and Germany were finally formed as nations. Wars were pathetically frequent. In such conflicts a nation's efforts involved the average citizen to a degree unknown in previous centuries. No longer were wars fought largely by professional soldiers for a king. Now the cause was one's country. In short, the times were a good incubator for nationalism in the arts.

The language of the directions does not affect the actual sounds, but it offers an idea of the composers' outlook toward their music.

In their efforts to assert their independence from foreign influences, some composers indicated the tempo markings and other musical directions in their native language rather than the more internationally accepted Italian. So Debussy wrote *Vif* instead of *Vivace*, Wagner wrote *Schnell*, and some American composers in this century wrote *Lively* or *Fast*, to cite a few examples.

THE RUSSIAN FIVE

Until well into the nineteenth century, Russia had little musical tradition of its own. The czars imported French and Italian opera as well as French ballet. Michael Glinka (1804–1857) was the first Russian composer to write an opera on a Russian theme. Today he is generally considered to be the father of Russian music.

More important was a group of five Russian composers, known as the Russian Five, who lived in the latter half of the Romantic period. The leader of the informal group was Mily Balakirev ("Bal-*lah*-kee-ref," 1837–1910). He himself was not a talented composer. Instead he had a different but important role: to persuade other Russian composers that they didn't need to imitate the German style in order to compose good concert music. He urged them to draw on the musical resources in traditional Russian music. Four composers especially listened to Balakirev's advice: Modest Mussorgsky, César Cui (1835–1918), Aleksandr Borodin ("*Bor*-o-deen," 1833–1887), and Nikolay Rimsky-Korsakov (1844–1908).

Most of the Russian Five had little formal training in music. Balakirev was self-taught. Cui, an engineer, was not a particularly successful composer.

Borodin was a celebrated chemist and an excellent composer. Had he been able to devote more time to composing, his name would be far better known in the music world than it is today. His Second Symphony is performed often, as are *In the Steppes of Central Asia* and String Quartet No. 2. His greatest work was an opera, *Prince Igor,* which was completed after his death by Rimsky-Korsakov and Alexander Glazounov (1865–1936).

Steppes are the treeless tracts of land in southeastern Europe and Asia.

Rimsky-Korsakov represents a phase of Romanticism called *Exoticism.* Like many other Romantic composers, he felt drawn by the mystery and splendor of Eastern cultures. For example, his best-known work is *Scheherazade,* a tone poem based on the Persian legends in *A Thousand and One Nights.* His "Song of India" from the opera *Sadko* and "Hymn to the Sun" from *Le Coq d'Or (The Golden Cockerel)* are other works that reveal his keen interest in Asia. Rimsky-Korsakov also wrote nationalistic music and worked avidly to advance the cause of Russian music.

For a while Rimsky-Korsakov was a sailor in the Russian navy, during which time he visited many foreign countries.

MUSSORGSKY'S *BORIS GODUNOV*

Of the Russian Five, the most original was Mussorgsky. He chose an army career and later became a clerk in the engineering department. He was perhaps the least skilled technically of the five, but he is the one whose music best represents Russian character and culture.

His most significant work, his opera *Boris Godunov,* is derived from a play by the great Russian writer Aleksandr Pushkin. It does not follow a sequential plot, as do most operas. Pushkin's play contained twenty-four scenes. Mussorgsky adapted the libretto himself, using only seven scenes and changing them extensively.

Later research has indicated that Boris was innocent of the crime.

The story is about Czar Boris, who ruled from 1598 to 1605. The plot assumes that Boris had the young Prince Dimitri murdered in order to gain the throne, and the murder is presumed to have taken place before the opera begins. Boris's feelings of guilt are central to the

Modest Mussorgsky

During his lifetime **Modest Mussorgsky** (1839–1881) was considered to be clearly the least accomplished and important of the Russian Five. Today, because of his innovative style and the rugged Russian quality of his music, he is considered the greatest of the five.

He was born into a prosperous landowning family. He showed much talent at the piano at an early age, but he refused to practice and did not seem headed toward a musical career. Instead he entered a military academy. Soon he began drinking heavily, and his skill at the piano and good singing voice made him popular at parties. While still in the military, he met Borodin and Balakirev. They sparked his interest in composing, and he soon left the army.

Mussorgsky's musical genius was not recognized at the time, partly due to his own personality. First, there was the heavy drinking and occasional bizarre behavior in public. His drinking led to delirium tremens and his death at the age of forty-two. Second, he was undisciplined about his work and rarely finished anything he started. Much of his music was finished and revised by Rimsky-Korsakov, and the twentieth-century Russian composer Dmitri Shostakovich (1906–1975) revised his opera *Boris Godunov.*

Best-Known Works
Opera:
 - *Boris Godunov*
 - *Khovanschina*
Orchestra:
 - *A Night on Bare Mountain*
Piano:
 - *Pictures at an Exhibition* (later orchestrated by Maurice Ravel)

A scene from *Boris Godunov*

A generation later
Debussy, who first heard
Mussorgsky's music while
in Russia, used whole tone
scales in his music.

A listener's score for
the coronation scene
from Mussorgsky's *Boris
Godunov* is provided in
the *Study Guide*.

plot, and they finally lead to his death. There is a scheming Polish princess, who with an ambitious pretender to the throne seeks to capture the Kremlin, the huge Moscow fortress from which the czars ruled.

The scene of Boris's death is one of the most moving in opera. The original final scene has a simpleton beggar alone on the stage, having been tricked out of his most valued coin by a gang of ruffians. He seems to symbolize that the real losers are the Russian people, who suffer from the greed and ambition of those who want to be czar.

The music reveals Mussorgsky's innate musicianship and his flair for the dramatic. The prologue features the Russian people. Afraid for their future after the death of the czar, they pray for a ruler for their land. To encourage a public clamor for himself, Boris sends one of his lieutenants (Prince Shuisky) to tell the crowd that he still refuses to become czar. A chorus of religious pilgrims approaches and sings before the curtain falls.

The coronation scene, which follows the prologue, is one of the best-known scenes in the operatic repertoire. It takes place in a courtyard in the Kremlin; the Cathedrals of the Assumption, Annunciation, and the Archangel flank the stage.

In several ways Mussorgsky was ahead of his time, musically speaking. Twice in the coronation scene a scale containing only whole steps is implied. The scale (called the *whole tone scale*) would be used quite often twenty-five years later in the music of Impressionistic composers. In addition, there are places in the coronation scene in which two-beat against three-beat meter is implied. Again such combination of meters (called *polymeters*) would become much more common in the twentieth century. At several places in the orchestral portions of the coronation scene, Mussorgsky has adjacent chords harmonically as far apart as possible. For example, a C major chord is followed by one built on F-sharp. Again, this portends the breaking away from tonal harmony by twentieth-century composers.

The coronation scene from *Boris Godunov* has several notable features:

◆ The music has a virile, masculine quality. It exudes the rugged, hardy character that one associates with the peasantry of Russia at the beginning of the seventeenth century. Mussorgsky's admiration for the vigor of the Russian people has found its way into his music.

◆ The words, music, and drama fit together very effectively. Boris's solo is expressive and flexible. It suggests an aria and recitative in which the union of words and music fits perfectly. His prayer sounds somewhat like a chant, which is appropriate because chant is a feature of Russian Orthodox worship.

◆ The resonant sound of Boris's bass voice gives the impression of a mighty man, the leader of all Russia, a man who can bend steel with his bare hands.

◆ The scene is filled with color, both visually and musically. A coronation is an impressive event to see.

Mussorgsky's innovations and fresh, nationalistic approach were almost too much for the audience in 1872; even his friends and admirers had trouble understanding *Boris Godunov*. It was rejected twice for performance by the Imperial Opera. Only after two revisions and a performance of three of its scenes at a benefit concert was all of *Boris Godunov* performed.

Modest Mussorgsky: Coronation scene from *Boris Godunov*
CD ④ Track 26

0:00   26 The music opens with the gong and tuba sounding two long, low notes, which are then followed by long chords played by the brasses.

0:16   The woodwinds and the strings playing pizzicato sound a running series of notes at a loud dynamic level.

0:50   After a silence the gong, tuba, and brasses repeat the opening music.

1:00   Again the running series of notes are played by the strings and woodwinds.

1:36   After another silence the trumpets herald Prince Shuisky, who sings:

> **Shuisky:** Long live and reign, Czar Boris Feodorovich!
>
> **Chorus:** Long live our great and noble Czar!
>
> **Shuisky:** Praise him!

1:55   After a short orchestral introduction, the chorus sings a melody based on a Russian folk song:

> As the sun lights all heavens
> So reigns our great and noble Czar Boris!
> Hail to Boris, lord of Russia,
> Hail to our sovereign Boris!
> Long live our Czar!
> Czar, our father, hail.
> We hail thee, our father,
> Our gracious Czar, thou our gracious Czar!
> Great and glorious will thy reign be,
> Father of Russia!

2:45   The music changes often between two- and three-beat meter to fit the text:

> Sing, rejoice ye, people!
> Sing, rejoice ye, Russian people!
> Sing, rejoice ye, faithful people!
> Sing, rejoice ye, people!
> Come, exalt our Czar!

3:11   The trumpet heralds the words of the Boyars, the noblemen of Russia:

> **Boyars:** Hail to thee Czar Boris Feodorovich!
> Long life to thee!
> As the sun lights all heaven,
> So reigns our great Czar, glory!

3:27   The pattern of running notes from the opening of the scene is played again, and the chorus continues. Soon the parts imitate one another:

> Czar, our father beloved!
> Long life to thee!

4:03   The original Russian folk song melody returns:

> As the sun lights all heaven,
> So reigns our great Czar, glory!
> Sing the glory of the Czar of Russia, glory!
> Glory! Glory!

4:45　The music becomes quiet as the horns hold a long note. The troubled Boris sings of his torment:

> My soul is sad!
> Against my will strange tremors and evil premonitions oppress my spirit.
> O saint long dead,
> O thou my royal father!
> Thou see'st in heaven the faithful servant's tears!
> Look down on me and send a blessing from on high upon my kingdom!
> May I be true and merciful, as thou,
> And justify my people's praise.

6:37　After a short passage played by the clarinet, Boris decides to go ahead with his coronation:

> Now let us go and kneel in prayer before the tombs of Russia's kings.
> And then the people all shall feast.
> Come, ev'ryone from nobleman to serf;
> All shall find room, all find an honored welcome!

7:19　A flurry of sound is heard from the orchestra, and the sopranos sing, "Long live and reign our great and noble Czar!"

7:30　**27** At this point Mussorgsky specified that church bells should sound freely without any other music.

7:38　The music that opened the scene is played again. The sopranos, altos, tenors, and basses enter in imitation singing, "Thou our gracious Czar!":

> Long life to thee, Czar Boris Feodorovich!
> Hail to thee!
> As the sun lights all heaven,
> So reigns our great Czar of Russia,
> Glory and long may he reign!
> Glory! Glory! Glory!

9:16　The scene concludes after a final "Glory" sung by the chorus and two closing chords played by the orchestra as the chimes continue.

Bedřich Smetana

Bedřich Smetana (1824–1884) was born in a small town in Bohemia, the seventh child of a music-loving brewer. Family activities included string quartet playing at home. Smetana studied for a while in Prague, served as music master for a rich family, and later became pianist for Kaiser Ferdinand, who had abdicated the throne and was living in Prague. After about ten years, Smetana moved to Gothenburg, Sweden. He earned a good living there, but the climate was bad for his wife's failing health, so he moved back to Prague several years later.

Like Beethoven, Smetana became deaf toward the end of his life. Some of his best compositions were written when he was deaf.

Smetana once said that he simply could not write absolute music. Perhaps his feelings of nationalism were too strong to allow him to think of music in absolute terms.

Best-Known Works
Opera:
 ■ *The Bartered Bride*
Orchestra:
 ■ *Má vlast (My Fatherland),* which includes *The Moldau*

BOHEMIA

There is no country of Bohemia today, although at one time it was a distinct area of central Europe with its own language and cultural identity. Most of it lies in the Czech Republic. This rather small area produced two important composers who promoted its music: Antonín Dvořák and Bedřich Smetana. Throughout most of the nineteenth century, Bohemia was part of the Austrian empire, so the style of Dvořák and Smetana does not differ all that much from the prevailing Romantic style of the time. But its nationalism is expressed in the use of folk melodies and native subject matter.

SMETANA'S *MOLDAU*

The Moldau is the best known of Smetana's series of tone poems called *Má vlast*. The program that Smetana placed in the score reads:

> Two springs pour forth in the shade of the Bohemian forest, one warm and gushing, the other cold and peaceful. Coursing through Bohemia's valleys, it grows into a mighty stream. Through thick woods it flows as the gay sounds of the hunt and the notes of the hunter's horn are heard ever closer. It flows through grass-grown pastures and lowlands where a wedding feast is being celebrated with song and dance. At night, wood and water nymphs revel in its sparkling waves. Reflected on its surface are fortresses and castles—witnesses of bygone days of knightly splendor and the vanished glory of martial times.

The Moldau River

The stream races through the St. John's Rapids, "finally flowing on in majestic peace toward Prague and welcomed by historic Vysehrad," the legendary castle of ancient Bohemian kings. "Then it vanishes far beyond the poet's gaze."

LISTENING GUIDE

Bedřich Smetana: *The Moldau* from *Má vlast*
CD **5** Track **1**

0:00   **1** Two flutes are featured as murmuring sounds are heard.

0:26   Two clarinets join the flutes, apparently to represent the second spring that contributes to the Moldau River.

1:07   **2** The strings play a lyrical, flowing melody, part of which is repeated.

3:00   The brasses play fanfares to represent the hunters in the forest.

4:06   **3** The sounds of dance music at a wedding are heard; first the French horns play long notes, and then the string and woodwinds join in, playing the dance tune.

6:00   **4** The music becomes very soft, slow, and lyrical to give the impression of nightfall. Murmuring sounds are heard, indicating the water nymphs playing in the moonlight.

8:39   The main theme for the Moldau returns.

9:30   The brass and timpani are heard prominently as the music takes an urgent quality indicating the St. John's Rapids.

10:44   **5** The music becomes powerful and noble and is played by the full orchestra. A chorale-like melody is soon heard as the river flows past historic castles.

12:05   The river begins to fade into the distance far beyond the poet's gaze.

12:44   *The Moldau* concludes with two forceful chords.

O THER NATIONALISTIC COMPOSERS

Norway

Edvard Grieg (1843–1907) was the leading proponent of Scandinavian music. Among his well-known works are the *Peer Gynt Suites*, which were originally composed as incidental music for Henrik Ibsen's play. He also wrote a melodious piano concerto, as well as many shorter piano pieces and chamber works.

Finland

Jean Sibelius ("Yon Si-*bay*-lee-us," 1865–1957) was Finland's most famous composer. Most of his more nationalistic music was composed early in his career. One of the themes from his tone poem *Finlandia* became the national anthem of Finland. He also used native themes as the basis for program works such as *The Swan of Tuonela* and *Pohjola's Daughter*. The themes in many of his symphonies often have a folklike quality, even if they are not actually folk melodies.

England

The music of Edward Elgar (1857–1934) strikes a consonant note in the hearts of English audiences. Although his music is not very different from that of other Romantic composers, nor is it particularly nationalistic, it possesses a distinctively English quality. Elgar is the composer of *Pomp and Circumstance,* the stately march that is played at so many graduations. His best-known work is *Enigma Variations* for orchestra. Elgar wrote on the score the initials of the friend or family member who is associated with each particular variation. Guessing that person's identity becomes the puzzle or enigma. Fortunately, listeners today can enjoy the beauty of the music without the need to figure out who is being represented.

Several English composers in the early part of the twentieth century are also nationalistic. The most important of these is Ralph Vaughan Williams (1872–1958). He helped revive interest in English folk music and also contributed to the improvement in the music of the Church of England. He selected texts for his many vocal works from England's finest poets and used themes from earlier English composers in such works as Fantasia on a Theme by Tallis. Other important works of Vaughan Williams include Symphony No. 2 ("The London Symphony") and Fantasia on "Greensleeves."

His family name is *Vaughan Williams,* not just *Williams.*

Italy

Italian nationalism in the nineteenth century was largely confined to opera. Nationalism in instrumental works did not become evident until the twentieth century in the music of Ottorino Respighi ("Res-*pee*-gee," 1879–1936). His *Pines of Rome* and *Fountains of Rome* are definitely nationalistic. His style is strongly Romantic, even if the composition dates from the twentieth century.

Verdi's role in Italian nationalism is discussed in chapter 30.

Spain

Spanish nationalism is found in the music of Isaac Albeniz (1860–1909), Enrique Granados (1867–1916), and Manuel de Falla ("*Fi*-ya," 1876–1946). Each of these composers exploited the rhythms of Spanish dance and the colorful sounds of its music. Although their careers extended into the twentieth century, their music is essentially Romantic in character.

France

As the Romantic era progressed, French composers began to develop a style that was different from the prevailing German style. A truly distinct French style did not appear, however, until the Impressionistic music of Debussy and Ravel, which is presented in chapter 33.

United States

Nationalistic music was slow to develop in the United States. In fact, very little existed prior to 1900. The nationalistic music that developed in the twentieth century is discussed in chapter 42.

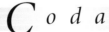

C o d a

*Mussorgsky, Smetana, and a host of other nationalistic
composers mined the musical riches of their native lands.
In doing so, these composers contributed
much to the world of music.*

33 Impressionism and Post-Romanticism

Over the years all artistic movements, even highly successful ones like Romanticism, spend themselves out. A point is reached where they can be carried no further. Eventually, something has to change.

Post-Romanticism and Impressionism represent two types of change from the German/Austrian style that dominated the nineteenth century. Post-Romanticism was an attempt to pump life into Romanticism by doing more—making the works longer and for larger groups. In contrast, Impressionism focused on the subtle, delicate, and fleeting inner impressions of an outer world. It represented a more substantial change in outlook toward works of art and music, one that called for a different view of the arts.

CHARACTERISTICS OF IMPRESSIONISM

Impressionism probably owes its name to painter Claude Monet, who in 1874 exhibited a picture called *Impression—Sunrise*. Critics took up the term to make fun of the new movement.

Impressionism was an artistic viewpoint in which poets, painters, and composers tried to capture something incomplete, of the moment, a sensation. It is based on the belief that experiences in life are largely impressions rather than detailed observations. To achieve this, Impressionists stressed informality and rarely carried a moral or message. They were also fond of nature and commonplace scenes—sunsets, people in casual poses, water lilies in a pond, and the like.

Several Impressionistic painters, for example, tried to catch the atmosphere of a particular time and place by making rough sketches at two or three different times during the day, because the impression of a scene changed with different lighting. The painting would often be finished in the studio. They also avoided hard outlines and used subtle blending of primary colors.

A picture in a book or newspaper is made up of thousands of tiny dots.

Some painters used a technique called *pointillism* in which dots of paint are placed close together. Seen up close, the picture looks like a newspaper photo when viewed through a magnifying glass; when viewed from a short distance, however, the dots appear to blend.

Impressionistic poetry and drama were highly symbolic. These writers tried to capture fleeting moments by presenting a sequence of images in words. They intentionally kept their poems in an inconclusive and fragmented condition, which left the meaning up to the reader. Impressionistic writer Maurice Maeterlinck wrote in one of his essays, "Beneath all human thoughts . . . there lies the vast ocean of the Unconscious. All that we know, think, feel, see, and will are but bubbles on the surface of this vast sea."

In one sense, Impressionism represented French nationalism, although it was more of a cultural nationalism than the usual political type. Many works by Impressionistic composers are programmatic. What makes Impressionistic music different from most other program music written in the nineteenth century is that the nonmusical associations are with impressions, not stories or characters.

Monet's Impressionist painting of Rouen Cathedral From his vantage point in a window opposite the church, Monet painted at least thirty nearly identical versions of this scene at different times of day and under varying weather conditions.

The Impressionistic movement was unique in the extent to which writers, artists, and musicians knew each other and often worked together. And they held a similar point of view about the arts. The painter wanted to capture a fleeting moment on canvas, the author in the printed and spoken word, and the composer in the transitory world of musical sounds. These artists shared a common fondness for subtle nuances of light and shadow, vague contours, and veiled thoughts.

Impressionistic composers achieved the goals of Impressionism in several ways:

Impressionistic composers were especially fond of the piano, with its many tonal possibilities, as well as the harp and flute.

♦ They used fewer instruments in their orchestral works.

♦ They made much use of the tonal colors of instruments and used a particular chord or combination of instruments because they liked that sonority.

♦ They had chords move in parallel motion, something that had been forbidden in traditional harmony.

♦ Often they were subtle and complex in their treatment of rhythm.

♦ Sometimes they made the tonal center obscure through the use of whole tone and pentatonic scales.

♦ They made little use of traditional forms.

♦ They did not seek to impart any deep messages in their works. Rather, they viewed musical works as something simply to be enjoyed.

Claude Debussy   *Maurice Ravel*

Best-Known Works of Debussy
Opera:
  ▢ *Pelléas et Mélisande*
Orchestra:
  ▢ *La Mer*
  ▢ *Nocturnes*
  ▢ *Prelude to the Afternoon of a Faun*
Piano:
  ▢ *Children's Corner Suite*
  ▢ *L'isle joyeuse*
  ▢ *Images*, Sets 1 and 2
  ▢ *Suite bergamasque*

Claude Debussy ("Deb-yew-*see*," 1862–1918) was born in a small town near Paris. He entered the Paris Conservatory at the age of eleven, where he often revolted again the rules of composition his professors tried to teach him. When he was twenty-two he won the Prix de Rome, which included study in Italy. Although he did go to Rome, he much preferred the bustle and gaiety of Paris. He also valued the company of painters and writers.

Debussy's early admiration for Wagner faded after a second visit to Bayreuth in 1889, and he developed a dislike for things Germanic. He wrote a number of articles about music, which offered him a chance to vent his feelings. Regarding Wagner, he wrote, "The French forget too easily the qualities of clarity and elegance peculiar to themselves and allow themselves to be influenced by the tedious and ponderous Teuton." He considered the

The Teutons were one of the ancient German-speaking peoples.

development of themes dull "musical mathematics," and he claimed that "beauty must appeal to the senses, must provide us with immediate enjoyment."

Debussy was a careful craftsman. He added much to music composition by writing parallel chord movements, chords with added notes, and new timbres. His piano compositions were especially Impressionistic.

The fact that **Maurice Ravel** (1875–1937) followed Debussy both chronologically and stylistically has tended to place him in the background despite his many fine compositions. He was born into the family of a mining engineer who had once aspired to be a musician himself. Ravel studied at the Paris Conservatory and, though highly qualified for the award, was four times passed over for the Prix de Rome. The arbitrary nature of these decisions caused a public furor that eventually led to the resignation of the Conservatory's director.

A French patriot, Ravel drove an ambulance along the front lines during World War I.

Best-Known Works of Ravel
Orchestra:
  ▢ *Bolero*
  ▢ *Concerto in D for Piano (left hand)*
  ▢ *Daphnis et Chloé Suite No. 2*
  ▢ *La valse*
  ▢ *Ma Mère l'Oye (Mother Goose)*
Piano:
  ▢ *Gaspard de la nuit*
  ▢ *Le tombeau de Couperin*

After the war he was recognized as France's greatest composer. He died at the age of sixty while undergoing surgery for a rare brain disease that had seriously affected his speech and motor coordination.

One of his best-known works, and certainly the most unusual, is the hypnotic *Bolero*, in which the same melody and rhythm pattern continue throughout the seventeen minutes of the work.

DEBUSSY'S *FÊTES* FROM *NOCTURNES*

In 1899 Claude Debussy composed a three-section work for orchestra titled *Nocturnes*. The first section is *Nuages (Clouds)*, *Fêtes (Festivals)* is the second section, and the third is *Sirènes (Sirens)*. In a true Impressionistic manner, he does not provide specific information about any particular festival for *Fêtes*. That is left for listeners to fill in for themselves. Perhaps it is a Mardi Gras type of event.

Sirènes is inspired by the mythical beautiful women whose hypnotic songs lured sailors to their destruction on the rocks.

Fêtes offers the musical feeling of a festival, an event filled with bustling sounds and disorganized activity. Because the overall title of the work is *Nocturnes*, referring to night, the image of a festival at night is implied. The work is separated into sections, something like seeing different scenes at a festival. The music is colorful, with a middle section that sounds like a march played by a band that begins far away and moves toward the listener. The final section of the music seems to fade away—as if the festival is over.

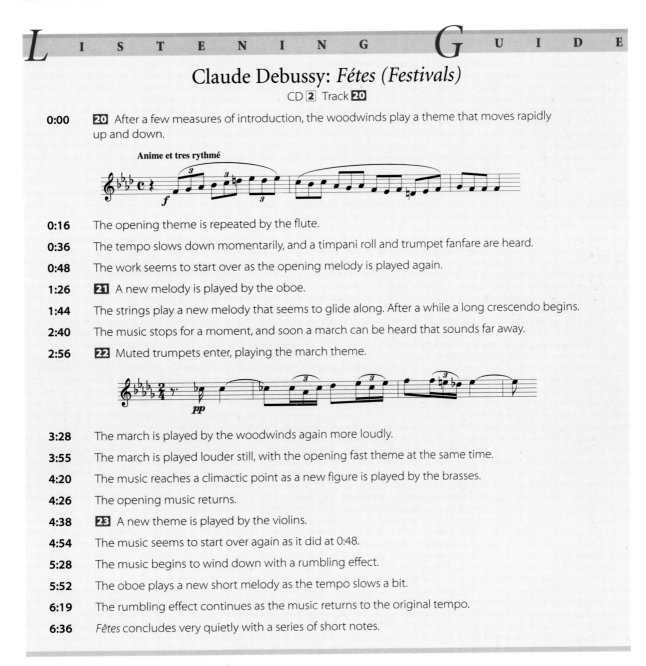

LISTENING GUIDE

Claude Debussy: *Fétes (Festivals)*

CD **2** Track **20**

0:00	**20**	After a few measures of introduction, the woodwinds play a theme that moves rapidly up and down.

0:16	The opening theme is repeated by the flute.
0:36	The tempo slows down momentarily, and a timpani roll and trumpet fanfare are heard.
0:48	The work seems to start over as the opening melody is played again.
1:26	**21** A new melody is played by the oboe.
1:44	The strings play a new melody that seems to glide along. After a while a long crescendo begins.
2:40	The music stops for a moment, and soon a march can be heard that sounds far away.
2:56	**22** Muted trumpets enter, playing the march theme.

3:28	The march is played by the woodwinds again more loudly.
3:55	The march is played louder still, with the opening fast theme at the same time.
4:20	The music reaches a climactic point as a new figure is played by the brasses.
4:26	The opening music returns.
4:38	**23** A new theme is played by the violins.
4:54	The music seems to start over again as it did at 0:48.
5:28	The music begins to wind down with a rumbling effect.
5:52	The oboe plays a new short melody as the tempo slows a bit.
6:19	The rumbling effect continues as the music returns to the original tempo.
6:36	*Fêtes* concludes very quietly with a series of short notes.

Fêtes is successful in projecting a general idea or vision. It also has a very French quality about it. No one familiar with art music would confuse it with Brahms or Wagner or Mussorgsky.

Impressionism partly bridged the change from the Romantic style of the nineteenth century to the music of the twentieth century. It represented a significant break from the predominant Germanic style through its use of added notes in chords, parallel chord movement, and subtle rhythms. But it did not leave all its Romantic tendencies behind. Rather, it exemplified the French love of nuance and color, and in so doing pointed the way toward the future.

French Impressionism seems to have a noticeably lighter quality than German or Russian music.

POST-ROMANTICISM

The Romantic outlook did not go quietly into the night. In fact, elements of it are still found in music being written today—and probably always will be. Some composers who lived near the end of the nineteenth century and into the twentieth continued the Romantic tradition by composing works that were more massive and extensive than those of their predecessors.

RACHMANINOFF'S RHAPSODY ON A THEME OF PAGANINI

Rhapsody on a Theme of Paganini is one of the best loved of Sergei Rachmaninoff's compositions. It is based on a theme written by the legendary nineteenth-century violin virtuoso Niccolò Paganini. The work opens with a short introduction and one variation before the theme is presented by the violins. It is essentially a simple melody: The same melodic and rhythm pattern is heard on the tonic or home chord, then the dominant chord, then a return to the tonic, and two concluding notes on the dominant. That portion of the theme is repeated before the second half of the theme appears. This half maintains nearly the same melodic pattern and the same rhythmic ideas presented in sequence.

At first the variations are modest in scope. The piano plays decorative versions of theme that little by little move farther from it. Variation 7 combines the theme played by the low strings and the Dies irae theme played slowly by the piano. Variation 10 again opens with the Dies irae played by the piano, which is then taken up by the orchestra.

The following Listening Guide begins with variation 18 and goes to the conclusion of the work.

$\mathcal{L}$ I S T E N I N G $\mathcal{G}$ U I D E

Sergei Rachmaninoff: Rhapsody on a Theme of Paganini
excerpt
CD 2 Track 24

0:00   24 Variation 18 is based on the inversion of the theme. This variation has a very sensuous quality.

2:46   Variation 19 has a quick tempo, with the piano playing rapidly moving notes. The accented notes contain the outline of the theme.

3:12   25 Variation 20 is built around a two-note figure taken from the theme. The violins accompany it with continuously running sixteenth notes.

3:48   Variation 21 features the piano playing notes constructed around the notes of the chords.

4:14   26 Variation 22 is soft and marchlike until halfway through, when the orchestra enters. Then the music becomes smoother, and the piano plays many rapidly moving notes.

5:12   Variation 23 restates the theme played by the piano and then the orchestra.

5:33   The piano plays a short cadenza.

5:50   Variation 24 begins softly, with the piano playing notes built around the chords implied by the theme. As the music increases in speed, the theme is played again by the woodwinds and violins.

6:36   27 The coda begins as the theme is played very rapidly by the piano.

7:17   The Dies irae theme is played by the brasses.

7:39   The work concludes somewhat quietly with two short chords.

For a number of reasons, this work represents post-Romanticism well. First, it was composed in 1934, well after the Romantic style had been predominant. Second, the theme is by Paganini, who in some ways was the quintessential Romantic musician. Third, the work includes a quotation of the Dies irae theme, which is associated with death and mystery—favorite topics of Romanticists. Fourth, it is a basically a rhapsody containing a free expression of feelings, even though it is in the form of a theme and variations.

Gustav Mahler and Anton Bruckner (1824–1896), an earlier Romantic composer, both exhibit one of the traits of Romanticism: a tendency toward musical elephantiasis. Mahler's Third Symphony holds the dubious distinction of being the longest ever written. It takes about one hour and thirty-four minutes, with the first movement alone requiring nearly forty-five minutes to perform. His Eighth Symphony is sometimes called the "Symphony of a Thousand" because it requires so many people to perform it: a huge orchestra, additional brass, and male, female, and children's choirs. Mahler is nevertheless able to handle these musical resources with skill and discretion.

Sergei Rachmaninoff

Sergei Rachmaninoff (1873–1943) was well known during his lifetime as a composer and pianist. Like several post-Romantic composers, he tended to be in the shadow of someone else's musical style. In the case of Rachmaninoff, it was Tchaikovsky. At times, Rachmaninoff equalled Tchaikovsky in writing beautiful music, but he was not as consistent in doing so.

Jean Sibelius

Jean Sibelius was mentioned in chapter 32 for his Finnish nationalistic works. He is best remembered today for his symphonies and violin concerto. He was masterful at extending the development of a motive. His symphonies often contain the cyclical use of themes in which the same theme appears in more than one movement.

Gustav Mahler

Gustav Mahler (1860–1911) was a successful conductor as well as an excellent composer. He had a vocal outlook toward music. Not only did he write many songs, but his instrumental works often seem to be conceived vocally, and, indeed, some of them involve singers. He believed in the unity of the arts and often combined music, poetry, and philosophical ideas in his compositions. Much of the time, Mahler's music sounds so effortless and simple that listeners can easily miss his expertise in handling musical ideas.

Coda

Perhaps the length and bulk of Mahler's symphonies are omens of the frustrations that composers were feeling with the Romantic style. Skilled composers such as Debussy, Ravel, Rachmaninoff, Sibelius, and Mahler were able to create some great music, but the musical resources of Romanticism were fast being consumed.

Part VI

Twentieth-Century Music

Art in the Twentieth Century

For much of history, artists played the role that cameras do today. That is, they tried to create an accurate rendition of a person or a scene. But with the invention of photography in the nineteenth century, and especially with its widespread use in the twentieth, the goal of artists changed. Instead of producing good images of what was seen, artists became more interested in interpreting what they saw and creating visual objects that are of interest solely for their visual properties. Their use of shape and color has become somewhat like composers' use of sounds in music. This change led to a wide variety of types of artworks. It also occasionally led to charges that "My kid brother could have done better than that!" from people who wanted art to look like something.

As the twentieth century saw the return to certain techniques used in musical compositions written in earlier centuries, painters also revisited techniques of artists centuries earlier. One such technique was to eliminate the third dimension and to experiment with lines and colors on flat planes or cubes. Pablo Picasso's Three Musicians *is a type of Cubism called "collage Cubism," in which the impression is given that the portions of the painting are pasted-up like pieces of paper (which is what the word* collage *means in French). The separate pieces are fitted together firmly as little architectural blocks. More than pattern concerned Picasso in* Three Musicians, *however. He tried to project the image of musicians as traditional figures of the comedy stage. Their humanness is sensed behind the screen of costumes and masks.*

PABLO PICASSO. *THREE MUSICIANS.* FONTAINEBLEAU, SUMMER 1921. OIL ON CANVAS, 6' × 7' × 7' 3¾" (200.7 × 222.9 CM). THE MUSEUM OF MODERN ART, NEW YORK, MRS. SIMON GUGGENHEIM FUND. PHOTOGRAPH © 1998 THE MUSEUM OF MODERN ART, NEW YORK.

Wassily Kandinsky tried to do in art what composers do in music in terms of working with materials to create something of interest. In Improvisation 30 *he even took a term from music and also used a number instead of a title or name. The result was a series of patterns and shapes containing many brilliant colors. At first glance* Improvisation 30 *doesn't seem to have any unity or coherence— but look at it carefully for a while. Something about it really works.*

In spite of its title, Piet Mondrian's Broadway Boogie Woogie *is not an attempt to represent Manhattan. Mondrian developed a completely nonrepresentational, abstract style. He restricted himself to horizontals and verticals and a few simple colors with no shading. In this way it would be virtually impossible to paint a picture of something. In spite of these limitations, Mondrian succeeded in creating a lively, attractive painting. At first glance it may look easy to imitate Mondrian's style successfully but, actually, the limitations make it very difficult.*

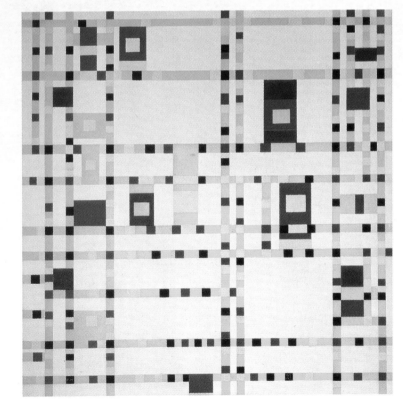

An important current in twentieth-century painting is fantasy. Many painters have become interested in "the inner eye"—the introspective look at imagination and feeling. Such a view seems to be the artistic counterpart to Freudian psychology and its interest in dreams and the subconscious. Marc Chagall appeared never to lose the memories and dreams of his childhood in a Jewish community in Russia. His painting Snowing *depicts some of that personal mystery and fantasy. Does it contain shades of the highly successful Broadway musical* Fiddler on the Roof?

Grant Wood's American Gothic *is one of the most famous American paintings. It graces doormats and T-shirts and is seen in cereal commercials on television. It depicts something very American in its matter-of-fact representation of life. It celebrates the homely, simple virtues of rural life, of America as it once was. The use of the term* Gothic *is intended as an ironic comparison with the massive and complex structures found in the European Gothic tradition. The pointed-arch window of the dwelling in the background is an example of what is sometimes called "carpenter Gothic," which is the American version of a European style carved ornately in stone.*

Music and art in the twentieth century have sometimes expressed a social or political message. *Quartetto* by the New York painter Ben Shahn is a political allegory showing a worker, a farmer, and a boss "harmonizing." Notice the simplicity and charm of the painting. It is based on no theories of art; instead it seeks to project its message in an imaginative way.

Roy Lichtenstein's *Whaam!* has no message. According to Lichtenstein, "Stylistically, my work is devoid of emotional content. And it's what I want." He and his musical counterpart, John Cage, created works that were so obvious that they invited no interpretation. They represent a complete rejection of the nineteenth-century belief in art as the conveyor of great ideas. The sounds in music and the shapes and colors in art are what they are—period.

Music in the Twentieth Century

34

*Twentieth-century music may at times be confusing
and difficult to understand, but dull it is not. It's as fascinating
and challenging as twentieth-century life itself.*

THE TREMENDOUS AND TUMULTUOUS CENTURY

The twentieth century has not been for the faint of heart, either socially or artistically. It has witnessed two world wars and numerous lesser conflicts, a great economic depression and general prosperity, and thousands of discoveries and inventions ranging from organ transplants to computers to exploration in space.

Most of these changes have had both benefits and liabilities. For example, as the peoples of the world seem to be drawing closer together, at the same time they seem to be becoming more aware of their differences, and in many regions various groups of people are striving to assert their particular identities.

Nor have the marvels of technological progress made people any happier. Information can now be passed along in milliseconds to almost anyplace in the world, but the quality of what is said often is no better than what hundreds of years ago was written with a quill pen and delivered by hand. Astronauts have traveled into space, but they must return to earth and its many problems.

As the end of the twentieth century draws to a close, the pervasive influence of technology grows stronger in many areas of life. It has had a major impact on the amount and type of music people hear, as well as how they think about music. It has also played a very important role in the production and reproduction of music. But, again, it has had both positive and negative results. People today hear much more music than ever before, but they seem to listen to it less and less carefully.

Diverse and complex factors also exist in twentieth-century art music. It seems to be divided into numerous camps. Some of these subgroups are designated by words that end with *isms,* such as Neoclassicism, Serialism, Primitivism, Expressionism, and Minimalism. Other types are folkloric, experimental, avant garde, and what is considered mainstream. Each of these types represents a view about music and has played a role in the development of twentieth-century music.

If twentieth-century music is marked by diversity, dramatic change, and expansion, those same qualities mean that it is also musically very rich. For instance, some twentieth-century music:

♦ Contains expanded continuation of musical elements in earlier music

♦ Is influenced by new sources of music such as Africa and Asia

♦ Is the result of sophisticated intellectual efforts

♦ Is a revival of musical practices that were in fashion several centuries earlier

♦ Is a repudiation of nineteenth-century music

♦ Probes new and largely untested ways of creating musical works

As was pointed out in chapter 1, there is a big difference between just hearing music and really listening to it.

DESCRIBING TWENTIETH-CENTURY MUSIC

With the Baroque, Classical, and Romantic periods, it is possible to describe their main intellectual and artistic features. That is a much more difficult task with twentieth-century music. Perhaps part of the problem is the lack of perspective; we are simply too close to it.

Part of the reason for the lack of cohesion in twentieth-century music is probably due to the diversity and fragmentation in twentieth-century society itself. Core values and beliefs that prevailed in the Classical and Romantic eras no longer seem to be in effect.

Equally important is the fact that there is so much music to consider in this century. No longer can an understanding of music be confined to art music of Europe and America. Music from every part of the globe is now available, as are all types of folk and popular music. Also, more universities and conservatories now offer instruction in composition, so more people are writing and making music than ever before. What's more, ever since the Romantic period, composers have tried consciously to avoid writing music that sounds too much like any other composer's style. Imitating someone else flies in the face of the idea of creativity as conceived over the past two centuries.

Another reason why it is hard to name one set of standard features for music in this century is its ever-changing character. For instance, Stravinsky's *Rite of Spring* was modern and novel when it premiered in 1913, but that certainly is not true today. In fact, it was not even true for Stravinsky a decade later; he had moved on to another style. And Stravinsky is not alone among composers in changing styles.

Some labels are helpful in understanding twentieth-century music, just as period labels such as *Baroque* and *Romantic* are useful in learning about the music of earlier centuries. But such designations should be used with care when discussing twentieth-century music. Composers usually do not like being categorized. They consider their pieces unique works that should be evaluated on their own merits, which is only fair. Still, the use of classifications—the *isms,* for example—can aid in looking at and thinking about the art music of this century.

WHAT'S NEW IN TWENTIETH-CENTURY MUSIC?

What features are found in much of the concert music of the twentieth century? How does it differ from the music of the past?

Rhythm

Rhythm is a much more important element in twentieth-century music than it had been in previous centuries. Some (not all) of the music composed in the twentieth century has broken away from the idea of regular metrical patterns. The "tyranny of the bar line" is long since gone. Composers have felt free to mix meters, either by actually changing the signature or by displacing the accents. At one point in Stravinsky's *Rite of Spring,* the meter changes with each measure: 3/16, 5/16, 3/16, 4/16, 5/16, 3/16, and so on.

Measures traditionally contained two, three, or four regular beats. New asymmetrical patterns are found in some twentieth-century works. Measures with five or seven beats per measure are used, as well as measures in which the beat pattern is not regular, as in this 8/8 pattern:

$$\text{♩. ♩. ♩} = 3 + 3 + 2$$

Furthermore, musicians have felt free to have more than one rhythmic pattern sounding at the same time, what is termed *polyrhythm.*

There is an old saying about "not being able to see the forest for the trees."

Stravinsky's *Rite of Spring* is presented in chapter 36.

By using phrase markings and accent signs, a composer or arranger can change the meter of the music without actually changing the meter signature.

Polyrhythms are presented in conjunction with African music in chapter 9.

Some composers have consciously tried to return to rhythmic devices found in folk/ethnic music, such as rhythmic ostinatos—the persistent repetition of short rhythm patterns.

The increased attention given to rhythm has a corresponding increase in the importance of percussion instruments. More percussion instruments are used, and they are featured much more. In fact, some works have been composed for percussion ensemble; others have featured percussion instruments.

Melody

The concept of melody has expanded far beyond potentially singable melodies in the traditional major and minor tonalities. Melodies are often no longer warm and flowing as in the preceding century. In fact, melody as such seems to be less important in twentieth-century works. Melodies are often conceived nonvocally in their use of wide, awkward leaps and irregular phrases. Sometimes no actual melody can be found in a work. Yet some beautiful melodies exist in the music of this century.

Twentieth century composers have broken away from the balanced patterns of phrases found in Baroque and Classical music. No longer are four measures complemented by another four measures. The clearly defined structure of melodies has been loosened considerably.

Harmony and Counterpoint

Romantic harmonies are rich and colorful, and chords were built around the traditional pattern of thirds. Twentieth-century composers have frequently broken away from that pattern and have written chords in fourths, fifths, and seconds. More often, however, they have added notes to chords just because they want that particular sound at that particular place in the music.

Examples of chords:
Seconds—C D E F
Thirds—C E G
Fourths—C F B♭
Fifths—C G D

Chord progressions in traditional harmony provide a syntax that helps organize the music. Twentieth-century composers have not completely abandoned traditional tonal progressions, but they certainly have been far less concerned about following them. In fact, not only have they been much less interested in tonal centers, but some composers have also deliberately composed music with no tonal center whatsoever.

Music without a tonal center is presented in chapter 38.

Some twentieth-century composers have written music in two or more keys that sound at the same time. The term for this technique is *polytonality*. For example, at one point in *Rite of Spring* Stravinsky writes an F♭ A♭ C♭ chord in the lower pitches and an E♭ G♭ B♭ D♭ in the upper pitches, a sonority that includes all seven pitches of the C-flat major scale.

Some twentieth-century music is written not in the major/minor keys of the preceding three hundred years, but in the modes that prevailed in the Renaissance and earlier periods. This is especially true of music that draws on folk sources.

As the attention given to harmony has decreased in the twentieth century, the amount of counterpoint has increased. At times the counterpoint sounds like it was written by a resurrected J. S. Bach. Other twentieth-century counterpoint is very different, because it is filled with dissonance and complex rhythms.

Dissonance

The changes in harmony have led to one of the things people notice first about twentieth-century music: dissonance. Other composers have carried the idea of dissonance to its limit, for example, by asking the pianist to push an elbow down on the keyboard or by specifying a stick that is 14⅜ inches long and pushing it down on the keys. Often dissonance is used to add a certain color to the music, not to create or resolve tension, as it had been traditionally employed. In any case, the amount of dissonance in twentieth-century music is much greater than at any time in history.

Such groups of pitches are known as *tone clusters*.

The principle of dissonance resolving to consonance that has prevailed for more than 200 years is sometimes not followed in twentieth-century music.

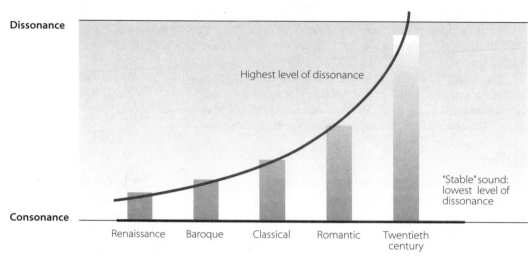

The increasing use of dissonance in music through history

Timbre

Twentieth-century composers have opened up a new world in terms of timbre with the synthesized sounds and effects available through technology. Even without technology, composers have freely milked every possible sound from conventional instruments and the human voice—shrieks, babbling, tongue-clucking, banging, squeaking, buzzing, and sounds made with parts of the instrument removed. Some works for piano call for placing thumbtacks, rubber bands, coins, and other objects on the strings to create different timbres.

The idea of timbre has become the central element in some works that consist of organized series of tone colors rather than themes and melodies.

A synthesizer can produce almost any sound. It is not limited to the standard timbres of instruments.

The technique is called *prepared piano*.

Form

A few composers have written works in sonata and other forms. But formal patterns seem not to be very important to most twentieth-century composers. Some have attempted other approaches to organizing their music, and several of these are described in the following chapters.

Tone rows are presented in chapter 38, and chance and electronic music in chapter 39.

Sources

Musicians in this century know more about music from every historical age and part of the globe than their predecessors. Ease of communication and improved scholarship into the world's treasure trove of musics has made this possible. Twentieth-century music is pancultural and panhistorical as no other music has been before. A number of twentieth-century composers have drawn heavily on elements of music from non-Western cultures, as well as from past times.

The advent of tape recordings made possible a knowledge of many kinds of music that had not been known before. Also the field of ethnomusicology has researched many types of music.

C o d a

*Because of its diversity and richness, twentieth-century
music offers something for just about every musical taste. And because of its
wide diversity, probably few people like every kind of music that has been
created since 1900. Whether a particular type is for you,
all of it merits exploration and explanation.*

The Mainstream

35

Much twentieth-century music is an expansion and
evolution of previous musical styles. It is hard to know what
to call this body of "conventional" music. Some writers have coined the
word *folkloric,* because the music is partly derived from folk or ethnic
sources, but that is not true of even a majority of this style. *Traditional* is
not an accurate word, because most twentieth-century composers broke
with nineteenth-century traditions to some extent. *Cosmopolitan* or
eclectic are not accurate descriptions either, since many composers
did not attempt to integrate a variety of musical styles in their
compositions. *Mainstream* seems to say it best; it refers to
music that is neither experimental nor committed to any
one particular approach to writing music.

Three mainstream works are discussed in this chapter: Concerto for Orchestra by
Béla Bartók, the "Aria" from *Bachianas Brasileiras No. 5* by Heitor Villa-Lobos, and
the Dies irae from *War Requiem* by Benjamin Britten.

BARTÓK'S CONCERTO FOR ORCHESTRA

Bartók composed his Concerto for Orchestra in the summer of 1943 for a $1,000
commission from the Boston Symphony Orchestra. "The general mood of the work,"
he wrote, "represents, apart from the jesting second movement, a gradual transition
from the sternness of the first movement and the lugubrious death-song of the third
to the life-assertion of the last." The work is called a concerto because single
instruments and sections are treated in a concerted way, as in Baroque music. There
is also an element of virtuoso performing skill in the concerto. It is one of the
masterpieces of twentieth-century music.

As pointed out in chapter 17, *concerto* refers to the contrast between groups of instruments. Sometimes the difference is size and sometimes it is the kinds of instruments.

First, Second, and Third Movements

Although the movements are independent and no themes are carried over from one
movement to another, Bartók considered them as leading from one to another, as
was just pointed out. The opening theme of the first movement is based on the interval
of a fourth, with appearances of the theme separated by shimmering chords played
by the strings. The main theme ascends and descends rapidly and contains a
syncopated figure. The second half of this theme is nearly the exact inversion of the
first half, with the interval of a fourth being prominent.

Bartók used many timbrel effects in his music.

The second movement is entitled "Games of Pairs," because the wind instruments
are paired off at specific pitch intervals: the bassoons in sixths, the oboes in thirds,
the clarinets in sevenths, the flutes in fifths, and the muted trumpets in seconds.
This is the jesting movement that Bartók mentioned in his synopsis. After the five
short sections featuring pairs of instruments, the brasses play a chorale accompanied
by the snare drum with its snares not engaged. The opening music of the movement
follows the chorale, which gives the movement a three-part form.

The third movement is the "lugubrious death-song." The melody is folklike and
is played by the oboe. The music is rhapsodic and seems to rise to a peak moment
of tragedy.

Fourth Movement

Bartók called the fourth movement "Interrupted Intermezzo." The opening melody has a Hungarian folk quality. The first six complete measures of the theme all begin on the same note—A-sharp—and the five-note pentatonic scale is used. The second melody sounds almost like a waltz, but not quite. Its meter changes often, usually by adding or subtracting half a beat. It gives the music a certain awkward charm. This melody also has a Hungarian folk character and is a reworking of a folk song.

> Hungarian folk music often uses the pentatonic scale.

The third theme is different. Bartók adapted a theme from the Seventh Symphony by the Russian composer Dmitri Shostakovitch. That symphony, often referred to as the "Leningrad Symphony," is a somewhat programmatic work that Shostakovitch composed in 1941 during the siege of Leningrad (St. Petersburg today) by the invading Nazi Germans. Bartók wanted to express his revulsion at Nazi Germany, which had taken over Hungary several years before and caused him to flee his native land. The theme is interrupted by rude noises, which seem to represent the "rough, booted men," as Bartók referred to the Nazi occupiers.

> Leningrad suffered terribly, and thousands of its citizens died in the long siege. Shostakovitch served as a fireman during those years.

LISTENING GUIDE

Béla Bartók: Concerto for Orchestra
Fourth Movement
CD 2 Track 28

0:00   **28** After a short introduction, the oboe plays the *A* theme.

1:00   **29** The violas play the *B* theme, and then the violins play it.

1:42   The *A* theme returns, played again by the oboe.

2:05   **30** The clarinet introduces the *C* theme, which was adapted from Shostakovitch. Rude noises follow the theme, played by the trumpets and woodwinds.

2:27   The violins play a parody of the *C* theme, after which more blatant noises are heard.

2:41   The *C* theme is played in inversion by the violins, again followed by more rude noises.

2:53   The *B* theme returns, played by the violas.

3:27   The *A* theme returns, played by the English horn, flute, and clarinet.

4:15   The movement concludes quietly with three quick notes.

Béla Bartók

Béla Bartók (1881–1945) was born in a small city in Hungary. His mother was his first music teacher. After Béla's father died, she became a schoolteacher. They moved quite often, but finally settled in Pressburg (today Bratislava), where Béla studied piano and composition. After finishing his studies at the Royal Conservatory, he concertized throughout Europe.

Bartók and another important Hungarian composer, Zoltán Kodály ("Koh-*die*-ee"), first became recognized outside of Hungary as collectors of Hungarian folk music. They lugged their early recording equipment from one village in Transylvania to another, recording the music of the people. In 1907 Bartók became a professor of piano at the Royal Conservatory and spent most of the next thirty years of his life in Budapest. His compositions received little attention outside of Hungary until the late 1920s.

After the rise of Hitler and the subsequent collaboration of Hungary with Nazi Germany, Bartók felt impelled to leave his homeland. In 1940 he came to the United States to live. He was appointed to a position at Columbia

> When he left Hungary, he could take almost nothing with him, so commissions for compositions were an economic necessity.

University, primarily to continue his folk music research. He received a few commissions from ASCAP and from jazz clarinetist Benny Goodman.

> *ASCAP* stands for American Society of Composers, Authors, and Publishers.

Bartók's earlier compositions were often barbaric, with many thick, dissonant chords. His most recognized works were composed between 1926 and 1937. One of the more interesting is his *Mikrokosmos*, a set of 153 piano pieces in six volumes that are arranged so that the music progresses from simple pieces to works of awesome difficulty.

During the latter part of his life, Bartók appeared to mellow. His music became less dissonant and more accessible. He died of leukemia, with his true stature as a composer still not fully appreciated.

Best-Known Works
Chamber music:
- String Quartets Nos. 4, 5, and 6

Orchestra:
- Concerto for Orchestra
- Music for Percussion, Strings, and Celesta
- Piano Concerto No. 3

Piano:
- *Mikrokosmos*

Fifth Movement

The fifth movement is in a large three-part form. It features a theme of nearly continuous running notes and much contrapuntal writing, especially in the *B* section. The theme of that section is treated fugally, and it appears again at the conclusion of the movement.

HEITOR VILLA-LOBOS: *BACHIANAS BRASILEIRAS*

The Brazilian composer Heitor Villa-Lobos was a man of tremendous energy who adopted musical ideas from many sources. His greatest inspiration was the music of the Brazilian people. Although his eleven hundred works are of uneven quality, many of them are fascinating and very beautiful. His *Bachianas Brasileiras* and *Chôros* are filled with rich sounds that alternate between being romantic and boldly dissonant.

Villa-Lobos composed nine *Bachianas Brasileiras*, in which he tried to combine the style of Bach with the indigenous music of Brazil. Villa-Lobos wrote: "This is a special kind of musical composition based on an intimate knowledge of J. S. Bach and also on the composer's affinity with the harmonic, contrapuntal, and melodic atmosphere of the folklore of the northern region of Brazil." The Aria of *Bachianas Brasileiras No. 5* was composed in 1938; in 1945 he added a second movement to it.

A wordless song is called a *vocalise*.

To project the sound of humming, trained singers hum with their teeth apart and their lips barely closed.

The Aria is for a soprano accompanied by eight cellos—hardly a typical instrumentation. The music is not typical either. During the first third of the work, the singer just vocalizes a luscious melody, first on "Ah" and then for the last third by humming.

The middle section is somewhat like a Brazilian popular song, with its syncopation and frequent changes of tempo. The soloist's melody has an improvised quality.

L I S T E N I N G   G U I D E

Heitor Villa-Lobos: Aria from *Bachianas Brasileiras No. 5*
CD 5 Track 6

0:00   6 The cellos play a short introduction.

0:12   The soprano, doubled by a cello, vocalizes the melody on "Ah."

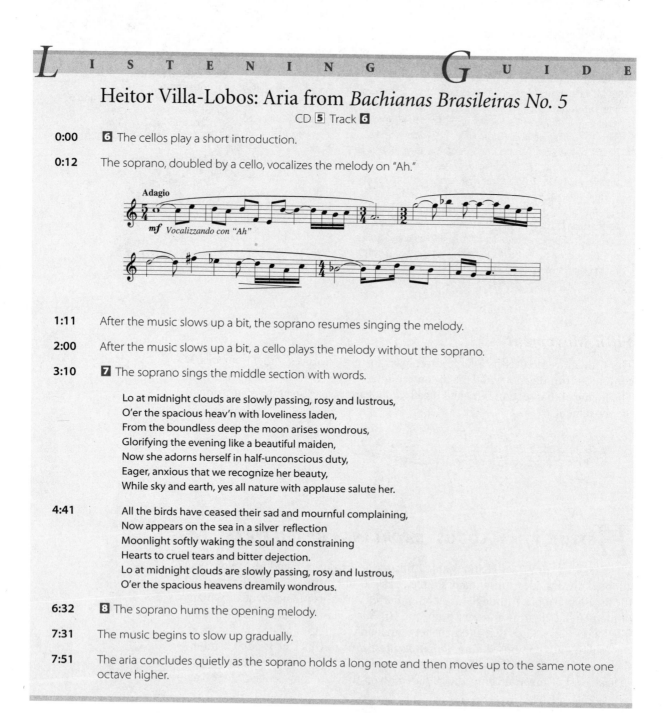

1:11   After the music slows up a bit, the soprano resumes singing the melody.

2:00   After the music slows up a bit, a cello plays the melody without the soprano.

3:10   7 The soprano sings the middle section with words.

> Lo at midnight clouds are slowly passing, rosy and lustrous,
> O'er the spacious heav'n with loveliness laden,
> From the boundless deep the moon arises wondrous,
> Glorifying the evening like a beautiful maiden,
> Now she adorns herself in half-unconscious duty,
> Eager, anxious that we recognize her beauty,
> While sky and earth, yes all nature with applause salute her.

4:41
> All the birds have ceased their sad and mournful complaining,
> Now appears on the sea in a silver reflection
> Moonlight softly waking the soul and constraining
> Hearts to cruel tears and bitter dejection.
> Lo at midnight clouds are slowly passing, rosy and lustrous,
> O'er the spacious heavens dreamily wondrous.

6:32   8 The soprano hums the opening melody.

7:31   The music begins to slow up gradually.

7:51   The aria concludes quietly as the soprano holds a long note and then moves up to the same note one octave higher.

Heitor Villa-Lobos

Heitor Villa-Lobos (1887–1959) was born in Rio de Janeiro, the son of a librarian who was an avid amateur musician. He taught his son cello and strongly encouraged him in music. When Heitor was twelve, his father died, and he composed a piece in his father's memory. Soon Villa-Lobos began playing cello professionally. As a young man, he traveled throughout Brazil and heard the music of its people. Although he never collected folk music in a systematic way, he seemed to absorb it, and it had a major impact on the more than eleven hundred works he composed during his lifetime.

In the 1920s he made two trips to Paris, where he met a number of the composers who were living there at the time. He studied their compositions and absorbed some of their techniques. In the 1930s he was director of music education for Brazil. He drafted a curriculum for its schools and organized several mass concerts, one of which involved forty thousand children! He made several journeys to the United States in the 1940s and founded the Brazilian Academy of Music.

His music is a blend of Brazilian folk music and Western art music that seems to incorporate the best elements of each.

The influence of folk or ethnic music in art music is termed *folkloric*.

Best-Known Works
Instrumental:
- [ ] *Bachianas Brasileiras Nos. 1, 5, and 9*
- [ ] Concerto for Guitar and Orchestra
- [ ] Etudes for Guitar (12)

BRITTEN'S *WAR REQUIEM*

Saint Michael's Cathedral had stood in Coventry, England, since medieval times. During World War II, it was bombed and burned out. Only its walls remained with their mute, empty windows. Rather than rebuild using the former shell of Saint Michael's, it was decided to leave the ruined shell there as a reminder of war's devastation. The new cathedral was dedicated on May 30, 1962, and Benjamin Britten was commissioned to write a work for that occasion.

Britten decided to use the traditional Mass for the Dead, or Requiem, as it is more commonly known. But he wanted his *War Requiem* to convey the message of tragedy and despair over the horrors of war. Therefore, he interspersed the words of the Latin Requiem with the antiwar poems in English by Wilfred Owen. Owen was an English soldier who was killed just before the end of World War I. His poems were published posthumously and they speak to the harshness and futility of war:

> My subject is War, and the pity of War.
> The Poetry is in the Pity . . .
> All a poet can do today is mourn.

Appropriately, Britten dedicated his *War Requiem* to four friends who died in World War II.

War Requiem is a monumental work in six sections, the same ones found in the traditional Requiem Mass. The work requires about eighty-three minutes to perform and calls for orchestra, chorus, boy choir, and three soloists. Its music is neither grand nor glorious, but rather is stark and often quite dissonant. It is highly effective in expressing its message.

The Dies irae is the second section of the *War Requiem,* and only the first portion of it is included in the Listening Guide. Its music is not flowing; instead each syllable seems chopped off from its adjacent one. The meter is an asymmetrical seven beats in each measure. The musical effect is one of a limping, twitching march that belies the "wondrous trumpet" phrase in the text and emphasizes "trembling," which is also contained in the text.

The entrance to the new cathedral is through the shell of the old one.

The sections of the Requiem Mass are:

1. Requiem aeternam
2. Dies irae
3. Offertorium
4. Sanctus
5. Angus Dei
6. Libera me

Britten used the text of the Dies irae but not the same chant melody that Berlioz and Rachmaninoff used in their works, which were presented in part V.

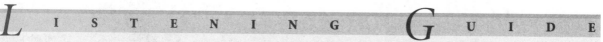

Benjamin Britten: Dies irae from *War Requiem*
excerpt from beginning
CD **2** Track **31**

0:00   **31** The French horns and trumpet exchange short passages rather quietly.

0:28   The men in the chorus sing the first three lines of the text:

Dies irae, dies illa	Day of wrath, day of anger
Solvet saeclum in favilla,	The world will dissolve into ashes,
Teste David cum Sibylla	As witness David and the Sibyl.

0:50   The horns and trumpets exchange more passages as the music becomes somewhat louder.

1:20   The women in the chorus sing the second three lines of the text:

Quantus tremor est futurus,	What trembling there will be
Quando Judex est venturus,	When the Judge shall come;
Cuncta stricte discussurus!	All shall thoroughly be shattered!

1:41   The brasses and percussion play a more extensive passage.

2:15   **32** The entire chorus, with the brasses continuing to play figures, sings the next three lines of the text:

Tuba mirum spargens sonum	The wondrous trumpet, spreading its sound
Per sepulchra regionem	To the tombs of all regions,
Coget omnes ante thronum.	Will gather all before the throne.

2:40   The brasses (with trombones muted) continue.

3:13   The chorus sings the final three lines of the text somewhat softly:

Mors stupebit et natura,	Death will be stupefied, also nature,
Cum resurget creaturam,	When all creation arises again
Judicanti responsura.	To answer to the Judge.

3:45   After the brasses play a few more figures, the section closes quietly.

Soldiers attending a service in the ruins of Coventry Cathedral on May 13, 1945, a few days after the war had ended in Europe.

Benjamin Britten

Benjamin Britten (1913–1976) was born in the seacoast town of Lowestoft, England, the son of a dental surgeon and a musical mother. He began putting patterns on paper before he was five, but by the age of six or seven the notes became associated with what he had in mind. By the age of fourteen, he had composed a number of works for piano and voice. He was given a scholarship to the Royal College of Music, and by the age of twenty-one was largely earning his living as a composer.

He emigrated to the United States in 1939 but returned to England in 1942. He toured America again several times, usually giving performances with his lifetime companion, tenor Peter Pears.

Britten wrote for every medium and for varied levels of musical difficulty. He once said of composing: "It is the easiest thing in the world to write a piece virtually or totally impossible to perform—but . . . that is not what I prefer to do; I prefer to study the conditions of performance and shape my music to them."

Best-Known Works
Opera:
- *Peter Grimes*
- *Albert Herring*
- *Billy Budd*
- *The Rape of Lucretia*

Orchestra and voice:
- *War Requiem*
- Serenade for Tenor, Horn, and Strings

Choral:
- *A Ceremony of Carols*

Orchestra:
- *The Young Person's Guide to the Orchestra*

Lili and Nadia Boulanger

Two Influential Twentieth-Century Musicians

The odds were against the Boulanger sisters. Both lived in France at a time when it was very difficult for a woman to make her mark as a composer or conductor.

Lili Boulanger (1893–1918) suffered from poor health for much of her short life, so the odds were even more difficult for her. She won the Prix de Rome at the age of nineteen, however, becoming the first woman to be awarded that coveted honor. She composed about twenty-one works, many of which are available on recordings. Her last composition, Pie Jesu, was dictated to her sister, Nadia, because she was no longer able to hold a pen. She died at the age of twenty-four from Crohn's disease.

Nadia Boulanger (1887–1979) had a greater impact on the world of music. Although she composed only a few works herself, she combined a dynamic personality and a photographic memory for music to become one of the most influential composition teachers of the twentieth century. She taught two generations of composers at the Paris Conservatory, the École Normale de Musique, and especially at the American Conservatory in Fontainebleu. It was there that she taught Aaron Copland (see chapter 42) and a long list of prominent American composers.

Nadia did not limit herself to just teaching composition. She was a highly successful conductor and was the first woman prior to World War II to conduct the Paris Philharmonic, the New York Philharmonic, the Royal Philharmonic in London, the Philadelphia Orchestra, and the Boston Symphony. She promoted a number of old and neglected works such as music by Monteverdi. Fortunately, Nadia lived a rich and full life of ninety-two years.

OTHER MAINSTREAM COMPOSERS

Russia

Dmitri Shostakovitch (1906–1975) was born in St. Petersburg and spent most of his life in Russia when it was under the control of the Communist regime. He entered the Conservatory at St. Petersburg when he was thirteen and composed his First Symphony when he was nineteen. Several times in his career he had problems with the Communist Party because his works were well liked in the West. Public apologies and some politically correct works were required from Shostakovitch to get himself back in good standing. Before he died he completed his Fifteenth Symphony, making him the first major composer since Beethoven to write more than nine.

England

Ralph Vaughan Williams and Edward Elgar are mentioned in chapter 32. In addition to these composers, England produced a number of others who contributed to its great tradition of choral music, including William Walton (1902–1983).

France

Following World War I, France went through a strong anti-Romantic reaction. The informal leaders of this movement away from Romanticism were a poet, Jean Cocteau (1889–1963), and an eccentric musician, Erik Satie ("Sah-*tee*," 1866–1925). Satie reacted to past music in his own inimitable way by writing little compositions entitled, for example, *Three Pieces in the Shape of Pear, Three Flabby Preludes for a Dog,* and *Dried Embryos.* The purpose of such titles was to satirize the seriousness of Romantic composers.

On one occasion Satie composed some music *not* to be listened to. When the audience listened to it, he became irritated and urged them not to.

From this stream of irreverent thought came a group of French composers known as The Six. The most important of these were Darius Milhaud ("*Mee*-yo," 1892–1974), Arthur Honegger ("*Own*-eh-gair," 1892–1955), and Francis Poulenc ("Poo-*lahnk*," 1899–1963).

Milhaud lived for a while in Brazil, where he became acquainted with Latin American music. He also visited New York City and heard jazz, which made a lasting impression on him. He was a prolific composer, especially of small works.

Honegger was more conservative than Milhaud. One of his compositions is a tone poem, *Pacific 231,* which depicts a steam engine. By the time he composed it, tone poems had become passé. His most successful works were large in scope, with the oratorio *Le Roi David (King David)* being the best known.

Poulenc's music more clearly expresses the Cocteau-Satie outlook. It is charming and pleasant. Most of it was written for small groups, although he also composed two operas.

Latin America

Villa-Lobos is discussed earlier in this chapter. Carlos Chávez (1899–1978) was Mexico's leading composer. His *Symphonia India* is based on Inca music, and his Toccata for Percussion Instruments is an exciting, rhythmic work.

Chávez's Toccata for Six Percussionists is probably the best-known work for that type of ensemble.

Alberto Ginastera ("*Hee*-nah-stair-ah," 1916–1983) was an Argentine composer who achieved fame for his instrumental and vocal works. His music sparkles with Latin American qualities.

C o d a

The composers cited in this chapter are but a sample
of the many in the twentieth century whose mainstream music merits
attention. Most of these composers' music is not inaccessible and radically
different. This fact is especially true when it is listened to carefully
with an understanding of its qualities.

36 Expressionism and Primitivism

People seem to have known it all along,
but in the twentieth century it has been brought out into
the open and explored as never before: Human behavior is a
complex matter that is influenced by competing, contradictory,
and sometimes concealed forces. Are humans basically good or
fundamentally bad? Is the glass half full or half empty? Is everything
folly and meaningless, as the writer of Ecclesiastes says, or does
the writer of Psalm 100 have it right with the words
"For the Lord is good and his love endures forever"?

Even a saint like Paul had trouble doing what he should and not doing what he shouldn't. (See Romans 7:15.)

Pax Romana refers to the peace that prevailed in Europe when the Roman Empire ruled it.

Events in Europe in the first twenty years of this century especially caused people to wonder about the nature of the human race. World War I raged from 1914 to 1918. It was a particularly horrible and senseless war, with the use of poison gas and a million casualties in the trenches of France and elsewhere. And for what purpose? No good seemed to have come from it; no Pax Romana resulted that provided political and economic stability. Instead, the ruling houses of Austria, Germany, and Russia were deposed, only to be replaced with confusion and turmoil that soon led to takeovers by repressive totalitarian regimes. It was a great time to be cynical and to see humans as weak and attracted by evil.

It was also a time of intellectual questioning of the established ways. In Germany, Friedrich Nietzsche's philosophy of "might-makes-right" was respected and believed. In Vienna, Sigmund Freud was developing his psychoanalytic theories of neuroses, which focused attention on the dark and inexplicable aspects of the human mind. Charles Darwin's theories of evolution and the survival of the fittest had challenged the assumptions about the dignity and place of human beings in the scheme of things.

EXPRESSIONISM

Because one role of creative artists is to be commentators on and give expression to the attitudes and feelings of society, it is logical that art and music would reflect European society of that time. The chief artistic style for doing this was *Expressionism*. In a sense, Expressionism was the opposite of Impressionism: Where Impressionism had been essentially happy, bright, and outward-looking, Expressionism was morose, dark, and inward-looking.

Expressionist painters included Franz Marc, Wassily Kandinsky, Oskar Kokoschka, and Edvard Munch, whose painting *The Scream* is shown here. They tried to shock their viewers with distortions and blatant colors.

Expressionist writers centered on the dark side of people. Elements of Expressionism found their way to the United States in the writings of Franz Kafka. This

***The Scream* by Edvard Munch** The fascination with the macabre still thrives in America today in the form of horror movies, television shows, and the attention given such lurid events as the O. J. Simpson trial in 1995.

tradition continued with the American writers William Faulkner and Tennessee Williams and the introspective and profound Irish writer James Joyce.

The poem "The Sick Moon" by the Belgian Albert Giraud is typical of Expressionist poetry. Its first stanza is:

> *You nocturnal deathly sick moon,*
> *Up there in the heavens' dark pillow,*
> *Your look too full with fever*
> *Captivates me like a strange melody.*

The poem attracted the Expressionist composer Arnold Schoenberg, who included it in his set of songs *Pierrot Lunaire (Moonstruck Pierrot)*, which he composed in 1912. The music calls for eight instruments and one singer, who uses a speech-song style called *sprechstimme*. The written pitches in the music for the singer are only approximate, and no sustained pitches are to be produced. Schoenberg's intent was to merge the spoken word and music as much as possible. The effect is eerie and nonvocal in the traditional sense.

Expressionism and Impressionism did have one point in common: Both had a natural affinity among writers, artists, and composers who knew each other. Some were talented in more than one art. The painter Kandinsky wrote plays and poetry, and the composer Schoenberg painted and even exhibited in several shows of Expressionist art.

It would be a mistake to dismiss Expressionism as just a passing fad. Because it touches on and explores a side of human nature, it merits a place in the world of the arts.

> Impressionism was very much associated with France; Expressionism was associated with Germanic thought.
>
> Expressionism emphasized subjective expression of the artist's inner experiences.
>
> Arnold Schoenberg is discussed in conjunction with his tone row music in chapter 38.
>
> Several twentieth-century works are based on the sad clown figure known variously as *Pierrot, Petrushka,* or *Pagliacci.*

BERG'S *WOZZECK*

Berg composed *Wozzeck* ("*Vot*-tzek") between 1917 and 1921. He adapted the libretto himself from a play by Georg Büchner, which he saw in 1914. The opera follows a carefully worked-out plan, one that is partly symphonic in nature:

Act I	Exposition
Act II	Development
Act III	Catastrophe

These sections differ from the usual exposition/development/recapitulation of sonata form.

Alban Berg

Alban Berg (1885–1935) was born in Vienna, the son of a factory worker. At the age of fourteen, he took up composing, an interest that occupied his time when he was confined by asthma and poor health. His father died the next year, leaving the family in difficult financial straits; only the help of a well-to-do aunt allowed Alban to remain in school. After graduation from high school, he took a position as an accountant for the government.

He was largely self-taught until the age of nineteen, when he answered a newspaper ad placed by Schoenberg for composition students. Schoenberg accepted the young man and, because Berg was poor, did not charge him for more than a year. From then on the lives of the two men seemed woven together. They were mutually supportive of each other when most of their works were received coolly by audiences.

Actually, sometimes audiences were extremely hostile to their works.

Berg's place in history is largely the result of his opera *Wozzeck*. Never in good health, Berg died as a result of complications following a bee sting.

Best-Known Works
Chamber music:
■ Lyric Suite
Opera:
■ *Lulu*
■ *Wozzeck*
Orchestra:
■ Concerto for Violin

Each of the three acts contains five scenes that are organized around a specific musical form or compositional technique. For example, act III—the one discussed here—is organized as a theme and variations.

Scene 1   Variations on a theme
Scene 2   Variations on a single tone
Scene 3   Variations on a rhythm pattern
Scene 4   Variations on a chord
Scene 5   Variations on continuous running notes

A short orchestral interlude is heard between the scenes. Berg did not intend for listeners to be conscious of these forms or techniques. Instead, he wanted the audience to be caught up in the drama and its emotional impact. The techniques used in each case, however, contribute to the dramatic and musical effect.

The story in no way resembles one that Mozart might have used for one of his operas!

The story of the opera is about Franz Wozzeck, a poor and rather incompetent soldier. He is persecuted by his sadistic captain and used as a guinea pig by the company's somewhat demented doctor. He is betrayed by his mistress, Marie, who sleeps with another man. Driven to madness, Wozzeck stabs her and later drowns trying to wash the blood off the knife and his hands.

Prior to act III, Wozzeck has been driven to desperation by Marie's unfaithfulness, a beating from the man who slept with her, and the actions of the captain and doctor.

The libretto with an English translation of the original German for act III, scene 2, appears in the Listening Guide. In it Marie and Wozzeck walk by a pond. She is anxious to get back home, but he wants to sit and talk. They comment on the blood-red color of the moon in the sky. After tenderly kissing her, he pulls a knife and plunges it into her throat. Throughout the scene one note is softly but persistently heard. As Marie is stabbed, it is sounded over and over by the timpani. In the orchestral interlude that follows, it becomes overpowering as it increases to two ear-splitting crescendos. The rhythm pattern of the interlude becomes the musical basis for the next scene.

Wozzeck and Marie shortly before he stabs her in a jealous rage.

L I S T E N I N G   G U I D E

Alban Berg: *Wozzeck*, act III, scene 2

CD **5** Track **9**

(Forest path by a pool. Dusk is falling. Marie enters with Wozzeck, from the right.)

0:00   **9** **Marie:** Dort links geht's in die Stadt.
         's ist noch weit. Komm schneller!

Wozzeck: Du sollst dableiben, Marie.
    Komm, setz' Dich.

Marie: Aber ich muss fort.

                  They sit down.

Wozzeck: Komm. Bist weit gegangen, Marie.
    Sollst Dir die Füsse nicht mehr wund laufen.
    's ist still hier! Und so dunkel.—Weisst noch, Marie,
    wie lang' es jetzt ist, dass wir uns kennen?

Marie: Zu Pfingsten drei Jahre.

Wozzeck: Und was meinst, wie lang' es
    noch dauern wird?

                  She jumps up.

1:23   **Marie:** Ich muss fort.

Wozzeck: Fürchst Dich, Marie?
    Und bist doch fromm? Und gut! Und treu!

    He pulls her down again on the seat; he bends over her, in deadly earnest.

Was Du für süsse Lippen hast, Marie!

                  He kisses her.

Den Himmel gäb' ich drum und die Seligkeit,
wenn ich Dich noch oft so küssen dürft!
Aber ich darf nicht! Was zitterst?

Marie: Der Nachttau fällt.

2:41   **10** **Wozzeck:** Wer kalt ist,
    den friert nicht mehr! Dich wird
    beim Morgentau nicht frieren.

Marie: Was sagst Du da?

Wozzeck: Nix.

        A long silence. The moon rises.

Marie: Wie der Mond rot aufgeht!

Wozzeck: Wie ein blutig Eisen!

           He draws a knife.

Marie: Was zitterst?

           She jumps up.

Was willst?

Marie: The town lies over there.
    It's still far. Let's hurry!

Wozzeck: You must stay awhile, Marie.
    Come, sit here.

Marie: But it's getting late.

Wozzeck: Come! So far you've wandered, Marie.
    You must not make your feet so sore, walking.
    It's still, here in the darkness.—Tell me, Marie,
    how long has it been since our first meeting?

Marie: At Whitsun, three years.

Wozzeck: And how long, how long will
    it still go on?

Marie: I must go!

Wozzeck: Trembling, Marie? But you are good
    (laughing) and kind and true!

Ah! How your lips are sweet to touch, Marie!

All heaven I would give, and eternal bliss,
if I still could sometimes kiss you so!
But yet I dare not! You shiver?

Marie: The night dew falls.

Wozzeck *(whispering to himself)*: Whoever
    is cold will shiver no more in the
    cold morning dew.

Marie: What are you saying?

Wozzeck: Nothing.

Marie: How the moon rises red!

Wozzeck: Like a blood-red iron!

Marie: You shiver?

What now?

3:55	**Wozzeck:** Ich nicht, Marie! Und kein Andrer auch nicht!	**Wozzeck:** No one, Marie! If not me, then no one!

He seizes her and plunges the knife into her throat.

Marie: Hilfe!   **Marie:** Help!

She sinks down. Wozzeck bends over her. She dies.

Wozzeck: Tot!   **Wozzeck:** Dead!

He rises to his feet anxiously and then rushes silently away.

4:50	Scene change—orchestral interlude *(B)*.

There are no DNA tests in operas!

The rhythm pattern has a hypnotic effect and contributes to the sense of horror.

Scene 3 takes place in a tavern. Wozzeck is almost out of his mind and tries to forget his crime. The music is a dissonant and distorted version of barroom dance music and is played on an out-of-tune piano onstage. Marie's friend Margret sings a weird-sounding folk tune. After a while she notices blood on Wozzeck's hands and sleeve and she thinks it smells like human blood. He flees in terror as people in the tavern close in on him. The mood of the scene is increased throughout by the twitching, persistent rhythm pattern first heard in the previous interlude. Only the tempos at which it is performed are altered to suit the needs of the drama.

In scene 4 Wozzeck returns to the site of the murder to get rid of the knife. The orchestra adds a macabre, almost surreal tonal backdrop of sounds for his shrieks and shouts. The moon and pond seem to turn to blood as he loses his sanity. He wades into the water to wash the knife and himself.

Berg once admitted that he wanted the music to appeal to the compassion of the audience.

The captain and the doctor—his two tormentors—happen to walk by and hear someone drowning. They offer no help, commenting that the sound of someone drowning "is not good to hear." As Wozzeck drowns, the sounds of the orchestra seem to engulf him. The orchestral interlude that follows is much longer than the other interludes. It presents musical motives associated with Wozzeck's life and it seems to sob to a close.

Scene 5 is an epilogue that takes place the next morning outside Marie's house. A group of children sing ring-around-the-rosy. The child of Marie and Wozzeck rides a hobby horse. One of the children cruelly taunts the boy: "Hey! Your mother's dead!" At first the child does not understand and continues to ride the horse. The children decide to go see the body. They run off. The child continues to ride for a few more moments, and then he also runs after the other children. The opera does not end with a clear-cut conclusion. The music simply stops.

Many twentieth-century works of music do not have clearly developed endings.

What is so moving and compelling about *Wozzeck*?

♦ It is gripping drama. Its unvarnished realism has a hard-hitting impact that grabs and keeps one's attention.

♦ The music is excellently crafted to add to the impact of the drama. What the music lacks in traditional beauty is more than made up for in its dramatic power. The audience usually feels emotionally wrung out when *Wozzeck* concludes.

♦ The music is ingenious in terms of its use of forms and compositional techniques.

PRIMITIVISM

Primitivism was not so much a point of view about art and life as it was a fascination with the art and music of non-Western and nonliterate societies. African sculpture and masks began to interest the artistic world, as did Paul Gauguin's paintings of Polynesian culture. Nineteenth-century writers, artists, and composers had been attracted by the beauty and mystery of the "long ago and far away"; twentieth-century artists admired the power and vitality of the arts of these societies.

Paul Gauguin believed that the renewal of Western art and civilization must come from "the Primitives" such as the Polynesian natives he painted in the South Pacific.

STRAVINSKY'S *RITE OF SPRING*

The high point of Primitivism in music was probably reached in 1913 with the premiere of Igor Stravinsky's ballet *La Sacre du Printemps (The Rite of Spring)*. The music was written for a production of Sergei Diaghilev, impresario of the Ballet Russe. Each year he brought a new and stunning ballet production to Paris. With keen artistic judgment and calculated showmanship, he decided in 1913 to capitalize on the Parisians' interest in primitive art. He chose to produce a ballet about prehistoric ceremonies that culminated in the sacrifice of a human being—a real change from the usual lovely stories found in ballet prior to that time.

Excerpts from the music for *The Rite of Spring*, act I, are presented in the Listening Guide. The work opens with a bassoon solo in its upper range, giving the music a haunting quality. The pitches of the melody keeping returning to the opening note, and the rhythm pattern is irregular, with frequent stops and starts. The introduction contains dissonant, strange sounds with coloristic effects.

In the "Dance of the Adolescents" that follows, Stravinsky unleashes the force of rhythm. The effect is like the wild beating of savage drums. Much of the music is quite dissonant, and the rhythm patterns are irregular. A steady series of eighth notes begins with this irregular pattern:

1-2-3-4   1-2-3-4-5   1-2   1-2-3-4-5-6   1-2-3   1-2-3-4   1-2-3-4-5

The "Dance of Abduction" is even wilder. A scampering tune is played by the woodwinds and answered by a French horn call. The meter signatures change often. Polyrhythms are also part of the rhythmic interest of the music.

What Is Beautiful? What Is Fascinating?

A modern performance of Igor Stravinsky's *Rite of Spring*

Stravinsky's Rite of Spring *premiered at the Théâtre des Champs Elysées in Paris on May 29, 1913. Stravinsky had written two previous ballets for the great impresario Sergei Diaghilev and the Ballet Russe, and both had been successfully performed in Paris, so both men were already well known there. The premiere was an event of importance among Parisian society; the theater was filled with dignitaries, royalty, and renowned musicians.*

None of them could have anticipated what would happen that May evening. Instead of the expected lovely music, beautiful costumes, and toe dancing, the audience was subjected to some harsh-sounding chords and dancers in not-so-pretty costumes making angular, rough motions. No one knows what set off the audience more, the dancing or the music, but the audience reacted—to an extreme. One writer reported:

> *A certain part of the audience, thrilled by what it considered to be a blasphemous attempt to destroy music as an art, and swept away with wrath, began very soon after the rise of the curtain to whistle, to make catcalls, and to offer audible suggestions as to how the performance should proceed . . . The orchestra played on unheard . . . The figures on the stage danced in time to music they had to imagine they heard.*

One critic yelled as loudly as he could, "The music is a colossal fraud!" The ambassador from Austria laughed derisively. One lady reached out into the adjoining box to slap the face of a man who was hissing. Another lady rose majestically in her seat and spat in the face of one of the noisemakers. The eminent French composer Maurice Ravel alone shouted, "Genius!" Backstage, Stravinsky held on to the choreographer, Waslaw Nijinsky, to keep him from going into the audience and fighting with those who disapproved.

Probably no one that evening thought about it in this way, but they were violently disagreeing about the nature of art. Must it always be beautiful? Can't art sometimes stir the emotions and affect people deeply? Can art be of life, or must it always be better than life?

If nothing else, Expressionism demonstrated that art goes much deeper than beauty in the sense of being pretty. There is nothing pretty about Berg's Wozzeck and many sections of Stravinsky's Rite of Spring, but they continue to attract listeners again and again. The poet Keats was right when he wrote, "A thing of beauty is a joy forever," but were he writing today he might have revised that line to read, "A thing of human feeling is a fascination forever."

Igor Stravinsky: *The Rite of Spring*
excerpts from act I
CD 2 Tracks 33 and 36

0:00 33 The "Dance of the Adolescents" begins with the orchestra playing persistent, driving chords with irregular beats.

0:19 The trumpet plays a short melodic figure that descends by half-steps.

0:48 The bassoon plays a simple melody derived from the previous rhythm pattern.

1:19 The persistent rhythm is broken by some held notes played by the brasses, but the rhythmic dance music soon starts again.

1:43 34 The French horns sound a short melodic figure that is gradually taken up by other instruments.

2:20 The trumpets play a third short melody in the "Dance of the Adolescents" as the music grows more active.

3:23 35 The "Dance of Abduction" begins with the brasses holding long notes that soon give way to music with a rapid tempo and irregular meter.

3:35 The French horns play a primitive-sounding figure that is heard often in this dance.

4:19 A passage containing solo notes for the timpani is heard; other instruments respond to the timpani in irregular metrical patterns.

4:45 The "Dance of Abduction" ends with a long trilled note played by the flute.

★ ★ ★ ★ ★ ★

0:00	**36** "The Dance of the Earth" begins very quietly with the bassoon holding a long note as the basses and timpani sound a two-note pattern.
0:20	The bass drum, which is soon joined by the timpani, begins a crescendo as the tempo becomes very fast. The orchestra barks out chords in an irregular pattern.
0:57	The French horns begin playing many repeated notes and are soon followed by the cellos and the trumpets. The rest of the orchestra joins them as various instruments pop in and out, playing repeated notes.
1:38	"The Dance of the Earth" and act I conclude with a tremendous crescendo.

Igor Stravinsky

Igor Stravinsky (1882–1971) was born in St. Petersburg, Russia, where his father was a singer with the Imperial Opera. Although he studied music, his parents hoped that he would become a lawyer. He studied law at the University of St. Petersburg and composition with Rimsky-Korsakov at the same time.

Stravinsky soon became associated with Sergei Diaghilev, manager of the famous Ballet Russe, who signed the twenty-eight-year old composer in 1910 after hearing only one of his works. The ballet he composed for the Ballet Russe was *The Firebird*. It was so successful that he was commissioned to write another, which turned out to be *Petrouchka*. Both ballets are based on Russian folk tales. He was then given a third commission for a ballet, *The Rite of Spring*.

Just before World War I, Stravinsky moved to Switzerland. The revolution in Russia cut off his income, and the Ballet Russe disbanded for a while. He lived in Switzerland for eight years while recovering from a serious illness.

After the war ended, Stravinsky settled in Paris. He became a French citizen and traveled widely as a conductor and pianist. He continued to compose, but he abandoned the style he had used for the three ballets with the Ballet Russe. In 1939 he came to the United States to lecture. World War II prevented his return to Europe, so he settled in Hollywood and became an American citizen. He retained his esteemed position as one of the greatest composers of this century.

Despite superficial changes of style, Stravinsky remained true to his objective concept of music: Because a musical work is something a composer creates, it is essentially an object, not a manifestation of his psyche. Therefore, a composer's works do not need to be consistent personal creations. Skill at composition is what matters; the composer's personality is irrelevant.

When he was eighty, Stravinsky was the honored guest of President John F. Kennedy at the White House. He was also the subject of a special one-hour program on national television.

Best-Known Works
Ballet:
- *The Firebird*
- *Petrouchka*
- *The Rite of Spring*

Chamber music:
- *Octet*
- *L'Histoire du soldat*

Choral:
- *Symphony of Psalms*

Opera:
- *Oedipus the King*
- *The Rake's Progress*

"Round Dances of Spring" brings some relief from the frenzied music that precedes it. The tempo is slow, and the flutes and other woodwinds play a melody that resembles an American Indian tune.

The music becomes energetic again in "Games of Rival Tribes." The idea of competition is expressed by pitting one section of the orchestra against another, each with its own distinctive music. The music is bitonal in a number of places.

Bitonal refers to music that is in two different keys at the same time.

The "Entrance of the Sage" brings back the main thematic material with a thick orchestration. The music becomes slower and more majestic at this point.

Act I ends with "Dance of the Earth." It also suggests violence and upheaval.

The ballet must be seen with this part of the music to appreciate the full impact of the work.

The second and final act of *The Rite of Spring* depicts the sacrifice of a young maiden so that the God of Spring will be satisfied. It is similar in style to the first act, but is rarely played apart from the ballet. Just the opposite is true of the music for act I.

To listeners hearing it for the first time, *The Rite of Spring* may sound like a jumble of random notes. It may even seem that the players can play anything they want and no one would notice the difference. Such an idea is of course incorrect. Stravinsky carefully planned everything in the score and wrote detailed instructions for playing each part. He tells the timpanist when to change from hard to soft sticks, the French horn players when to tilt the bells of their instruments upward, and the cellists when to retune a string so that a chord can be played on open strings to achieve a more raucous effect.

Musicians generally consider Stravinsky's *The Rite of Spring* to be one of the masterpieces of twentieth-century music. Why?

♦ Its exploitation of rhythm is exceptional. Stravinsky had an uncanny sense of when to accent notes or change the metrical pattern.

♦ The themes are used in an imaginative and interesting way. What Stravinsky often did was create a short tune and then repeat it many times, but each time with slight changes. Like every composer whose music has lasted over the centuries, Stravinsky was able to manage the tension between the needs for unity and variety in his music.

♦ Although a traditional symphony orchestra plays the work, Stravinsky demonstrates great ability to find new timbres and create new sounds.

♦ Dissonance is also handled in a masterful way. Some chords are very dissonant, but many are not. It's not just that Stravinsky employs dissonant sounds; rather it is that he knew *when* to use dissonance—and when not to.

Primitivism also appealed to other composers in the years just before World War I. Béla Bartók composed *Allegro Barbaro* for piano in 1911, and several of his other works are wild and rhapsodic. Some of Sergei Prokofiev's early works have driving rhythms and blatant harmonies. Ernest Bloch's Violin Sonata, written in the 1920s, has a hard-driving character.

Sergei Prokofiev is discussed in chapter 37.

C o d a

Expressionism and Primitivism seemed to burn themselves out in about a decade. But what powerful music was created in these two movements!

Neoclassicism

Styles of music seem to move toward being either products of emotion and feelings or the result of thoughtful intellectual effort. The Baroque style was more emotional than that of the Renaissance. The pendulum then swung back toward intellectual control in the Classical period, but after a few generations it swung back again toward the highly subjective music of the Romantic period.

NEOCLASSICAL PERIOD

The twentieth century has seen the dichotomy between thought and feeling continue in its music, but with a definite swing toward more intellectually oriented music. This approach to music is called *Neoclassicism*. It seeks to capture the spirit and attitude of the Classical writers, artists, and musicians of the eighteenth century, who in turn looked back to ancient Greece and Rome for inspiration.

The prefix neo means "new."

The Neoclassical attitude is evident in Pablo Picasso's painting *The Lovers*. If you were to imagine what a picture with such a title would look like, it probably would *not* depict a man and a woman in the cool, detached attitude seen in Picasso's painting. Emotional and passionate it is not. Delicate, sensitive, balanced, and thoughtful it is.

Notice that a minimum of lines and shadings are used, but they achieve the desired effect. Notice also that the figures are dressed not in modern clothing but rather garments that seem more like those of the ancient Greeks or Romans. The painting projects an attitude of tender love yet in a restrained way.

NEOCLASSICISM IN MUSIC

After *The Rite of Spring*, Stravinsky changed to shorter, more concise music written for a limited number of instruments. Why did he do this? Because of his beliefs about what a composer should do with sound. He wrote: "What is important for the clear ordering of the work, for its crystallization, is that all the . . . elements . . . should be properly subjugated to the role of law before they intoxicate us." In Stravinsky's eyes, writing a musical composition is like solving a problem; it is a task to be done by applying the brain. Therefore, music is intended to do nothing except demonstrate the composer's ability to contrive interesting tonal and rhythmic combinations of sounds.

Sometimes Neoclassicism in music has been given the euphonious name "Back to Bach." Several Baroque

***The Lovers* by Pablo Picasso** recalls the cool, quiet, classic quality of ancient Greek and Roman art. The figures seem like delicately posed statuary in an art museum.

By the word *intoxicate* Stravinsky does not mean "drunk," but rather "out of control."

forms such as the concerto grosso were revived during this time, and there was a renewed emphasis on counterpoint; the harpsichord has also enjoyed a rebirth of interest, so the allusion to Bach is reasonable.

PROKOFIEV'S *CLASSICAL SYMPHONY*

The *Classical Symphony* is Op. 25 in Prokofiev's list of works, so it is an early work but certainly not one of his first. To have this symphony follow the style of Mozart and Haydn, he made a number of musical decisions:

Prokofiev composed his *Classical Symphony* in 1916–1917.

♦ It would not be long. The first movement, for example, is just over three and a half minutes—a fraction of the length of most nineteenth-century symphonies.

♦ It would be for small orchestra. The score does not call for trombones, or for percussion other than timpani, and only two instruments are featured on each of the other brasses and the woodwind parts.

♦ It would contain the type of themes typically found in the Classical style. And, sure enough, the themes are collections of short melodic ideas that are connected together. The harmonies are less rich and complex than those found in music of the nineteenth century.

One of the themes in the first movement is marked to be played *con Eleganza*— "with elegance."

♦ It would call for a style of playing that is neat and precise.

♦ It would follow traditional forms. The first movement is in sonata form, the second movement follows a large three-part form, the third is a stylized dance, and the fourth returns to sonata form.

First Movement

The first movement is presented in the Listening Guide.

Sergei Prokofiev

Sergei Prokofiev (1891–1953) was born in a village in southern Russia. His mother taught him to play the piano and encouraged him to compose music. By the time he was nine, he had written a three-act opera. After his family moved to Moscow, Prokofiev studied with outstanding teachers of composition, including Rimsky-Korsakov.

His early compositions were rather dissonant, and his teachers thought him somewhat of a musical revolutionary.

After the Communist revolution, he left his homeland and lived in Paris, where he continued to compose and give concerts. In 1933 he decided to return to the Soviet Union, where he was greeted warmly by the public

and initially by the government. As he grew older, his music became more mellow.

Following World War II, Prokofiev and Shostakovitch were accused of being "formalistic," a charge meaning that their music was considered too sophisticated by government officials. He did not allow governmental pressure to interfere with his work, however.

His style could vary from Neoclassical in the *Classical Symphony* to Neo-Romantic in his ballet *Romeo and Juliet*. He clearly was able, in Stravinsky's words, to subject his compositions "to the rule of law." That fact allowed him to be as Classical or Romantic as he wished at any moment in each musical work. Sergei Prokofiev was one of the giants of twentieth-century music.

Best-Known Works

Ballet:
- *Cinderella*
- *The Love of Three Oranges*
- *Romeo and Juliet*

Orchestra:
- *Classical Symphony*
- *Lt. Kijé Suite*
- Piano Concertos Nos. 1 and 3
- Symphony No. 5
- Violin Concerto No. 2

Piano:
- Sonatas (10)

Sergei Prokofiev: *Classical Symphony*, Op. 25
First Movement

CD 5 Track 11

Exposition

0:00   **11**   The movement opens with a short introduction, which is quickly followed by the first theme, played by the violins.

0:21   A transition consisting of short melodic fragments is begun by the woodwinds but is soon passed among several sections of the orchestra.

0:48   **12**   The second theme begins, played in a very light, quiet style by the violins accompanied by steady short notes on the bassoon.

1:19   A short codetta concludes the exposition.

Development

1:33   **13**   After a silent measure, the violins play part of the first theme as the music modulates often.

1:42   A fragment of the transition is played by the woodwinds and violins, which is followed by a fragment of the first theme.

1:58   The second theme is played by the strings and followed by other sections of the orchestra as the woodwinds continue playing continuously moving notes. This time the theme is not light and elegant but loud and forceful.

Recapitulation

2:34   **14**   The first theme returns, played lightly by the violins.

2:43   The transition is played again by the woodwinds and followed by other sections.

3:04   The second theme is played very quietly at a high pitch level by the violins.

3:29   The coda begins, with the woodwinds and violins outlining chords.

3:44   The movement closes in a rush of sound.

Second Movement

This movement is quiet and songlike. The main melody seems to be the epitome of delicate, refined beauty.

Third Movement

The third movement is a gavotte—sort of. It does have all the features of the gavotte of earlier times, but is actually quite twentieth century in its free use of keys. The form is interesting. The movement opens and closes with the same music. Between the two appearances of that music, there are two sections of contrasting music, each repeated. When the second of these sections is repeated, the oboes add a line of counterpoint.

The stylized dance form used in the symphonies of Haydn and Mozart was the minuet. Prokofiev parted from the Classical tradition a bit in this movement.

Fourth Movement

The movement is marked *Allegro vivace* with a metronome marking of 152 beats per minute. In other words, the notes fly by, especially for the violins. Prokofiev reveals his twentieth-century harmonic thinking with a number of interesting key changes. The codetta presents a third theme, which is used prominently in the development section.

It is hard *not* to like Prokofiev's *Classical Symphony*. It has all the attributes of the music of Mozart and his contemporaries—the tuneful themes, the well-thought-out forms, the neatly balanced phrases, and generous amounts of charm and beauty. But Prokofiev has taken those characteristics and added a richer palette of harmonies and treatment of melodies.

OTHER NEOCLASSICAL WORKS

Prokofiev was by no means the only composer attracted to Neoclassicism. Stravinsky has already been discussed; the milestone Neoclassical work by him was his Octet for Wind Instruments, which he composed in 1923. Other works by Stravinsky that reveal strong Neoclassical tendencies include a ballet *Apollo (Apollon Musaagète)*, *Jeu de cartes (Game of Cards)*, *Oedipus Rex*, *Pulcinella*, Suites Nos. 1 and 2 for Small Orchestra, and *Symphony of Psalms*.

Paul Hindemith (1895–1963) was a composer whose Neoclassical works had a Germanic quality. He composed sonatas for virtually every instrument and a large amount of chamber music. He also wrote a number of motets and choral works. A few of his works were large in scope, including his program symphony *Mathis der Mahler (Matthias the Painter)* inspired by three paintings by Mathis Grünewald on the altar at Isenheim, Germany.

Hindemith believed in "useful, functional" music (in German *Gebrauchsmusik*) that could be played by competent amateurs. He composed many of his sonatas with that goal in mind.

A number of twentieth-century composers wrote some of their compositions in a Neoclassical style. Although known first for his compositions on Jewish themes, Ernest Bloch (1880–1959) composed two concerti grossi and a number of suites. Several twentieth-century French composers adopted the Neoclassical approach as well. Among them were Jacques Ibert (1890–1962), Francis Poulenc, and Darius Milhaud. A number of American composers also took a Neoclassical approach. They are discussed in part VII.

C o d a

Neoclassicism offered a fresh approach, one that had been neglected for more than a century. Of course, it was not possible or desirable to compose musical works that were just rewrites of Haydn and Mozart. The new music in the Classical style had to offer listeners some of the features of twentieth-century music as well as the outlook of the Classical period. And that is exactly what Prokofiev, Stravinsky, and other Neoclassical composers did.

Tone Rows and Serialism

It had worked for almost three hundred years. Music from popular songs to symphonies had a tonal center around which it functioned. The key of a work may have strayed and for a time become lost, but inevitably it was there and the music returned to it. This principle of a tonal center and the movement of chords in relation to that tonal center seemed as necessary to music as the law of gravity seems to us.

But was it? Arnold Schoenberg did not think so. He and other composers initially wrote works (mostly Expressionistic ones) that centered around no particular key. In short, that music was *atonal*. But Schoenberg was not satisfied. No longer did the old forms such as fugue or sonata work with atonal music. He felt the need to develop a new system for composing. About 1923 he devised a means of "composing with twelve tones," as he termed it.

TONE ROW MUSIC

Although at first glance the idea may seem limited, it has been calculated that there are more than 479,001,600 rows available!

The heart of Schoenberg's system was its *tone row*. The basic row, which the composer determined before writing the composition, includes the twelve different pitches of the chromatic scale, with no pitch being repeated before the row was complete. In this way no tonal center could be implied because all the notes in the chromatic scale were treated equally.

Tone row music is linear, although it does contain some chords. The predetermined row is treated in four ways: (1) the *original*, (2) the *retrograde* (backward, in reverse order), (3) the *inversion* (all intervals reversed from their original direction), and (4) the *retrograde-inversion* (reverse pitch direction and reverse order). Any of the forms of the row can be transposed.

SCHOENBERG'S VARIATIONS FOR ORCHESTRA

Flutter tonguing is actually created by a fluttering motion of the tongue.

In Germany the musical note *H* is B natural, and *B* is B flat. Therefore, the four notes of Bach's name in music are B-flat–A–C–B-natural. Several composers have since written works based on his name as a tribute to him.

As its title implies, the work is a set of variations on a theme. There certainly was nothing new about that. What was new was the use of the tone row theme and the ways in which it is varied.

The overall plan for Variations for Orchestra consists of an introduction, the theme, nine variations, and a finale. The introduction contains a series of sounds including tremolos in the violins and *flutter tonguing* by the flute. It also includes a time-honored motive built around the notes B-flat, A, C, and B-natural, which in German spells *B A C H*. Bach himself used this pattern of notes to spell his name as a fugue subject in his last composition, *The Art of Fugue*.

The variations are short, sometimes only twenty-three measures long. They often feature small groups of instruments, not the entire orchestra. The finale is longer than any of the variations. The work closes after a final statement of the B A C H motive.

Here is the basic tone row for Variations for Orchestra:

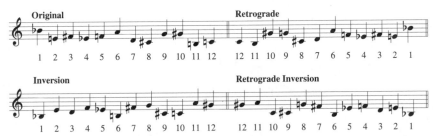

The structure of the music is very carefully planned. For example, the chords are derived from one version of the row, and the number of notes in the melodic phrases corresponds to the number of notes in the chord.

Tone row compositions present problems for listeners not familiar with this type of music. The concept of the row is not hard to understand, but the row itself can seldom be heard in the composition. Furthermore, its chromatic nature makes it hard to remember. Actually, the row is mainly a compositional technique or approach for composers; hearing the row as such is not necessary for listeners.

The idea of manipulating timbre also fascinated Schoenberg and other Expressionist composers. He devised a technique for doing that, which he gave the German name *Klangfarbenmelodie*. It involves changing the timbre along with the pitch changes. This is accomplished by giving different instruments various notes of the melody so that while the melody is present, it is not heard in its complete form played on just one instrument.

Klangfarbenmelodie literally means "manufactured tone color melody" in German.

Schoenberg vigorously denied that his music was cold and intellectual. When the requirements of tone row composition are considered, that denial may seem inaccurate. His music does contain much activity crammed into most of its measures. It seems as if he compressed the dimension of time, causing what happens to the sounds to be much more concentrated than in previous music. During most of his career, Schoenberg obviously did not conceive of music in the rambling dimensions of the Romantic period.

Arnold Schoenberg

Arnold Schoenberg ("*Sh(r)n*-bairg," 1874–1951) was born in Vienna. He began studying violin when he was eight and became an avid participant in amateur chamber music performances. After his father's early death, he went to work as a bank clerk. He had little formal training at an advanced level.

For many years he had shown an interest in composing, and that interest increased until he decided to make it his life's work. He spent two years in Berlin as music director for a cabaret, and then returned to Vienna. He served in the Austrian army for two years during World War I. In 1925 he was appointed professor of composition at the Berlin Academy of Arts, where he remained until Hitler came to power. Because of the anti-Semitic actions of the new regime, he decided to leave Germany for the United States, where he taught at the University of California at Los Angeles (UCLA) until his death.

Schoenberg is important in the world of music as much for his leadership and innovative ideas as for his compositions. Prior to 1908 he stood in the tradition of Wagner and composed large romantic works. About 1908, however, he started turning to music for smaller groups. His music became more contrapuntal and much more chromatic. Over a period of time, he began to write music that had no tonal center. He also moved even further toward Expressionism.

About 1923 he devised the tone row system, which he followed for most of the remainder of his life. This was a system that was to leave its mark on the world of music.

Best-Known Works
Chamber music:
- *Pierrot Lunaire*
- Trio for Strings
Orchestra:
- Chamber Symphony No. 1
- Variations for Orchestra
- *Verklärte Nacht*

LISTENING GUIDE

Arnold Schoenberg: Variations for Orchestra
excerpt
CD 2 Track 37

0:00   **37** The cellos begin with the original version of the row, which is the theme of the work.

0:13   The retrograde-inversion of the row is played, but beginning on a different note from the original.

0:31   **38** The retrograde of the row is played, based on the same note as the original.

0:43   The inversion of the row is played, based on the same note as the retrograde-inversion.

1:00   The theme concludes quietly.

SERIALISM: BEYOND TONE ROWS

Since 1950 a number of other composers turned to tone rows. This movement can be attributed primarily to the influence of a quiet student of Schoenberg's: Anton Webern.

Webern expanded the concept of tone row music with the introduction of *Serialism*. In it the principles of tone row music are carried further with the development of one or more series of pitches within the row. The idea was subsequently extended to rows or series of articulations, dynamic levels, and rhythmic values. Serialism represented additional intellectual control over musical sounds.

For example, consider the basic row for Webern's Concerto for Nine Instruments:

Brackets have been placed over the four subrows.

The row can be divided into four subrows. In turn, each of these subrows can be divided into three segments, each consisting of two adjacent notes and one that is either a line or a space farther away. The first three notes can be thought of as a miniature row, followed by its transposed retrograde-inversion, retrograde, and inversion.

Anton Webern

Anton Webern ("*Vay*-burn," 1883–1945) was born Anton von Webern, but he dropped the royal *von* from his name after the 1918 revolution in Austria that deposed the Hapsburg monarchy. His father was a mining engineer, who provided young Anton with lessons in cello, piano, and music theory.

Webern's style moved away from the influence of Wagner when he met Schoenberg. He studied with Schoenberg for about two years and maintained a lifelong friendship with him, even after Schoenberg moved to America.

Webern began his career as a conductor, but in 1920 shifted to private teaching. For a while he worked for the Social Democratic Party and conducted a workers' chorus. In 1927 he was appointed conductor and adviser for Radio Austria, a position he held until his political party lost power. He composed actively throughout his adult life, even during World War II. At the time of his death, he was largely unknown to the general public but highly esteemed by a few other composers.

Although he composed in the same style as Schoenberg, Webern's music is more austere and economical. Of his thirty-one compositions, the longest is just ten minutes, and all his music can performed in less than three hours! His dynamic levels are often very soft, and his frail tone row melodies are subtly passed from one instrument to another. If he had written more sparsely, it seems like the music would disappear completely.

> Webern was accidentally shot by an American soldier near the end of the war, when he lit a cigarette in the dark during a strict curfew.

Best-Known Works
Orchestra:
- [ ] Five Pieces for Orchestra
- [ ] Six Pieces for Orchestra

Chamber music:
- [ ] Concerto for Nine Instruments

The Concerto for Nine Instruments begins:

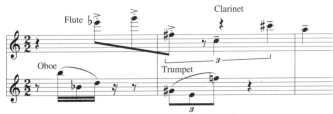

In this example the groups of three notes are retained, although with *octave displacement,* which is the technique of sounding a pitch in an octave higher or lower from most of the others in the row. The first group is played by the oboe, the second by the flute, the third by the trumpet, and the fourth by the clarinet. In addition, a different rhythm is associated with each three-note group, and different articulations are specified.

Webern's Concerto for Nine Instruments has no actual themes. It is held together by the rows and the three-note motives.

A number of composers, including Stravinsky, have been attracted to the principles of tone row and serial music and have used them in some of their compositions. Other composers made tone row or serial music their dominant style.

Articulation refers to tonguing, slurring, and the style with which notes are played.

Stravinsky made some modifications in Schoenberg's ideas when he wrote works using a tone row.

Coda

What is enjoyable about listening to the tone row music of Schoenberg and the serial music of Webern? The pleasure lies not in listening for its emotional appeal, but rather in listening to music that is so thoughtfully crafted. It is truly mind over music, presenting a musical challenge that can be enjoyable when approached in an intellectual way.

39 New Sounds and New Techniques

With the end of World War II in 1945, the world moved
into a new era. In a faltering manner, the nations and peoples of
the world started to rebuild in both a physical and an emotional
sense. Most people realized that whatever might happen in
the future, things would never be the same again.

Along with the monumental changes that have come about
in the more than fifty years since that time, a new generation of
composers has been active. New ways of making music have
become available through technological advances, and different
attitudes about music and music listening have evolved.

From about 1945 to 1960, the competition for leadership in the world of art
music was between those who favored strict control of musical sounds through
Serialism and those who favored only a few specifications through chance music
and improvisation.

EXTENSIONS OF SERIALISM

Tone row music may have
been originally rejected
because of its association
with Expressionism.

Although Schoenberg devised the tone row system in the 1920s, until about 1950
only a few of the major composers were attracted to it. The tone row approach began
to find more favor after 1945, partly because of the influence of Webern.

As mentioned previously, Webern extended the idea of a row beyond pitches to
include series of articulations, dynamic levels, and rhythmic values. The leading
proponents of what is described as *total Serialism* were the French composers Pierre
Boulez (b. 1925) and Olivier Messiaen (b. 1908). In one of his works, Messiaen uses
one series for the melody, another for the dynamics, and another for the rhythm;
each of the series is a different length.

Other composers who favored highly controlled works in the 1950s were
Luciano Berio (b. 1925) in Italy, Milton Babbitt (b. 1916) in the United States, and
Karlheinz Stockhausen (b. 1928) in Germany. The music they created during those
years is very complex, so it is difficult for listeners to perceive and performers to
render accurately. Over the years some of these composers have changed their
approaches to composing.

CHANCE MUSIC

The term *aleatory* comes
from a Latin word meaning
"dice" or "gambler," which
in the ancient world
signified chance.

The American John Cage (1912–1992) was a major promoter of *chance* or *aleatory
music*. In such music the sounds are partly the result of chance, and so they are
unpredictable. A player might be instructed to play anything that comes to mind
or just rest. Or the notes can be the result of throwing dice or dropping pages of
music on the floor.

At first glance, such musical practices may seem like a put-on, but they are not.
They are the application in music of an existential outlook on life. For centuries

Western civilization believed in progress, the idea of moving toward a goal. Through increased knowledge—which in turn led to such practical outcomes as improved medical care, more food, and increased leisure—it was thought that the human race was progressing. However, the idea of progress has come under attack in the twentieth century from proponents of existential philosophy and from advocates of Asian religious beliefs. The idea of progress is false, they maintain. There is only change, not progress.

The implications of the only-change, no-goal-toward-which-to-progress philosophy are enormous. It is like removing the goal lines and uprights on a football field and ceasing to keep score or time: The game just happens. About the only assumption that can be made is that the players will eventually tire and stop playing.

Composer John Cage said of his music, "I have nothing to say and I am saying it."

This philosophical position rejects the idea that works of art must have meaning. As Cage said, "My purpose is to eliminate purpose." Depicting a can of Campbell's soup or creating a painting that looks like it came from a comic book is not, as some people believe, a comment on the vulgarity of contemporary civilization. The content of such works is so obvious that it no longer encourages interpretation by the viewer, which is the way the artist wants it. A picture is a picture—and that's all.

In his book *Silence,* Cage urges the composer to "give up the desire to control sound, clear his mind of music [in the usual sense] and set about discovering means to let sounds be themselves rather than vehicles for man-made theories or expressions of human sentiments." Using chance devices to determine sounds is one way in which Cage and others try to get listeners to just consider the sounds and not attempt to read meaning into them.

The epitome of Cage's views was his work *4' 33",* which premiered in 1955. The pianist simply sits at the piano that long but never plays a note!

These ideas have been attempted by a number of composers, including Karlheinz Stockhausen. In a complete change from his electronic works of the 1950s, Stockhausen's *Originale* (1961) is based on a series of simultaneous, incoherent "happenings." In one scene the directions are: "Pianist and percussionist put on clothes brought in by cloakroom attendant. The pianist takes off his cultic robes and puts on Oriental female costume . . . When he is ready, he begins to brew up tea at the piano."

*E*LECTRONIC MUSIC

As music moved into the 1960s, both serial and chance music faded and electronic music began to receive much more attention. Prior to that time, technologically created and produced music had been confined to a few expensively equipped studios. When the cost of such equipment dropped enough in price, many more composers started to work with computers and synthesizers.

There are two general types of electronic music. One is *musique concrète.* Recordings are made of actual sounds—parts of human speech, the buzzing of an insect, the soothing sound of water running, the shrill sound of a whistle, and so on. Then the recording, which in the 1960s was on magnetic tape, is manipulated by the composer:

The term *musique concrète* means "concrete music" in French.

♦ It can be speeded up or slowed down.

♦ It can have other sounds added by splicing or editing.

♦ Some of the partials of a sound can be filtered out.

♦ The order in which sounds appear can be arranged and altered.

Digital editing equipment has made splicing tape no longer necessary.

An American advocate of *musique concrète* was Valdimir Ussachevsky (1911–1990), who was one of the founders of the Columbia-Princeton Electronic Music Laboratory in New York City. *Musique concrète* has been used successfully as background music for movies, plays, and ballets, especially when eerie music is appropriate.

Another type of electronic music consists of sounds produced on electronic equipment such as synthesizers and computers. Such music had its beginning in the Studio for Electronic Music of the West German Radio in the 1950s, but today is actively pursued throughout the Western world.

Technology offers a composer total control over the music, for several reasons:

Sometimes composers have made up graphics to describe their electronic music, but that is not necessary.

♦ There are no performers to alter the music, either intentionally or unintentionally by making mistakes. Once the right button is pushed, the equipment plays exactly what the composer entered into it. Therefore, there is no longer any need for music notation.

♦ Any pitch is possible, including ones so high that most humans cannot hear them, as well as *microtones,* which are intervals closer than the half-steps found on keyboards and many instruments.

♦ Any combination of pitches is possible.

♦ Any rhythm is possible, no matter how complex, including multiple rhythms occurring at the same time.

♦ Any timbre is possible. Electronic devices can filter out or increase partials in a sound to achieve any tone quality the composer wishes.

♦ Any dynamic level is possible. The sounds can be almost inaudibly soft or so loud that they cause physical damage to the loudspeakers (and listeners' eardrums!). Crescendos and decrescendos can be regulated exactly.

The line between *musique concrète* and electronic music is by no means clear-cut.

♦ Any electronically created sound can be combined with any recorded sound in any way the composer desires. Actual sounds of instruments can be *sampled* (recorded) and incorporated into electronic compositions.

♦ The computer can be programmed in conjunction with other electronic equipment to make some of the decisions in the creation of music. When this happens, the creator of the program becomes to some extent the "composer of the composer."

The world of electronic music has changed rapidly, and it has been around only a few decades in anywhere near the form in which it is found today. No solid repertoire of such music exists. Each new work is to some degree an experiment.

Varèse's *Poème Électronique*

Poème électronique by Edgard Varèse comes as close as any work to being a masterpiece of this type of music. It was created in 1958 for the Brussels World Fair and was a part of the pavilion designed by the Swiss architect Le Corbusier for the Philips Radio Corporation. Not only did Le Corbusier design the exterior, he used a planned sequence of colored lights and images to be projected on the interior walls while Varèse's three-track tape was played through 425 loudspeakers.

The interior of the pavilion contained many different shapes and angles. When visitors walked through the building, they were greeted with different colors, images, and musical sounds. Varèse realized that people would not go through the pavilion according to an establish path; they were free to move about as they wished, which meant that there was an element of chance in what they encountered. The reactions of the visitors in 1958 to what they saw and heard ranged from anger and fear to curiosity and awe.

There was a concensus that it was really *very different!*

The Listening Guide helps in learning about the content of this highly imaginative musical work.

L I S T E N I N G G U I D E

Edgard Varèse: *Poème électronique*
beginning
CD 5 Track 15

0:00	15 Sounds of a large bell, wiggling sounds, and sirens are heard.
0:43	Driplike sounds are heard, followed by something sounding like squawks.
0:56	A three-note pattern ascends three times.
1:11	A low sound is sustained along with a rattling sound, then a siren, and more squawks.
1:33	The three-note ascending figure is heard again, followed by more squawks and some chirps.
2:04	The sound of percussion instruments is heard, as well as a siren.
2:35	A large bell sound is heard again, along with sustained tones.
2:50	Recording fades.

Edgard Varèse

Although he was born in France, **Edgard Varèse** (1883–1965) lived most of his life in America. Appropriately, his first composition after he moved to his new country was entitled *Amériques*. It called for an orchestra plus an unusual combination of percussion instruments: drums of different types and sizes, siren, rattle, sleighbells, castanets, glockenspiel, and xylophone. Ten years later he composed a work that is better known today—*Ionization*—which uses thirty-seven different percussion instruments played by thirteen musicians.

Varèse came to music via a different route than most composers. He was trained in engineering and mathematics. His scientific leanings led to his contact in 1927 with engineers at the Bell Telephone Company laboratories to urge them to create machines that would synthesize musical sounds.

Notice the year and how far ahead of his time Varèse was.

When magnetic tape recorders became available in the 1950s, he was the first to explore their potential for music making. Those efforts led to *Poème électronique* in 1958.

Best-Known Works
Electronic:
☐ *Poème électronique*
Flute:
☐ *Density 21.5*
Instrumental:
☐ *Ionization*

The use of electronic music in conjunction with visual images has fascinated both art and popular composers. The potential of electronic music has barely been tapped. It offers vast possibilities for working with sounds and images, and many composers today are exploring this new medium.

ECLECTICISM

Although contemporary music is very pluralistic, with composers writing in widely divergent styles, some composers use what they think is the best of each style. They take various elements from different styles and synthesize music that is uniquely their own, a practice known as *Eclecticism.* They owe allegiance to no musical system or viewpoint, and their compositions are not easily classified.

Whether or not Eclecticism is successful depends on the abilities of the particular composer. One composer who seems to have achieved an effective synthesis of various types of music is the American Alan Hovhaness.

HOVHANESS'S *AND GOD CREATED GREAT WHALES*

Written in 1970, *And God Created Great Whales* seems like the epitome of twentieth-century eclectic music, containing all of the following features:

It was unusual for Hovhaness to include taped sounds in his musical works.

♦ A large amount of *musique concrète* in the form of actual recordings of whale sounds. They are integrated into the total composition at four different points. The only change in what the whales actually made occurs in the third appearance, when the sounds have been lowered in pitch to better fit the music.

Hovhaness did not usually indicate that performers could make choices about what to play or sing.

♦ Portions of the music are aleatory or chance music. Before the appearance of the whales, the orchestra members are instructed to "continue repetition, rapidly and not together in free non-rhythm chaos." Later they are directed to play "very wild and powerful."

Hovhaness was strongly influenced by music of Asia.

♦ A haunting melody in the pattern of the five-note pentatonic scale that sounds as though it came directly from China or Japan.

Alan Hovhaness

Alan Hovhaness Chakmakjian (b. 1911) was born in Somerville, Massachusetts, of Armenian-Scottish parents. Early in his career, he dropped his long last name. From the beginning he seemed destined to bring together the best of two worlds, the Occident and the Orient. His musical training in his younger years was largely confined to Boston and the New England Conservatory of Music. In addition, he studied astronomy and Far Eastern music and religions. For a time he taught theory and composition in Boston and was church organist at an Armenian church in Watertown, Massachusetts.

Hovhaness began receiving public attention for his compositions in the late 1940s. He won several awards and grants to study music and compose. These grants took him to India, Japan, and Korea. He responded with a steady outpouring of compositions.

His musical interests are very cosmopolitan and wide-ranging. He once wrote: "I admire the giant melody of the Himalayan Mountains, seventh-century Armenian religious music, classical music of South India, orchestra music of Tang Dynasty China about A.D. 700, opera-oratorios of Handel." And he admires great whales too!

Best-Known Works
Orchestra:
- *And God Created Great Whales*
- *Prayer of St. Gregory*
- *Armenian Rhapsodies Nos. 1, 2,* and 3
- Symphony No. 2 ("Mysterious Mountain")
- Symphony No. 50 ("Mount St. Helens")

◆ Much attention to various tone colors and combinations of sounds. Hovhaness often referred to "points of color" in his music that make it more attractive and interesting. He also explored other sounds from conventional instruments, such as the slide or *glissando* produced by the trombones and strings.

◆ An admiration for the great whales that inhabit the oceans of the world. In a real sense, this work is one of the first of the few "environmental" compositions in the concert repertoire.

Hovhaness composed this work long before "Save the whales" became a popular cause.

And God Created Great Whales also reveals the mystic, Romantic side of Hovhaness. He writes:

> Free rhythmless passages, each string player playing independently, suggest waves in a vast ocean sky. Undersea mountains rise and fall in horns, trombones, and tuba. Music of whales also rises and falls like mountain ranges. Song of whales emerges like a giant mystical sea bird. Man does not exist, has not yet been born in the solemn oneness of Nature.

The opening third of *And God Created Great Whales* is included in the Listening Guide.

L I S T E N I N G   G U I D E

Alan Hovhaness: *And God Created Great Whales*
beginning
CD 5 Track 16

0:00	**16** The strings begin quietly with many rapidly moving notes in a free aleatoric style. This leads to a large crescendo as the music progresses.
0:16	The brasses play the opening theme, which is pentatonic. The music grows louder and then tapers off.

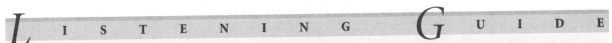

0:44	The strings quietly begin the accompanying sounds for the second theme.
0:53	**17** The second theme, which is also pentatonic, is played without accompanying chords by the violins. Some of the strings play pizzicato notes along with the melody.

1:27	As the second theme is being repeated many times, the low brasses take up the first theme again in long notes. The music gradually grows louder.
2:41	The low strings play a "busy" section consisting of many repeated notes.
2:47	**18** The recording of actual whale sounds begins.
4:39	The strings again take up the rapidly moving notes in a free style.
4:54	**19** The first theme is played again by the brasses as the music grows louder and some "points of color" are heard.
5:23	The trombones play glissandos (sliding sounds).
5:53	The music comes to a silent measure just before the second appearance of the whales.

INTO THE TWENTY-FIRST CENTURY—AND BEYOND

In *A Tale of Two Cities* Dickens was writing about the time of the French Revolution in 1789.

Charles Dickens began his *A Tale of Two Cities* with the well-known phrase, "It was the best of times, it was the worst of times . . ." This observation seems especially appropriate for the world of art music today.

It is the best of times in terms of the number of persons composing music, the number of orchestras, public and private financial support, freedom to compose what one wishes, and availability of music of all types at almost all times and in all places.

But it also seems like the worst of times in terms of the communication and understanding between composers and audiences. As a result, composers sometimes appear to be increasingly elitist and aloof, and the public responds with apathy toward new music.

Although an important topic, a discussion of the contemporary music scene is beyond the scope of a music appreciation textbook.

The situation is aggravated by the enormous changes that have been wrought by technology, which also have good and bad results. Music is far more available than ever before, so now people have become saturated with music. For many people it is no longer an art but rather a disposable commodity.

What is the future of music in the twenty-first century and beyond? No one knows, of course. But two predictions seem safe:

♦ There will be music. Humanity has found sound and its manipulation too intellectually fascinating and too emotionally satisfying to abandon it. In fact, the indications are that music and the other arts will be valued still more in the years to come. They offer people a counterbalance to a world that often seems impersonal and unfeeling.

♦ Music in the future will differ from it was in the past and is today. Creative minds are restless and forever unsatisfied with previous accomplishments. They want to experiment, to try new ways. Truly creative people are simply unable to accept imitations or be content with the efforts of others.

Coda

*By definition, creativity involves bringing forth
something new and unique. And so in the art of music, as in any
creative undertaking, there will always be something new. And when
music is the product of imaginative and skilled musicians, it will
be both a fascination to listen to and a joy to understand.*

Part VII

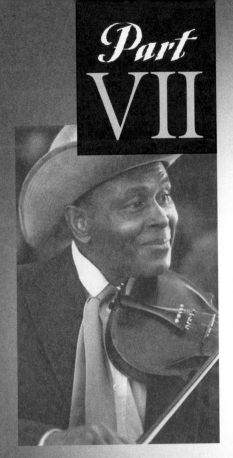

Music in the United States

Music in Colonial America

The United States has a unique history. North America was only thinly populated by Native Americans until the arrival of Europeans in the early part of the seventeenth century. And when Europeans did arrive, they came to stay, not just to take the gold and other treasures and head back home, as happened in Central and South America. For the first century and a half after the first settlements, the question was not would America be a colony, but whose colony it would be. The English, Dutch, Spanish, and French all laid claims to it at one time or another.

New York was once called New Amsterdam, Louisiana was named for King Louis of France, and *Florida* comes from a Spanish word referring to "the land of flowers."

There were no democratic nations in the seventeenth century. The belief in the equality of all people was a revolutionary idea that developed in America.

The first edition of the *Bay Psalm Book* published in 1640 had no music. Music was not included until the ninth edition in 1698.

Until well into the twentieth century, it was believed that an aspiring artist, composer, or performer should spend some years studying in Europe.

America represented a fresh start, a chance to develop a new country that was largely unfettered by ties to the past. It was a circumstance that has rarely happened in history. This situation led to the fruition of ideas that today we take for granted—ideas such as all people are created equal and government should function democratically.

While the American experience was good for democratic government and the common good of its citizens, it was not so helpful in the development of the arts. They had a slow start in America, and did not really flourish until the twentieth century.

Why were the arts slow to develop in America? There were several reasons:

♦ For much of the first three hundred years of its history, its people were occupied with practical matters related to making and settling a new land. Except for a tiny number of prosperous families on the eastern seaboard, they had little time for the arts.

♦ Rightly or wrongly, the Puritans, who were among the earliest settlers, thought that art and theater were undesirable. At best they considered them worthless diversions; at worst they were products of the devil. The only music permitted in church was the unaccompanied singing of psalms and hymns. Not surprisingly, the first book published in America was the *Bay Psalm Book.*

♦ America had almost no titled families to patronize the arts. This fact contributed much to the development of a democratic society, but it removed an important source of patrons for composers and artists.

♦ Initially, Americans brought their language and arts with them from their former lands. They thought that European art and music were superior to whatever might be developed in the colonies or in the young nation. For hundreds of years, the attitude was one of transplanting the superior culture from Europe, not of developing a culture that was distinct and indigenous. In short, Americas suffered from a cultural inferiority complex, a condition that has not entirely disappeared even today.

In spite of its slow start, American music is a rich and rewarding type of music to know and understand, especially, of course, for Americans. It is an essential part of a course that covers music listening today.

American music can be divided into three broad categories: folk, popular, and art. American folk music is discussed in chapter 8. The latter two types are presented in the following chapters.

THE EIGHTEENTH CENTURY

The most sophisticated music written in the American colonies before the Revolutionary War was the product of the Moravian communities around Bethlehem, Pennsylvania, and Winston-Salem, North Carolina. These people had come from what is today part of the Czech Republic, bringing with them a rich musical heritage. Besides music for church services, they also wrote chamber works. There were several active composers among the Moravians, but John Frederick Peter (1746–1813) was the most skilled. He emigrated to America in 1770.

Probably the first native-born American composer was a musical amateur, Francis Hopkinson (1737–1791), a friend of George Washington and a signer of the Declaration of Independence. In 1788 he published some songs, for which he also wrote the words. He dedicated the book to Washington. Hopkinson's most famous song was "My Days Have Been So Wondrous Free."

Washington was humble in his response to Hopkinson:

> I can neither sing one of the songs, nor raise a single note on any instrument to convince the unbelieving, but I have, however, one argument which will prevail with persons of true estate (at least in America)—I can tell them that *it is the production of Mr. Hopkinson.*

William Billings (1746–1800) was a tanner by trade, and later one of a talented number of singing-school masters. He had an insatiable drive to write music and was a firm believer in American music for Americans. He explained in his first collection, *The New England Psalm Singer* (1770), that he would follow his own rules for composition. One of the techniques he used in his hymns was "fuguing," which was an impressive name for simple imitation.

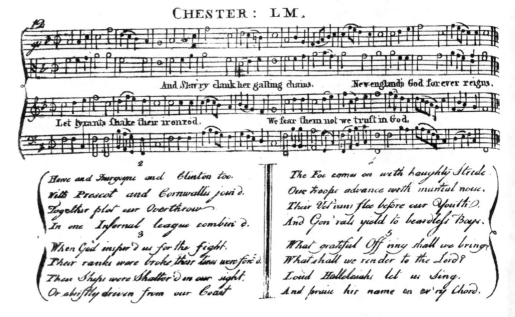

Whatever Billings lacked in training was offset by his natural musical ability. Despite some rough places, his music possesses a vigor that has fascinated many musicians and listeners in this century. A number of Billings's tunes are performed today. The tune "Chester" is one of his best known. A version of it from Billings's *Singing Master's Assistant* is shown here. The melody is in the tenor part, which is the third line from the top. The music has a plain and direct quality.

During the eighteenth century, music in America was not confined to religious situations; a folk music tradition was also developing. Much of this music, as was pointed out in chapter 8, consisted of adaptations of music from England and much of it was not published.

Billings was not modest in making claims about fuguing:

> [Fuguing] is twenty times as powerful as the old slow tunes. Each part striving for mastery and victory. The audience entertained and delighted. Now the solemn bass demands their attention; next the manly tenor. Now here, now there, now here again! O ecstatic! Rush on, you sons of harmony.

"Chester" was the theme for one of the movements in William Schuman's *New England Triptych*, which was written in 1956.

Coda

America did not lack for a cosmopolitan and interesting beginning. One portion of it consisted of the music of the Moravians from Bohemia. Then there was the gentleman amateur composer Francis Hopkinson. Finally, there was the leather tanner who loved music, William Billings, an amateur with little musical training. What a wonderfully diverse start!

America's Patriotic Songs

As is true of a great deal of American culture, much of its patriotic music consists of songs with European roots. The origin of "Yankee Doodle" is unknown, but it was introduced in the colonies by a British doctor named Shackburg about twenty years before the Revolutionary War began. It was first sung by the British to ridicule the New Englanders, who promptly took it over as their own song by adding new verses.

 The melody of "The Star-Spangled Banner" was adapted from a popular English drinking song "To Anacreon in Heaven." This song to an ancient Greek poet was probably composed by John Stafford Smith (1750–1836). The words were written by an American lawyer, Francis Scott Key. During the War of 1812 between the Americans and the British, Key went aboard a British ship in Chesapeake Bay to negotiate the release of a Dr. William Beames, who was being held prisoner by the British. On September 13, 1814, the British fleet sailed up the bay to bombard Fort McHenry, which guarded Baltimore harbor. Before the battle began, Key, Beames, and a companion were transferred to a small boat behind the fleet.

All night Key paced the deck, wondering if the American flag would still be there in the morning. If it were, it would mean that the fort had withstood the challenge and that Baltimore had been saved. "By the dawn's early light" Key could see the Stars and Stripes still flying and he was moved to begin the poem that is sung today. By that afternoon he had finished it, and a week later it appeared in the Baltimore American. The words were sung for the first time by an actor in Baltimore. It was not officially made the national anthem until 1931.

"My Country 'Tis of Thee" ("America") is sung to the same melody as the British national anthem, "God Save the King (or Queen)," which was written by the English composer Henry Carey (1685–1743). The words sung in this country were written in 1832 by the American Samuel Francis Smith (1808–1895), somewhat by accident. Lowell Mason was searching for music to arrange for children to sing in church. He had been given a collection of songs used in German schools. Not knowing German, Mason had asked Smith, a student at Andover Theological Seminary, to set English words to them in his spare time. It took Smith only half an hour one February day to write his words to the tune, which he did not realize at the time was "God Save the King."

"America, the Beautiful" is sung to a hymn tune, "Materna" ("O Mother, dear Jerusalem"), by Samuel A. Ward, an obscure organist from Newark, New Jersey. The words were the creation of Katherine Lee Bates (1859–1929), a professor of English at Wellesley College and author of a number of books and poems. She was so impressed by her first visit to the summit of Pike's Peak in Colorado that the opening lines of the poem seemed to just come to her. They were printed in a magazine called The Congregationalist on July 4, 1895, and were subsequently set to several different tunes, but the "Materna" melody is the only one heard with the poem today.

John Philip Sousa's "The Star and Stripes Forever" is discussed in chapter 41. "Hail Columbia!" is another patriotic march. Feeling the need for a song to help unify the young nation, in 1798 Joseph Hopkinson wrote the words and set them to a melody that had been written as an inaugural march for George Washington nine years earlier. The composer of the march is generally believed to be Philip Phile. In those days America was often referred to as Columbia (the feminine form of Columbus), as can be seen in the designation District of Columbia for the national capital area.

Art Music in America to 1920

41

When the nineteenth century began, the former colonies had been the United States of America for little more than a decade. Its population was just over 5 million people, who lived almost entirely east of the Appalachian Mountains. Most of its goods were still imported from Europe, and there were serious doubt that the young nation would survive. The arts were still in a largely embryonic state. Over the next hundred years, these conditions would change dramatically.

The population of the United States was fifteen times larger by the end of the nineteenth century.

THE NINETEENTH CENTURY

The name *Mason* is an important one in American music. Lowell Mason (1792–1872) wrote many hymns, including "Nearer, My God to Thee," and conducted the Handel and Haydn Society in Boston. Two of his sons founded the piano-manufacturing company of Mason and Hamlin, and a third son became a famous music teacher. Mason led a campaign against some of the religious music of his day, which came into being after the decline of Billings's "fuguing tunes." As part of this effort, Mason published a large number of music collections.

Lowell Mason is considered the father of public school music in the United States. He was able to institute music instruction in the Boston elementary schools in 1837.

Not only did America import much of its music, it also imported musicians. European virtuosos found it profitable to tour the United States. The most sensational of these was the singer Jenny Lind, who was advertised by her brilliant promoter, P. T. Barnum, as "the Swedish Nightingale."

An early American piano virtuoso was Louis Moreau Gottschalk (1829–1869). He was a handsome man who cultivated some of the mannerisms of Liszt. He often left his white gloves on the piano for his female admirers to fight over. He wrote sentimental pieces with such tear-jerking titles as "The Last Hope" and "The Dying Poet." "The Banjo," which is based on American rhythms and melodies, became very popular in Europe in the 1850s.

Gottschalk was from Louisiana, and he toured the Caribbean extensively as well as Europe.

Louis A. Jullian (1812–1860) chose a different approach. He kept his white gloves on as he conducted with his jeweled baton. He played some high-quality music, including some by American composers. But his biggest success was a number titled *Fireman's Quadrille,* during which, as flames burst from the ceiling, the local fire department would rush into the hall to dramatically quench the blaze.

For sheer spectacle no one equalled Patrick Gilmore (1829–1892), a bandmaster who organized supercolossal extravaganzas. One was the Great National Peace Jubilee in Boston in 1869. The performers included a chorus of 10,000 and an orchestra of 1,000, with cannons and 100 firemen pounding anvils in the "Anvil Chorus" from Verdi's *Il Trovatore!* The only way for Gilmore to top that was to organize a World Peace Jubilee, which he did. For this event he brought Johann Strauss from Vienna to lead his *Blue Danube Waltz.* Although the orchestra was restricted to 1,000 players, the chorus was increased to 20,000 singers!

In a letter home, Strauss described his feelings of terror as he stepped before the huge aggregation.

From Jullian's orchestra came a young German violinist named Theodore Thomas (1835–1905), who organized his own orchestra in 1862. Thomas maintained high standards of performance and tried to educate his audiences. In so doing he laid the foundation for the symphony orchestras of today. He traveled widely throughout the United States and for a time was the conductor of the New York Philharmonic. Later he organized the Chicago Symphony and was its conductor for many years.

The political upheavals in Europe, and especially Germany, in the mid-1800s brought thousands of immigrants to the United States. Some were musicians who soon became affiliated with orchestras and opera companies throughout the country. The European immigrants constituted an audience for the German symphonic music that Thomas's orchestras performed for them.

Late in the nineteenth century, several American composers began to write longer and more-sophisticated works. Most of these composers lived around Boston, and almost all of them had studied in Germany at one time or another. For this reason most of their music sounded similar to works of European composers. The "Boston" or "New England" group included George W. Chadwick (1854–1931), Horatio Parker (1863–1919), Arthur Foote (1853–1937), John Knowles Paine (1839–1906), and Amy Chaney Beach (1867–1944), who was the first American woman to write a symphony. She is probably the best known of these composers today.

Edward MacDowell (1861–1908) had excellent musical training. He studied at the Paris Conservatory when he was eleven years old. After his return to America, he became a professor of music at Columbia University. Most of his works are for piano, including the often played "To a Wild Rose" from *Woodland Sketches*. He also wrote four piano sonatas and two piano concertos. His Suite No. 2 ("Indian Suite") is a landmark because of its early use of Native American music.

Amy Beach followed the custom of using her husband's first and last names. She signed her works "Mrs. H. H. A. Beach."

MacDowell was a classmate of Debussy at the Paris Conservatory. Later he played for Liszt at Weimar.

THE EARLY TWENTIETH CENTURY

Soon after the turn of the century, the popularity of German Romanticism began to recede in America, only to be replaced by attempts to imitate French Impressionism. The best-known American who wrote in this style was Charles Tomlinson Griffes (1884–1920). He started out composing in the German tradition, but later switched to the Impressionistic style of Debussy and Ravel. "The White Peacock" from his *Roman Sketches* is frequently performed. Charles Martin Loeffler (1861–1935) also wrote Impressionistic-sounding music.

John Philip Sousa on the cover of his most famous work. Sousa wrote more than ninety marches which are still widely performed today. Much of his music was patriotic.

Sousa and Wind Band Music

Not all music at the turn of the century in America was heard inside concert halls. Some of it was band music that was enjoyed while relaxing on the grass in a park or town square on a warm summer's evening. In the early 1900s, most Americans lived on farms or small towns. Most small towns had a bandstand from which local bands performed, often with more enthusiasm than skill.

The popularity of the band as a concert ensemble—very much an American musical institution—encouraged the development of a number of virtuoso performers such as Arthur Pryor on trombone and Herbert Clarke on trumpet. It also resulted in a number of composers who wrote marches and overtures for wind bands. The person most recognized for his contributions to band music is John Philip Sousa (1854–1932), who was often referred to as "the March King."

Sousa was born in Washington, D.C., of a Portuguese father and a Bavarian mother. The first ten years of his career were spent as a violinist in a theater orchestra. In 1880 he became leader of the U.S. Marine Corps Band. After twelve years he left that position to form his own band. It was very popular (and financially successful) and toured extensively until his death forty years later. He helped develop the sousaphone, a version of the tuba that can be carried over the shoulder while marching. Despite his busy schedule, Sousa found time to compose operettas and marches, as well as write novels and an autobiography.

"The Stars and Stripes Forever" is easily Sousa's best-known march. He thought it out in his mind on a ship while returning from Europe. He then wrote it down verbatim when he reached shore. The march follows the traditional march form, except for the addition of a *break*, or *dogfight*, before returning to the main melody of the trio. This march is also famous for the decorative countermelody played by the piccolo when the melody of the trio reappears after the dogfight.

Although the melody of the trio may seem simple, it is not. It consists of two sections that are each sixteen measures long. These are further divided into four smaller phrases. The rhythm of two notes on the upbeat leading to one longer note pervades throughout the melody. Other than one instance of syncopation, the melody is rhythmically quite straightforward.

Dogfight is term band directors often use to describe a part of a march in which there is a rapid exchange of musical material among sections of the band.

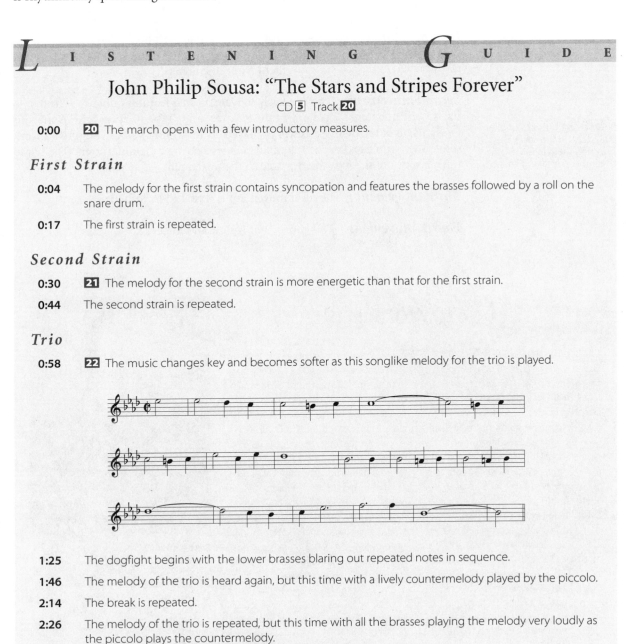

L I S T E N I N G   G U I D E

John Philip Sousa: "The Stars and Stripes Forever"
CD **5** Track **20**

0:00   **20** The march opens with a few introductory measures.

First Strain

0:04   The melody for the first strain contains syncopation and features the brasses followed by a roll on the snare drum.

0:17   The first strain is repeated.

Second Strain

0:30   **21** The melody for the second strain is more energetic than that for the first strain.

0:44   The second strain is repeated.

Trio

0:58   **22** The music changes key and becomes softer as this songlike melody for the trio is played.

1:25   The dogfight begins with the lower brasses blaring out repeated notes in sequence.

1:46   The melody of the trio is heard again, but this time with a lively countermelody played by the piccolo.

2:14   The break is repeated.

2:26   The melody of the trio is repeated, but this time with all the brasses playing the melody very loudly as the piccolo plays the countermelody.

3:06   "The Stars and Stripes Forever" ends with a short, abrupt, loud chord, which band directors often call a "stinger."

One reason for a modest-sized group was to hold down expenses.

A string bass could be used because Sousa's band only played concerts; it did not march.

Sousa's bands were not large, ranging between 48 and 52 players. They consisted of about 25 clarinet and saxophone players, 16 brasses, 6 percussion, and 1 string bass. Sousa did not perform his marches at as fast a tempo as some directors take them today. He gave them a dignified, not a harried, sound.

IVES'S SYMPHONY NO. 2

Ives composed his Second Symphony between 1897 and 1901. It is a rather early work and is somewhat conservative for Ives. Except for having five movements, it is a relatively standard symphony.

First movement   The movement has a moderate tempo and consists mostly of music for strings. In several respects it is a long introduction, including the fact that it is attached to the second movement without a break.

Sheaves are bundles of grain stalks; but in the song, bringing them in is a metaphor for saving souls.

Second movement   This is a lively movement that features quotations from two old American hymns: "Bringing in the Sheaves" and "When I Survey the Wondrous Cross." The latter of these tunes is played in long note values (augmentation), sometimes with portions of the other themes serving as counterpoint. The hymn tunes are two of the four themes used in the movement.

Third movement   The third movement is slow and melodious.

Fourth movement   This movement is slow and majestic.

Charles Ives

Charles Ives (1874–1954) was born in Danbury, Connecticut, the son of a bandmaster. His father was no ordinary town band leader. He encouraged his son to listen carefully and to experiment with different tonal effects. "Stretch your ears" was his advice. So Charles tried such things as retuning the piano and writing for two bands playing different pieces of music while marching toward each other.

Ives attended Yale University as a music student. After graduation he went to New York City, where he made a fortune in the insurance business. He composed his music alone and had little contact with other musicians. Because he had no need to make money, he did not try to have his compositions

> Ives studied composition with Horatio Parker at Yale, but the conservative Parker and the experimental Ives had quite different ideas about what music should be!

published and sold. For this reason, for many years almost no one knew about them. Many of them sat in the barn at his country home in Connecticut. Partly because of health problems, he stopped composing around 1915, almost forty years before his death.

Shortly after the turn of the century, Ives was writing novel harmonies and rhythms that did not appear in Europe for another decade. He experimented with such techniques as polytonality, dissonant counterpoint, atonality, polyrhythms, chords with added notes, unusual melodic intervals, and *sprechstimme*. Ives was also fond of weaving fragments of familiar tunes into his works. He seemed to thrive on the element of surprise and what was novel.

Ives's Symphony No. 3, composed between 1901 and 1904, was awarded the Pulitzer Prize in 1947. The insurance man Ives took the seed of American music planted by the tanner Billings a century before and made it flourish. But until the 1940s, no one knew it.

Best-Known Works
Orchestra:
- Symphonies Nos. 2 and 3
- *Three Places in New England*
- *The Unanswered Question*

Organ:
- Variations on "America"

Piano:
- Sonata No. 2 ("Concord")

Songs:
- "The Cage"
- "Lincoln, the Great Commoner"

Fifth movement　　In this movement Ives quotes from American folk and patriotic songs, in contrast to the second movement and its quotations from hymns. One of the songs is Stephen Foster's "Camptown Races," and another is "Columbia, the Gem of the Ocean." Another song sounds a bit like Stephen Foster's "Old Black Joe," but it is not. Instead it is from a work titled *The American Woods* by Brookfield. A fragment of the bugle call "Reveille" is also used.

Stephen Foster is discussed in chapter 43.

　　This movement is presented in the Listening Guide.

Charles Ives: Symphony No. 2
Fifth Movement
CD **2** Track **39**

0:00	**39**	The movement opens at a rapid pace, with the violins scurrying through eighth and sixteenth notes.

0:23		The French horns play a fragment of Stephen Foster's "Camptown Races."

0:57		A portion of "Camptown Races" is played by the trombone.
1:47	**40**	The music becomes quieter and less active. The French horn plays a tender melody that sounds somewhat like Foster's "Old Black Joe."

2:35		The French horn repeats the slow melody; later the orchestra begins playing transitional material.
3:51		The scurrying theme that opened the movement returns.
4:09		A fragment of "Camptown Races" is played loudly by the French horn as the rapidly moving notes continue in the violins and woodwinds.
4:31	**41**	A short section of "fife and drum" music is played by the percussion and piccolo.
4:43		A fragment of "Camptown Races" is played by the trombones and bassoons.
5:25		The trombones play a portion of "Columbia, the Gem of the Ocean." This portion is taken up by other instruments as the music progresses.

5:43		The slow melody returns, played by the cellos, as the flute plays contrasting melodic figures. The orchestra plays the transitional material again.
8:19		The trumpet plays part of the bugle call "Reveille."
8:22	**42**	The music reaches a very loud level as the trombones play a sizable portion of "Columbia, the Gem of the Ocean" while the orchestra provides a vigorous accompaniment.
9:08		Immediately after another fragment of a bugle call played by the trumpet, the movement ends with a portion of "Columbia, the Gem of the Ocean" and two dissonant chords.

IVES'S "THE THINGS OUR FATHERS LOVED"

One of the characteristics of Ives's music is an unabashed nostalgia. It occurs in his instrumental music in the form of quotations of old songs. But Ives also composed more than a hundred songs, and in some of these he looks back fondly to the things he once knew. The words of "The Things Our Fathers Loved" reveal this side of Ives. Written either by Ives or his wife, they speak longingly of the past.

LISTENING GUIDE

Ives: "The Things Our Fathers Loved"
CD **5** Track **23**

0:00	**23** The song begins: I think there must be a place in the soul all made of tunes, of tunes of long ago;	
0:28	I hear the organ on the Main Street corner, Aunt Sarah humming Gospels; Summer evenings,	
1:02	The village cornet band, playing in the square. The town's Red, White, and Blue, all Red, White, and Blue—	Notice the references to bands playing in the town square.
1:16	Now! I hear the songs! I know not what are the words But they sing in my soul of things our Fathers loved.	
1:56	The song closes very softly.	

Musically, "The Things Our Fathers Loved" has the voice and piano parts combine to give the song the twilight feeling of recalling dim memories. Each phrase presents a different vision—the serenity of Aunt Sarah's humming gospel tunes, the excitement of seeing the American flag, and finally the invigorating effect of hearing the old songs. The piano part begins somewhat simply, but soon provides a furious backdrop to the words "I hear the songs! I know not what are the words but they sing in my soul."

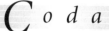

Coda

Although World War I was to leave the United States a world power, it was still timid about realizing its musical potential. Nevertheless, American music had come a long way from Hopkinson and Billings.

Art Music Since 1920

42

What changes have taken place in American art music
in the eight decades following World War I? In a word, *plenty!*
To begin with, American composers and American performers came
of age. Over the years, they shed their feelings of musical
inferiority and gradually assumed a leadership role in
the world as performers and as composers.

Part of the reason for the rise of American music was its good fortune in coming out of both world wars with its land virtually unscathed. True, in both wars thousands of American young men died in combat, but in nowhere near the numbers that the nations of Europe and Japan suffered, and the battles took place thousands of miles away from the shores of the then-forty-eight states. America did not become exhausted in a struggle for survival or have its cities decimated, as was true of England, Germany, Japan, Russia, and a host of smaller countries.

In addition, a number of outstanding musicians fled to the safety and freedom of the United States prior to and during World War II. These musicians and composers provided America with an enormous musical infusion.

Over the years, America's training of musicians also became better, until it reached a point where it was no longer necessary to study in Europe to achieve success. Of the three composers featured in this chapter—Aaron Copland, Ellen Taaffe Zwilich, and John Adams—only Copland studied overseas for any length of time, and he was almost two generations ahead of Zwilich and Adams. In fact, today thousands of students from Asia and Central and South America, plus some from Europe, come to the United States to study music at American universities and music schools.

The quality and quantity of art music in the United States has also been advanced by the National Endowment for the Arts (NEA), which was established in 1965. The NEA represents the first promotion of the arts by the federal government. A sizable portion of the NEA's funds are passed on to state arts councils, which in turn cooperate with and support arts efforts in large and small communities throughout the nation. A number of major foundations have also continued or increased their support of music.

The United States and Japan have led the world in the development and use of technology for music making and listening. Starting with the phonograph invented by Thomas Edison in 1877 through radio, television, tape, long-playing records, compact-disc players, and now CD-ROM, with its music and images produced in conjunction with computers, the procession of technological advancement has significantly affected, and continues to affect, the music that people hear and how they listen to it.

Although it is impossible for any three works to give the total picture of the wonderfully rich and diverse conglomeration of American music since 1920, Copland, Zwilich, and Adams each represent important aspects of its rich musical fabric.

Stravinsky, Hindemith, and Schoenberg were but three important composers who came to America.

A performance at the Kennedy Center in Washington, D.C. The center has contributed to the growth of American music at the national level, as has the Public Broadcasting System (PBS).

NATIONALISM

Although nationalism was one of the features of nineteenth-century Romanticism in Europe, it did not appear in American music until well into the twentieth century. Besides, until this century only a small amount of art music was being composed in America, and those few composers were attempting to emulate European models. The greatest interest in nationalistic music occurred from the 1930s through the 1950s. Composers most associated with this movement were Samuel Barber (1910–1981), Howard Hanson (1896–1981), Roy Harris (1898–1979), William Schuman (b. 1910), and especially Aaron Copland (1900–1990).

Barber composed *Knoxville: Summer of 1915* and Adagio for Strings. Hanson wrote an opera, *Merry Mount,* and promoted American music as director of the Eastman School of Music for forty years. Harris composed Symphony No. 4 ("Folksong Symphony"). Schuman wrote *New England Triptych* and an opera, *The Mighty Casey.*

> Although Charles Ives revealed strong nationalistic tendencies in Symphony No. 2, his music was almost unknown until the 1940s.

COPLAND'S *FANFARE FOR THE COMMON MAN*

A *fanfare* is usually a rather short work for brass instruments, sometimes with percussion included, too. It's the kind of music associated with the appearance of royalty. But Copland had a more democratic idea. When asked to compose a fanfare for the Cincinnati Symphony Orchestra to play in its 1942/43 season, during which the United States was involved in World War II, he decided to recognize the common people. Copland sought to honor the people who may not do heroic deeds or carry a royal title but who struggle daily to lead useful, productive lives. This fanfare certainly achieved his goal.

LISTENING GUIDE

Aaron Copland: *Fanfare for the Common Man*
CD 5 Track 24

0:00	**24**	The music opens with the bass drum, gong, and timpani sounding notes followed by rests. Copland instructs the players to let the sounds of their instruments ring into the rests.
0:22		The trumpets enter playing the theme, which contains many notes that are rather far apart. The music is marked *nobile*—to be played with a noble quality.

Very deliberately (♩ = ca. 52)

0:49		The bass drum and timpani play a short version of the opening material.
0:54		The trumpets and French horns play the theme.
1:26		The bass drum, gong, and timpani play some of the same music that opened the work.
1:37	**25**	The trombones play the theme, which is quickly imitated by the timpani. Then the trombones are imitated by the trumpets and horns.
2:00		After the timpani plays the theme in augmentation, the brasses play a series of accented notes.
2:18		The trombones, with horns and trumpets imitating, very forcefully play the theme followed by the steady series of notes.
2:43		The trombones and trumpets play the theme in augmentation.
3:12		*Fanfare for the Common Man* concludes with full, massive chords leading to a large crescendo on the final note.

COPLAND'S *APPALACHIAN SPRING*

Copland composed *Appalachian Spring* in 1943/44 for the outstanding choreographer and teacher Martha Graham. It is about the courtship and wedding of a couple in rural Pennsylvania in the 1800s. Copland writes some very American-sounding melodies for it, in addition to using the Shaker song "Simple Gifts." The overall spirit of the ballet is calm and its music often hymnlike, which suits the character of the people being portrayed.

"Simple Gifts" is presented in chapter 3.

Today *Appalachian Spring* is heard in an orchestral suite that Copland himself arranged.

Copland provides this synopsis of the score:

1. *Very slowly.* Introduction of the characters, one by one, in a suffused light.

   The bride enters, then the groom, a neighbor, and a revivalist and his flock. The music is built around a motive derived from a major chord. Soon a hymnlike melody emerges.

The interval between the notes of the theme is often four or five steps, which adds to the open, simple sound of the music.

2. *Fast.* A sudden burst of unison strings in A major arpeggios starts the action. A sentiment both elated and religious gives the keynote of this scene.

   The theme is a lively one that sounds like it could have come from no other county than the United States.

Copland soon combines the high, rapidly moving part with the long notes in the trombones and basses as the flute plays a contrasting line.

A scene from Copland's ballet *Appalachian Spring*

3. Duo for bride and her intended—scene of tenderness and passion.

4. *Quite fast.* The Revivalist and his flock. Folksy feeling—suggestions of square dance and country fiddlers.

5. *Still faster.* Solo dance of the bride—presentiment of motherhood. Extremes of joy and fear and wonder.

   The music of this section is particularly sensitive and tender.

6. *Very slowly* (as at first). Transition scene to music reminiscent of the introduction.

   Some of the music of this section is derived from the second section.

7. *Calm and flowing.* Scenes of daily activity for the bride and her farmer husband. There are variations on a Shaker tune.

   This section of *Appalachian Spring* is presented in the Listening Guide.

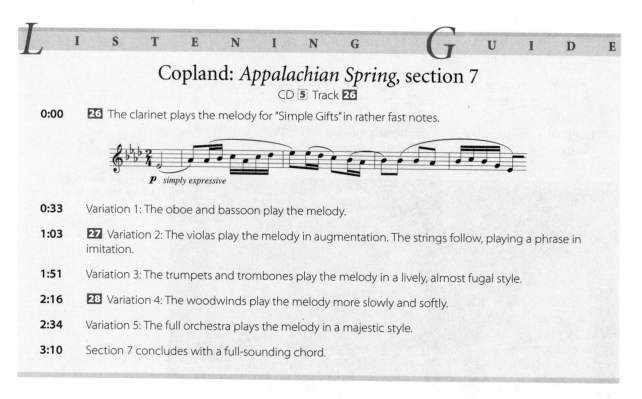

L I S T E N I N G   G U I D E

Copland: *Appalachian Spring,* section 7
CD **5** Track **26**

0:00	**26** The clarinet plays the melody for "Simple Gifts" in rather fast notes.

p simply expressive

0:33	Variation 1: The oboe and bassoon play the melody.
1:03	**27** Variation 2: The violas play the melody in augmentation. The strings follow, playing a phrase in imitation.
1:51	Variation 3: The trumpets and trombones play the melody in a lively, almost fugal style.
2:16	**28** Variation 4: The woodwinds play the melody more slowly and softly.
2:34	Variation 5: The full orchestra plays the melody in a majestic style.
3:10	Section 7 concludes with a full-sounding chord.

Variation 5 of the preceding section was for many years the theme music for CBS News.

8. The bride takes her place among her neighbors.

   This section is a quiet coda that balances the introduction. The neighbors depart, and the newlyweds remain "quiet and strong in their new house." The music closes with a serene passage for strings, which sounds, in Copland's words, "like a prayer."

   Copland succeeded in writing music that sounds very American. In it he captures the simplicity and strength of a part of American life from its past.

NEOCLASSICISM

In the decades following World War II, a number of composers in America moved toward a more intellectual, Neoclassical style of music. Most of them composed absolute music. The major composers in this group include Roger Sessions (1896–1985), Elliott Carter (b. 1908), and Ellen Taaffe Zwilich (b. 1939).

ZWILICH'S SYMPHONY NO. 1

Zwilich's First Symphony, composed in 1982, was awarded the Pulitzer Prize in 1983. In the preface to the symphony, she writes: "The first movement begins in a contemplative mood, with a 'motto': three statements of a rising minor third, marked accelerando. Each time the 'motto' appears in the first movement, an accelerando occurs, prompting slight evolutions of character until an *Allegro* section. After the *Allegro,* the movement subsides in tempo and ends as quietly as it began."

As Zwilich's remarks indicate, the movement consists of three broad sections. The first is introductory and centers around the motto. The second section of the movement is the allegro. It contains many thematic ideas and is more dramatic than the other two sections. The final section is somewhat like a coda as the music becomes more calm and the motto returns.

Zwilich's music is built on the idea of "all the same but always different." The movement of her Symphony No. 1, to use her word, *evolves.* It is not marked by clear-cut sections and themes; it has a continuous quality about it. Furthermore, the melodic ideas appear rapidly in the music, and often they alternate between sections of the orchestra. The music is very compact and concentrated.

Zwilich's Symphony No. 1 is outstanding for several reasons:

♦ Its superb craftsmanship. Zwilich is masterful at working with musical ideas and shaping them into music that is rewarding to listen to. Her skill in doing this is similar to what Brahms did in his Fourth Symphony, which was presented in chapter 31.

♦ Zwilich is not only careful in working with intervals and sounds, she is also able to give her music an architectural quality in its overall design. The first movement grows in both intensity and tempo and then tapers off and concludes as quietly as it began.

♦ Like other outstanding composers in the past, Zwilich is ingenious in developing and transforming musical ideas. What is different about her music is that those ideas are conceived in a twentieth-century idiom.

The technique of building a musical work around a particular interval or pattern of notes is by no means new with Zwilich. Bartók used the idea in some of his music, and both Elliott Carter and Roger Sessions (two of Zwilich's teachers) also made extensive use of the technique. What Zwilich did was to use this principle of composing in a highly effective way.

First movement   This movement is presented in the Listening Guide.

Second movement   This movement begins slowly and softly with much melodic imitation. The melody contains many wide leaps. The basic form of the movement is *A B A.*

Third movement   This movement has the character of a scherzo. It begins with the timpani playing a rhythm pattern, but other instruments soon join in. The movement contains several stops and starts.

Zwilich was the first woman to receive this honor for composition.

A *motto* is a motive that grows as the musical work progresses.

Ellen Taaffe Zwilich

Ellen Taaffe was born in 1939 in Miami, Florida, the daughter of an airline pilot. She studied music at Florida State University and the Juilliard School before playing violin for several years in the American Symphony Orchestra under Leopold Stokowski. She also studied composition with Roger Sessions and Elliott Carter. In 1969 she married Joseph Zwilich, who died ten years later.

Her career since 1975 has been a series of commissions, awards, and performances by major symphonies under highly esteemed conductors. In addition to the Pulitzer Prize for Symphony No. 1, she has been awarded the Elizabeth Sprague Coolidge Chamber Music Prize and the Arturo Toscanini Music Critics Award, as well as having received two Grammy Award nominations. She has received grants from the New York State Council on the Arts, the Martha Baird Rockefeller Fund for Music, the National Endowment for the Arts, and a Guggenheim Fellowship.

Best-Known Works
Chamber music:
☐ String Quartet
Orchestra:
☐ Concerto Grosso
☐ Concerto for Trombone
☐ Symphonies Nos. 1 and 2

LISTENING GUIDE

Ellen Taaffe Zwilich: Symphony No. 1
First Movement
CD [2] Track [43]

Introduction

0:00   [43] The motto built on an ascending third is played quietly three times by the strings and harp, which are soon joined by the flute and English horn. The interval of a third increases to a fifth, then a tenth (an octave and a third). The rhythm is essential to the character of the motto, as it is traded among the parts.

0:29   The motto is played by the winds while the violins play a smooth contrasting theme.

0:55   The upper and lower strings alternate in playing the motto as the French horns play a contrasting melody.

1:26   The strings play the motto in contrast to a melodic line played by the winds that gradually ascends in pitch.

1:44   [44] The trumpets play the motto, answered by the violins and flutes as the music becomes more dissonant.

2:03   The motto is played by the trumpets, French horns, and trombones.

2:14   The music grows more intense and the tempo faster, leading to a short break.

2:21   Long chords are punctuated by a four-note motive.

Allegro

2:33 🔢45 A broad melody is played by the French horns and then the trumpets, accompanied by the strings playing repeated notes in pizzicato style.

2:54 A fragment consisting of four descending notes is passed among various instruments, followed by several strong chords.

3:10 🔢46 The motto is played again by the violins, followed by the snare drum sounding repeated notes leading to silent measures.

3:40 The four-note figure is heard ascending and descending at the same time between the trumpet and trombone.

4:00 The motto idea is heard again, played by the low strings and bassoons as the four-note figure continues.

4:42 The energy of the music is reduced as a single note is sounded by the chime along with a sustained chord.

Coda

4:53 🔢47 The four-note figure is sounded by the woodwinds and piano.

5:24 The sustained chord dies away as a rocking motive continues softly in the violins.

5:43 The motto is played quietly by the oboe and brasses against a sustained melody played by the cellos.

5:59 🔢48 The cellos play a melody based on the motto in long notes.

6:20 The rocking motive alternates with the motto as the movement closes peacefully.

6:54 The movement concludes with a soft chord.

MINIMALISM

At times, twentieth-century composers have seemed intent on seeing how *much* they can work into their compositions in terms of techniques and musical ideas. *Minimalism* is a reaction against the technical complexities and highly charged emotional content in much of the art music of the past two centuries. Minimalist composers are intent on seeing how *little* they can do in their music and yet create something interesting and satisfying to listen to. They take a small amount of musical material and repeat it over and over and over, usually with small modifications.

The effect on listeners of the continual repetition of minimalist patterns is almost hypnotic. And with good reason. Minimalist music changes very little and does so at a slow rate. These conditions also contribute to the considerable length of most Minimalist music. Minimalist musicians do not think of their musical works as finished products, but rather as processes. What happens during the music is considered more important than the final result.

Minimalism in music has been largely confined to America. Composers associated with this type of music include Philip Glass (b. 1937), Steve Reich (b. 1936), and John Adams (b. 1947). Glass, who attended the Juilliard School, worked in New York for two years before moving to Paris. While there he

Minimalism is sometimes referred to as "trance music," a name that is rejected by Minimalist composers.

Philip Glass

Although both Javanese and African music contain much repetition of musical material, Minimalism has been almost exclusively developed by American composers.

Indian music and the sitar are discussed in chapter 10.

was employed copying music for Ravi Shankar, the well-known sitar player. Shankar's Indian music gave Glass an appreciation of the idea of "change within repetition."

Minimalism didn't exactly take off with audiences and critics. Glass had to drive a cab in the daytime and rehearse his group of six players at night. But success did come over time, including music for the award-winning movie *The Thin Blue Line* (1988) and a song collection, *Songs from Liquid Days* (1986) with Paul Simon and Linda Ronstadt. Rock star David Bowie also made a Minimalist pop album called *Low* in 1977.

ADAMS'S *SHORT RIDE IN A FAST MACHINE*

The work was composed in 1986 for the Great Woods Festival in Mansfield, Massachusetts.

Short Ride in a Fast Machine exudes energy and fun. It is a short work for orchestra and two synthesizers. When asked about the title, Adams responded, "You know how it is when someone asks you to ride in a terrific sports car, and then you wish you hadn't." Appropriately, he uses the descriptive term *delirando,* meaning "frenzied," for the work.

Adams shows his Minimalist approach to music by having the brasses play a very rhythmic pattern that evolves as the music flies along:

changes to

changes to

changes to

changes to

John Adams

Best-Known Works
Opera:
  ☐ *The Death of Klinghoffer*
  ☐ *Nixon in China*
Orchestra:
  ☐ *Harmonielehre*
  ☐ *Harmonium*
Piano:
  ☐ *China Gates*
  ☐ *Phrygian Gates*

John Adams was born in 1947 in Worcester, Massachusetts, and grew up in Vermont and New Hampshire. He majored in composition at Harvard, earning both his bachelor's and master's degrees there. In 1971 he accepted a position at the San Francisco Conservatory of Music. From 1978–1985 he was composer-in-residence for the San Francisco Symphony. Adams has spoken of himself as "a minimalist who is bored with minimalism."

He has written for a wide range of media: orchestra, opera, video, film, and dance. His most widely seen stage events are his two operas, *Nixon in China* (1987, which was telecast on PBS) and *The Death of Klinghoffer* (1991). The former is about President Richard Nixon's historic visit to China after nearly a quarter century of no formal contact between the two nations. The latter concerns the murder of an elderly New York businessman when a Mediterranean cruise ship is taken over by Palestinian terrorists.

Adams may feel bored with Minimalism, but he gives his music tremendous vitality.

The repetition of rhythmic motives, which mutate as the music moves along, are the basis for the work. Then there are the insistent sounds of the woodblock. The music tends to propel itself to its frenzied conclusion.

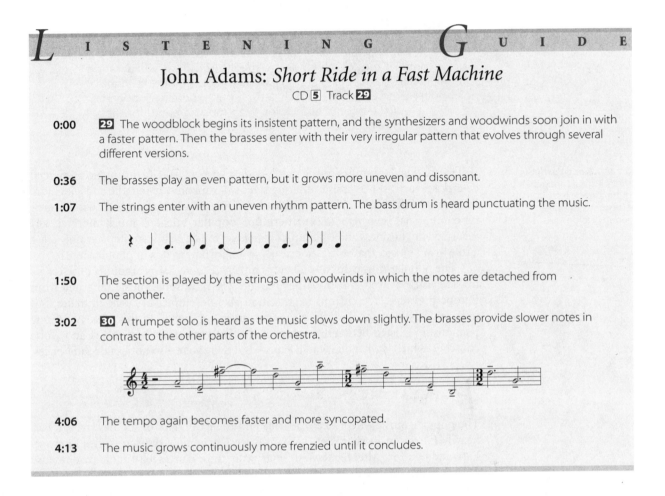

L I S T E N I N G   G U I D E

John Adams: *Short Ride in a Fast Machine*
CD 5 Track 29

0:00 **29** The woodblock begins its insistent pattern, and the synthesizers and woodwinds soon join in with a faster pattern. Then the brasses enter with their very irregular pattern that evolves through several different versions.

0:36 The brasses play an even pattern, but it grows more uneven and dissonant.

1:07 The strings enter with an uneven rhythm pattern. The bass drum is heard punctuating the music.

1:50 The section is played by the strings and woodwinds in which the notes are detached from one another.

3:02 **30** A trumpet solo is heard as the music slows down slightly. The brasses provide slower notes in contrast to the other parts of the orchestra.

4:06 The tempo again becomes faster and more syncopated.

4:13 The music grows continuously more frenzied until it concludes.

C o d a

Listeners considering the American art music scene are like people standing in front of a magnificent buffet table filled with interesting and attractive foods. Which delicious foods should they put on their music plates today? The new-Classicism of Zwilich, the quotation music of George Crumb (b. 1929), the Postminimalism of Adams, the experimental music of Cage, the electronic music of Morton Subotnick (b. 1933), the nationalistic music of Copland, the cosmopolitan-Asian sounds of Hovhaness, or the new-Romantic works of Howard Hanson and Samuel Barber? What an abundance! What wonderful musical opportunities are waiting to be enjoyed!

And, best of all, listeners can return as often as they wish to the banquet!

Popular Music and Jazz to 1950

Music critic Sigmund Spaeth has asserted that the history of popular music "is an index to the life and history of a nation." All music is an index to some extent, of course, but the popular and folk types seem more closely attuned to experiences of a majority of the people of a nation than music created for the concert hall. In any case, it merits investigation.

The terms *popular music* and *folk music* are general. There are always exceptions to these generalizations.

The term *popular* implies music that is widely known, usually through commercial enterprises such as sheet music publishers, record companies, and radio and television. In contrast, folk music is passed among the people on an informal basis with little or no commercial involvement. Furthermore, popular music is much more closely involved with business and economics than is art music. While money certainly plays a role in art music, that role is not nearly as important as it is in popular music.

The popular music discussed here is mostly secular. Large amounts of religious music existed as well, but in white churches the traditional music inherited from Europe prevailed. A rich musical tradition also developed in black churches, but only recently have scholarly investigations been conducted in this area. A definite relationship existed between religious and secular music in both black and white churches, which is what one would expect, but there were also noticeable differences.

POPULAR MUSIC BEFORE 1850

The popular music of colonial America and the early days of the new nation was heavily European in character. Its dances were originally the same ones found in Paris and London. After the Revolutionary War, these dances fell out of favor because of their association with European monarchies, and country dances largely replaced them. For example, a dance imported from France, the cotillion, became the quadrille. It eventually developed into the square dance, which became very popular in nineteenth-century America.

Not much is known about the popular music in the early days of America. Secular songs were not published with words and music together until nearly 1700. Prior to that time, song sheets contained only words. The people then must have been guided by an oral tradition regarding which tunes to sing with which set of words, because often the sheets did not indicate a tune. Even if a tune was indicated, that information is of limited usefulness to researchers today, because sometimes the same tune was known by different names.

As mentioned previously, the words to popular songs were printed on sheets of paper called *broadsides*.

The *parlor song* was an important type of popular music in early nineteenth-century America. These songs were purchased in sheet music form and sung in the homes of the rapidly expanding middle class. They generally required only modest music-making skill. All of them were in major keys—even the sad songs. The accompaniments, which were usually played on the piano or small pump organ, were rather easy. Many of them were based on Irish folk melodies, which can partly be explained by the large number of Irish immigrants who came to the United States during those years.

The texts and moods of parlor songs were usually sentimental and filled with nostalgia, and they often dealt with death. One well-known song of this type was "The Ocean Burial," which began with the words "O! Bury me not in the deep, deep

Stephen Foster

The most popular composer of the time was **Stephen Collins Foster** (1826–1864). He was the ninth child in a prosperous family that lived near Pittsburgh, Pennsylvania. He revealed his sensitive, artistic nature as a boy, but his interest in music was discouraged by his family, who simply could not understand it. In 1846 he went to Cincinnati to work as a bookkeeper for his brother. In his spare time, he wrote songs. About half of them were for the popular minstrel shows, and the other half were the more sentimental parlor songs. In 1848 Foster sold "Oh! Susanna" for $100. It quickly became a hit with the Forty-Niners on their way to the goldfields of California.

Foster's music is generally associated with the South, even though he lived for only a few months in Bardstown, Kentucky, about forty miles south of Louisville, and made

> "Oh! Susanna" was so popular that soon twenty editions of it appeared, nineteen of them pirated!

only one boat trip to New Orleans. But something about the African American songs he heard along the Ohio River and around Bardstown must have made a great impression on him. Some of his songs idealized life in the South, but his attempts at black dialect

> Foster never saw the Suwannee River in northern Florida. He liked the sound of its name, which he changed slightly to "Swannee."

in some of them can at times obscure their melodic charm.

By 1860 Foster seemed to lose his ability to compose attractive songs. He moved to New York to give his career a boost, but the move did not help. He began drinking heavily, and his wife left him. He died in 1864 at the age of thirty-eight after an accident in a Bowery flophouse. A piece of paper with the words "Dear friends and gentle people" was found in his pocket. Perhaps it was an idea for another song by the composer of some of America's favorite music.

Best-Known Works
Songs:
- "Beautiful Dreamer"
- "Camptown Races"
- "Hard Times"
- "Jeannie with the Light Brown Hair"
- "My Old Kentucky Home"
- "Oh! Susanna"

sea." Later this song was transformed into "O Bury Me Not on the Lone Prairie," and it became one of the more popular cowboy songs.

A few popular soloists or groups toured America prior to the Civil War. One was the Englishman Henry Russell (1812–1900). Although he spent only about seven years in the United States, he greatly influenced Stephen Foster and the Hutchinson Family Singers.

The Hutchinson family consisted of three brothers and their sister, and they reached the height of their popularity in the 1840s. Many songs sung by Russell and the Hutchinsons promoted social causes. One song, "The Maniac," drew attention to the terrible conditions in mental asylums at the time. Other songs dealt with women's rights, the abolition of slavery, and the evils of alcohol. Sometimes the music of the Hutchinsons and similar performers was presented in melodramatic scenes that included acting.

It is hard for us today to understand the appeal of sentimental music, just as it would be difficult for people who lived in the nineteenth century to understand why songs today often have so little sentimental quality.

People today would find such melodramatics comical, but audiences at the time were impressed.

FOSTER'S "BEAUTIFUL DREAMER"

"Beautiful Dreamer" is a good example of the sentimental parlor song that was popular in the nineteenth century. Its gentle, quaint text seems to us to come from another time, which in fact is the case. The song nevertheless has a tender charm and beauty that is still appealing.

Hoping to cash in on Foster's death, his publisher claimed that this song was his last, which it was not. The publisher had bought the song from Foster and had the plates engraved a year or so before he died, but for some unknown reason had not yet released it.

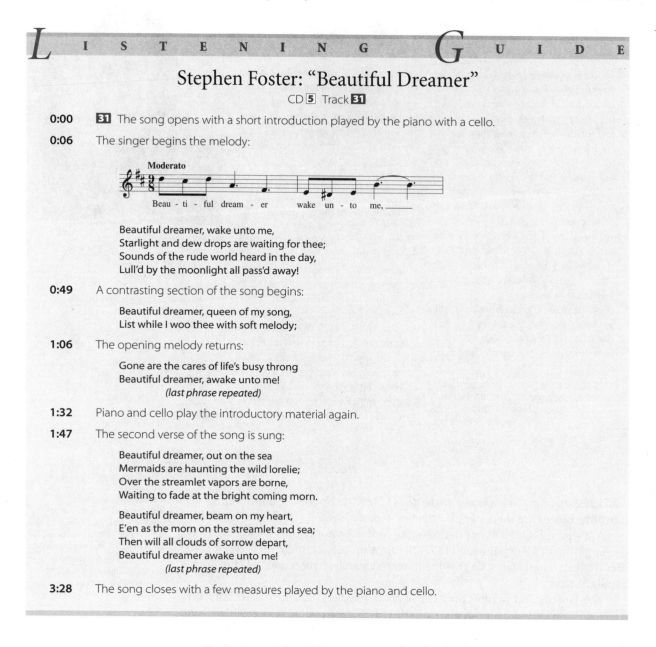

LISTENING GUIDE

Stephen Foster: "Beautiful Dreamer"
CD 5 Track 31

0:00   **31** The song opens with a short introduction played by the piano with a cello.

0:06   The singer begins the melody:

Beau - ti - ful dream - er   wake un - to   me, _____

Beautiful dreamer, wake unto me,
Starlight and dew drops are waiting for thee;
Sounds of the rude world heard in the day,
Lull'd by the moonlight all pass'd away!

0:49   A contrasting section of the song begins:

Beautiful dreamer, queen of my song,
List while I woo thee with soft melody;

1:06   The opening melody returns:

Gone are the cares of life's busy throng
Beautiful dreamer, awake unto me!
(last phrase repeated)

1:32   Piano and cello play the introductory material again.

1:47   The second verse of the song is sung:

Beautiful dreamer, out on the sea
Mermaids are haunting the wild lorelie;
Over the streamlet vapors are borne,
Waiting to fade at the bright coming morn.

Beautiful dreamer, beam on my heart,
E'en as the morn on the streamlet and sea;
Then will all clouds of sorrow depart,
Beautiful dreamer awake unto me!
(last phrase repeated)

3:28   The song closes with a few measures played by the piano and cello.

Some Civil War songs had two sets of words, one for the Union and the other for the Confederacy. Even the melody of "The Star-Spangled Banner" had different words set to it.

By the time of the Civil War (1861–1865), a popular music-publishing industry was in place. Sheet music was to popular composers at that time what recordings are to popular music today. Without sheet music, it would have been impossible for most people to know the music of Foster or other songwriters.

The Civil War spawned quite a few new songs, or old songs with new words. A few of these, especially Julia Ward Howe's "The Battle Hymn of the Republic" and Dan Emmett's "Dixie," are still sung today.

TOWARD TIN PAN ALLEY AND RAGTIME

The transcontinental railroad linking the east and west was completed only four years after the end of the Civil War.

Following the Civil War, America witnessed rapid territorial and economic expansion. It was also a time of social unrest and of social causes such as the antisaloon movement. During these years there was much victimization of Native Americans, and the robber barons who built the railroads amassed their fortunes. For the first twenty-five years following the Civil War, popular songs looked to the past more than to the future.

Tin Pan Alley

Beginning about twenty years before the turn of the century, popular music changed with the emergence of a nationwide music industry for the promotion and publication of songs. The center of this industry was New York City, which dominated both musical theater and popular music. The origin of the term *Tin Pan Alley* has never been clearly determined, and neither has its location. Essentially, it referred to the popular music industry, much as the word *Hollywood* refers to the motion picture industry today.

Tin Pan Alley started at 28th Street, then moved to 42nd Street, and finally to the Brill Building on 47th Street.

It was (and still is) the nature of the commercial music industry to issue a huge number of songs, most of which had very short lives. Most of the songs barely paid their printing costs. But every so often, a song came along that made its composer and publisher wealthy. The first to reach into the millions in sales was the early 1890s song "After the Ball" by Charles K. Harris.

"After the Ball" sold 10 million copies at about fifty cents a copy.

To amass large numbers of sales, publishers hired "pluggers" to go into music and department stores to play and sing the publisher's music for the customers. A number of well-known songwriters began as pluggers—Irving Berlin, Jerome Kern, George Gershwin, and others. In addition, publishers made outright payments to performers, who were then mostly in vaudeville, to perform particular songs.

The payment to performers was an early version of a now illegal practice later known as *payola*.

Vaudeville is discussed in chapter 45.

Tin Pan Alley songs of the 1890s were remarkably similar to one another. They were set in 3/4 waltzlike meter, had a form that consisted of a lead-in verse and a chorus in thirty-two-measure form (*a a b a*, each with eight measures), and simple harmony. Some of these Gay Nineties songs include "Meet Me in St. Louis" (a song promoting the World's Fair there in 1904), "In My Merry Oldsmobile," and "The Bowery." There were some songs about women betrayed ("Only a Bird in a Gilded Cage") and some Irish American songs ("My Wild Irish Rose" and "Who Threw the Overalls in Mistress Murphy's Chowder").

The decade of the 1890s was termed the *Gay Nineties* because it was relatively prosperous and trouble-free.

The lyrics of "The Bowery" tell of the naughty things people say and do there. It is said that the song reduced property values in that part of lower Manhattan for a while.

Ragtime

Ragtime existed in two related forms. One form consisted of popular songs; it was popular between 1890 and 1920. The other form was for piano and was a forerunner of jazz. Ragtime songs were usually peppy tunes in 2/4 meter with a lot of syncopation. Some of the better-known titles include "Hot Time in the Old Town," Irving Berlin's "Alexander's Ragtime Band," which is basically a march instead of a rag, and "Way Down Yonder in New Orleans."

"Hot Time in the Old Town" is reported to have been based on a song heard in a famous St. Louis bordello.

Three major developments in the 1920s brought an end to ragtime and major changes in the popular music industry:

1. The rapid demise of sheet music sales and a corresponding rise in the sale of recordings.

2. The advent and development of commercial broadcasting. In January 1922 there were 28 broadcasting stations; by December of that year there were 570.

3. The introduction of sound motion pictures in 1927. Within two years of that date, there were 320 songwriters and composers working in Hollywood.

Another musical phenomenon affected American popular music in a profound way in the 1920s and 1930s: the popularization of jazz.

Although thousands of ragtime songs were written, today it is known almost exclusively as solo piano music. The most recognized composers of piano rags were Ben Harney (1871–1938), Tom Turpin (1873–1922), and, most notable of all, Scott Joplin (1868–1917). Although piano rags became a national fad within two decades of their introduction, some that are highly regarded today were not very successful at the time. Of all Joplin's rags, only "Maple Leaf Rag" was widely popular during his lifetime.

Scott Joplin

Joplin's opera *Treemonisha* was awarded a Pulitzer Prize posthumously in 1976. Interest in his music increased greatly after his rag "The Entertainer" was used in the soundtrack for the movie *The Sting.*

Piano rags, as many a pianist has discovered, are not easy to play well. Both Harney and Joplin wrote instruction books for playing them.

Joplin was a versatile musician who played cornet and piano, as well as being a bandleader. He also composed some stage works. Today he is remembered as the premier composer of piano rags.

The rise of piano rags paralleled the rapid increase in the sales of pianos in America between 1890 and 1920, after which a decline began. Piano rags also benefitted from the development of the mechanical player piano, which was operated by small holes punched in rolls of paper that were pulled across pneumatic tubes connected to the keys. In fact, some rags existed only on piano rolls and not on sheet music.

Ragtime did not follow the path through Tin Pan Alley to the public, as did most popular music. Instead, its home was the large and small cities of the Midwest— St. Louis, Sedalia, and Kansas City, Missouri; Moline, Illinois; New Albany, Indiana; Oskaloosa, Iowa; as well as Memphis and Indianapolis.

BLUES

The *blues* began as folk music (their musical characteristics are discussed in chapter 8), but a few words listing musical features can't provide the true flavor of the blues. Beyond their lowered notes in the scale and *a a b* pattern of lines covering twelve measures, there is something about a singer's tone quality, small shadings of intonation, and basic melancholy feeling that makes the blues sound "blue." The vocalist always sings alone of his or her personal and usually unhappy feelings; the blues are not for a vocal ensemble.

Bessie Smith is often referred to as the "Empress of the Blues."

The first publication of blues dates back to 1912, but the high point of their popularity came in the 1920s and early 1930s with performances by vaudeville singers. The best-known blues singers were Ma Rainey (Gertrude Pridgett, 1886–1939) and Bessie Smith.

SMITH'S "LOST YOUR HEAD BLUES"

Bessie Smith recorded "Lost Your Head Blues" in 1926. She is joined on the recording by two other jazz greats: Fletcher Henderson on piano and Joe Smith on trumpet. Although each *a* line is repeated, Smith varies it slightly.

Bessie Smith

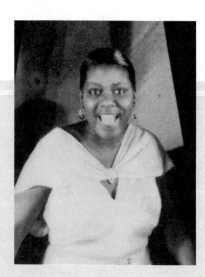

Bessie Smith (1894–1937) was born in Tennessee but was "discovered" singing in Selma, Alabama. She was contracted by Columbia Records in New York. Between 1924 and 1927, her recordings of the blues sold more than 2 million discs, making her the highest-paid black performer of the time. She died as the result of an automobile accident in 1937.

In popular music, and certainly in the blues, the performer is far more important than the writer of the music; often he or she is hardly mentioned. Smith was successful because she projected a magnetism that comes through even though the recordings of the 1920s lack the fidelity of recordings today. But her success can be attributed even more to her expressive singing voice and style. She adjusted her tone quality and added subtle nuances in pitches to make her singing memorable.

LISTENING GUIDE

Bessie Smith: "Lost Your Head Blues"
CD **5** Track **32**

0:00 **32** The recording begins with a short introduction.

0:11 The *a* line of the song is based entirely on the tonic, or I, chord. A short trumpet break follows Bessie's singing.

> I was with you baby when you did not have a dime.

0:22 The repeat of the *a* line is mostly based on the subdominant, or IV, chord, but returns to the tonic at the end, and another trumpet break is heard.

> I was with you baby when you did not have a dime.

0:32 The *b* line is mostly based on the dominant, or V, chord, but concludes on the tonic, which is followed by a trumpet break.

> Now since you got plenty money you have throw'd you good gal down.

The rest of the verses follow the same pattern of lines and chords, except for the last verse when the breaks also occur in the middle of the lines.

0:43 Once ain't for always, two ain't for twice. *(Repeat)*
When you get a good gal, you better treat her nice.

1:16 When you were lonesome, I tried to treat you kind. *(Repeat)*
But since you've got money, it's done changed your mind.

1:47 I'm gonna leave, baby, ain't gonna say goodbye. *(Repeat)*
But I'll write you and tell you the reason why.

2:19 Days are lonesome, nights are long. *(Repeat)*
I'm a good gal, but I've been treated wrong.

2:52 The song concludes quietly.

JAZZ

The roots of *jazz* are complex, but certainly some of them reach back to the African heritage of African Americans. Other influences include minstrel show music, work songs, field hollers, blues, French-Creole and Latin American music, and especially ragtime.

The traditional beginning of jazz lies with the brass bands that played for funerals in New Orleans. As a part of the procession to the gravesite, the band played solemn versions of hymns like "Nearer My God to Thee." After the burial, the band would assemble a couple of blocks away from the cemetery and break into a ragtime version of a hymn or tune like "Didn't He Ramble." The bands were competitive in their ability in *cutting* or *bucking*, the terms for such playing. The style eventually moved to the red-light district and the bordellos of New Orleans.

These bands were small by today's standards.

The "jazz funeral" is still practiced in New Orleans today.

Like folk music, jazz was created by generally untrained musicians who could not have written down what they played or sang, even had they wanted to. But it differs in two ways: (1) It sprang up in the cities, so its roots are urban; and (2) only a few people perform jazz, while many listen.

Some of the early jazz musicians didn't want to learn to read music because they claimed it might hinder their creative abilities.

Elements of Jazz

Melody   The most notable feature of jazz melodies are the *blue notes*. These notes are created by altering the major scale by lowering the third, fifth, or seventh steps. The chords that accompany these notes are not altered, however, so there is a dissonance between the lowered melody note and the note in the chord. The result, however, is not so much dissonance as it is a particular tonal effect.

Harmony   Traditional jazz harmony is as conservative as a church hymn. Most chords consist of the three primary triads used for harmonizing most simple songs: tonic (I), dominant (V), and subdominant (IV). As jazz matured, however, its harmonic palette became much richer and more sophisticated.

Rhythm   Jazz assumed many of the rhythmic characteristics of ragtime—a meter of two beats per measure combined with a countless variety of syncopated melodic figures. Jazz rhythms cannot be written precisely in traditional notation. Jazz musicians make small deviations in timing and emphasis, which most trained musicians cannot execute without guidance and practice.

The plunger mute was originally a rubber sink plunger.

The idea of "note bending" was a vocal technique derived from field hollers. It was picked up by instrumentalists and used in jazz.

Timbre   Jazz has its own tonal colors. Certain instruments and certain styles of playing have become associated with jazz. The saxophone was intended to be a concert instrument, but jazz players took it up and produced a different timbre. Brass instruments in jazz often use mutes. Some of these mutes have distinctive names, such as *cup, wah-wah,* and *plunger.*

The style of singing jazz is quite different from that used for singing an art song or a folk song. Jazz singers employ more colors and "bend" the pitch for expressive effect.

Form   Jazz has no overall form that applies to all its styles. The form generally consists of a series of variations on a simple harmonic pattern. As mentioned previously, the blues have a traditional pattern of three lines set in an *a a b* pattern. Sometimes the singer does not sing all the way through a section, and an instrumentalist fills in with a short solo called a *break.*

Improvisation   Making up music on the spot is fundamental to jazz. Traditionally, jazz was not written down, but as it developed it was often arranged with at least some of the music notated. The extemporaneous creation of music gives jazz an ever-fresh quality. Improvising in jazz is based on the chords of the tune. Players are not confined to just the notes of the chords, especially as jazz has evolved, but they are aware of them and make up their music accordingly.

The key can be decided in a few seconds. Jazz musician are usually "easy" about such things.

Typically, the players in a jazz performance agree that they will play a certain piece in a particular key. They also agree on an order in which each player is featured, although it can be changed during the performance by a nod of the head. Each player in turn improvises a chorus while keeping in mind the harmony of the song. Often for the final time through the piece, everyone joins in simultaneous improvised counterpoint. Only the musical instincts and good ears of the players, as well as the basic chord patterns of the piece, keep the music together.

Often during jazz improvisation, the melody can no longer be detected in the mosaic of sound. This happens because players sound many notes in addition to the former melody, and the tune becomes pretty well obscured.

Types of Jazz

The U.S. Navy had Storyville shut down because it was concerned about its impact on the physical and moral health of the servicemen.

Until the end of World War I, jazz had been mostly confined to the South, especially New Orleans. A number of factors led to the movement "up the river" to St. Louis, Chicago, and other cities in the North. One was the closing of Storyville, the red-light district in New Orleans. Many jazz musicians who worked in the bordellos lost their jobs and had to seek work elsewhere.

In addition, during World War I many young men, who had previously never thought they would see much more than the area where they grew up, were assigned to military camps and bases all over the United States. Furthermore, travel between cities by train was easy and not too expensive, if one were willing to ride coach class. If a jazz piano player lost his job in New Orleans, he could buy a ticket and head for St. Louis or Chicago. One of the best-known bands to make such a move was Joe "King" Oliver's Creole Jazz Band.

Joe "King" Oliver's Creole Jazz Band

Dixieland   The predominant type of jazz in the 1920s was *Dixieland*. It consisted of music in two beats to the measure with a strong upbeat, and a "busy" quality when several players were improvising at the same time. The bands were small, usually four to seven players. Originally, they did not include drums; keeping the beat was the piano player's job. Drums were added in later years. Dixieland bands loved to describe their music as being "hot," which meant that it was somewhat faster and louder than people were accustomed to at the time.

What was "hot" in the 1920s seems rather tame to most listeners today.

The song "Come Back, Sweet Papa" is a good example of Dixieland style. The tune was written by Paul Barbarin and Bob Russell, but in jazz what the players do with a tune is much more important than the original tune. If a recording had been made of "Come Back, Sweet Papa" a day or even a few minutes after the version in the Listening Guide, it would be similar but not exactly the same, because the players make up some of what they play as they go along.

"Come Back, Sweet Papa" was recorded by Louis Armstrong and His Hot Five in Chicago on February 22, 1926. On the recording Armstrong plays cornet. Other instruments heard on the recording are trombone, sax/clarinet (the same player doubling), piano, and banjo. The recording has a twangy quality, due largely to the inadequacies of recording equipment in 1926. It could be remastered today to sound "warmer," but why? Part of its charm lies in its original timbre.

Notice that there are no drums in the Hot Five.

Scat singing was an instrumental style of singing introduced by Armstrong in a recording of a song called "Heebie Jeebie." It sets syllable sounds without meaning to an improvised vocal line. The sounds are usually sung quite quickly.

The most famous scat singer was Ella Fitzgerald.

LISTENING GUIDE

Louis Armstrong: "Come Back, Sweet Papa"
CD [5] Track [33]

0:00	[33]	The trumpet and saxophone play a short introduction.
0:07		The chorus is played by the sax.
0:28		The sax repeats the chorus.
0:48		The trumpet takes up the chorus as the trombone adds some melodic figures.
1:08		The trumpet plays the chorus again.
1:27		The trombone plays sliding notes (glissando) and the trumpet continues. The clarinet improvises a contrasting part.
1:49		The piano plays a chorus.
2:08		The trumpet and trombone join together in playing the chorus.
2:31		The piece concludes with a characteristic rhythm pattern.

Boogie-woogie   After the Great Depression hit in 1929, for economic reasons people often hired only a piano player rather than a six- or seven-piece band. This situation encouraged the development of a type of jazz piano playing called *boogie-woogie*. It features a persistently repeated bass figure over which the player improvises trills, octave tremolos, and other melodic figures. Boogie-woogie was often called "eight to the bar," because the repeated bass part has eight notes per measure.

Octave tremolos are the rapid alternation between two notes an octave apart.

Swing   By 1935 jazz had progressed from small groups improvising in Dixieland style to intricate arrangements for bands of twelve to nineteen players. Much of their music was written down. Many pieces were played in four rather fast beats per measure, and the chords were far more complex than they had been in earlier jazz. The term *swing* may well have come from the bouncy quality of the music.

The Swing Era was a time when audiences danced. Its concert halls were such places as the Roseland Ballroom in New York and the Palladium in Hollywood. It was also a time when the more successful bands had regular broadcasts over national radio networks.

The Swing Era was also known as the Big Band Era.

Improvisation was still an important part of swing. Arrangers marked places for a soloist to *ad lib*—to improvise at liberty or at will. And there were many outstanding soloists: Gene Krupa on drums, Harry James on trumpet, Coleman Hawkins on saxophone, Artie Shaw and Benny Goodman on clarinet, and others. It was also the era of outstanding bands: Glenn Miller, Paul Whiteman, Les Brown, Count Basie, Woody Herman, and especially Duke Ellington. These bands had outstanding arrangers who had as much to do with the musical results as the composers of the tunes.

LISTENING GUIDE

Duke Ellington: "Take the 'A' Train"
CD 2 Track 49

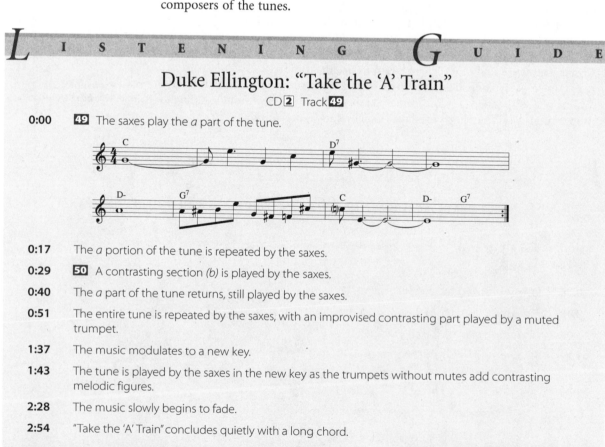

0:00   **49**   The saxes play the *a* part of the tune.

0:17   The *a* portion of the tune is repeated by the saxes.

0:29   **50**   A contrasting section (*b*) is played by the saxes.

0:40   The *a* part of the tune returns, still played by the saxes.

0:51   The entire tune is repeated by the saxes, with an improvised contrasting part played by a muted trumpet.

1:37   The music modulates to a new key.

1:43   The tune is played by the saxes in the new key as the trumpets without mutes add contrasting melodic figures.

2:28   The music slowly begins to fade.

2:54   "Take the 'A' Train" concludes quietly with a long chord.

Louis Armstrong

Duke Ellington

Armstrong was once asked to define jazz. He replied to the effect that "If you don't know, I can't explain it."

Armstrong's first name is pronounced "*Loo*-ie," which indicates the French tradition in his native New Orleans. He also acquired the nickname "Satchmo" for "satchel mouth."

Louis Armstrong (1900–1971) was born on the Fourth of July into a poor and unstable New Orleans family. As a boy he became involved with street life and at the age of twelve was sentenced by the juvenile court to the Colored Waifs' Home. It was there that he learned to play the cornet. After two years in the home, he was released; he did odd jobs and played whenever the opportunity presented itself.

Good fortune struck when Joe "King" Oliver took an interest in Armstrong, including sending him jobs that he couldn't accept himself. In 1919 Oliver moved to Chicago, and Armstrong was recognized as the best trumpet player in New Orleans. Two years later Oliver telegraphed Armstrong to join him in Chicago. Two years after that, Fletcher Henderson offered him a job with his outstanding band in New York.

After leaving Henderson's band some years later, Armstrong lead several groups of his own, including the Hot Five. By the 1940s he was featured on many radio shows and appeared in a number of films. His last movie was *Hello, Dolly!* In his later years, he sang as much as he played. He served as a goodwill emissary for the U.S. State Department on a number of worldwide tours.

Armstrong is considered the first great improvising soloist. He established a high standard of performance that has lasted for generations. In so many ways, he caught the elusive quality and joy of jazz.

Edward Kennedy "Duke" Ellington (1899–1975) lived a very different life from that of Louis Armstrong. Ellington was born in Washington, D.C., into the middle-class family of a butler. He studied both art and music when he was young, and his piano lessons included instruction in the popular ragtime style of the day. Although he was successful in his art studies, he decided on music and formed a band that played at social events in the Washington, D.C., area.

In 1923 he joined a five-piece combo called The Washingtonians and went to New York. Success didn't come easily, but three years

Ellington once commented that they were so poor he would buy one hotdog and split it five ways.

later he was playing at the Cotton Club, which at that time was the most expensive nightclub in Harlem. It catered to white audiences who wanted to hear good jazz.

Over the years, Ellington's band was responsible for many musical innovations, including echo chambers in recordings to increase reverberation (which became standard

Ellington's interest in art shows in a number of his song titles that mention colors, including "Mood Indigo" and "Black, Brown, and Beige."

practice later), the flatted fifth, the amplified bass, and the baritone saxophone. By the 1950s his group seemed to be declining after twenty years, but a stunning performance at the Newport Jazz Festival in 1956 revived it. He composed a number of sacred works in his later years and made goodwill tours for the U.S. State Department.

Ellington's compositions were partially group efforts. He would begin playing a musical idea on the piano, and other members of the band would join in and add ideas. He would then massage these ideas into a final composition. Duke Ellington and his band left a legacy of elegant jazz.

Jazz bands were noted for a high turnover rate. Not so with Ellington. For example, Harry Carney, his baritone sax player, was with him for forty-seven years!

C o d a

From the broadsides of colonial days, to the parlor songs of the nineteenth century, to the piano rags at the turn of the century, to the big-band arrangements of jazz in the middle of the twentieth century, American popular music has paralleled the changes in American society. It has indeed been an index of life in the United States.

44 Popular Music Since 1956

In many ways America today is not all that different from America at midcentury. Its governmental structure and economic system are virtually unchanged, and most of its core beliefs and values are still somewhat intact. But in other ways, America has moved far from what it was in 1950.

A number of these changes have had a major impact on music, and especially on popular music.

- The population of the United States has nearly doubled since 1950. Therefore several segments of it easily became large enough to draw the attention of the media and make the marketing of specially oriented products, including music, well worthwhile.

- The decade of roughly 1947–1956 saw a huge increase in the number of children born, partly because veterans of World War II had to delay having families until after the war. The number of births in these years accounted for roughly half of the total increase in population.

- The general economic level of the United States reached new heights. Most teenagers are able to buy records, movie tickets, and clothes and other products especially created for them as never before.

- Television replaced radio as the prime form of mass media entertainment. Network radio, which in the 1930s and 1940s had been an extremely important cultural force, almost disappeared except for its news function. Instead, hundreds of local radio stations sprang up, many of which catered to audiences of a particular age level or ethnic group. Most of these stations survived (and often thrived) by playing recordings of popular music interspersed with spot commercials.

- Recordings could be produced and marketed by small companies, which greatly reduced the influence of the few large record companies that had controlled the industry in the previous decades. These small companies were much more innovative and responsive to changes in audience tastes than the established companies. Without these new companies, many of the developments in popular music would have happened much more slowly, if indeed at all.

- America's minority peoples became much more conscious and proud of their particular identities. For quite a few years, most whites could not understand the feelings that the "Black is beautiful" slogan and the words of Malcolm X evoked in African Americans. The awareness of ethnic and racial identity greatly influenced people's choices in popular music.

Like American society, its popular music is a fascinating mix of many kinds of music influenced by many factors. No discussion of it, even one the size of an entire book, can do it justice. To make an examination of it more manageable, however, popular music can be divided into three broad categories: soul, country, and rock.

Baby boomers are a very large and significant age group in the population of the United States.

BLUES AND SOUL

Two of the main types of American popular music were born in the rural South. And just as the South was segregated on the basis of race until a few decades ago, its popular music also had strong racial associations. The *blues* was the music of the blacks, and *country* was the music of the whites.

Blues began as a type of folk music, as described in chapter 8. As many African Americans migrated over the years from the South to the cities of the North, the blues moved with them. It spoke of the harsh life that they encountered in the northern cities. The acoustic guitar was replaced by the electric guitar, and piano, drums, and other instruments were added to accompany the singers. The music became louder than before, and blues singers often adopted a shouting style, even though they usually used a microphone. The style of piano playing was similar to what was used in boogie-woogie, with its heavy left-hand repeated patterns. Drums were eventually added as well.

Rhythm and Blues

By the 1950s saxophones and backup vocal ensembles had completed the migration of the blues from the country to the city. And it had acquired a new commercial name: *rhythm and blues*. Entertainers such as Chuck Berry (b. 1926) and Bo Diddley (Elias McDaniel, b. 1928) created a music that became the basis of rock and roll, which began to appear in the mid-1950s.

Motown Records was a major force in promoting rhythm and blues. It was founded in Detroit in 1958 by then auto worker and part-time songwriter Barry Gordy, with $700 he borrowed from his credit union. At first success was limited. The real breakthrough happened in 1964 with a recording of "Where Did Our Love Go?" by the Supremes.

Motown Records carefully developed its stars and their recordings, including choreography and arrangements slicked up for white audiences. In addition to the Supremes, its major stars were Smokey Robinson, The Temptations, and Stevie Wonder. In 1988 Motown Record Corporation was sold to MCA, Inc., for $61 million.

The name *Motown* is a contraction of "Motor Town," a nickname sometimes given Detroit.

Gordy once described the Motown sound as "rats, roaches, struggle, talent, guts, love."

That's 87,142 times the value of Gordy's initial investment!

Chuck Berry, The Supremes, and Stevie Wonder

Soul

Rhythm and blues gradually gave way to a more general concept of African American music: *soul.* This term is somewhat nebulous, but it is strongly associated with the racial and cultural identity of African Americans, and is created primarily for them. Musically, it is a synthesis of blues, jazz, and gospel. On the surface its prominent musical characteristics are not all that different from those of rock. But underneath there lies a wealth of subtle tonal and rhythmic nuances that make soul distinctive and highly expressive.

Rap

Rap music began in the 1970s as a product of the streets of the South Bronx in New York City. It features rapid-fire talking in a singsong, patter style over a rock rhythmic background. Its words are often on social or political topics.

In a sense, rap continues a tradition of versifying and impromptu speaking that goes back to African American preachers, the "talking blues," and the street culture. The group Run DMC was largely responsible for making rap a commercial success with its recording "Raising Hell." The popularity of rap has continued with a group called N.W.A. (Niggas with Attitude). Rap has also had its white artists such as the Beastie Boys, Marky Mark, and Vanilla Ice.

In 1990 "As Nasty as They Wanna Be" by 2 Live Crew became the first recording to be ruled obscene in a U.S. district court.

COUNTRY MUSIC

Country music was (and still is) the "people's music" among the whites in the South. It began as folk music but evolved into a national phenomenon and a huge commercial enterprise.

Characteristics of Country Music

Singing style The style of singing is a direct carryover from the style used for folk songs. It has a lonesome quality and is sung with a clear tone and no vibrato. It tends to be nasal and slightly tense or strained. Often singers let their voice "break" to add emotion to a moment in a song. Yodels are sometimes added, especially in the west. Above all, the singing projects sincerity, or else it is just not country music.

Instruments Country music is traditionally played on stringed instruments—the fiddle, dulcimer, guitar, banjo, and mandolin. The *fiddle* is a violin played in a distinctive way with a straight, penetrating tone, short and rapid bow strokes, and much sliding from one note to another. Some country music festivals have fiddling contests. Often fiddlers perform tricks such as playing the instrument behind their backs, holding the bow between their legs while moving the fiddle with their hands and arms, and similar antics. The *mandolin* is associated with Italy, but became widely used in some types of country music.

Melody and harmony Country music is simple and direct. As it became more popular, major and minor scales replaced the extensive use of the older modal scales. Its songs are mostly harmonized with the three primary chords found in so much music in the Western world: tonic, dominant, and subdominant.

Rhythm The rhythm is simple, with only a little syncopation. Most of the songs are two beats to the measure.

Texts The texts of country songs are an interesting blend of realism and sentimentality. Topics include death, drinking, nostalgia, loneliness, and, the perennial favorite, broken love.

Development of Country Music

The move of country music away from its folk status to the world of popular music coincides with the widespread use of recordings and radio in the 1920s. Record companies realized the commercial potential of what was then called *hillbilly* music. They recorded singers such as Uncle Dave Macon from Tennessee, the Carter Family from Virginia, Gid Tanner and his Skillet Lickers from Georgia, and especially Jimmie Rodgers from Mississippi.

Radio broadcasts were vital to the growth of country music, because a large part of its audience lived in remote, rural mountainous areas. The radio show that eventually became the Grand Ole Opry started in 1925 on WSM in Nashville with two unpaid performers and no commercial sponsor!

The first major country music star was Jimmie Rodgers (1897–1933) from Meridian, Mississippi, who was known as the "Singing Brakeman." His career was short—only six years. But during those years, he recorded 111 songs and sold 20 million records, an amazing feat for that time. He was quite eclectic in the music he performed, which included work songs, white blues, love songs, and melancholy ballads.

Country music had a close cousin in country-western music. Part of the commercial success of this music was due to the popularity of movies about cowboys and the music performed in them. Some performers became well-known in these films: Gene Autry, Ernest Tubb, Maurice "Tex" Ritter, and the Sons of the Pioneers, which at that time included Roy Rogers (Leonard Slye).

Country music grew rapidly after World War II. The most important name in country music from the early 1950s was Hank Williams (1923–1953), who like Jimmie Rodgers had a short career. He and his band, the Drifting Cowboys, recorded such perennial favorites as "Your Cheatin' Heart," "I'm So Lonesome I Could Cry," and "Hey, Good Lookin'." Other important names include Johnny Cash, Tennessee Ernie Ford, Merle Haggard, Patsy Cline, and Loretta Lynn, whose life's story was made well known in her autobiography and subsequent movie, "The Coal Miner's Daughter."

The "Wabash Cannonball" as performed in 1947 by Roy Acuff (b. 1903) and His Smokey Mountain Boys is typical of country music at the time. A special feature of the music is the use of train whistles to represent the fact that the song is a narrative about a famous train.

The lack of a sponsor seems unbelievable today.

A brakeman was one of the crew on a locomotive.

Gene Autry later became owner of the California Angels baseball team. Roy Rogers became a star in his own right.

Notice the use of a western name for Williams's group.

LISTENING GUIDE

Roy Acuff: "Wabash Cannonball"
CD 5 Track 34

0:00	**34** Song begins with an introduction played by the guitar and train whistles.
0:14	The singer begins verse 1; it is built around paired phrases in question-and-answer form.
0:34	Verse 2 is sung using the same paired phrases.
0:53	An instrumental segment is played, featuring the harmonica and train whistles.
1:15	Verse 3 is sung using the same paired phrases found in verses 1 and 2.
1:35	Verse 4 begins and follows the same pattern of phrases as the previous one.
1:56	An instrumental segment is played with the steel guitar taking the lead as train whistles are heard again.
2:12	The fifth and final verse is sung following the same pattern as the earlier verses.
2:33	The "Wabash Cannonball" concludes.

Country greats Hank Williams, Bill Monroe, and Loretta Lynn

Types of Country Music

The success of country music led to several variants in its style. *Rockabilly,* as its name suggests, was strongly influenced by rock. It was mostly the product of Sun Records and was represented by Carl Perkins (b. 1932), Elvis Presley (1935–1977), and Jerry Lee Lewis (b. 1935).

Another variant is sometimes referred to as *honky-tonk.* It centered around Austin, Texas, and its most recognized performer is Willie Nelson (b. 1933).

A third variant, *bluegrass,* attempted to return country music to its traditional roots. Only acoustic (nonelectric) instruments are used, and its song topics return to the less commercial ones of early years. Bluegrass music can largely be credited to one man, Bill Monroe (1911–1996), who grew up in Kentucky. Monroe was a virtuoso performer on the mandolin.

Country music's growth has made Nashville "Music City, USA," complete with a new Grand Ole Opry House in 1975, television and recording studios, publishing houses, agents, and amusement parks. Names such as Dolly Parton, Emmylou Harris, Barbara Mandrell, Randy Travis, Kenny Rogers, and a host of others are familiar to the many millions of people who enjoy country music today.

ROCK

It would be easy to say that rock is the musical progeny of a union between blues and country music, because it contains important elements of both. But it is much more than that.

Rock often vents strong feelings of revolt. As one writer has said, rock "expressed a visceral impatience with sociopolitical norms." Although rock first appeared in the mid-1950s, it did not begin to dominate the popular music scene until the mid-1960s. The fact that these years also witnessed the emergence of the baby boomer generation as college-age young people at the same time as the turmoil over the Vietnam War can hardly be a coincidence.

Rock had its start with a Cleveland disc jockey named Alan Freed, who played rhythm and blues. He probably coined the term *rock and roll,* as it is used today, as he called his radio program "Moondog's Rock and Roll Party." Later Freed moved to New York City as a disc jockey for WINS, which soon became that city's leading popular music station.

At about the same time, white groups began recording their own versions of rhythm and blues. The first such hit was Bill Haley's (1925–1981) "Rock Around the Clock." Elvis Presley was soon to follow with songs such as "Heartbreak Hotel," which

Bluegrass has no songs about truck drivers or urban situations.

"Rock Around the Clock" was the theme song for the 1955 motion picture *Blackboard Jungle* in which rebellious students smashed the teacher's valuable collection of jazz records. Later it was the theme for the popular television show *Happy Days.*

in 1956 succeeded in both the black and white segments of the market—something that rarely happens.

Presley is easily the most remembered country-rock star. His dynamic singing and personal magnetism greatly enlarged the audiences for both country and rock music. His recordings have sold an astounding 1 *billion* worldwide, with 111 albums or singles going gold, platinum, or multiplatinum. In addition, he appeared in thirty-three films and sang hundreds of concerts. The public's fascination with Presley continues. His home, Graceland, in Memphis is the second most visited home in the United States; only the White House exceeds it.

Characteristics of Rock

Rhythm   The heart of rock is its strong beat. Often the beat is incorporated in a simple melodic figure played in the bass parts. Another feature of rock rhythm is its prominent *backbeat.* In some types of rock, this backbeat is incorporated with other rhythm patterns to create a complex combination of rhythms.

Elvis Presley, the King In the years since his death, he is reported to have been seen in hundreds of different places.

Melody and harmony   The melodies and harmonies of rock are strongly influenced by folk music. It has an elemental simplicity. Rock has more songs written in the modes than other types of music, which again reveals some of its folk heritage.

Timbre   The tonal qualities of rock depend on the particular style. "Hard" rock is very loud with distorted sounds, which is not true of "soft" or "pop" rock. Rock's sounds are almost always amplified electronically, which affects the timbre of the music. The style of singing can vary from raucous, almost shouted sounds of undetermined pitch to energetic but tuneful. Singers work hard at developing individual styles that listeners can easily identify.

The *backbeat* is what audiences clap along with: 1-**2**-3-**4**, 1-**2**-3-**4**.

Lyrics   The form of a rock song is usually built around its lyrics. Songs are often strophic and have more verses than traditional Tin Pan Alley songs. Often lines of text are freer in phrase lengths than the usual thirty-two measures in *aaba* form. Some rock music uses sophisticated lyrics in terms of rhyme schemes and frame of reference, and sometimes the lyrics do not follow metrical patterns.

Performances   Most rock musicians are very conscious of visual effects. Some have experimented with subjective mental states in concerts and on videos, or what has often been termed "psychedelic" rock. Some of these images have been fantasy, some subliminal, and some probably influenced by drugs. Because of the enormous amount of money that top rock stars earn, they can afford the best in terms of lighting and other visual and sound effects. Rock concerts are usually more than just music. They include stunning lighting and dramatic effects to captivate their audiences.

Developments in Rock Since 1965

British influence   The close relationship between British and American popular music has a long history. Therefore it was not surprising when two British groups, The Beatles and the Rolling Stones, became very influential in the American rock music scene. In fact, after the mid-1960s the rock music styles of the two countries became almost indistinguishable from each other.

John Lennon once said of The Beatles' music, "We're kidding you, we're kidding ourselves, we're kidding everybody. We don't take anything seriously except the money."

The Beatles

The Beatles—John Lennon, Paul McCartney, George Harrison, and after 1962, Ringo Starr—were all born in Liverpool, England, of working-class parents during World War II. Lennon, who was halfheartedly studying art at a local institute, met McCartney and Harrison, and they decided to form a group. At the time, they were just one of the three hundred such groups around Liverpool earning about $15 a week and hoping to make it big someday. They tried a number of different names, but the name changes seemed to make no difference.

If the changes of name didn't help, the acquisition in 1961 of Brian Epstein as manager certainly did. He had become interested in the group when customers came into his father's department store, asking for its records. First he designed a pseudo-choirboy outfit to replace the beatnik garb they had used in the past. Next he took them to London to interest a record company in the group. After a few rejections, Epstein talked EMI (Electrical Music Industries) into producing "Love Me Do." It sold respectably. The EMI executives had an idea: Bring in a new drummer—Ringo Starr.

In the fall of 1962, The Beatles made their debut on British television with Starr on drums, and it was soon uphill at a dizzying pace. By April 1963 they had their first British gold record and, in the next nine months, thirteen more television appearances, plus a royal command performance. Young people loved their odd hairdos, charming irreverence, and brashness.

The Beatles did not enter the American rock scene until early 1964. By February of that year, they came to the United States in person for an appearance on The Ed Sullivan Show. They could hardly be heard over the screaming teenagers at their live performances. But their main means of performance was through recordings. By 1967 The Beatles had sold more than 20 million singles and an equal number of long-playing records.

The Beatles' early music and approach was infectious good fun. But in later works, they took an eclectic approach, not confining themselves to just one style, but covering the musical gamut from synthesized sounds to Indian ragas to Renaissance music. Their music grew in sophistication, culminating in the Sgt. Pepper's Lonely Hearts Club Band album in 1967.

The decline for The Beatles began in 1967 with the accidental death of their brilliant manager, Brian Epstein. Some of their business ventures turned sour, and tensions developed among the four men and their wives and girlfriends. They disbanded in 1971 and went their separate ways, never again to enjoy the success as individuals that they had as a group. Tragedy struck when Lennon was murdered in New York in 1980 by a deranged fan.

Folk-rock poet and performer Bob Dylan

Folk rock   Rock had its urban folk form in the music of Bob Dylan (Robert Zimmerman, b. 1941), who was associated with Greenwich Village in New York City. He infused his music with both folk qualities and social protest lyrics. Other singers of folk rock included Judy Collins and Joni Mitchell.

Fusion   The combination of two or more different musical styles is called *fusion*. The fusion of rock with other styles was inevitable, given its enormous popularity. One fusion occurred between rock and jazz. Several groups successfully blended these two types of music. Two groups stand out in doing this: Blood, Sweat and Tears, and Chicago. The combination of styles is heard particularly in the treatment of rhythm. Some of these works were considerably longer than the usual rock song.

Another fusion involved the influence of classical music in rock. Three British musicians or groups achieved recognition for this type of music: Keith Emerson, the Bee Gees, and Deep Purple. Emerson, with Greg Lake and Carl Palmer, also produced popular versions of music by such composers as Copland and Mussorgsky.

George Harrison and The Beatles were among the first, if not *the* first, to include elements of Asian music in their rock works. Indian music especially attracted Harrison.

Satire and punk   One piece of evidence regarding the maturing of rock was its increasing use of satire. Frank Zappa (b. 1940) and the Mothers of Invention engaged in theatrics and put-ons that caused audiences to wonder about the seriousness of it all. Zappa himself kept interviewers guessing about the nature of his artistic intentions with his rambling and unclear statements.

While Zappa may have been having fun with audiences, *punk* rock was deliberately being rebellious. The feelings of rebellion were directed at both the norms of society and the rock establishment, which these performers thought had sold out to commercial interests. The musical impact of these groups was probably less than their social impact, as they sometimes engaged in repulsive behavior in their performances.

Some rock groups vary their style quite a bit, which blurs their classification.

An art form has evolved to a more mature state when it can poke fun at itself.

Punk rock groups did not lack for interesting names, including: Weirdos, Sex Pistols, the Lewd, the Mutants, the Ghouls, Flesheaters, Slash, Search and Destroy, Circle Jerks, Crime, Damage, and Destroy All Music.

MUSIC VIDEOS

The present generation of young people is sometimes described as "the Video Generation." It has grown up with visual images provided by television and other technology. And these images are not just pictures or designs, but frequent, often rapid-fire moving images that flash across a screen.

Even on network television, one shot is almost never maintained for more than four seconds. The time span is shorter yet in music videos.

It was only a matter of time before popular music began to combine music and visual images. This effort led to the establishment of MTV (Music Television) in the early 1980s. Initially, the purpose of the videos was the promotion of recordings. One of the early and most widely recognized music videos was Michael Jackson's "Thriller," which was taken from his 1983 album of the same name.

Music videos can be divided into four main types:

♦ Videos that present a performer in a concert format

♦ Videos that present music in a dance format

♦ Videos that present a story, which may or may not relate directly to the lyrics of the song

♦ Videos that present fantasy images, often on the premise of a dream

Music videos rely heavily on the manipulation of images, using computers and other technological equipment.

Any survey of a musical style is limited in the amount of information it can provide and in the conclusions it can draw. This seems especially true of rock, because it changes so rapidly and because it is a complex social-psychological-musical phenomenon. Whatever else may be said of rock, it is truly a fascinating topic and a creative type of music.

OTHER TYPES OF POPULAR MUSIC

Although soul, country, and rock cover much of the popular music scene since 1950, they certainly do not account for all of it. Several other types of popular music were influential as well.

Latin American

A *rumba* is a dance in a rapid two-beat meter with an intricate contrasting part played by the percussion. It is Afro-Cuban in origin.

Salsa means "sauce" or "spice."

Latin American music has influenced the popular music of the United States since at least the 1920s, when the husband-and-wife team of Vernon and Irene Castle popularized the tango. By the 1930s the *rumba* had become a popular dance. Cuban music soared in popularity as "The Peanut Vendor" recorded by Don Azpiazú became the first Cuban hit record. Also Xavier Cugat, who was born in Spain but lived most of his life in Cuba, and his band were appearing in a number of motion pictures.

Interest in Latin American music reached a high point in the 1950s and 1960s with the popularization of the *mambo*. The person most responsible for the interest in this dance music was Tito Puente, who was born in New York City of Puerto Rican parents. His most successful recording from this period was "Dance Mania."

The 1970s saw the advent of a "hot" style of Latin American music called *salsa*. It originated in the Cuban nightclubs in the 1940s, from where it spread to the rest of the Caribbean and then on to the United States. Three cities became known as the "salsa triangle": San Juan in Puerto Rico, Miami, and New York.

Another type of Latin American music is associated with the American West. Austin, Texas, became the center for an amalgamation of Mexican and country music called *Tex-Mex*.

Tito Puente

The best-known singer of Latin American music in the 1970s was Linda Ronstadt. She grew up in Tucson, Arizona, the daughter of a part-Chicano father.

While *reggae* originated in Jamaica in the 1960s, it did not become widely known in the United States until fifteen or so years later. Reggae features accents on the backbeat with simple melodies and few chord changes. Bob Marley (1945–1981) and the Wailers presented colorful sounds that became popular with the 1976 song "Roots, Rock, Reggae."

The interest in Latin American music is very strong. In 1992 Puente recorded "Numero 100," his one hundredth recording. The Miami Sound Machine with Gloria Estefan is another example of Latin American music that appeals to a wide audience.

Gloria Estefan

Modern Jazz

Jazz reached a turning point in the 1950s: It became more sophisticated—gone was the strong beat that people could dance to. In its place was a music that began for the first time to be considered seriously as art music by its audiences and many of its performers. No longer was it music for the players; instead it became music for listeners. In the process, jazz lost its appeal to the young people, who moved to rock and rhythm and blues.

The change began with a style of jazz called *bebop* or, more common, *bop*. It was the product mainly of Charlie "Bird" Parker (1920–1955) and Dizzy Gillespie (John Birks, 1917–1993). Bop contains nearly continuous syncopation, dissonant chords, and freely developed melodies. Bop groups were usually small combos, not the big bands of the 1940s. The string bass was often responsible for maintaining the beat. Some of its musical passages were played in unison, often with lots of notes.

Miles Davis (1926–1991), Dave Brubeck (b. 1920), and the Modern Jazz Quartet turned toward a "cool" style of jazz. Their music was more intellectual and well ordered, and it was also performed by small groups.

A less well understood type of jazz is called *free jazz*. It was first developed by Ornette Coleman (1926–1967) about 1960. Other practitioners of this style include John Coltrane (b. 1930) and Cecil Taylor (b. 1933). Free jazz usually involves collective improvising, no predetermined chord progressions or tonality, playing deliberately out of tune, and expanded forms that are longer than those usually encountered in jazz.

Some jazz composers, notably Miles Davis, moved to electronic sounds and changes that made their works jazz-based compositions. Davis's "Bitches Brew," created in 1969, uses a number of electric instruments and an almost rocklike rhythm pattern that is ornamented with Latin American figures. In 1995 Wynton Marsalis (b. 1961) and his Septet followed in Davis's footsteps with "Citi Movement," a thirty-seven-minute-long ballet. These are jazz compositions that represent high artistic aspirations. Jazz has indeed moved far from what its founding fathers back in New Orleans had started early in the twentieth century.

The share of the radio and record market occupied by jazz slipped to about 2 percent.

Dizzy Gillespie defined bop by saying that in bop you go *Ba*-oo *Ba*-oo *Ba*-oo instead of *Oo*-ba *Oo*-ba *Oo*-ba.

Coda

All the various types of popular music in America have come a long way in five decades. It has developed new and different variants of its old styles, and it has acquired much economic and social importance as well. Because they are continuously evolving, the various types of popular music are as fascinating and complex as American society itself.

Music for Stage and Film

Music for stage performances and films is somewhat different from concert music. Such music does not stand alone. It always involves a visual element and usually drama. Composers therefore face somewhat different requirements when writing for stage or film. They need to create music that is effective in tandem with the action and story with which they are working. In spite of this apparent limitation, this requirement has produced a body of beautiful and interesting music.

EARLY CONCERTS

Public performances of music in the 1700s were mostly confined to four cities: Philadelphia, New York, Boston, and Charleston. These performances were hardly concerts in the current sense of the word. They included songs, dances, recitations, card tricks, and even balancing acts. Audiences were noisy, and performers often had to request them to be quiet. In fact, for many years part of the audience was allowed to sit onstage.

On bad nights the audience threw nuts, fruit, and even bottles at the performers!

No clear division existed between popular and art music in stage productions, a situation that lasted until about 1830. Songs were almost always included in early public performances, but few of those songs have survived.

A few types of musicals existed. Most of these had skeletal plots around which composers created some songs, but most of the music for these stage productions has been lost.

MINSTREL SHOWS

An indigenous American type of stage show is the *minstrel show*, which developed in the decades before the Civil War. These shows enjoyed enormous popularity and existed well into the twentieth century.

After the Civil War, blacks became the main performers in minstrel shows.

The banjo played melody, not chords as it usually does today.

The *bones* were two small clappers played with the fingers that were originally animal bones but were later made of hardwood.

The well-known song "Dixie" has each of these characteristics.

Minstrel shows featured the exaggerated portrayal of black people by white performers wearing blackface. The shows consisted of songs, dances, jokes, skits, and satirical speeches. Originally, there were only four performers seated in a semicircle. They didn't sit still for long, however; they were almost constantly in motion, even when sitting. Banjo and fiddle players occupied the middle two seats. The other two performers were logically called "end men." They played the bones and tambourine, as well as engaged in entertaining horseplay. The music for minstrel shows was generally in a major key, had a lively tempo, and contained much repetition of short motives.

Two names are especially associated with minstrel shows: Stephen Foster, who is discussed in chapter 43, and Dan Emmett (1815–1904). Emmett composed "Dixie" while working with a minstrel show company.

VAUDEVILLE

Late in the 1800s, a new and important form of stage entertainment appeared: *vaudeville.* It descended from minstrel shows, the English music hall, and the "burlesque" type of entertainment offered in saloons. Vaudeville usually consisted of a succession of individual acts—singers, dancers, jugglers, magicians, and animal acts. They were typically headed by a well-known comedian or singer.

By the turn of the century, vaudeville was playing in thousands of theaters across the United States. It thrived into the days of silent movies, with which it often shared the stage. Many persons who later became famous through the movies, radio, or television got their start in vaudeville: Sophie Tucker, George M. Cohan, Jimmy Durante, Jack Benny, and Ed Wynn, to name a few. Interestingly, vaudeville left no discernible body of music.

The origin of the word *vaudeville* is French. It refers to light or satirical texts sung to already-existing tunes. Later the term was applied to a comedy with music.

MUSICAL COMEDY AND BROADWAY MUSICALS

The Black Crook, first produced in 1866, is often credited with being the first American musical. Actually, it was quite European in character; the more American musical comedies were at least a generation in the future. Along the way, three European-born and -trained composers contributed much to the development of this genre of music: Victor Herbert (1859–1924), Rudolf Friml (1879–1972), and Sigmund Romberg (1887–1951). Their stage works, called *operettas,* were filled with beautiful melodies, and their stories were pure escapism. Many of them were placed in exotic locations and times.

Probably the richest time period for musical comedy was the thirty years between Jerome Kern's *Show Boat* (1927) and Leonard Bernstein's *West Side Story* (1957). Other notable composers of musical comedies during this time include Richard Rodgers and Oscar Hammerstein II, Frederick Lowe and Alan Jay Lerner, Cole Porter, and Irving Berlin. The stories became more real, and the music was integrated more logically into the story line. No longer were songs just strung together around a flimsy plot. These musicals consisted of one good tune after another. Some of the songs were not only quite expressive, they were also rather sophisticated. Artistic dance scenes were often incorporated as well.

The movie version of *West Side Story* won the Academy Award for Best Picture in 1961.

Some of the musical comedies during these years had quite serious stories, along with some comedy—*South Pacific, Showboat, Lady in the Dark, Carousel, The King and I,* and others.

BERNSTEIN'S *WEST SIDE STORY*

West Side Story (music by Leonard Bernstein and lyrics by Stephen Sondheim) is an updated version of Romeo and Juliet. Instead of rival families, however, it's rival gangs; one is Puerto Rican and the other native New Yorkers. Maria is Puerto Rican and Tony is of Polish descent. They meet and fall in love at a dance, but the obstacles to their happiness cannot be overcome. Tony unintentionally kills Maria's brother in a gang fight. Then Tony is told falsely that Maria has turned against him, and so he allows himself to be stabbed. He dies in Maria's arms.

The sequence titled "The Dance at the Gym" contains a mambo and a cha-cha, which are Latin American dances. The mambo demonstrates the excitement that rhythm can achieve in music. It does this with a fast tempo and the use of several rhythm patterns at the same time.

In Shakespeare's play, Romeo comes from the Montagues and Juliet from the Capulets. The two families hated each other.

Scene from "The Dance at the Gym" from the movie version of *West Side Story*

Rhythm is not the only feature of the mambo. The orchestra provides the music with a kaleidoscope of timbres, including trumpets played in Latin American style and percussion instruments. The cha-cha is quiet and controlled. Its rhythmic interest lies in the silences, finger snaps, and especially the three quick notes that almost seem to say "cha cha cha."

Leonard Bernstein

Leonard Bernstein (1918–1990) was born in Lawrence, Massachusetts, of Russian-Jewish parents. His businessman father moved the family to Boston shortly after Leonard's birth, and he graduated from the Boston Latin School and Harvard University. Later he studied at the Curtis Institute in Philadelphia.

During his career he developed a number of successful television programs on musical topics, appeared as a piano soloist, and composed a variety of types of music. For a decade he was conductor of the New York Philharmonic Orchestra.

Best-Known Works
Ballet:
■ *Fancy Free*
■ *On the Town*
Musical:
■ *West Side Story*
Orchestra:
■ *Candide: Overture*

L I S T E N I N G   G U I D E

Leonard Bernstein: "The Dance at the Gym" from *West Side Story*

CD 5 Track 35

0:00	35	The music begins with tremendous energy with drums and cow bell playing.
0:07		The trumpets join in.
0:10		The dancers onstage join in by shouting, "Mambo!"
0:32		The trumpets play a two-note descending figure as the drumming continues.
0:49		The dancers add hand clapping to the music.
1:43		The music begins to grow quieter and slower.
1:47	36	The cha-cha begins quietly, played by the violins. Three quick notes (frequently accompanied by finger snaps) followed by a short silence are often heard at the end of phrases.
1:57		The song "Maria" is played in short notes by the strings being plucked.
2:27		The violins play a contrasting part of "Maria."
3:00		The music concludes quietly after several consecutive soundings of three quick notes followed by a short silence.

Since *West Side Story,* musical comedies have moved away from the emphasis on the composer and the songs. The librettist, director, and choreographer have assumed new importance. Some musicals are built more around a concept rather than a story. *Chorus Line* and *Cats* are two such "concept" musicals.

OPERATIC MUSICALS

A noteworthy trend in music for the stage in recent years is a growing number of the successful musicals that are virtually operas—every word in them is sung. Three examples of this trend are *Phantom of the Opera* by Andrew Lloyd Webber and *Les Misérables* and *Miss Saigon* by Claude-Michel Schonberg. There are, however, several differences between them and the operas of Mozart, Verdi, and other composers as performed by the major opera houses of Europe and the Americas.

♦ The style of singing is more like what is heard in musicals.

♦ The singing is amplified, although no microphones are visible and the sound levels are not particularly loud.

♦ The vocal parts are technically less demanding; no virtuoso singing ability is required.

♦ The accompanying orchestra is rather small.

♦ They are sung in English in English-speaking countries.

♦ They contain one or more humorous sections and characters.

♦ The action onstage moves at a faster pace.

Les Misérables uses a rotating stage. It makes sixty-three turns in each performance.

These musicals have international roots; they are no longer just Broadway musicals. Webber is British and Schonberg is French. Furthermore, they opened in London and Paris, respectively, and came to New York after having enjoyed much success overseas.

Phantom of the Opera is based on a story about a phantom (who is actually a man with a terribly scarred face) who haunts the Paris Opera House. It has been made into at least two movies and a stage play. The plot revolves around the love of the phantom for a beautiful young soprano. He sabotages the efforts of the opera managers to promote her place in the company. He also tries to win her affection and keep her from her fiancé. Fortunately, he fails. *Phantom* is quite theatrical and at times it contains elements of old-style film music, with its sinister theme and crashing chandelier.

Schonberg's *Les Misérables* and *Miss Saigon* were both originally written in French with the text by Alain Boubil. English translations were carefully prepared later.

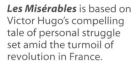

Les Misérables is based on Victor Hugo's compelling tale of personal struggle set amid the turmoil of revolution in France.

Les Misérables is probably the world's most popular musical, with an audience approaching 40 million. It has been translated into fourteen languages and has won thirty-one awards.

Les Misérables is based on the great novel by the French writer Victor Hugo. It tells of a man, Jean Valjean, who while young committed a petty crime for which he spent several years in jail. Although initially bitter after his release, his feelings change after being befriended by a kindly priest. He eventually adopts a new name and becomes a factory owner and mayor of his town, but is still pursued by an unrelenting police inspector. One of his good deeds is to raise as his own an illegitimate girl, Cosette. Her mother had worked for a while in Valjean's factory, but she had fallen on hard times and died while Cosette was quite young.

Times are hard in France in the 1830s, and Valjean joins a band of students who hope to bring about another revolution to better the lives of the poor. The revolution fails because the people do not rise up as they did in 1789. Valjean saves Cosette's fiancé, who was one of the revolutionaries, by carrying him unconscious through the sewers of Paris to safety. The young man recovers and the couple marry. Finally, they learn the truth about all that Valjean has done for them. *Les Misérables* closes with Valjean being escorted into heaven by Cosette's mother and the stirring marching song of the revolutionaries.

A Listening Guide for the finale of *Les Misérables* is included in the *Study Guide*.

Miss Saigon is a much more contemporary story about Chris, a U.S. Marine in the war in Vietnam, who falls in love with a Vietnamese girl named Kim. Despite his best efforts, he is forced to leave her behind when the Americans withdraw. Two years later, now married to an American woman, Chris learns that Kim is alive and that he has a young son in Vietnam. He returns to see her and the child. Kim, realizing that the best hope for her son's future is with his father in America, decides to give him up to Chris. In her grief-stricken state, she commits suicide, dying as Chris bends over her in anguish and the curtain falls.

Each of the three musicals mentioned here is filled with memorable music. All are well worth knowing.

Miss Saigon contains many parallels to Puccini's opera *Madame Butterfly,* the story of an American naval officer who fathers a child with a young Japanese woman while on tour in Japan and then abandons her.

A Listening Guide for the duet "I Still Believe" from *Miss Saigon* is included in the *Study Guide.*

AMERICAN OPERA

Opera has never held the attention of the American public as it has of those in many European countries. Some of the reasons for this are mentioned in chapter 21, but certainly the lack of operas in English is significant. Another probable reason is the lack of an American aristocracy to fund and support opera.

It is not that American composers have failed to write several first-rate operas. Rather, it is that only a few of them seem to have achieved a permanent place in operatic repertoire. One candidate for this permanent status is Howard Hanson's *Merry Mount,* which is based on a story by Nathaniel Hawthorne set in New England.

Another candidate is *The Medium* by Gian-Carlo Menotti, who was born in Italy but emigrated to the United States when he was seventeen. *The Medium* is based on a grisly story of a devious old lady who claims to communicate with the dead in fake séances. Eventually, her conscience begins to bother her, and she imagines that something clutched her throat during a séance. Disaster follows. Menotti's *Amahl and the Night Visitors* was one of the first operas composed for television. After its premiere on the *Hallmark Hall of Fame* in 1951, it became an annual Christmas telecast for nearly two decades.

In the late 1800s and early 1900s, many American cities had "opera houses," but they were used mostly for concerts and other events, not operas.

The Medium uses only five singers and an actor who plays the role of a deaf mute. Its orchestra is very small, there is no chorus, and it lasts for less than an hour.

GERSHWIN'S *PORGY AND BESS*

The opera that has secured for itself a solid place in American operatic repertoire is not a true opera, but rather in the composer's words a "folk opera." *Porgy and Bess* by George Gershwin is based on a story by DuBose Heyward set in Charleston, South Carolina. It is about a handicapped beggar named Porgy, who gets around in a goat cart. Gershwin could see the dramatic possibilities in the story and he decided to compose an opera based on it.

To make the story as real as possible, Gershwin has the characters speak many of their lines instead of singing recitatives. He also incorporates the music of the black people of Charleston—the blues and features of jazz—into the opera. Although he does not include actual folk songs, the music has a folklike quality. Its jazz elements are written down, rather than made up on the spot as they usually are in jazz.

The story of *Porgy and Bess* is filled with tragedy. Porgy leads a lonely life; Bess, a loose-living woman, comes to town with her lover, Crown. Neither Bess nor Crown is accepted by the people of Catfish Row. Crown kills a local man in a fight, and Bess takes refuge from the police in Porgy's shanty. Their relationship grows into genuine love.

The U.S. Department of State has on several occasions supported overseas tours of *Porgy and Bess.*

The area of Charleston in which Heyward's novel takes place is Catfish Row (originally Cabbage Row). It is only a few blocks from the city's historic district.

When Crown learns of Bess's love for Porgy, he sets out to kill him. In the fight between the two men, Crown is stabbed and dies. Porgy is taken off to jail on suspicion of murder.

Now is the moment the character Sportin' Life has been waiting for. He represents the easy, evil life that Bess left behind when she moved in with Porgy. Because Porgy may never be freed from jail, Sportin' Life is able to persuade Bess to go back to New York with him. But Porgy is released and when he returns home, he find Bess gone. "Where is she?" he asks. "New York," answer his neighbors. *Porgy and Bess* closes with the pathetic scene of Porgy climbing into his goat cart to go to New York to find Bess.

The song "Summertime" appears near the beginning of the opera and helps establish the opera's setting. The mood is lazy and relaxed as the mother sings her baby to sleep. The accompaniment suggests a gentle rocking motion. The song includes some vocal devices such as a slide, or glissando, and a little catch on the word *cry*.

The legal system for blacks in the South in the 1930s was hardly affected by what today is considered due process or impartiality.

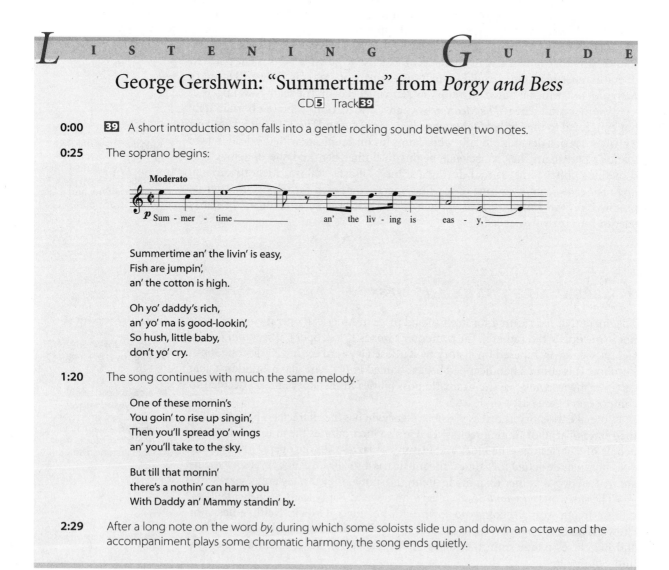

LISTENING GUIDE

George Gershwin: "Summertime" from *Porgy and Bess*
CD 5 Track 39

0:00 **39** A short introduction soon falls into a gentle rocking sound between two notes.

0:25 The soprano begins:

Moderato
p Sum - mer - time ___ an' the liv - ing is eas - y, ___

Summertime an' the livin' is easy,
Fish are jumpin',
an' the cotton is high.

Oh yo' daddy's rich,
an' yo' ma is good-lookin',
So hush, little baby,
don't yo' cry.

1:20 The song continues with much the same melody.

One of these mornin's
You goin' to rise up singin',
Then you'll spread yo' wings
an' you'll take to the sky.

But till that mornin'
there's a nothin' can harm you
With Daddy an' Mammy standin' by.

2:29 After a long note on the word *by*, during which some soloists slide up and down an octave and the accompaniment plays some chromatic harmony, the song ends quietly.

George Gershwin

George Gershwin (1898–1937) was born and educated in Brooklyn, New York. His family was poor, but was able to afford piano lessons for him. At the age of sixteen, he was employed as a song-plugger by a Tin Pan Alley publisher, and his career in music began. He often collaborated with his brother, Ira, who wrote the lyrics for many of George's songs.

Although successful and now financially well off, Gershwin was ambitious about composing concert music. His first big success came with *Rhapsody in Blue* in 1924. He originally composed it for piano and jazz orchestra; later he asked Ferde Grofé to arrange the orchestral part. Whatever he lacked in developing musical ideas he more than made up for in his sparkling tunes and moving melodies.

George Gershwin died in Hollywood of a brain tumor after unsuccessful surgery to save him.

Best-Known Works

Orchestra:
- *American in Paris*

Orchestra and Piano:
- Concerto in F
- *Rhapsody in Blue*

Opera:
- *Porgy and Bess*

Musicals:
- *Of Thee I Sing*
- *Girl Crazy*
- *Strike Up the Band*

A Scene from *Star Wars*
Music played an important part in the film *Star Wars*, establishing characters and deepening the audience's emotional responses.

MUSIC FOR FILMS

In a sense, commercial movies have almost never been silent. In the small, low-priced theaters a pianist pounded out music at appropriate places as the film flickered by on the screen. In upscale theaters small- to medium-sized orchestras played music especially composed for the film. This body of theater music has now been largely forgotten.

Role

Today, of course, music is an integral part of almost every commercial film, even showings of old silent movies. Why? Because music contributes to a film in a number of ways.

♦ It creates a more convincing atmosphere of a particular time and place. A scene with a ship sailing through the seas calls for one kind of music, and a scene in a crowded western saloon requires another.

In many ways music can express such feelings better than words.

♦ It gives the viewers cues about the unspoken thoughts of the characters or the yet unseen implications of a situation. If a man is looking at a woman and he is filled with feelings of love and desire, the music can project his feelings.

♦ It provides neutral filler or background sound. Although such music is of little interest in itself, it does fill the empty places in a film.

♦ It helps build a sense of continuity in a motion picture. This is done by associating certain music with a particular character or situation.

Almost no movie ends in silence, even if it lacked much of a musical score.

♦ It supports and contributes to the buildup of a scene, including giving the film a solid ending.

Development

It wasn't much of a beginning back on October 6, 1927, with *The Jazz Singer,* the first motion picture with music. The sound portion consisted of just five songs, including Irving Berlin's "Blue Skies." Its sound quality was vastly inferior to what we are used to today. To help the picture succeed, Warner Brothers picked a well-known vaudeville performer, Al Jolson. Impressive by today's standards or not, *The Jazz Singer* opened the door and soon "all-talking, all-singing, all-dancing" films would follow.

It was as though a great divide had been reached that separated silent movies from films with sound. Within a few years of *The Jazz Singer,* Hollywood was attracting top musical talent for its productions. Many of the best Broadway composers and arrangers worked there—George Gershwin, Jerome Kern, Irving Berlin, Cole Porter, and Harold Arlen.

At first glance, composing some music to serve the five purposes described earlier would seem to stifle creative quality. After all, the music must match the film to the second, so little development of musical ideas is possible. Either because or in spite of these limitations, a number of excellent composers established their professional reputations through their film music—Miklos Rozsa, Erich Korngold, Henry Mancini, Alfred Newman, Dimitri Tiomkin, James Horner, Max Steiner, Jerry Goldsmith, Maurice Jarre, Bernard Herrmann, John Williams, among others. Some of their music has found a life apart from the movie for which it was made in terms of commercial recordings. Some of it has almost assumed a folklore status, such as the shrieking sounds from the violins that Herrmann wrote for the soundtrack for Alfred Hitchcock's *Psycho* and Williams's ominous throbbing sounds for the shark in *Jaws.*

Both Miklos Rozsa and John Williams have pointed out that music for a film has to be immediate in its effectiveness. Musical ideas cannot be introduced gradually.

WILLIAMS'S "STAR WARS: MAIN TITLE"

"Star Wars: Main Title" was presented in chapter 1. As we revisit it this time, notice how your understanding of music has increased in view of the information that has been presented in the preceding forty-four chapters.

Also notice the following features as you listen to Williams's music:

◆ The sensuous, richly romantic character of the music; its roots go back to nineteenth-century Romanticism. The fact that the music for a space-age epic is Romantic may seem like a bit of a contradiction in a film filled with technology and futuristic scenes. But love and conflict exist, whether the actors are wearing jeans and riding a horse or wearing spacesuits and floating through space.

◆ The attraction of the music lies in its overall massive and colorful sounds and timbres and its energetic rhythms.

◆ Something is happening in the music almost all of the time. Something in addition to the themes can be heard—a rhythm pattern, swirling notes played by the violins, points of tonal color added by the harp, and so forth. It contains elements of the English composer Gustav Holst (1874–1934) and several other composers.

The movement titled "Mars" in Holst's *The Planets,* which was composed about 1915, is quite similar to parts of "Stars Wars: Main Title."

◆ The form of the music is rather sectional. It is not music that takes a theme and works with it in the manner of Beethoven or Zwilich. Nor does the music feature much counterpoint in the manner of Bach or Palestrina. The reason for the sectional character of "Star Wars: Main Title" is the need to fit with the different scenes and characters of the film.

LISTENING GUIDE

John Williams: "Star Wars: Main Title"
CD 1 Track 1

0:00	**1** The music opens with a short introduction containing a fanfare figure.
0:08	The first section (a) of the main theme (A) is played by the brasses. The theme has a massive, heroic quality and is accompanied by energetic, irregularly sounded chords, with the percussion contributing to the rhythmic quality of the music.
0:26	The strings play portion b of the main theme.
0:49	The a part of the main theme is played again by the French horns over rhythmically punctuated chords.
0:59	The trumpets add a colorful melodic figure.
1:11	A repeating rhythm pattern is played by the orchestra.
1:18	Pairs of rich-sounding chords are played as the music slows down and grows softer.
1:28	The piccolo plays a short, tender melody.
1:46	A repeated rhythmic figure is played by the brasses as the music grows slower and louder as dissonant chords are heard.
2:01	**2** The "battle" theme (B) is played against swirling notes played by the violins and a persistently repeated rhythm pattern.
2:21	The A theme returns, played by the French horns over an energetic rhythmic accompaniment.
2:37	The strings again play the b section of the A theme.
2:55	The French horns take up the a portion of the main theme.
3:13	The cellos play a warm, passionate theme associated with Princess Leia.
3:59	A climactic moment is reached by the brasses and strings.
4:05	The first part of the A theme returns, played by the trumpets.
4:22	The strings again play the b section of the A theme and extend it.
4:38	The brasses twice play a figure containing two quick notes that descend to a third note.
5:02	The strings play a passionate-sounding series of chords.
5:16	The brasses begin the coda section.
5:46	After punctuated, full chords and a snare drum roll, "Star Wars: Main Title" concludes in a decisive manner.

MUSIC AND VISUAL IMAGES

Technology is opening up an easy union of music with visual images. One attempt at doing this is MTV, which was discussed in chapter 44. Sometimes the role of movies in the promotion of music, especially popular music, has been overlooked. The film versions of Broadway musicals did much to further that type of music, which is also true of Latin American music and some of the big-band music of the Swing Era. But videotape and videodisc now offer even more intriguing possibilities.

Coda

The situations presented on a stage or in a film have often inspired composers to create music with much emotional impact. The challenge of fitting the dramatic scene seems to have been a good incubator for many interesting and beautiful works of music.

A P P E N D I X
The Notation of Music

RHYTHM

Beat   The basic pulse that underlies the rhythm. The beat recurs regularly in music and is accented periodically. The beat is also the unit of measurement by which listeners judge the duration of a musical sound.

Tempo   The rate of speed at which beats recur.

Meter   The way in which beats are grouped together and measured, or the pattern created by accented and unaccented beats. Meter requires attention to the heaviness or lightness of the various beats. For example:

beat-beat **beat**-beat **beat**-beat   suggests a grouping of twos

beat-beat-beat **beat**-beat-beat   suggests a grouping of threes

Note values   Symbols to indicate the passing of time in music. Various kinds of notes each represent a particular duration. The duration of a note is always figured in relation to the beat.

Whole note	o	usually lasts for four beats
Half note	♩	usually lasts for two beats
Quarter note	♩	usually lasts for one beat
Eighth note	♪	usually lasts for half a beat
Sixteenth note	♪	usually lasts for a quarter beat

The mathematical relationships among these note values are illustrated by the following chart. The arrows here represent the passing of time; they do not appear in actual music notation.

Rest   A sign to indicate silence for a certain period of time. For each kind of note, there is a rest with the same name and time value.

—	▬	𝄽	𝄾	𝄿
Whole rest	Half rest	Quarter rest	Eighth rest	Sixteenth rest

Time signature or meter signature   The two numbers at the beginning of a piece of music. The meter signature indicates the meter or basic rhythmic grouping of the beats. This grouping is indicated by vertical bar lines in the music itself; the areas marked off by bar lines are called *measures*. The top number of the signature tells how many beats are in each measure. The bottom number tells what kind of note lasts for one beat. A *4* on the bottom stands for a quarter note, a *2* stands for a half note, and an *8* stands for an eighth note.

The meter signature is not a fraction; *3/4* does not mean three-fourths, because it does not represent a portion of anything. Two abbreviated time signatures are seen often:

ℭ	(common time)	means	$\frac{4}{4}$
₵	(cut time or *alla breve*)	means	$\frac{2}{2}$

Pitch

Note   A symbol placed on the staff to indicate the pitch and duration of a particular musical sound.

Staff   The five horizontal lines and four spaces on which the notes are written.

Ledger lines   Short horizontal lines indicating the pitch of notes too high or too low to be placed on a regular staff. Ledger lines extend the range of the staff.

Clef   A sign placed on a staff to show the exact pitches of the notes written on the staff. The two most common clefs are:

treble clef—generally for notes above the pitch middle C.

bass clef—generally for notes below the pitch middle C.

The treble and bass clefs indicate definite pitches, all named with letters of the alphabet from *A* to *G*:

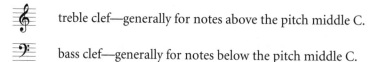

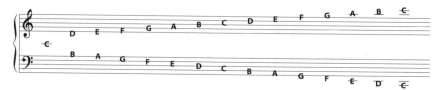

Another clef sometimes encountered in instrumental music is the alto clef (or C clef, because it indicates the position of middle C):

Sharp ♯ A sign placed to the left of a note to raise the pitch one half-step.

Flat ♭ A sign placed to the left of a note to lower the pitch one half-step.

Natural ♮ A sign placed to the left of a note to indicate that it is neither raised nor lowered. This sign cancels a sharp or flat previously applied to the note.

PITCHES ON THE PIANO KEYBOARD

The black keys of the piano are found in groups of twos and threes. All white keys are identified in relation to these groups of black keys. For example, every C on the piano is a white key immediately to the left of a group of two black keys; every F is a white key immediately to the left of a group of three black keys. The white keys are named consecutively from left to right, using the letters *A* to *G:*

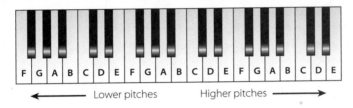

To find the sharp of any white key on the piano, find the black key touching it on the right. To find the flat of any white key, find the black key touching it on the left. If there is no black key where you are looking, the nearest white key in the appropriate direction is the sharp or flat.

Middle C, the note midway between the treble and bass staffs, is also the C nearest the middle of the piano keyboard. Using this as a guide, you can look at any note on the staff and find the exact pitch it represents.

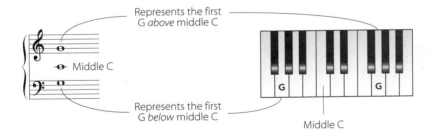

Interval The distance between two notes. The name of an interval is determined by the number of letters it includes, counting the lower note and the higher note. Examples:

Second   Fifth   Third   Octave   Prime or unison

Interval names are not fractions; they are not portions of anything. The name is written in full: *a sixth* rather than *1/6.*

Half-step The smallest interval that can be played on the piano.

Whole step An interval of two half-steps.

MAJOR KEYS

Scale   A series of pitches ascending or descending by a specific pattern of intervals. A scale can be built on any note, which is then called the *tonal center, tonic,* or *keynote*. A scale usually consists of eight notes, the eighth note having the same letter name as the first, or keynote. Numbers are often used to indicate the successive steps of the scale.

Key   The effect created when several tones are related to a common tonal center. If these notes are arranged to form a scale, the starting note of the scale (step 1) is the name of the key.

Key signature   A group of sharps or flats placed after the clef at the beginning of the staff. Every sharp or flat in the key signature is applied to its particular note throughout the composition, unless the composer or arranger later cancels it with a natural. The key signature indicates the tonal center of the composition.

Accidental   A sharp, flat, or natural used within a composition to show a pitch not indicated by the key signature.

Modulation   Changing the key within a composition, usually with no break in the music.

Transposition   Changing the key of an entire piece so that it is performed at a higher or lower pitch level.

MINOR KEYS

Minor key   The effect created when the third step above the keynote is lowered. Other notes may be lowered also, but a lowered third step is a consistent feature of music in minor keys.

HARMONY

Chord A combination of three or more notes sounded at the same time.

Root The note on which a chord is built.

Triad A chord of three notes. The harmony most familiar in Western culture is based on the triad. In any key, there are three triads that are basic because they occur so frequently. They can be understood better when they are related to the scale:

In any key:

◆ The triad built on step 1 is called I or the *tonic* triad.

◆ The triad built on step 4 is called IV or the *subdominant* triad.

◆ The triad built on step 5 is called V or the *dominant* triad.

Although the I, IV, and V triads are the most common, triads can be built on any step of the scale and are named accordingly: II, VI, and so on.

Seventh chord A chord of four notes, consisting of a root plus intervals of a third, fifth, and seventh above the root.

Inverted chord A chord that does not have its root sounding as the lowest tone. *Inversion* does not affect the name or function of the chord.

Glossary

absolute music Music that is free of extramusical associations.

a cappella Unaccompanied music.

accent The emphasis placed on a note, usually by playing it louder.

accidental A sharp, flat, or natural sign written in the music notation to indicate a departure from the prevailing key signature.

aerophone Any instrument that generates sound by vibrating a column of air.

air A song or instrumental work in song style.

aleatory music Music in which the sounds are partly or entirely the result of chance.

allemande A Baroque dance in moderate tempo and two-beat meter.

alto (contralto) The lower, heavier female voice.

aria An accompanied solo song, usually of some length and complexity, in an opera, oratorio, or cantata.

art music Music intended for careful attention to its sounds and expressive qualities.

art song A musical setting of a text by a composer for solo singer and piano.

atonality Music that is not in any key or tonality.

augmentation A compositional technique in which the note values of a theme are all lengthened proportionally.

ballad An English narrative song told in simple verses.

ballade A short, melodic piano piece.

bar *See* measure.

Baroque The style of music the prevailed from 1600 to 1750.

bass The lower, heavier male voice.

basso continuo *See* continuo.

beat The pulse or throb that recurs regularly in music.

behop *See* bop.

bel canto Literally, "beautiful singing" in Italian. Often it refers to a style of opera in the first part of the nineteenth century that featured much vocal technique and beautiful singing.

berceuse Instrumental pieces in a moderate tempo and accompaniment reminiscent of rocking a cradle.

binary form Two-part form, *A B*.

bitonality Two keys occurring simultaneously.

bluegrass A type of country music in which acoustic instruments are used in an attempt to better capture the original qualities of country music.

blue note A note in major scale—usually the third, fifth, or seventh—that in jazz is lowered one half-step while the harmony remains in major.

blues A type of song associated with African Americans in which a solo singer sings about some hardship; the usual form of the blues is *a a b*.

bolero A Spanish dance adapted by the Cubans, who made its rhythm more complex.

boogie-woogie A jazz piano style featuring a repeated figure in the bass part and a highly decorated melody line.

bop (bebop) An advanced jazz style for a small group, involving nearly continuous syncopation and a flowing melodic line.

bourrée A Baroque dance with two quick beats per measure.

broadside A ballad printed on one sheet of paper, with a text often discussing political matters.

broken chord The notes of a chord one after another rather than simultaneous.

cadence A melodic or harmonic formula that gives a sense of phrase ending. In poetic usage it sometimes refers to beat or tempo.

cadenza A section in which a soloist plays a free paraphrase on the themes of the work.

call-and-response The form found in African music in which phrases of music are exchanged between soloist and group.

canon Music in which one or more lines imitate one another for almost the entire work.

cantata A vocal composition in several movements for solo voices, instruments, and usually a chorus; it is usually based on a religious text.

cantus firmus A preexisting melody that is used as the basis for a polyphonic vocal work.

chaconne A work featuring variations on a pattern of chords repeated throughout the work.

chamber music Instrumental music in which each part is performed by only one player.

chanson (1) A French polyphonic song of the seventeenth century. (2) The French word for song.

chantey An English or American sailors' song.

character piece A short keyboard work expressing a mood or idea, composed during the Romantic period.

chorale A stately hymn tune used in the German Lutheran Church.

chord The simultaneous sounding of three or more pitches.

chordophone Any instrument that produces sound by vibrating strings.

choreographer The person who designs the movement of dancers.

chorus (1) A sizable group of singers that sings choral music. (2) A section of an opera, oratorio, or cantata sung by a chorus.

chromatic Melodic or harmonic movement by half-steps.

chromatic scale The scale that includes all twelve tones of the octave; the tones are a half-step apart.

classical music The popular term for art music.

Classical period The prevailing style of music from 1750 to 1820.

clavier A general term indicating any keyboard instrument.

coda (codetta) The concluding portion of a section or movement, usually giving the impression of an ending.

concert overture An overture not associated with an opera or drama.

concertmaster (concertmistress) The first-chair player in the first-violin section of an orchestra.

concerto A multimovement work consisting of music that contrasts a soloist with an orchestra or band.

concerto grosso A multimovement work contrasting a small instrumental group with a large group.

consonance A group of simultaneous sounds that seems agreeable or restful.

continuo (basso continuo) A bass line for keyboard and other instruments in which the player is given only a succession of single notes and other symbols from which to fill out the remainder of the harmony. Also the instruments that play the continuo part.

corrido A Mexican narrative song.

countermelody A melodic idea that accompanies a main theme.

counterpoint Two or more independent lines with melodic character occurring at the same time.

countersubject The secondary theme in a fugue.

country music A type of music containing folklike qualities that is especially popular with the white culture of the American South.

courante A lively dance in triple meter, usually containing running notes.

crescendo (cresc.) The music should gradually become louder.

cyclical form The appearance of a theme from one movement in another movement of a multimovement work.

decrescendo (decrec.) The music should gradually become softer.

development (1) The manipulation of themes in a musical work. (2) The section in sonata form devoted to the development of themes.

diminution The proportional reduction all note values in a theme.

dissonance A group of simultaneous sounds that seems disagreeable or harsh.

divertimento A pleasant but not very complex instrumental work, usually consisting of stylized dances.

Dixieland A jazz style for a small group of players, consisting of two beats per measure and a rather lively tempo.

doctrine of affections (doctrine of affects) The Baroque practice of attempting to project states of feeling and ideas in music.

dodecaphonic music *See* tone row music.

dominant chord A chord built on the fifth step of a major or minor scale.

double (1) A variation of a stylized dance. (2) The addition of a different instrument or voice on a part.

double stop The sounding of two different pitches at the same time on a string instrument.

downbeat The first beat of a measure.

drone A low, continuous sound that lasts throughout a piece of music.

drum roll The rapid successive sounding of notes on a drum.

dynamics The amount of loudness in music.

ensemble An instrumental or vocal performing group.

episode Sections of a fugue in which the subject is not present.

equal temperament A system of tuning, in which the intervals are adjusted to divide the octave into twelve equal parts.

ethnic music Music that is characteristic of a particular culture or group of people.

étude A short instrumental work stressing some technical aspect of playing the instrument.

Exoticism A phase of Romanticism that draws on scenes from Asia and the Middle East.

exposition (1) The opening section of a fugue. (2) The opening section in sonata form.

Expressionism An early-twentieth-century style that emphasized subjective and often disturbing emotions.

fantasie A short, free-sounding instrumental work.

figured bass A shorthand system of numbers and accidentals used by keyboard players in Baroque music for indicating chords.

finale (1) The concluding movement of some musical works. (2) The last piece in an act of an opera or musical.

fine arts Type of art in which objects are created only for the psychological satisfaction that people find in them.

folk music The music of the common people of a society or geographical area.

folkloric A type of twentieth-century music that contains folklike qualities.

form The pattern or plan of a musical work.

free jazz A sophisticated type of jazz containing few stylistic guidelines.

frets Metal strips on the fingerboard of a guitar and similar instruments that help the player in finger placement.

fugue A composition in which the main theme (subject) is presented in imitation in several parts.

fusion The combination of two or more musical styles.

gamelan A Balinese instrumental ensemble.

gavotte A dance with moderate tempo in two-beat meter.

gigue A Baroque dance in 6/8 meter performed at a quick tempo.

Gothic motet An unaccompanied work composed during the Gothic period for voices using a cantus firms from Gregorian chant with other parts in vernacular languages added and often containing complex rhythmic and melodic relationships.

Gothic period The style of music that prevailed from approximately 1100 to 1450.

grace note A short decorative note that has no assigned rhythmic value.

Gregorian chant (plainsong) The liturgical chant of the Roman Catholic Church.

ground bass A variation form in which a bass line is repeated over and over while the melodies above it change.

half-step The smallest interval on keyboard instruments.

harmony The simultaneous sounds of several pitches, usually in accompanying a melody.

homophony The texture consisting of a line of melody with accompaniment.

idée fixe (fixed idea) A theme that is transformed at various places in a composition.

imitation The immediate repetition of a theme in another part or line.

Impressionism An artistic viewpoint that emphasizes overall impressions rather than detailed or intellectual observations.

impromptu A short piano composition in an improvised-sounding style.

improvisation Music that is made up on the spot, usually according to stylistic guidelines.

incidental music Music composed to be performed in conjunction with a drama.

interval The distance between two pitches.

inversion (1) Turning a melody upside down so that an ascending interval descends and vice versa. (2) Rearranging the notes in a chord so that its basic note is no longer the lowest one.

jazz An African American style of music developed in twentieth-century America that is characterized by improvised playing and syncopated rhythms.

key (1) *See* tonality. (2) A part of a wind or keyboard instrument that is manipulated by the player's fingers.

key center *See* tonic.

Kyrie The first section in the Ordinary of the Mass.

leitmotiv A motive or theme that is associated with a particular character or idea in the music dramas of Richard Wagner.

libretto The text of an opera or oratorio.

Lied The German word for art song. The plural of *Lied* is *Lieder*.

liturgy A ritual for public worship.

madrigal A free, secular, imitative work for voices.

march A musical composition designed to accompany marching, usually in two-beat meter.

Mass (1) The celebration of Holy Communion (Eucharist) in the Roman Catholic Church. (2) The musical setting of the Ordinary of the Mass.

measure A group of beats marked as a separate unit in music notation.

melody A series of consecutive pitches that form a cohesive musical entity.

membranophone Any instrument that produces sounds from a skin or other membrane.

meter The pattern of stressed and unstressed beats.

meter signature The two numbers, one above the other, at the beginning of a piece or section of a longer work that indicate the metrical pattern and how it is notated.

microtone An interval of less than a half-step.

minuet and trio A three-part form in three-beat meter and the style of a minuet.

modes As used today, scale patterns containing seven pitches other than major or minor.

modulation Changing the tonal center as the music progresses, usually without a break.

monody The type of homophonic texture associated with the early seventeenth century, consisting of a single melody accompanied by a few chords.

monophony One melodic without any accompaniment.

motet A sacred composition for voices.

movement A large independent section of an instrumental composition.

musical (musical comedy) A type of theater that features music as well as actions, scenery, and costumes.

musique concrète Natural sounds that are recorded and then modified and organized by a composer into a musical composition.

mute A device for muffling or dampening the sound of an instrument.

nationalism A deliberate, conscious attempt to develop artworks that are characteristic of a particular country or region.

Neoclassicism "New classicism"—works that attempt to emulate the techniques and flavor of those created in the Classical period.

nocturne A type of nineteenth-century character piece for piano; originally, the word meant "night music."

octave A pitch that has twice or half the frequency of vibrations of another; usually, the two pitches have the same letter designation.

octave displacement Using a note with the same letter name as a previous note but in another octave.

Op. (opus) Meaning "work" in Latin, it usually appears with a number to indicate the order in which the composer's works were written.

opera A drama set to music in which the lines of text are sung with orchestral accompaniment.

opera buffa Comic opera of the eighteenth and nineteenth centuries.

opera seria Dramatic opera, usually dealing with serious subject matter.

oral tradition The process in which music is preserved by people through hearing the music, remembering it, and then performing it.

oratorio A sizable work for chorus, soloists, and orchestra, usually on a religious topic, that is performed without scenery, costumes, or acting.

Ordinary The parts of the Mass that are ordinarily included regardless of Church season: Kyrie, Gloria, Credo, Sanctus, and Agnus Dei.

ostinato A short, persistently repeated melodic, rhythmic, or harmonic pattern.

overture An instrumental introduction to a vocal work or an orchestral suite.

pandiatonicism The selection of notes in chords without regard for traditional harmonic function.

passacaglia A repeated set of variations based on a melodic ostinato in the lowest-pitched part.

passion An oratorio based on the suffering of Jesus on Good Friday, according to one of the four Gospels.

pedal point A note that is held for a long time despite changes of harmony.

pentatonic scale A five-note scale, usually with the pattern of whole steps and half-steps encountered on the black keys of the piano.

phrase A rather short, logical segment of music; it is comparable to a clause or phrase in language.

pitch The perceived highness or lowness of a musical sound.

pizzicato Notes on a string instrument that are played by the player's fingers plucking the string instead of using the bow.

plainsong *See* Gregorian chant.

polanaise A stately stylized dance of Polish origin.

polymeter The presence of two or more meters at the same time.

polyphony Music in which two or more melodic lines of approximately equal importance are sounded at the same time.

polyrhythm Two or more rhythm patterns occurring simultaneously.

polytonality Two or more tonal centers sounding at the same time.

post-Romanticism Works in the Romantic style composed after it was the prevailing style.

prelude (1) A short instrumental work. (2) A piece to be played as an introduction.

prepared piano A practice sometimes used in twentieth-century music in which tacks, chewing gum, paper, and other objects are placed in the mechanism of the piano so that it sounds different timbres.

Primitivism Music that seeks to contain rhythmic power and blatant expression.

program music Instrumental works associated by the composer with an extramusical idea or object.

program symphony A multimovement programmatic work for orchestra.

progressive jazz A sophisticated type of jazz usually for big bands involving dissonant chords.

punk rock Rock music that deliberately expresses rebellion.

quotation music Music that makes extensive use of quotations from other music.

raga A melodic formula used in the music of India.

ragtime A forerunner of jazz, usually for piano in a marchlike style.

rap A type of African American music that consists of rapid delivery of words in a singsong style.

recapitulation The section of sonata form in which the themes from the exposition are repeated again.

recitative A style of singing that covers its text expressively, usually in an economical and direct way.

Requiem The funeral Mass of the Roman Catholic Church.

retrograde The reverse version of a melody or tone row, in which the first note becomes the last, and so on.

retrograde-inversion The upside-down and backward version of the tone row.

rhythm The flow of music in terms of time.

rhythm and blues A term for African American popular music.

rhythmic modes The constant repetition of certain rhythm patterns, much as poetic meters.

ritornello form The orchestral form in which themes at the beginning of a concerto gross return later in the movement.

rock (rock and roll) A popular style of music that contains features of both rhythm and blues and country music.

Rococo The decorative, light style prevalent in the eighteenth-century courts, especially France.

Romantic period The style of music that was prevalent from about 1820 to 1910.

rondo A form in which the theme appears three or more times with contrasting sections between its appearances.

rubato A performer's slight deviations from a strict tempo.

sarabande A slow dance of Spanish origin that is used in many Baroque suites.

scale A series of pitches that proceeds upward or downward according to a prescribed pattern.

scherzo (1) The third movement of some symphonies and other works, usually in a playful style. (2) An independent work for piano composed during the Romantic period.

score The complete notation of a work involving a number of different vocal or instrumental parts.

secular music Music that is worldly or nonsacred.

sequence The immediate repeating of a phrase or figure at a different pitch level from the original.

Serialism The application of the principles of tone row music to elements such as dynamic levels and articulations.

sforzando A loud, accented note or chord; it is indicated by the letters *Sfz*.

sonata (1) A Baroque multimovement work for solo instrument. (2) A multimovement work for piano and another instrument, or for piano alone.

sonata form A form consisting of an exposition section, followed by a development section, and then a recapitulation of the themes from the exposition.

soprano The higher female voice classification.

soul A general term for several types of African American music.

sprechstimme A vocal style that is a combination of speaking and singing.

staff The five horizontal lines and four spaces on which notes are written.

strophic form A song in which several verses of words are sung to the same melody.

subject The main theme of a fugue.

suite (1) A collection or group of stylized pieces of dance music. (2) A collection of parts of a larger work such as a ballet or opera.

suspension A nonharmonic, dissonant note that was consonant in the preceding chord and that eventually resolves downward to become consonant.

swing A type of popular music containing many jazz influences that was arranged for big bands.

symphonic poem *See* tone poem.

symphony A large multimovement work for orchestra.

syncopation The displacement of an accent so that it occurs where it is not normally expected or does not occur where it is expected.

tala A rhythmic cycle of beats found in the music of India.

tempo The speed of the beats in a piece of music.

tenor (1) The higher, lighter male voice. (2) The line in a Gothic motet that contains the phrases from Gregorian chant.

terraced dynamics Abrupt changes in levels of loudness.

text painting (word painting) The compositional technique of having the musical sounds reinforce the words being sung.

texture The basic setting of the music: monophonic, homophonic, or polyphonic.

theme A central melody in a musical work.

theme and variations A work consisting of a theme and altered versions of that theme.

theme transformation The alteration of a theme that retains its characteristic intervals of melody or rhythm pattern.

through-composed song A song that contains no repetition of lines of music.

timbre Tone quality or tone color in music.

time signature *See* meter signature.

toccata A showy work, usually for keyboard instrument.

tonality The centering of pitches around a particular pitch.

tone clusters Chords in twentieth-century music made up of notes a half-step or whole step apart.

tone poem A sizable orchestral work of program music.

tone-row (twelve-tone or dodecaphonic music) A composition based on row of pitches that uses each of the twelve tones in an octave.

tonic The specific pitch around which a piece of music is centered.

tonic chord A chord built on the first degree of a major or minor scale.

transcription An adaptation of a musical work for an instrument or voice for another instrument or voice, or for a group of either.

transposition Rewriting or playing a piece at a different level of pitch by retaining the same intervals among the pitches.

tremolo (1) The rapid repetition of a tone on a string instrument by moving the bow rapidly back and forth. (2) The rapid alternation between two octaves on the piano.

trill A melodic ornament consisting of the rapid alternation between the written note and the note immediately above it.

triplet Three equal notes on one beat.

trio sonata A Baroque sonata written for two players on melody and the basso continuo line.

twelve-tone music *See* tone-row music.

unison A single line of music performed by the entire ensemble.

variation A section of music in which the melody, harmony, or rhythm of a theme is repeated with some changes.

vibrato Slight, rapid fluctuations of pitch.

virtuoso A very technically skilled performer.

vocalise A song sung without words, usually sung on a single vowel sound.

voice (1) The human voice. (2) A part in an instrumental composition, especially a fugue.

western music Music of the American West.

Western music Music of Europe and the Americas.

whole-tone scale A scale in which the octave is divided into six whole steps.

wind band (wind ensemble) An ensemble comprising wind and percussion instruments.

INDEX OF
Composer Biographies

Listening Guides

INDEXED BY COMPOSER

Index

Photo and Art Credits